SATISFACTIONS

.

SATISFACTIONS

7 RELATIONSHIP SKILLS YOU NEED TO KNOW

PETER K. GERLACH, MSW

To order additional copies of this book, contact:

Xlibris Corporation

1-888-795-4274

www.Xlibris.com

Orders@Xlibris.com

5362

CONTENTS

To Autumn, Deanna, and Tabatha – learn and model these skills for your precious children and all who will spring from them!

Acknowledgements

I've studied human relations, including communication dynamics, for 43 adult years. I've learned much from my roles as a son, brother, engineer, marketing rep, husband, stepfather, corporate manager, trainer, consultant, and since 1981, psychotherapist. Those roles leave me deeply indebted to a group of communication and relationship theorists and teachers, and clients in my psychotherapy practice. I'm glad to thank people in each group who have helped me write this book. The key people who have helped me learn about internal and interpersonal human relationships are acknowledged in "Who's *Really* Running Your Life?" (Xlibris, 2000).

My gruff high school algebra teacher, Benjamin "Shoey" Shoemaker, modeled a way of effective thinking that has probably influenced my views on relationships and communications more than I know. Other science and Stanford engineering instructors helped me to see how *systems* work. This is a great help in understanding the complex relationship and communication dynamics within us and between us.

The writings of several communication masters profoundly shape what you'll read here. Principal among them are Dr. Milton Erickson, and some of his teachers, students, and colleagues who founded the paradigm of indirect clinical hypnosis: Gregory Bateson, Jay Haley, John Weakland, Richard

Fisch, and Paul Watzlawick. Steve Lankton, Paul Gilligan, Jeffery Zeig, Francis Barber, Fritz Perls, and Ray Robertson taught me more about the mysterious communications between our conscious and unconscious minds. Writings by Mara Selvini Palazzoli and her Milanese colleagues helped me understand the power of applied paradoxical communication. In their writings on Neurolinguistic Programming (NLP), Richard Bandler and John Grinder taught me to appreciate the preferred communication styles of different people. Carl Roger's and Virginia Satir's teachings about our human need for dignity and respect permeate these pages.

Intrigued by the title "Inner Family Systems Therapy," I attended a Chicago seminar by psychologist Richard Schwartz in 1988. That led to two externships with him and a group of fellow clinicians, which revealed the amazing world of our ceaseless *internal* communications. Since then, three books by *Voice Dialog* pioneers Hal and Sidra Stone (e.g. "Embracing Our Selves,") amplified what I was learning with Schwartz and colleagues.

Ann Moir and David Jessel ("Brain Sex"), and Deborah Tannen ("You Just Don't Understand") helped clarify and illuminate the wonderful, vexing communication differences between typical "male brains" and "female brains." The year I spent studying and teaching with Robert and Dorothy Bolton and fellow communication trainers at Ridge Associates adds significantly to what you'll read here.

Over 1,000 therapy clients and communication-class students have motivated me to write this book. I've spent two decades empathically witnessing the pain, anger, frustration, confusion, anxiety, distrust, and agony that result when mates, parents, kids, and co-workers can't communicate effectively, internally and with each other. I've experienced those often, personally and professionally.

So I gratefully acknowledge the hundreds of contributors to this book. My pleasant task is to meld and present their teachings coherently, so you may fill more of your daily needs by communicating *effectively*, in ways that please you and the people around you

Introduction

This chapter answers . . .
Why does this book exist?
What's unique about this book?
Is it for you?
What's in it?
Why read it?
How can you best use it?

Why Does This Book Exist?

Living things communicate to meet their current *needs*. After 30+ years' study and teaching these seven skills, I believe _ most people haven't a clue on how to resolve the constant stream of problems (needs) _ inside them and _ between them and other people. This includes Ph.D.s, astronauts, hobos, CEOs, rock stars, Queens, legislators, and the people you live and work among. Most people don't know what they don't know about how to get their needs met via communicating more effectively. They—you—settle for communicating far below their potential, not knowing what they're capable of. A silent tragedy is that this promotes their—your—dependent kids to live similar stunted, stressful lives.

It doesn't have to be that way, starting with *you*!

What's Unique About This Book?

I assume you're reading this because you're interested in communicating "better," or helping someone else do that. There are already scores of how-to books and tapes for adults, kids, and business people on "effective interpersonal communications." Why write another one?

Four factors guarantee that the ideas you'll read here will be significantly different than those in any other media on the same topic:

My unusual combination of engineering, business, teaching, and psychotherapy training and experience, including clinical hypnosis;

My 11 years' experience studying and teaching *inner*-family communication dynamics;

My 15 years' experience recovering emotionally and spiritually from a low-nurturance childhood; and . . .

My unique life experience, personality, vocabulary, and style of thinking and writing.

These factors blend and provide a unique mix of practical ideas here, including . . .

The concepts of personality splitting and *inner* families, and how they affect communication and relationship effectiveness. These concepts are summarized in Chapter 1, and explored in depth in the companion volume "Who's *Really* Running Your Life?" (Xlibris, 2000).

The inner-family idea leads to the premise that your **interpersonal communication is really three simultaneous exchanges** among _ your and _ your partner's respective *inner* families (personality subselves), and _ between these two families. This idea provides new options toward assessing and resolving your most vexing or stressful "communication problems."

I've added premises on clear thinking (Chapter 3), and "digging down" below surface needs (Chapter 4), to Bob and

Dorothy Bolton's useful scheme of five related communication skills. Other authors I've studied don't explore the premise that most internal and social conflicts are really surface clashes. Few people in conversation are aware of the *true* needs that they and their communication partners are trying to fill. The dig-down technique helps you learn what you and your partners really need, and who's really responsible for filling them.

The true-need idea generates another unique feature of this book: identifying the **six discomforts (needs) we all ceaselessly try to lower by communicating**. Awareness of these six creates a vital concept I've never seen in any other communication material. It's called the "**R message**" here. R-messages and psychological wounds largely determine the effectiveness of any interaction you have within yourself, or with another person. Few people are aware of either of them.

Four more unique aspects of this book are . . .

. . . **the** Reality check and Status check exercises throughout the text,

. . . **the** pointers [..**/****.htm] to supplemental articles and worksheets in the non-profit Web site at [http://sfhelp.org/],

. . . **the** Glossary of over 350 communication and relationship terms; and

. . . **the** skill-summaries, recommended readings, and index in the Resource section.

I've acquired and/or developed these practical resources over 30 years of teaching communication and other classes to individuals, couples, and kids. With the text, they'll help you discover how to assess, understand, and solve most communication (relationship) problems inside you, and with your partners.

Pause for a moment, and breathe comfortably. Can you describe your thoughts and feelings objectively now, like a reporter would? What are your "inner voices" saying about what you just read? Do you know who's "speaking" them?

Why Read This Book?

All living things evolve communication strategies to fill current *needs*; i.e. to reduce discomforts, and increase current pleasure. Is that your experience? Whether you're a mute hermit or a famous global leader, I suspect that communicating with yourself and with other people largely determines how content you are as you prepare to sleep. Can you think of another learned skill that affects your daily achievements and contentment as much as "communicating" does?

Imagine an earnest stranger saying . . .

"If you're interested, I can show you a safe, practical way to—oh, maybe double your daily verbal and written communication effectiveness. That means regularly getting many more of your small and major needs met, and feeling good about how you do that."

How would you respond? Skepticism? Interest? Anxiety? If you have kids in your life, what if the stranger added . . .

"Oh, and once you learn this 'way', you can teach it to your kids. That will significantly increase their happiness, safety, and success across their lives, which will nourish your great fan of unborn descendents."

And if you supervise, manage, or work for other people, what if this stranger said . . .

"Here's another payoff: if you choose to learn and apply this seven-skill 'way' of communicating, the morale, productivity, and harmony inside and among you and your co-workers will probably rise and stay high, despite unexpected problems. That means you'll wake up most mornings with hope, confidence, and zest for what the day brings you."

How are your inner voices responding to these ideas; what's your "self-talk"? Does this sound too good to be true? Perhaps one of your voices is saying, *"Come on, what's the catch? Nothing comes for free—nothing."* Our stranger smiles and says,

*"Yep, you're right. In order **to get these payoffs, you'll have to do at least five things:***

Get to know your *inner* **family**, and who's *really* running your life these days.

Accept that one adult in the universe is responsible for filling your daily and long-term true needs: *you.* Your favorite villain or abuser really isn't to blame for reducing your discomforts. Sorry, no substitutions or stand-ins, unless you're a child. And you'll need to . . .

Learn that you're probably used to communicating at under half of your potential effectiveness, and realize fully what that has meant. And . . .

Commit to changing some cherished personal priorities, habits and attitudes, and adopt some alien new ways of thinking and behaving. Finally, to get the prizes above . . .

You must study and integrate some ideas that can be boring, tedious, "intellectual," and seem irrelevant, at times. The TANSTAFL principle rules here: "There Ain't No Such Thing As Free Lunch."

So to richly profit yourself, your kids, and co-workers by communicating "better," you'll have to get to know your *inner* family, learn and apply a set of new ideas, and change some comfortable, familiar aspects of your inner and outer life.

As you've guessed, I'm the "earnest stranger." The "new way (to communicate)," the benefits, and the five "catches" above pertain to *you.* Restated: if you seriously try the communication concepts in this book over time, your life will surely improve in major ways. Learning skill with a harmonica or a tennis racket probably won't change your basic life philosophy. Learning to use these seven skills will. To get their priceless benefits, the skills will guide you toward making some basic second-order (core attitude) changes to the way you live.

Scan this book, to sense whether it may be worth it to you to experiment with these life changes. If that seems likely, then read this book for meaning, *use* the tools, and notice the effect on your daily satisfactions.

Now you have a sense of what's unique in these pages, and why read them. You may wonder . . .

Is This Book For You?

I write this to several groups of people:

Average women and men, with or without college education, who spend "significant" time each day thinking and communicating with other adults and kids. I specially have you in mind here if you're in a primary relationship, or you want to be; and/or if you're nurturing one or more minor kids part time or full time. Your young ones are learning how to communicate, specially when stressed, by watching and listening to *you*. This book is the second in a series slanted towards co-parents in troubled, absent-parent, and remarried families. If you're not in one of these family types, trust that the concepts and skills illustrated here apply equally to your own situation.

All people in the human service and "helping" professions: student and practicing clinicians; clergy; caseworkers; educators; consultants; medical professionals; lawyers, police, mediators, and judges; human-resource specialists; and those who train, supervise, support, and evaluate them. If you serve other people in person, professionally or not, the ideas and tools here can improve your days and results, over time.

And finally, I write to . . .

Researchers trying to grow our understanding of human development, behavior, and relationships, individually and in groups, including neighborhoods, congregations, teams, races, and nations.

If you're among these groups, there's one more requirement before you can benefit: you must be displeased with your communication outcomes now, or motivated to improve them even if you aren't. Restated: you must seek to improve your relationships with yourself and other people in your home and life.

Do you see yourself here? Do you know others in these groups?

What's In This Book?

You'll learn **clear, practical answers to vital life-skill questions** like these:

1) How can I tell if my true Self is in charge of my personality at any time; and what do I do if s/he isn't?

2) What are the six needs I and other adults and kids try to fill by communicating?

3) What are my options if the current communication needs of me and another person don't match?

4) What two outcomes determine whether I and any partners feel our communication was *effective*?

5) What are the two most important variables that determine communication effectiveness in any situation?

6) Why is it impossible for two people in a relationship to "not communicate"?

7) What are over 20 common communication blocks, and what can I do about each of them?

8) What are the four universal interpersonal-communication situations, and which of the seven mental/verbal skills should I use in each one?

9) What does childhood have to do with how effective a communicator I, my kids, and important others, are?

10) What are the ~30 everyday factors I can learn to help me assess and improve my communication successes? Examples: "flooding," double messages, defocusing, assuming (mind reading), intellectualizing, and generalizing. Of these 30, which are the most important?

11) What's a "Bill of Personal Rights?" How can thoughtfully

building one of my own significantly improve my effectiveness at asserting and problem solving?

Reading this book will also help you develop useful answers to . . .

12) Which is the only one of the 16 possible outcomes of any communication exchange that allows both partners to feel "successful"? Knowing the answer is critical, if you want to become adept at identifying how often you and key others communicate *effectively*.

13) What's the vital difference between listening, and listening with my *heart*?

14) What are the keys to my giving effective feedback, including praise, to strangers and loved ones?

15) Why are effective communications usually harder to achieve with family members than other people?

16) What's my gender got to do with how effective my social and intimate communications are?

17) What's the difference between fighting, arguing, and problem solving; and how can I tell which I'm doing?

18) How can I see below conscious surface needs to my *true* needs, and assert them effectively with others in a mutually respectful way?

19) What personal needs can only be filled by me—so it's conflictual and useless to ask or demand that other people fill them?

20) What's the simple key to asserting my needs with others *effectively*, including with people I distrust, dislike, or fear?

21) How can I learn to say "No" (assert my limits and boundaries) without feeling cold, selfish, anxious, apologetic, and/or guilty?

22) How can I spot *inner*personal conflicts, and how can I usually resolve them?

23) How can I graphically "map" (diagram) my key communication sequences and patterns, in order to spot

problems inside or between me and others, and permanently resolve them?

24) What's the most effective option I have with a communication partner who's too upset to hear me now?

25) How can I learn to express hurt, frustration, and anger safely, honestly, and productively—without undue anxiety (worry), guilt, and/or shame?

26) Why do I and others lie, at times? If I lie "too much," how can I reduce that safely? If key others lie to me, can I do anything to reduce that?

The first part of this book will introduce you to . . .

. . . **your** *inner* **family** and who leads it, and communication basics (Chapter 1).

. . . **seven skills** you can learn and use to fill your daily needs more often (Chapters 2–8).

. . . **how to use** these skills to reduce or resolve conflicts (need clashes) *inside* you (Chapter 9), and . . .

. . . **some premises** about healthy (high-nurturance) relationships (Chapter 10).

The Resources section summarizes communication basics and each of the seven skills, for reference ease. These summaries include Internet addresses to over 20 practice exercises, self-discovery worksheets, checklists, and articles. The section also includes _ a sample Bill of Personal Rights, _ a summary of 29 common communication blocks, and _ a unique 300+-term communication-relationship glossary. The book closes with a thorough index.

How to Use This Book

Scan these options, pick those that appeal you, and add your own . . .

Before reading this book, I encourage you to read the companion book "Who's *Really* Running Your Life?," [xlibris.com] or the Web articles at [http://sfhelp.org/pop/

assess.htm]. You'll learn about your *inner* family of personality subselves, and clarify who's been making your life decisions: your true Self, or someone else. If a protective "false self" controls you, you'll probably miss or distort key ideas in this book. I suspect that over half of any communication problems you experience are *inside you*. If your false self is controlling you, you may have thoughts now like . . .

"My communication is OK enough now."
"Sounds interesting, but I don't have time."
"Too much like work. No way!"
"This is just more pop psychology psychobabble."
"This stuff is probably too complicated. Forget it."

Thoughts like these come from distrustful subselves trying to protect you from some suspected discomfort or danger. You also really may have more important things to do now. If you experience strong inner resistance to reading or using the ideas here, I suspect a more worthy goal is learning if a well-meaning, myopic false self is holding you in protective custody.

If you're not in a place to read "Who's *Really* Running Your Life?" now, Chapters 1 and 10 here suggest what's possible.

A second way to best use this book is to coach yourself to **build and keep three key attitudes** as you read and experiment:

Curiosity: Choose the open, questioning, thoughtful, focused "mind of a student." The alternative is a rigid, cynical, or distracted (split) mind of a non-student. If a narrow-minded protective false self is controlling you, keeping an open, focused mind here will probably be hard. You'll learn (or confirm) who's controlling you in the next chapter.

Patience: Take a long-range view, as you read and try out these communication ideas. You've spent decades learning your present communication attitudes, values, and habits. It will take months of study, experimenting, and evaluation to make consistent changes in your communication outcomes. Good news: some benefits can happen quickly! Finally . . .

Experiment: Reading this book will not build your communication skills. *Doing* the many "Reality-check" exercises and *trying* the seven skills is the only way you'll experience their power and usefulness. Welcome "mistakes." They're useful guides to learning! Let yourself feel alien, awkward, and even phony with the skills, for a time, without guilt. Even Mozart wasn't a concert pianist his first time at the keyboard. As with any new skill, these seven will take practice, feedback, and patience before they become automatic and fully effective for you. Take two helpful slogans to guide you on your exploration:

"Progress, not perfection!", and . . .

"The road to success is always under construction."

If possible, practice with a partner. Having someone to share experiences and feedback with will speed your learning, and make it more fun. If you don't have a partner now, you can always ask trusted others for clear feedback on your communication behaviors. And you always have *inner* partners!

Avoid preaching: As these skills start enabling you to fill more daily needs, I suggest you avoid trying to persuade insecure or uninterested partners to try them. Kids are the exception. Though well meant, persuading resistant adults can imply that you're "1-up," and the receiver "needs fixing." This implication breeds resentment, defensiveness, and resistance. *Modeling* your expanding communication skills often raises others' interest, over time.

Expect some "unease" and distrust in others: Partners' first reactions to you communicating differently may be "unease": distrust, confusion, and anxiety. Shame-based and fear-based people can misjudge new behaviors like empathic listening as phony or gimmicky. They, i.e. their distrustful false selves, may believe that you're trying to "pull something" on them.

Using these seven skills to manipulate others, rather than communicate, is a form of aggression. Doing so inevitably erodes trust and respect. If your steady goals are . . .

"I want to hear you clearly, and I want both of us to get more of what we need here,"

. . . then these mental/verbal skills *will* enhance your relationships, starting within you. When your true attitude about your communication partner is "=/=":

"Your dignity and current opinions and needs are just as valid and important as mine,"

then these seven skills *will* get more of your needs met. Any other attitude will be sent by your voice tone, body, and face, and will dilute or block the skills' usefulness.

A tape or video recorder can help you learn these skills, and your present communication habits. Recorders can also help avoid the endless *"You said . . . No I didn't"* cycles that erupt when insecure people feel attacked or get confrontive feedback. Recording devices can also scare and distract uneasy partners from communicating freely. If such devices are used to trap, beat, or shame another person (*"See? You* do *swear all the time!"*), then relationships and self-esteem will suffer.

Option: Keep a log or journal: A core communication skill is *awareness*: learning to perceive and sense what's really going on inside you, and with others. Grow your awareness by regularly writing down your communication goals, experiments, thoughts, and feelings. Most men ("male brains") and emotionally-repressed women can benefit from periodically expressing their thoughts and feelings on paper. Doing this breeds confidence in acknowledging them to yourself, and expressing them clearly and confidently to others. Emotional and physical *feelings* signal what you really need now.

If an inner voice says *"Oh, I can't write,"* or *"What if someone reads my log?"* get interested in what protective inner-family member is speaking. I doubt that it's your wise true Self. I recommend Julia Cameron's excellent guide to keeping such a self-discovery log in *"The Artist's Way."* Her book is really about growing your inner awareness and honoring your self, more than being an artist.

To get the most from reading this book, use the tools. The resource section of this book offers you reference summaries, and points to many selected articles, self-discovery worksheets, checklists, and practice exercises. The book closes with a thorough index. You can learn as much from *using* the tools, readings, glossary, and index as from reading the Basics and Skills chapters.

Authorize yourself to **mark up the book** as you go: jot notes, circle or hilight key points, draw faces; bring a pen and markers, and dialog with me and the ideas in these pages!

Pick communication hero/ines. Some of us are more effective communicators than others. Identify one or more of the people you've known whom you feel are specially effective communicators. It may be useful to pick someone of your gender. Try to spot specifically why you single them out. In key situations, ask or imagine *"What would (my hero/ine) do here?"* If you do this, stay clear that you have a different personality, different values, and probably a different "style" than they do. The goal here is to notice who communicates well and who doesn't, not to become someone's clone. Beware of your *Inner Critic* comparing your efforts to their behaviors, and shaming your inner kids.

 # Reality check: Try it now: *Someone I know who is a specially effective communicator is . . .* Identify several reasons you choose her or him. If you can't think of a hero/ine now, what does that imply?

The options above can increase your rewards for using the ideas in this book. Because you're unique on Earth, reflect and add your own tips for yourself: e.g. *"Don't read this at night, when I'm tired and distracted."* You'll probably develop tips along the way, as your awareness grows.

This chapter summarizes what's unique about this communication-skills book, whom it's written for, why you should read it, and what's in it. It ends with nine options to help you get the biggest payback from your time and effort in reading these chapters.

Reflect: what are you aware of now that you weren't before you began reading this? *"I don't know," "I'm not sure,"* and *"Nothing"* are OK answers.

Now let's lay a foundation of basic definitions and concepts, before learning about each of the seven communication skills. Do you have "the (open, curious) mind of a student" right now? Are you ready to meet your *inner* family of subselves, and learn who's usually leading it?

BASICS AND THE 7 SKILLS

1) Inner family and communication basics

2) Communication *awareness*

3) Clear thinking

4) Dig down to true needs

5) Metatalk: talking about communicating

6) Empathic listening: hearing with your heart

7) Effective assertion

8) Problem solving (conflict resolution)

9) High-nurturance relationships . . .

10) Resolving *inner* conflicts

11) What would your life be like if . . .

1) Basics

"I know you believe you understand what you think I said,
But I'm not sure you realize that
what you heard was not what I meant."
—*Poster*

You're about to meet a cluster of ideas about *effective* inner and interpersonal communications. Each idea adds to the whole, and some are extra important. Add your own symbols, hilights, rephrases, and notes as you go. Make these ideas yours!

This chapter _ introduces *inner*-family basics, and _ outlines basic communication premises and definitions. To begin: **do you know who is *really* running your life?** You may be surprised . . .

Inner-family Basics

Have you ever loved and hated a person at the same time? Have you ever acted impulsively, and said later, "I don't know what got into me?" Do you ever have outbursts, spells, moods, or feel unusually clear or confused at different times? Have you had the experience of feeling like a kid in the presence of a parent or authority? Do you ever smile or chuckle when you're hurting, or sometimes do things "without knowing why?" Have you ever had a self-harmful habit that you couldn't "break," like overworking, overeating, using toxic drugs like nicotine or sugar, or exercising too much or too little? Have you ever been in an emotionally toxic co-dependent relationship? Do you have unusual or chronic guilts and/or fears?

Do you know adults and kids who have some or many of these traits? Do you dub yourself or them psychologically "crazy"? Do you know why we all do these things? Will I ever stop asking these questions?

Multiplicity is Normal

Some researchers propose a new explanation for these paradoxic, vexing realities about human nature: *multiplicity*. This is the natural ability of our neural system ("brain") to reprogram itself in response to injury or environmental threats, like a low-nurturance ("dysfunctional") early childhood. Multiplicity seems to be an built-in function that promotes our *survival* (vs. growth). The pop psychology term "split personality" refers to this. The media sensationalizes extreme cases of personality splitting ("Multiple Personality Disorder"). It doesn't recognize yet that we're *all* "split" to some degree.

You're in the first generation in history to be able to see living human brains in action. Positron Emission Tomography (PET) radiographic scans reveal that a simple experience like "I feel / smell / taste / see / understand the peach" simultaneously activates multiple regions of our brain. This happens all the time, without our control or awareness. It has been part of our "normal daily life" since we were late-stage fetuses.

Our short-term memory resides in one brain region, and long-term memory in another. One neural center decodes meaning from visual shapes, another center decodes colors, and a third identifies smells. While you're automatically "thinking," your brain is also dynamically regulating your breathing, digestion, blood composition and distribution; your body temperature, dividing and repairing cells; fighting off infections. These are all totally below your conscious awareness. Among the many implications of this *multiplicity* feature of your brain and nervous system, one is key here.

Before examining this implication, note another reality about you and the people you care for: **we all seem to have at least three minds**: conscious, semi-conscious, and unconscious. My study of clinical hypnosis illuminated some of the mysterious communications that go on in and between these three busy arenas. Our multi-faceted personality seems to live scattered in parts of all three domains, like relatives living in different geographic states.

Let's say your *personality* **is** "the collection of beliefs, attitudes, knowledge, values, memories, sensitivities, tendencies, habits, traits, and conscious and unconscious associations, and preferences that make you unique among all humans who ever lived." (Whew). Parents, teachers, ancestors, and the media usually teach us as kids that we have one body (true), one brain (true), and one monolithic personality (*false*). Through sensationalized media presentations, we're taught that people with "multiple personalities" _ exist, and _ are "crazy." Is that what you believe?

Thanks to new brain-scan technology and psychological research, the ancient one brain-one personality myth now seems as misguided as the once-unquestioned "fact" that the Sun revolves around the Earth. **Normal personalities now appear to be composed of a group of different** *parts*, **or** *subselves*, which may correspond to different areas of our brains. Your *Inner Critic* may be one set of neural areas, your *Procrastinator* another, and your *Rebellious Kid* yet another. This has profound implications for human behavior, social relationships, and effective communications within us, and between us.

I've studied and practiced "*Inner* Family Therapy" since

attending a seminar by veteran psychologist Richard Schwartz in 1988. What you're about to read is a digest of what I've learned from two externships with him and clinical colleagues, clinical writings and seminars on "dissociative disorders," and scores of inward-exploring therapy clients. For other views on your multi-faceted personality, see the book list on the Web at [http://sfhelp.org/11/resources.htm].

Are you ready to explore the amazing, unique Being called by your name?

Three or Four Groups of Subselves

Premise: normal personalities like yours are like orchestras, sports teams, or committees. They're composed of semi-autonomous *parts* or *subselves*. These . . .

. . . **have** their own values and priorities, thoughts, memories, goals, opinions, strategies, and allegiances;

. . . **can** learn new facts, and change their inner family roles and goals quickly, when that seems safe and reasonable; and our subselves . . .

. . . **all** mean us well, though at times their actions cause us and other people injury, pain, and even death. And our personality parts . . .

. . . **can** communicate with each other and our conscious mind in various ways: thoughts ("inner voices"), emotions, hunches, fantasies, day and night dreams, "intuition," "senses," inner images, and body sensations. These can include "nervous or tight stomach;" (some) "headaches;" "indigestion;" muscle aches, twinges, spasms, or tics; "shallow (or no) breathing;" skin tingling, flushing, and perhaps "goose bumps;" sighing; and automatic (unconscious) gestures facial expressions, and voice tones. I now believe "psychosomatic illness" (no identified organic cause) is real, and is one or more subselves urgently trying to tell us something.

Our inner troupe of subselves seems to be made up of **three or four functional groups**:

Regulars, who make our daily decisions when no inner or outer crises are apparent. Typical Regular subselves include a *Driver* or *Achiever* ("Get going!"), a *Historian*, an *Organizer-Planner*, a *Spiritual One*, a *Wise One*, a *Nurturer-Good Parent*, a *Health Director*, an *Analyzer*, an *Observer*, a *Creative One*, and an *Adult* ("Common Sense.") Each of these subselves has a main interest and strength, or talent, which it contributes to the whole family *when allowed to* by other subselves.

A key Regular is your true Self (capital "S"). My experience suggests that at birth, every neurally normal infant has the seeds of this personality part. Its innate, undeveloped talent is to coordinate all other subselves well, and make wholistically healthy short-term and long-term decisions.

As this subself matures and gains life awareness and confidence, it's increasingly adept at what effective human leaders do well: set clear goals, limits, and policies; learn, flex, direct, organize, forgive, delegate, decide, coordinate, support, give feedback, nurture, innovate, affirm, praise, encourage, team-build, evaluate, inspire, balance, and unselfishly develop other team members. Have you ever worked or studied with someone with many of these qualities? If you were so fortunate, how would you describe the ongoing effect this leader had on your group's morale and productivity?

Do you trust that you now have such a naturally gifted leader *within* you, who is motivated, skilled, and qualified to lead your inner crew if s/he is allowed to? When their Self is solidly in charge of their group of subselves, people spontaneously report feeling *centered, grounded, energized, aware, "up," clear, strong, calm, firm, focused, relaxed, compassionate, "light," purposeful, alive, and serene.* Remember the last time you felt a mix of those?

Premise: when your subselves trust your Self to lead them, you're most likely to communicate effectively.

This implies that you can practice the seven mental/verbal skills described here and still communicate ineffectively, if a "false self'" is making your life decisions. So improving your **communication effectiveness really starts with getting clear on who is *really* running your life.** If it's not your true Self, work on empowering him or her first! See the companion volume "Who's *Really* Running Your Life?" [www.xlibris.com].

Besides your staff of Regulars, the second functional group of normal personality parts is composed of your . . .

Vulnerables, or inner children (plural). These are developmentally young, naïve, impulsive, and reactive. They bring us intense emotions like love, joy, awe, curiosity, shame, guilt, lust, rage, loneliness, sadness, impatience, and terror. Our Vulnerables know little of the world, and are driven more by needs and emotions than logic. They usually have short attention spans, and seek gratification *now*. If one or more of these subselves control you, that often causes "trouble." The title *Vulnerables* notes that these young subselves can't protect themselves from emotional injury, just as unsupervised young boys and girls are vulnerable to dangers around them. This susceptibility generates a third functional group of personality parts: your . . .

Guardians, or Protectors. Depending on the number and traits of our Vulnerables, we each develop a unique squad of subselves in childhood. The lower the nurturance-level of our earliest years, the more Guardian subselves we develop. Their sole purpose is to soothe, comfort, and protect our young Vulnerable parts. Most of our troublesome personal and social behavior comes from these narrow-visioned Guardians "taking us over," to protect our inner kids. Here are some common Guardians, titled by their preferred strategies. Recognize any old friends here?

- Procrastinator
- Illusionist / Magician
- Idealist / Zealot / Bigot

- Bum / Loser / Failer
- Controller / Manipulator
- Hermit / Loner / Nun
- Professor / Mentor
- Con / Thief / Crook
- Murderer / Suicider
- Rescuer / Savior
- Distracter / Defocuser
- Plodder / Good soldier

- Predator / Stalker
- Daredevil / Risk Taker

- Lunatic / Crazy One
- Righteous One

- Perfectionist
- Inner Critic (Blamer)
- Addict / Obsesser

- Superstar / Winner
- Saint / Martyr / Victim
- Clown / Entertainer
- Seducer / Gigolo
- Liar / Deceiver
- Idiot / Dunce
- Numb-er / Anesthetist
- Warrior / Amazon
- Narcissist

- Rebel / Troublemaker
- Explorer / Adventurer

- Bitch / Bastard
- Worrier / Doubter

Reality check: Star or hilight which of these are significant in your life. If you have other favorite Guardian subselves, add them.

The fourth group of personality parts or energies is subject to personal experience, interpretation, and opinion. These are Spiritual or "Higher" Ones. They can include Guardian Angels, Higher Selves, Future Selves, Spirit Councils, personal Totems, "Watchers," "Guides," "Old Ones," and other transcendent beings or energies that seem to affect some humans in times of stress or crisis.

I was raised as an atheist, and first trained as an engineer. After 63 inquiring years on Earth and 15 years' recovery from a low-nurturance childhood, I now believe that "something" or "someone" *does* intervene for many of us at crucial or random times. Whether this is God or another element of the universe is beyond our scope. The point is: if some kind of *higher* energy does exist, it may communicate with you and others at times. That may affect your awareness, needs, and behavior, and your communication with your self and others.

Because our neurological *multiplicity* is an emerging concept, researchers don't agree yet on how many subselves typical people have; what to call them; why and how they originate, interact, and behave; and what to do if they're not well organized and led. Our current generation of personality pioneers is like the proverbial five blind people first encountering an elephant:

"*It's a boulder,*" says one, feeling the belly.

"*No, no, it's a snake,*" says another, exploring the waving trunk.

"*You're both wrong,*" said a third, feeling a massive leg, "*It's a tree!*"

"What are you saying? It's a vine or rope," says the person feeling the tail.

"*How can you all be so blind?*" said the fifth (with a smile?). Feeling the elephant's broad ear, he says, "*It's obviously a fan!*"

Some researchers suggest that it's normal, at least for people from low-nurturance childhoods, to have well over a dozen active and dormant subselves. Veteran researcher and clinician John Rowan suggests that people he's met seem to have an average of about seven subselves. One variable is that a subself may have more than one major trait. For example, one Vulnerable personality part may bring you feelings of anger, sadness, and fear at different times. All subselves, including your Self, appear to feel a range of emotions. Some parts "specialize" in bringing key emotions to your bodily awareness; e.g. "my enraged, defiant, *Inner Teen.*"

Currently, there's a healthy clinical debate about personality leadership. Some say there is a true Self, and others say, "*No, the personality-parts team is run by consensus, like a commune.*" My experience leads me to the former view, with a vital variation. To understand it, I need to present another inner-family premise.

Blending and Your False Self

After a decade of clinical research and experience, my instructor Dr. Richard Schwartz proposed that when one or more Vulnerables or Guardian parts "activate," or "get excited," **they blend with**, or infuse and "take over" (disable) your Self. Your Self can't prevent this, just as the conductor of a volunteer orchestra can't stop upset musicians from forcibly taking over the podium and baton.

When blending occurs, you feel, need, experience, and think what the activated subselves do. Their interpretation of sensory perceptions becomes "yours," so you, the person, behave the way they want you to. Until these excited parts calm down, they control your hormones, breathing, perceptions, thoughts, and muscles. At such times, **you (the person) are controlled by a *false self*:** two or more subselves who either don't know your Self exists, or they do, but don't trust him or her to take charge and gain the comfort and safety they need now. Your false self may be any mix of activated young Vulnerables and their dedicated, narrow-visioned Guardians.

Some people blend occasionally, in unusual situations. Others, usually survivors of low-nurturance childhoods, are blended or *split,* most of the time. The latter people aren't conscious of it, for it feels *normal.* Blending happens like lightning. Most kids and adults seem unaware of it when it happens, until they begin personal recovery from protective false-self dominance.

Psychological Wounds

After researching and recovering from the impacts from false-self wounds for 15 years, I conclude that average adults like *you* (and your partner, parents and siblings) may have a minor to significant mix of up to **six "inner wounds"** *and not know it* (denial and unawareness):

Being situationally or chronically ruled by a reactive, *protective* false self, rather than your wise true Self. This promotes inner family confusion, defocusing and fuzzy thinking, and . . .

Excessive shame ("I'm a disgusting, worthless, unlovable person") **and guilts** ("I break rules—do bad things."); and . . .

Excessive fears of the unknown (change), emotional overwhelm, "failure" (shame and guilt), success, and abandonment (aloneness);

Trust distortions: _ trusting toxic people or situations, and/ or _ distrusting safe ones. This includes *self* distrust, and trust in a benign, reliable Higher Power;

Reality distortions like denial, repression, minimizing, intellectualizing, projecting, hallucinating, and idealizing.

These five combine to promote:

Difficulty bonding (loving): an impaired ability to form normal emotional-spiritual *attachments* to certain or all people, or all living things. Sociopaths are the extreme example. If you know people who are "cold" and/or "can only show love by giving money and *things*," they probably have all six wounds.

When you read "false self" in the rest of this book, it stands for having some mix of these inner wounds. Does it seem credible to you that adults and kids suffering these unseen injuries have trouble nurturing themselves and others via communicating effectively? Low-nurturance relationships reproduce themselves and spread until sufferers get into true recovery.

Does "your *inner* family" mean more now? I suspect the idea that you are composed of a shadowy troupe, troop, clan, gang, squad, community, company, committee, or team of semi-independent personality subselves is new to you. If so, relax, breathe well, and listen for a moment to your *self-talk*: the mix of "inner voices" (thoughts), emotions, and body sensations you're experiencing right now. What do you hear? Paradoxically, "nothing" is something.

You're experiencing *inner* communications right now, between different areas of your brain (subselves); at least those acting in your conscious mind. You can't know what neural communiqués are flashing back and forth in your unconscious mind, though your body and mood may give you clues.

Reread the questions at the start of this inner-family introduction. Do those common human "foibles" now make more sense to you? Usually, every one of them is a symptom of a distrustful false-self blending with your Self. Note: if we were just one person(ality), proper English speakers would greet each other with "How *is* you?"

Are you wondering, "How can I learn if I'm controlled by a short-sighted false self, and if I am, how can I empower my true Self? The companion book "Who's *Really* Running Your Life" provides tools and recommendations to answer those questions, based on a over decade of my clinical research and experience.

False Selves and Your Communication Effectiveness

Are you wondering *"Why am I reading about subselves, inner kids and families, blending, and elephants, when I got this book to learn about communications?"* Here's why:

For most adults and kids, blending automatically occurs when two or more subselves experience significant discomforts. These can include shock, fear, emotional or physical pain, disorientation (confusion), guilt, despair, and/or shame. These may happen when you're alone (e.g. you cut yourself badly, or lose your keys), or with one or more other people. The latter is usually some form of conflict, confrontation, or embarrassment.

When a false self significantly controls you and/or a communication partner, you or they lose the calm wisdom and leadership of your true Self. Your inner communications are likely to become chaotic; e.g. subselves "yelling," interrupting, arguing, withdrawing, and catastrophizing. You, the person, lose your ability to hear and think clearly, and to make calm decisions, moment by moment.

False-self domination also promotes distorted perceptions and decodings of other people's intentions and behavior (*"I don't believe you, Maxine. I know you're badmouthing me behind my back to steal my job!"*) Acting on such distortions is likely to "upset" (split) your partner/s, so *their* thinking and behaving becomes distorted and reactive. Until everyone's true Selves can stop the inner and mutual pandemonium (*"Time out!"*), assess things, and effectively get their excited subselves to unblend, communications within and between the two groups of agitated subselves can escalate into a screaming match, a blame-and-shame contest ("power struggle"), or icy silence.

Each time that happens, both people lose some trust in their respective abilities to communicate effectively together. That puts their Vulnerable and Guardian parts on automatic alert any time communication is needed. That anxiety promotes quicker blending, and more of the same, unless both people start to study and use what you're reading here!

Recap: Your Inner Family

In the last generation, new radiographic technology shows living brains operating like a network of mini-computers exchanging simultaneous signals. Instead of having one personality as our ancestors believed, normal adults and kids have a group of semi-autonomous personality *parts*, or *subselves* that interact to produce our waking and sleeping experiences and behaviors. Some interactions are conscious ("inner voices"), and others are outside our awareness.

Your group of subselves can be called an inner family, for they interact just like parents, kids, and relatives. Subselves seem to fall into four functional groups: Regulars; young, reactive Vulnerables; their ever-vigilant Guardians; and probably some "Higher" spiritual energies. One of the Regulars is a talented natural leader: your true Self. When anxious or uncomfortable Vulnerables and/or Guardians don't know your Self, or don't trust him/her, they *blend* with that personality part and take it over. As a group, such usurping subselves are called (here) your *false self.* Many people live their lives dominated by a false self, *and never know it.*

When you and/or a communication partner are significantly blended, typically . . .

Your inner-family communication becomes chaotic, and your perceptions of your inner and outer worlds become distorted. That promotes . . .

Your words, voice dynamics, and body language (*"You're amazingly stupid for a college graduate."*) upsetting your partner's subselves, promoting their inner chaos to increase, and . . .

Acting in ways that escalate your inner ruckus. (*"I see we're into oversensitivity, defensiveness, and childish sarcasm again, eh?"*)

From this summary, notice at least three things. "Fights" and "disagreements" between you and other people are really three simultaneous conflicts in and between your inner families. Growing your inner-family awareness, and proactively empowering your true Self to harmonize and lead your inner crew in confusing times, will improve your half of this. If your partner does the same, s/he may improve her or his third of your communication action. If you *both* learn the seven skills in this book, you can improve the process in and *between* your inner families, over time. Note your self-talk now: what's your inner crew saying about this concept? If your false self is in charge now, you may be "hearing" (thinking) things like . . .

Scared Kid (Vulnerable): *"These ideas are weird. They're* *going to lead to something scary and bad. Stop reading!"*

Shamed Kid (Vulnerable): *"I knew it. No wonder I can't talk good with people, specially girls. I'm psycho, split, and nutso. I am so pathetic and weird. No one can ever love me."*

Pessimist *(Guardian): "Way, way too complicated and heady. Put the book down."*

Skeptic *(Guardian): "This is too far out. The author wants me to believe a gang of wacko 'subselves' runs me. I can see "splitting" in my sister the Olympic Dingbat, but not me. Forget this."*

Catastrophizer: *"Oh my GOD! I see it! My whole life, we've been split and have never let our Self be in charge! I've wasted my entire life. I don't even know what normal feels like! This is hopeless—I'll be held hostage by this gang of subselves that I don't even know for the rest of my days. I'll wind up on the street, alone, poor, and crazy. What ever possessed me to start reading this?"*

Observer: *"My, we're all upset, aren't we?"*

Addict (Comforter): *"Hey, a big chunk of (soothing high-fat) pizza would really taste good about now, huh? C'mon . . ."*

Distracter: *"Listen! What's that strange noise in the next room? Could it be . . ."*

Inner Critic: *"How come Mom and Dad never taught us about this stuff? I should have seen this about 25 years ago. Boy, talk about people controlled by false selves; what losers."*

If your Self were free to lead, s/he might say . . .

Self: *"Troops, how about calming down? Stop! Pull back from me (unblend), and let's talk this over. Let me understand what each of you wants here. Unless there's something you see that I don't, I think we ought to read a little more just to see what's here, before quitting the book . . ."*

Does your inner communication ever "sound" anything like this? What would make it *effective*? Do you identify with any of these subselves? If your troop needs a break now, why not take one? If you're making a communication log, consider jotting down your thoughts and awarenesses. We're about to shift gears, and start reviewing some basic communication premises and definitions.

Communication Basics

This section overviews what inner and interpersonal communication *is*, why and how we do it, and seven skills that can optimize it for you. The section ends with a premise on two factors that determine if your communication is *effective*.

In my experience, typical people like you don't know what they don't know about their communication values and habits. You and other people learned to listen, process, and talk from your families, teachers, heroes, friends, and persecutors. Few of them knew what you're about to learn here, so people like you are often unaware of your current communications *process*, and your choices. As our hands come to automatically tie bows, use a keyboard, or play an instrument, we talk and listen from habit, even if the results don't please us. Taking a "speech" class may grow diction, public speaking, or debating abilities, but probably won't cover the seven mental/verbal skills described here.

Years of practicing clinical hypnosis taught me profound respect for the mental and emotional power of individual words, and how they're said. My consistent experience is that when average people are asked *"What are they keys to a healthy relationship?"* many will say something like *". . . and partners need to have 'open and honest' communications."*

I use the adjective *effective* here to describe our communication-process outcomes, rather than *open and honest* or *good*. The phrase *good communication* implies that someone's judging for *bad*. That promotes people controlled by shamed subselves to blend. They lose their Self to a *Shamed* or *Anxious Child*, or their subself Guardians, who will distort their perceptions and thinking. *"I communicate badly"* can unconsciously generalize to "*I am an inept, bad person.*" This is a serious communication block, for self-respect is essential for effective inner and social communication. The rest of this book focuses on shifting your and your partners' communications from *ineffective* to *effective*, over time.

The following section summarizes the key concepts and terms underlying the seven mental/verbal skills you'll study in the following chapters. Learning these basics lays the foundation for the first of these skills: *awareness*. To see if you should learn these basics, take this . . .

Communication Quiz

What is "*effective* communication"?

What are the six needs you and others try to fill by communicating? Which one of them does each person always have in every social situation?

What are the four meanings we decode from each other's behavior all the time? Which one of these determines the effectiveness of any communication you have with another person?

What are the three "channels" that we all use to decode meaning from each other? Which of these channels is usually the most influential?

What are the seven mental/verbal skills you can learn to use in any communication situation, and how do they relate to each other?

What are the four common communication situations between two personality subselves or people, and which of the seven communication skills is best suited to each situation?

What two factors determine whether any internal or social communication exchange is successful? Why do people who don't know these basics have only about a 6% chance of success in critical exchanges?

How did you do? Please don't criticize yourself if you can't answer most of these questions. In the communication classes I've taught for 30 years and with my therapy clients, few people could, because their teachers (including parents) didn't know them either. A wonderful paradox is that we all depend largely on the skill of inner and social communication to fill our daily needs, yet few of us ever study how to "do it well." Hmm.

My experience is that most adults, including Ph.D.s and most relationship counselors, don't know what they don't know about what you're reading here. Therefore they don't read books or go to classes on communication skills. They (*you*) get along "well enough," without knowing what's possible. Among other things, that means their kids will probably inherit their unawareness" of answers to the quiz above, unless they're lucky enough to have a knowledgeable teacher. If you're a caregiver, can your kids answer the questions above yet?

Adopt the (open, curious) "mind of a student," and consider these premises . . .

What Are Communications?

What would you reply if a touring space alien asked, "What is this thing you humans do called 'communicate'?" I'd say "It's a dynamic series of emotional, spiritual, and physical interactions inside and between two or more humans who need something from each other." This view suggests that:

anything you do, or don't do, that causes a physical, emotional, spiritual, and/or mental change in another is "interpersonal communication."

It is a need-driven, cyclic sequence of cause > effect events: a process in which each person _ decodes meanings from the other's behavior, _ experiences two or more needs (discomforts) from the meanings, and _ seeks to fill them by responding verbally and nonverbally.

A key implication from this premise is that people in relationships can't *not*-communicate. The lack of a look, touch, sound, or note, causes meanings just as speech, touch, and eye contact do. If someone says, "*S/he didn't say anything*," or "*I got no response*," know that there probably were meanings assumed, like "*You don't care much about me right now.*" That may or may not be what the silent one meant, but that's often how the perceived absence of verbal, visual, and/or physical communication is decoded. Remember the last time you felt someone "didn't communicate?" Did you draw some conscious meaning from that, and/or have some emotional reaction?

Six Reasons We Communicate

Think of the last time you had a communication exchange with someone. What did you *need*? I believe there are only six needs that cause humans to communicate. In any exchange, each person tries to fill two or more of them. If both people succeed well enough in their own judgment, they rate their communications as *effective*. The six core needs are to . . .

Feel inner and outer **respect** (always present);

Give or get **information**;

Vent: release emotion, and receive empathy and acceptance;

Cause change or action; i.e. to feel potent, vs. powerless;

Cause excitement (end boredom), and/or to . . .

Avoid uncomfortable emotions and thoughts; e.g. end awkward silence, or deflect inner or interpersonal conflict.

Each of these communication motives aims to reduce some current emotional or physical discomfort. In any calm or conflictual situation, you and each partner need "enough" respect, plus one or more of the other five needs. Can you recall a time you needed three or four of these at once? Note that each of your inner-family members (subselves) need each of these too, so they communicate all the time!

To build your *awareness* (skill # 1), here's some perspective on each of these six core communication motives:

Need 1) The Universal Need for Respect

Comedian Rodney Dangerfield clowns, *"I don't get no respect!"* The media shows Mafia chieftains killing for lack of it. We all constantly need "enough" respect the comforting *feeling* of worth (value), acceptance, and approval that regulates our actions all the time. There are two sources for the respect we seek: inside us, and from other people. How our inner family reacts to our *Inner Critic* (subself) determines our "self esteem." Am I right in guessing you constantly decode the perceived behaviors of other people to determine if you feel respected enough by them? You may only be aware of doing this when someone seems *disrespectful*.

The need for respect, credible personal worth and dignity, is primal, powerful, and omnipresent in all people and situations. When one or more partners don't feel enough self-respect and social respect, communication effectiveness plummets. Is that your experience? A major implication: shame-based (false-self dominated) adults and kids will have trouble communicating with others, specially those with low self-respect. Shame-based co-parents often unintentionally raise kids with low self-respect, so excessive shame has been wryly called "the gift that goes on giving."

Reality check: think of someone you've had significant "trouble" communicating with: i.e. filling your six needs. How would you describe _ their self-respect, and _ the respect they seem to feel for you? Do you think s/he feels respected enough by you? Have you two ever talked together about how your inner and mutual respects affect your communication outcomes? Few of us communicators do, without coaching. This is specially tragic between unaware parents and minor kids.

Need 2) To Give or Get Information

George asks Sylvia "What's for dinner?" Sylvia says, "I'm afraid the pot roast is overcooked." Al asks Shannon "Did you finish your math homework?" The President asks, "How are we doing in the Iowa polls?" I write this book (give information), and you read it (get information). This instinctual communication need (discomfort) often focuses more on facts than emotions, except in intimate and therapeutic conversations. A key type of information we often want to communicate to others (and sometimes learn from them) is what we or they need right now.

Need 3) To Vent

Infants, kids, adults, and most animals need to *express* their thoughts, emotions, and needs at certain times. The last time you needed to vent, what discomforts were you trying to reduce? Why? What response did you need from your partner? The core communication tensions that cause venting are our normal human needs to _ release (express) emotions, and _ feel empathically heard, validated, accepted, and *respected* by one or more partners. Does that match your experience? Does venting without a partner satisfy your local needs?

Extreme versions of the need to vent occur when kids and adults have "rage attacks," "hysteria," or uncontrollable "weeping spells." These *always* indicate local dominance of a false self, and inner-family chaos. In such cases, subselves' need to release emotions is (temporarily) more important than keeping partners' respect and acceptance.

Need 4) To Cause Action and Feel Potent

Many times in an average day and night, you and your communication partners communicate to "get results" or changes. The changes you seek may be _ inside you ["I felt better (the change), after I told Jeff I felt he was lying"] and/or _ outside you: i.e. shifting the thoughts, feelings, needs, beliefs, and/or actions of another person. Ultimately, needing another person to change or do something is about raising *your* comfort.

Paradoxically, altruism ("selflessness") is real, and yet all communication is basically "selfish."

The need for action (change) manifests in all your relationships, as you and your partners constantly adjust the emotional and physical distance between you. The changes you seek range between _ come emotionally or physically closer (*"Could you give me a back rub?"*), or _ move further away (Jed stopped calling his sister), or _ stay right where you are. (*"No, I don't want to go to counseling with you."*)

The primal reason we communicate is to cause change: to lower current emotional tensions and/or physical discomfort within us. Sometimes our surface need to cause action implies a deeper need to feel potent (impactful, powerful, able), vs. helpless. This helps reduce uncomfortable anxiety that "I'm too weak or inept to change things, so I'm vulnerable and anxious!" As infants, you, the President, Billy Graham, and our respective parents, and I all felt that intense anxiety at times. Remember?

Need 5) To Generate Excitement

At times, adults and kids communicate to end deadening boredom. Do you know anyone who "loves a good debate (or fight)", or says "white" if you say "black"? Some use physical communications (pushing, pinching, tickling, caressing) to fill our need for excitement. Usually communicators with this motive aren't clearly aware their need for stimulation. Has anyone said *"I'm really* bored, *so I'm going to hassle you and generate some excitement, OK?"*

If you're not aware of their need for excitement (a form of distraction), you'll probably get frustrated trying to reason, explain, and use logic with them. They don't *care* about "making sense"! Usually people needing excitement and/or potency aren't conscious of it, until they learn to be self-aware.

The last reason you and I communicate is . . .

Need 6) To Avoid Discomfort

Jack won't met Jill's eyes. Marv lies to Alex about his poker losses. Jean "forgets" to call her controlling, critical mother. The stranger next to you says "Do you fly often?" as your plane waits to take off. Marsha says "It was OK," when her Dad asks about the school test she thinks she failed. Wendy thinks "I'll try balancing the checkbook again tomorrow." Think of the last time you behaved (communicated) to avoid some uncomfortable interaction with yourself (denial) or another person. How many times a day do you do that? One reason people avoid self-awareness is that it brings uncomfortable clarity on ("shameful") avoidances. Paradoxically, mental or behavioral avoidances often cause the discomfort of *guilt* ("You can run, but you can't hide.")

So I propose that you and the rest of us all communicate internally and socially to fill two to six current needs. Can you think of any other motives? Could you name the six before you read this? Communication success rises if you know what you (your inner family members) and your partner *need* at the moment, and over time. This is specially true in inner and social conflicts. As you'll see later, communication effectiveness drops when your mix of these six needs doesn't match mine: e.g. we each need to vent and have our partner *want* to listen to us now.

Now you know *why* your subselves and your partners communicate all the time. The next communication basic is to acknowledge the . . .

Three Ways We Exchange Messages

Filling our current needs is so vital that Nature provides three different ways to do that:

Verbal channel: spoken words and sounds (language);

Paraverbal channel: *how* the words are said (voice tone, pace, pitch, inflection, rhythm, volume, and accent); and . . .

Non-verbal channel (sight, smell, feeling, and *sensing*), including facial expression, eye contact, and body posture and movement.

These are like three different TV channels or radio stations we use concurrently to exchange information and *meaning*. Which of these do you think is the most powerful source of meaning in typical face-to-face communications? One study concluded that in a typical verbal communication, the words account for ~7% of the meaning we deduce, verbal dynamics supply ~23%, and non-verbal signals provide the remaining ~70%! If true, this implies that you and others often pay more attention to what you *see* or feel, tactilely, than what you *hear*. If your partner says, "*I'm* fascinated *by your explanation of how snails reproduce. Please go on*," and their face looks bored and/or they avoid eye contact, would you trust their spoken words to be true?

These three channels allow us an amazing array of communication nuances and shadings that we couldn't have with any one of them; hence "a picture (image of our partner's behavior) is worth a thousand words." The price for this is that if you're unaware of what your subselves are up to, you can send double messages that may harm your self-esteem ("*I don't communicate well*") and key relationships. Some sage said: "*Words may lie, but bodies don't.*"

Personality Parts Cause Double (Mixed) Messages

These confusing communications happen when we get a verbal message ("*I'm so glad to see you!*") that doesn't match the information on another channel (flat voice tone, expressionless face). When you get a mixed signal like this, how does your inner crew react? In my experience, most adults or kids respond semi-consciously with feelings of confusion, anxiety, and distrust. If you regularly receive double messages from a person, your distrust grows, and you may become "short" (uneasy), irritated, and frustrated with them. The communication skills of awareness (Chapter 2) and metatalk (Chapter 5) allow spotting and working to resolve local double messages. Inner-family therapy promotes reducing chronic double messages.

The *multiplicity* and *splitting* concepts explain our double messages. For instance:

Inner Teenager: *"I am bored out of my mind with Pat's endless explanation of how snails mate. If I don't leave or change the subject, I'll go berserk."*

Inner Judge: *"Hold it! Pat's a friend, and you know the rules. We have to be polite and respectful to friends, or else we're social morons. So just shut up and fake it."*

Analyzer: *"It's interesting that Pat is so fascinated with this subject. Let's figure out why, OK?"*

Guilty Child: *"I feel so bad! I shouldn't feel bored and critical of Pat, but I do. And I'm not supposed to lie . . ."*

Rationalizer (subself): *"Yeah, but in this case a little lie won't hurt. Actually it's a kindness."*

People Pleaser (Guardian): *"But we can't say we're bored, that would really hurt Pat. Come on, we have to be nice. It's only for a few minutes."*

Pleaser and *Rationalizer* cause you to say the words "*I'm fascinated by your explanation of how snails reproduce. Please go on.*" *Guilty Child* or an attentive Guardian subself makes you avoid eye contact, to lower the risk that your dishonesty will show. Your *Inner Teenager* causes the words to come out with false enthusiasm, tinged with sarcasm. Result: a double message. This all takes less than a second to happen, and it all occurs below your conscious awareness.

These activated personality parts have blended with (disabled) your Self. If this weren't true, you'd probably wait for an appropriate break, make comfortable eye contact, and say something like . . .

"Pat, I have to 'fess up. I'm not as interested in snails as you are, and my mind is starting to wander. I hope that doesn't offend you."

Your voice tone, expression, eyes, and words all convey the same meaning.

How often do you send double messages? To whom, and in what circumstances? Which members of your inner family are causing them? What internal and social responses do you usually get? You can learn the answers by developing your *awareness* (Chapter 2).

A third vital communication basic to know is the . . .

Four Messages We All Decode

In most (all?) communication exchanges, you and each partner simultaneously send, receive, and decode up to four types of information at once. Can you name them? For most people, this complex process is largely unconscious, until we focus on it. Three of the message-types are easy to identify. Paradoxically, the fourth is the most crucial, and the least known. In scores of communication classes, few of my adult students could name it. Neither could most of my therapy clients. Can you?

The "easy three" message-types we decode are what the other person seems to _ think, _ feel, and _ want and/or expect (need) from us now, and maybe long-term.

Think of a recent communication with someone. Did you form at least semi-conscious judgments about these three things about your partner? Sometimes one of these is more important than the other two, depending on the situation. In casual conversation, we don't need clear awareness of these. In conflicts or crises, we do.

Now, can you name the fourth message you and your communication partners constantly decode from each other? Recall the six needs that cause all human communication. The first one is the key: our ceaseless need for "enough" respect. The fourth signal we all instinctively decode may be called a *respect* **("R") message:** "What's your attitude now and over time about your worth vs. mine?" Restated: "Who's needs, opinions, and dignity do you seem to value more right now, yours or mine?"

Comedian Rodney Dangerfield invites us to laugh at what we all feel when other people behave in a way that implies, "*I value my needs and dignity more than yours now. I don't respect you.*" That's no laughing matter; specially if you inherited low self esteem as a person, a wo/man, or in a key role, from shame-based caregivers.

R(espect)-messages

A key dynamic to become aware of in important inner and social communications is the messages that each participant receives. The three possible decodings are . . .

"*You seem to feel "1-up" (superior). You care more about your needs, opinions, and feelings than mine right now.*" This inherently feels disrespectful, and roils the receiver's inner family.

"*You seem to feel '1-down' (inferior). You care more about my needs and feelings than your own, right now.*" This can be just as disturbing a message as "I'm 1-up," for it subtly invites discounting and disrespect. And . . .

"*You seem to genuinely value our respective feelings, worth, and current needs equally.*" When each partner's dominant subselves consistently hold this attitude, their communication exchange can be said to be "=/=," or "mutually respectful."

Notice the words "you seem to." The incoming R-message we decode may not be what our partner sent us. People controlled by false selves are at risk of sending mixed R-messages ("*I respect you equally*" and "*I care more about my needs than yours now*"), and misperceiving the R-messages from their partners.

I propose that the R(espect)-messages you send and perceive control the effectiveness of every communication exchange more than any other factor except false-self dominance of your inner family (personality). R-message sending and decoding are directly related to whether each person's Self is guiding their inner family or not. Generally, when false selves control and you have low self-awareness, you and others send or perceive 1-up or 1-down R-messages, and your communication effectiveness drops. Does this make tentative sense to you?

Reality check: Identify several of your most important relationships. In each one, are you aware of which of the three R-messages your partners usually receive from you? Now identify "unpleasant" or uncomfortable past or current relationships. With each one, mull which incoming R-message you've generally decoded from that person's behavior. I'd be startled if it was *"You seem to feel we're true equals in dignity and worth."*

Now imagine which R-message they usually received from you. Notice your self-talk (inner "voices," or thought streams) as you do. Becoming aware of the R-messages in your key internal and interpersonal communications opens up many useful options.

12 Simultaneous Messages

If we receive up to four messages from each other over three channels, then you and your communication partners are each constantly unscrambling up to 12 messages at once! Your conscious, semi-conscious, and unconscious minds are so adept at this, you're usually unaware of them sorting and decoding all these messages, unless you need more detail. Our amazing brains and subselves allow us to selectively focus on one channel and message at a time, as needed. From this view, does it make more sense that we're often unclear, confused, or mistaken about what our partner is really trying to tell us, and vice versa?

So far, we've reviewed . . .

What "communication" *is* (a mental-emotional-spiritual sequence of behavioral interactions),

Why do we do it (to reduce two to six current needs, or discomforts),

How (exchanging messages over verbal, paraverbal, and nonverbal channels concurrently), and . . .

What we communicate (up to four simultaneous messages).

Let's use these ideas to overview a set of communication tools you can learn and use to get more of your daily needs met, and help your kids and others to do the same.

Seven Learnable Relationship Skills

How would you define a *skill*? I propose that a skill is a mental, physical, and perhaps verbal activity you learn to control which achieves results that someone prizes (*"You* really *know how to can peaches!"*) Have you ever inventoried your scores of skills? Can you describe how you've developed each of them? Though we each have a preferred learning style (visual, audible, tactile, or action), building any skill involves interest (motivation) > conceptualizing > experimenting > practicing > evaluating > and adjusting, with or without a coach. You've used these steps many times to develop various abilities from making a sumptuous soufflé to selling an airplane to playing a concert cello, or whatever.

So you're already experienced with *how* to develop your skills at effective innerpersonal and interpersonal communications. Motivation and a clear concept may be all you need to start harvesting the benefits: i.e. satisfying more daily personal and social needs. **See if the next two sections clarify your concept of "communication skills."**

Premise: with, motivation, time, and practice, you can grow fluency in seven discrete, interrelated abilities that will significantly increase the effectiveness of your (1) thinking (inner-family communication) and (2) interpersonal communication with others. The skills are . . .

Awareness of what's "going on" _ inside each of you and _ between you now, and over time.

Clear thinking: consciously staying focused, minimizing distortions and distractions, checking for meanings, and using specific vs. vague or ambiguous terms.

"**Digging down**" to identify _ who *really* needs what now, and _ who is responsible for filling those needs.

"**Metatalk**": talking clearly about your thinking and communicating *process.*

Empathic listening: hearing with your *heart*;

Assertion: saying what you need and/or feel in a way your partner/s can hear you clearly, and . . .

Win-win problem solving, or conflict resolution.

Mastering each of these skills requires fluency the prior ones. For example, digging down depends on fluency in awareness and clear thinking. Effective listening requires *awareness* and *empathy* (another learnable skill). Successful assertion requires clear awareness + clear thinking + digging down + empathic-listening skill. General problem solving requires all six skills but metatalk. Resolving *communication* need-conflicts permanently requires all seven skills.

Were you ever taught these seven mental/verbal skills? Were your childhood caregivers and teachers? Was your partner? Your boss? Can any kids in your life describe each of these, and when to use each one? In my experience, our society generally takes "communicating" for granted, and ignores these vital skills and what they can achieve. Few people can name or describe them, so far. Here's some initial perspective on each skill:

Skill 1) Awareness

This is the foundation of effective communication. It's

learning to be being nonjudgmentally aware, moment-by-moment, of _ your and _ your partner's . . .

Key attitudes; and . . .

Physical and emotional **feelings** (including hunches and intuitions); **and** . . .

Thoughts ("inner voices"); and . . .

Current _ communication and _ underlying *true* **needs**; and . . .

If someone has a conflict (need-clash), what **kind of conflict** is it: internal, abstract, concrete, or communication-need; and . . .

How **you're talking** together, _ now and _ over time; and . . .

What you're talking about; and . . .

Outcomes: Who gets their true needs met, and how.

As you assess these factors, you dynamically choose which of the other six skills fit your present situation best. Use *awareness* in all key situations, including when you're alone. With practice, it becomes a habit. In important events, a useful awareness is your "awareness bubble": *"Right now, who am I, and who are you, aware of: just me, just you, both of us, or neither of us?"* One reason professional counselors and therapists exist is to provide the inner and social awareness that their clients and patients haven't developed themselves. Another is to provide respect and objectivity: an "=/=" attitude.

Skill 2) Clear vs. Fuzzy Thinking

How often in an average day do you *think*? Can you define *thinking*? Do you agree that this amazing inner process can range from "laser-clear" to "fuzzy" to "totally muddled and crazy"? Have you ever considered that thinking is a developed skill? Here, *thinking* means the ceaseless inner conversations going on between members of your inner family, including thoughts ("inner voices"), images, "senses," hunches, assumptions, "urges," memories, intuitions, and premonitions.

Premise: as you build your inner and outer *awarenesses*, you can intentionally improve the clarity of your thinking in key situations by . . .

Noticing, reality-checking, and correcting misperceptions and misassumptions; (*"You look sad now. Are you?"*); and . . .

Noting any defocusing from the topic at hand ("riding off in all directions"), and intentionally refocusing; and . . .

Noticing which of your inner-family members are talking, and how their styles (aggressive, submissive, placating, distracting) interact. And you can sharpen your thinking by . . .

Avoiding and replacing vague and ambivalent pronouns and phrases (*"I have a gigantic problem with you."*) with more specific, descriptive terms (*"I need you to want to stop interrupting me."*); and . . .

Noticing and avoiding or clarifying "hand-grenade" (emotionally-charged) words and phrases, in volatile situations; and . . .

Intentionally building your vocabulary, to help express yourself more accurately and impactfully.

In most situations, you don't need awareness of all these *thinking* (inner communication) factors. They become useful in resolving serious relationship conflicts and inner-wound recovery. Chapter 2 will introduce you to seven key awareness factors that can help resolve most local "problems" well enough. A*wareness* and clear thinking (Chapter 3) enable you to develop . . .

Skill 3) Dig Down to True Needs

Infants, kids, and adults communicate to ease local discomforts: i.e. to fill current needs. All important innerpersonal and interpersonal "problems" have *surface* needs (*"I need you to stop interrupting me"*) which overlay deeper *true* needs (*"I need to feel _ respected by myself, and _ that you value me enough to listen to me."*) Digging down to illuminate your and your partner's *true* needs usually reveals that only the adult feeling them can fill them, unless a partner has agreed to help. Kids really do need adults to help them fill key needs, until they're ready to live independently.

True needs usually come in clusters: for example: "*I need you to stop smoking*" (surface need) may *really* mean . . .

"*I need to reduce my fear of your getting cancer and slowly dying, and leaving me alone and insecure in old age*"; and . . .

"*I love you, and want the pleasure of seeing you live long and well. I need to avoid sorrowing over any pain, illness, and discomfort you feel;*" and . . .

"*I need to reduce my periodic discomfort over feeling powerless to get you to quit smoking, eat less fat and sugar, and exercise more often;*" and . . .

"*I need to reduce my guilt over semi-consciously disrespecting and resenting you for not valuing your own health, and causing me (and any kids) these discomforts.*"

Another example: "*You need to do your homework*" (surface need) can stand for . . .

"*I need to feel respected by myself (i.e. by my Inner Critic) and important other people, as being a 'good parent';*" and . . .

"*I need to reduce my anxieties about your school success, your self esteem, and your being eventually accepted at a good college;*" and . . .

"*I need to express my love and concern for you, and to feel satisfied with and proud of your achievements.*" *Alternative:* ". . . *and I need to avoid the personal and empathic pain of your possible scholastic 'failure';*" and . . .

"*I need to reduce or eliminate the 'stress' (inner-family criticism, resentment, and frustration) that I feel periodically from resenting that you seem too lazy and irresponsible (per my Inner Critic) to consistently do your schoolwork.*"

So "*You need to do your homework*" is code for four underlying true needs of *yours.*

Expecting kids or other adults to fill your *true* needs (e.g.

for *happiness*, or *security*) if they can't or won't, causes frustration, guilt, and conflict ("stress") for everyone. This skill may be the most difficult of the seven, for mastery requires you and other adults to take full responsibility for the quality and productivity of your own lives. That requires your true Selves to be consistently trusted by, and in charge of, your many other subselves.

Most of the conflicted mates I've worked with have gotten helplessly snarled in shame-and-blame contests (*"It's your fault!" No, it's yours!"*), because they're not clear and agreed on _ what true needs are unfilled, and _ who's really responsible for filling each of them. All such couples are _ psychologically wounded, and don't know it; and _ don't know these seven mental/verbal skills. Chapter 4 explains and illustrates this powerful "dig down" attitude and technique.

Skill 4) Metatalk

Building on the prior three skills, this one allows you to assess and identify local and chronic communication problems. *Metawriting* is writing about writing. *Meta-singing* is singing about singing. Metatalk is having honest, clear, and cooperative discussions with a partner about *how* you're communicating together, now and/or over time. It's based on mutual respect (shared =/= attitudes), and uses a special set of concepts and terms.

You can build your metatalk vocabulary by fitting the concepts and terms in this book to your own personal values and communication style. The Glossary (p. 418) is a collection of relationship and communication terms that can make your metatalk clearer and more effective. Metatalk identifies communication needs, assertion declares them, and problem solving helps resolve conflicts, and fill your *true* needs cooperatively. Have you heard of metatalk before? If so, do you *use* it?

Skill 5) Empathic Listening

You can listen with your head (intellectual understanding) and/or your *heart*. Listening with your heart involves empathizing with what your partner feels and needs now. This powerful skill is also called *mirroring*, and *active* or *reflective* listening. It starts with . . .

A mutual-respect (=/=) attitude, and a conscious decision to . . .

Suspend your opinions and other needs for the moment; and . . .

Periodically summarize your sense of your partner's main current thoughts, feelings, and needs as they express (behave); and . . .

Objectively note their physical, emotional, and cognitive **reactions** (via *awareness*) to your summaries.

Use empathic listening when your partner's emotions are so intense that they can't hear *you*. When used effectively, this powerful skill usually helps "upset" partners' chaotic subselves gradually calm down and listen to you, if you need something. It works just as well if an inner-family subself is too excited to hear your Self. A vital key:

Listening empathically does not mean you agree with your partner!

Growing your fluency in awareness and clear thinking can grow your empathic listening skill. When your Self leads your inner family, these can raise your effectiveness at asserting and problem solving. None of these skills work well when a false self dominates you.

Skill 6) Assertion: Say Clearly What You Need

This vital mental/verbal skill has been described as the art of telling other people what you need from them in a way that they can hear you. It starts with getting your Self in charge, and then . . .

Believing that your needs are as legitimate as anyone else's (self-respect); and . . .

Identifying clearly what you really *need* right now (awareness); then . . .

Requesting or demanding it, plainly, directly, and without guilt and anxiety; and then . . .

Calmly *expecting defensive responses* ("resistances"), listening empathically to them; and then . . .

Firmly repeating these steps until you either get agreement, an acceptable compromise, or new information. If the latter happens, switch to problem solving.

Three essentials for effective assertion are _ valuing yourself and your communication partner equally (=/=); _ firmly believing that your present needs and theirs are legitimate, and _ knowing if you're making a request (compromise and "no" are OK) or a demand (they're not OK).

Choose to assert when you need to _ prevent or _ resolve conflicts, and _ to give "unavoidable" praise.

Skill 7) Problem Solving, or Conflict Resolution

A *problem* is one or more unmet needs. A *conflict* occurs when two or more needs clash inside you, and/or between your and a partner's subselves. This seventh pivotal communication skill uses an =/= attitude and the other six skills to meet enough of everyone's underlying true needs. Problem solving involves (1) cooperatively uncovering what each person or personality part really needs now, and (2) creatively brainstorming all options to evolve a win-win solution. To be effective, problem solving requires _ your Self to be in charge, _ self and mutual respect (=/=), _ optimism, imagination, patience, and good will; and _ knowledge of all seven skills, and when to use each one. Do you have these requisites now?

Popular alternatives to effective conflict resolution are fighting, arguing, debating, manipulating ("controlling"), hinting, demanding, persuading, threatening, avoiding, and withdrawing (fleeing). Used with mutual respect, problem-solving skill's potential for good is *enormous*. How often do you use it? Did your parents use it? Do your kids know how to problem solve effectively yet?

When your true Self is leading your inner family, _ fluency in these seven skills, and _ knowing when to use each one, can help you go to sleep contented every night. Note that *you don't need to use these skills all the time*. Your ultimate goal is to grow automatic competence with them in important personal and social situations. You (your inner family) and your communication partners decide at any moment what qualifies as *important*.

Awareness and clear thinking are always useful. The other skills are best used in different kinds of situations. Here's a guide to . . .

When to Use Each Communication Skill

Most communication situations between two inner-family members, or between you and another person, are one of four types. To understand them, we need a new concept: **E(motion) levels**. Infants to oldsters all have fluctuating surges and periods of emotions as our inner and outer worlds unfold. Our wonderful palette of feelings has scores of variations, including shame, hope, despair, anxiety, lust, guilt, glee, terror, rage, and many more. When our emotional intensity rises like a thermometer's level, it distracts us (our inner family) from being able to stay focused on outer events, like listening empathically to a partner. If your or a partner's E-level rises "above your ears," you and/ or they can't *hear* the other person empathically, or at all.

Reality check: Is there someone in your life you often feel unheard ("misunderstood" and/or "ignored") by? Are there people that occasionally or regularly feel you can't hear them well, or at all? This is common when a parent, child, or spouse

is upset with their partner. When two people "fight," usually their inner families are chaotic, their E-levels are above their ears, and neither can clearly express their *true* needs, or really hear what the other needs. Does this make sense to you? If so, how can you use the seven mental/verbal skills to handle high-E-level situations?

Use awareness and clear thinking to determine which of four situations you're in. Then select the appropriate other skill/s, and use them *with an =/= attitude.* Here's the scheme:

Your and your partner's **E-levels are "below your ears."** Use awareness, clear thinking, and normal conversation.

Your E-level is low, and your partner's is high ("above their ears"). Use awareness, clear thinking, and empathic listening respectfully, until their E-level drops below their ears and they can hear you.

Your E-level is high and your partner's is low. Use awareness, clear thinking, respectful assertion, and empathic listening to tell them what you need them to hear, and keep their E-level down as you do; and . . .

Both of your E-levels are high. Use _ awareness to note this, and _ clear thinking and empathic listening to learn what your partner needs, and help them drop their E-level so they can hear you. Then _ use respectful assertion to say what you perceive, and what *you* need. Then _ invite your partner to use win-win problem solving on whatever conflict was causing your original upsets. If the main conflict has to do with your communication process or needs, _ use metatalk to help define it, and _ all seven skills to resolve it. Keep your Selves in charge, and use *awareness* throughout.

When your E(motion)-level is high, an important option is to use the seven skills *internally* to bring your own E-level down: i.e. to calm agitated subselves by listening to and validating them. Until you experience this working, it will probably make little sense to you. Generally, a sustained "high E-level" usually means that one or more personality parts have taken your or your partner's true Self over. If circumstances allow, that's a good time to focus your awareness on your or their inner-family's communications, and to learn who needs what, right now.

Does this four-situation scheme make sense to you? Do you feel that with practice, you could learn to assess your E-level combinations, and pick the most effective communication skills to use? If your motivation is strong enough, and your Self is leading your inner crew, I'll bet you can!

Now we have all the concepts we need to define . . .

What Is Effective *Communication?*

How can you tell if your communications "work well"? If you don't have a clear yardstick yet, it will be hard for you to identify communication problems, and to make and evaluate improvements. It will also be hard for you to teach your kids how and when to use these seven fundamental life skills.

Basic premise: you and other people communicate to fill current conscious and unconscious personal needs. Needs are fluctuating mixes of normal and special mental, emotional, spiritual, and physical "tensions." Moment by moment, you and each partner have major and minor needs that can conflict within you and between you (*"I want to both change my clothes, and to please you. You need us to leave now, and be on time."*) Awake and asleep, we strive to reduce these combined discomforts. So **communications succeed when** each subself and each person involved . . .

. . . **gets** enough of their present *true* (vs. surface) needs met, in their own opinion, and each . . .

. . . **feels** good enough afterwards about (respects) themselves, their partner/s, and the communication process between them.

This two-factor definition implies that all participants are *aware* of _ their current true, vs. surface, needs (Chapter 4), and of _ their emotions during and after the communication process. The learned skill of *awareness* (Chapter 2) provides both of these. In key situations, are you usually aware of these factors yet?

It's OK if this two-point definition doesn't work for you. To communicate well enough, however, you'll need a clear idea of what "well" means. So evolve a clear definition of effective communications that works for you, and then learn what your key partners' definitions are. If you (your false self) postpone this or choose not to do it, the ideas in this book will probably be much less helpful to you.

In the next chapter, we'll use this two-factor definition to discover why the odds of effective communication between two unaware people are about 6%: one chance in 16!

Recap

We've covered a lot of ground in this foundation chapter. These are the core premises underlying the rest of this book:

Each adult and child has an inner family of personality parts, or subselves. Together, they determine your fluctuating needs, perceptions, and feelings, and how you communicate. These subselves are semi-autonomous, and behave generally like "regular people." They rest or activate, have individual opinions, needs, goals, and strategies; ally or fight; and communicate regularly with each other and "you" (your Self and conscious mind) all the time. They do so via thoughts, dreams, hunches, "senses," images, and body symptoms.

Your subselves fall into four functional groups: Regulars, volatile young Vulnerables, Guardian subselves, and "others": spiritual and Higher energies. A core aspect of this inner-family concept is the ability of distrustful, upset subselves (a "false self") to blend with (disable) your true Self. When that happens, inner communications turn chaotic, which makes effective outer communications much less likely. This is specially so if your current partner's inner family is controlled by a false self also, and neither of you know it or what to do about it.

After this inner-family concept, we studied proposed answers to a set of questions on p. 44.

Does my proposal that most people don't know what they don't know about communicating make more sense now? If you can't answer each of these items yet, relax. When you need clarity on any of the answers, they're in this chapter, and summarized in Resource A. Use the index to quickly find what you need.

Pause and recall why you began reading this book. Remember with affection any of the comments your inner crew made when you first scanned these pages. What are they saying now about whether you may get something really worthwhile here? Each subself who adds an inner voice means well, in their own way. Each of their opinions is worth hearing and considering. The key question is: who's making your decisions right now: your true Self, or someone else? If you're using a communication journal or notebook, would you like to commune with it now?

Using these basics, the next chapters introduce you to each of the seven basic mental/verbal skills. The first one is fundamental to all inner and interpersonal communication situations: *awareness*. Before starting the next chapter, have a little fun. On a scale of 1 to 10, rank how aware of your _ inner world and _ your typical relationships with other people you are, most of the time. "1" is "*I never have a clue;*" and "10" is "*I'm a process-dynamics wizard. I am totally aware of what's going on inside me and around me at all times.*" For perspective, think of someone you feel is unusually *aware*, and adjust your numbers, if you wish.

Awarenesses: (or use your communication journal)

2) Communication *Awareness*

"Go within, or go without."
—Neale Walsch, Conversations with God

A contemplative friend once invited me to go to a Zen temple in Chicago. I was welcomed graciously, and given a small round, black cushion. The dozen other people and I placed our cushions on the hardwood floor about 18 inches from a wall, several feet from each other. After a brief centering ritual, we each sat cross-legged on our cushion and, under the watchful eye of an expressionless teacher, stared silently and motionlessly at the wall for about an *hour*. That Zazen experience, and reading several books on Zen Buddhism, introduced me to what *really* being aware can become. It is a mind-state, an art, a skill, and a spiritual doorway that has profound depths and scope.

Decades of observation and clinical experience since 1981 suggest to me that most Americans (most westerners?) are using a very small percentage of their potential levels of inner and environmental awareness. Unless you practice deep daily meditation or Tai Chi, that probably includes you. Few U.S. kids see their parents doing regular focused meditation (did you?), or are coached to value the serenity and wisdom that practicing it can gradually bring. We are a nation of sleepwalkers, moving mindlessly through our lives in a numbing kaleidoscope of media and activity distractions. We're largely unaware of what is *really* going on inside and around us. Most of us appear to be unaware of our unawareness. This profoundly hinders effective communications, key relationships, and living "on purpose."

 # Reality check: To make this premise more real, try this simple exercise. Read it through, and then close your eyes. Lie down, or sit with both feet on the floor, and your hands in your lap. Focus on the sensation of your breathing, without any judgment. Notice the faint sensations of your heart beating regularly, pulsing blood throughout your body. Notice any slight aches, discomforts, or temperatures, and the feeling of being supported by whatever you're sitting or lying on. Now for several minutes, mentally answer these questions factually and objectively like a scientist or reporter:

"Now I'm thinking . . ."
"Now I hear . . ."
"Now I feel . . ."
"Now my body is saying . . .
"Now I smell . . ."
"Now I need . . ."

Repeat this cycle slowly and calmly, pausing between each focus. Notice if you're breathing from your belly or your upper chest. Try to let go of any expectations, or a need to judge this as a "good" or "bad" experience. As you continue to repeat these observations, evolve an awareness of your awarenesses, over time . . .

"As I repeat this cycle, I notice . . ."

Do this for at least five minutes. Longer is better. Optionally, write about this experience in your journal when you feel "done."

What was that experience like? How did it contrast with the "normal" way you are throughout an average day? Which of your inner family members were the most expressive? What did they express, including bodily? What might you learn if you gave yourself quiet periods of even 10 minutes most days to reflect like that, and maybe journal about your experience?

If overall daily awareness is like a library, our project here (*communication* awareness) is like focusing on one aisle of books. For our purposes, awareness is a learnable _ attitude mind-state) and _ ability, and _ a set of communication-related concepts and focuses. **You can use the results in two ways:**
As input to metatalk (talking about communicating). That enables identifying and solving communication problems; and . . .
As the means of moment-by-moment appraisal about _ what your current communication situation is (e.g. *"My E-level is below my ears, and yours is above your ears . . ."*), and _ which skill you should best use (*". . . so I should use empathic listening until your E-level falls enough, and then switch to assertion and problem solving."*)
This first mental/verbal skill is essential for managing your key communication situations well, specially those among your inner selves. Each of the six other skills depends on your focus and clear *awareness.* Professional communicators and counselors try to be selectively aware of over 30 different factors inside and between communicators _ now and _ over time (Resource F). The good news is that you can greatly improve your communication effectiveness by paying attention to just seven dynamic factors inside you, inside your partner, and between you and them. Once you get the hang of it, you'll probably add more factors.
Note that you really only need these awarenesses in exchanges you or your partner feel are *important*, inside either of you or between you. The target here is to have this skill available if you feel local communication dynamics call for it.

Seven *Awareness* Questions

I propose that the single most important communication and relationship factor is . . .

Awareness **1) "Is either of us dominated by a false self?"** Have distrustful subselves disabled my true Self, and/or yours? If so, we're very likely to send double messages, avoid, defocus, distort reality, be distracted, mind-read (assume), misunderstand, send 1-up or 1-down R-messages, and be unaware of all this. If so, we'll hear our selves and our partner poorly.

The next most powerful communication factor is . . .

Awareness **2) "What R(espect)-messages are we exchanging now?"** Recall that we continually decode each other's behavior to fill our steady need for self and mutual *respect*. Any time one or both of us feels too little respect, we'll probably blend (lose our Self), raise our E(motion) levels, and stop hearing and thinking clearly.

Awareness **3) "Do our key communication needs match now?"** Which of the six reasons for communicating do you and I have now? Why are we each communicating? Restated: *"What do I need from you, and what do you need from me now, besides respect? Do our respective communication needs match?"* E.g. I need to get information and build our emotional closeness, now; and you need to vent. A mismatch would occur if we both needed to vent.

Awareness **4) "Where are we focused now, and do we stay focused or not?"** Is either of us so physically or emotionally uncomfortable that we can't stay centered on our joint communication process? If so, what are the distractions, and what would lower them? If neither of us is distracted, do we stay on one subject until we both feel finished enough? Are we focused on how we're communicating, or something else? There are at least four other *focus* questions you can use to build your awareness.

Awareness **5) "Where are our E-levels, and which of the other six skills should I use now?"** This awareness uses your knowledge of the four E-level situations, and which communication skills are best suited to each (p. 64).

Awareness **6) "What's our communication outcome?"** Who _ gets their needs met well enough (or not), and _ how do we feel about our joint process? If one or both of us doesn't get our needs met, what's in the way? See the summary of common communication blocks (p. 405).

The last basic awareness you can grow is . . .

Awareness **7) "What was our communication sequence, and what are our communication patterns over time?"** A communication *sequence* is a current string of (action > reaction > reaction > . . .) behaviors from which each participant decodes meanings. A communication *pattern* is a sequence of sequences, over time (*"Joanie, whenever I bring up money and the checkbook, we always get into a fight."*) Awareness and the technique of *mapping* outlined on p. 400 can help you answer this pair of awareness questions.

Reality check: Pause, and identify your three most important (vs. most satisfying) relationships. In each of them, how aware of these seven factors have you been, recently? How aware of the factors is each of your respective partners? How does your mutual awareness shape the effectiveness of your attempts to communicate, in general, and during conflicts? On a scale of 1 (ineffective) to 10 (very effective), how successful are your communications with each partner in _ peaceful and _ conflictual times?

Let's explore each of these seven awareness factors.

Q1: "Are our Selves in charge?"

In my experience, most ineffective communication comes from one or more people being unaware of _ the communication basics in Chapter 1, _ their inner family and false-self dominance, and _ how the latter degrades thinking and communicating. Many professional human-relations consultants can't communicate effectively because their true Self is disabled, and they don't know it, or what to do about it.

Chapter 1 summarizes the proposal that most (all?) of us are normally controlled by a group of semi-autonomous personality *parts*, or *subselves*. One is a naturally talented leader called (here) your true Self (capital "S"). If other subselves don't trust that part to coach and coordinate them, they "blend" (take over) and disable your Self. This contentious, shortsighted, reactive group of subselves (a "false self") unintentionally hinders perceptions, information decoding, and healthy decision-making, in many ways.

False selves seem to develop in early childhood. It's specially likely in families and settings low in emotional and spiritual nurturances, where adult leaders are significantly wounded. The resulting organization of personality parts, a false self, has felt *normal* for most of us wounded people all our lives. So the idea that a false self significantly controls you or any communication partner is probably alien. "Being guided by my true Self" has no experiential meaning for most such people, until they choose to become *aware*.

When they do, they (*you*?) notice that **when their Self is in charge of their inner team, they consistently feel** some mix of these emotions: *centered, grounded, "up," peaceful, focused, assertive, "light,". purposeful, compassionate, strong, resilient, clear, strong, serene, patient* and *alive*. People blessed with these feelings most of the time have been described as being "in the flow," "serene," and "at One with the universe." There are gradations of this splendid state that you can become adept at noticing, if your governing subselves wish to.

Alternatives to these inner-harmony symptoms are often feeling bored, apathetic, down, heavy, anxious, distracted, giddy, irritated, impatient, frustrated, numb, angry, depressed, empty, and so on. (Your Self can feel these too.) Awareness of these feelings in you and your partner is the key to answering this first pair of questions . . .

"Right now, am I experiencing a mix of these 'Self' feelings? Do you seem to be?

If you reflect and answer "No," or "I don't know," then **use** *awareness* to assess whether your partner's and/or your *inner* families are conflicted now, and/or over time. See these **self-assessment worksheets** on the Web for common symptoms of false-self dominance: [http://sfhelp.org/pop/assess.htm]. If *you* feel controlled by a false self (blended) occasionally, use your version of the ideas in Chapter 9. If you're blended often, confront your need for personal recovery. See "Who's *Really* Running Your Life?" [xlibris.com, 2000] for guidelines and options. If your *partner* seems blended, see the options in Chapter 10.

If one or both of you seems controlled by a false self (blended), _ reduce your expectation of effective communications now, without blaming either of you; and _ consider using metatalk (Chapter 5) to alert your partner to your observation, and then problem-solve together:

"Sarah, I've lost my Self. I need to take care of an inner conflict, before I can really hear you well. Can I get back to you by tomorrow on (the topic)?"

If your partner doesn't understand personality fragmenting and false selves, substitute something like *"I'm distracted by a personal matter"* for "lost my Self." If s/he does understand, you have the option of agreeing to shift your communication focus to putting the disabled Self or Selves back in charge before continuing.

Reality check: read the list of true-Self traits (p. 74) out loud, so you can experience *hearing* them as well as seeing them. Now reflect without judgment. Are you feeling some of those now? When your true Self is in charge, most people (who get quiet) *know* (sense) it. If you don't feel your Self is in charge now, who is? Can you recall times you have felt the Self-in-charge traits for a while?

If you omit this first awareness question in important behavior exchanges, or "forget to ask it" (false self in action?), the rest of these awarenesses will probably have limited benefits at best.

Q2: "What R-messages are we exchanging now?"

In key relationships and personal encounters, your and your partner's Guardian and Vulnerable subselves constantly decode how much the other person seems to respect you. We usually deduce others' attitudes about us more from their voice and body dynamics, than their words. Do you agree? Things people *don't* do (call us, send a card, follow up on a promise, listen, look at us) send R(espect)-messages just like things they do.

We each decode R-messages from our partners all the time, consciously and unconsciously. Our decoding depends on guesses about our partner's attitudes and meanings, based on our history with them and others, and our current beliefs about human nature. For example: *"Lack of eye contact means either shame, or lack of respect."*

Recall the **three R-messages**: *"Right now, you seem to feel that . . .*

You're 1-up, and I'm 1-down (inferior): i.e. your needs are worth more to you than mine." The extreme form of this is "You feel that I don't exist: my feelings, thoughts, and needs are of no interest or importance to you now." "1-up" R-messages from our partners are called discounts, insults, shots, slams, and putdowns.

We're equals in human dignity and worth. You see my current needs and yours as equally important now" (an "=/=" attitude); and . . .

You're 1-down, and I'm 1-up (superior): your present dignity and needs are less important to you than mine are, now."

Communications work well **only** *when all partners get credible =/= R-messages.* Beside false-self dominances, these embedded signals are probably the most powerful factors in internal and interpersonal communication exchanges. Without *awareness* skill, 1-up and 1-down R-messages are only vaguely noted, and sabotage well-meant communication. They usually produce hurt, defensiveness, resentment, misunderstandings, attacks, withdrawals, distrust, and confusion. Do you agree? Have you ever thought about the R-messages you send and receive with special people in your life? Do you know *how* you send key R-messages (verbal and/or nonverbal)? What would probably happen to your main relationships if you consciously chose an =/= (mutually respectful) attitude? What would that take (beside your Self at the helm)?

The Golden Rule of Communications

Effective communication skills spring from our present attitude about our partners and us:

"I now respect and value your spirit, dignity, needs, and opinions just as I would have you value mine."

Most people from low-nurturance childhoods are shame-based. Without healing, they lack healthy self-respect. Their *Inner Critic* routinely keeps their *Shamed Child* feeling 1-down. Unaware of this and false-self dominance, shame-based people often misread incoming =/= R-messages as *"You're 1-down"* (reality distortion). They feel hurt, defensive, and resentful, their E(motion)-level rises "above their ears," and they can't hear or problem-solve.

Most psychologically-wounded people react to misinterpreted R-messages by withdrawing resentfully, numbing out (*Inner Numb-er* at work), self-criticism, whining, explaining, or volleying back with an aggressive *"No, I'm 1-up!"* R-message. With any of these reflexes, E-levels (inner-family chaos) rise, effective communication drops, and mutual trust, and security and respect wither. Before true personal recovery, people controlled by a false self usually aren't aware of these inner and interpersonal dynamics. If they are aware, they may say later regretfully, *"I couldn't help it."* When did you last experience this fight-or-flight communication sequence?

You Can Run, But You Can't Hide . . .

Do you think average adults and kids can disguise disrespectful attitudes about each other for long? Words can be false and convincing for a while. Faces, bodies, hands, and voice dynamics speak the language of the unconscious, and never lie. **We "leak" our true attitudes about each other all the time.** We usually sense when others are faking respect and concern for us, unless our Guardian subselves need to distort reality via denial.

An anecdote about a communication hero of mine, Dr. Milton Erickson, illustrates our innate ability to read tiny cues from each other, and the degree to which we can learn to be aware of them. One day he was walking toward his psychiatric office when a co-worker approached and greeted him. As she began to walk past him, he said "Congratulations, Martha!" Startled, she turned and asked "For what?" Erickson smiled mischievously, and asked "Boy, or girl, do you think?" The woman was astounded. "How in the world did you know I was pregnant? I just found out yesterday, and I've told no one but my husband!" Erickson said, "It's perfectly obvious. The color of your earlobes has changed." He was serious.

As a boy on his family's Wisconsin farm, Erickson was paralyzed for a time by polio. All he could move was his eyes. He resolutely trained himself to *see*, long before his medical training. Later, he applied his extraordinary ability to notice and interpret tiny body and voice clues to become a legendary clinical hypnotist. As a boy, famed illustrator Norman Rockwell trained himself to *see* (be aware of) and later draw complex arrangements of objects in his hometown's department store window. Our anthem that begins "Oh say, can you *see* . . ." is a fine theme song for growing your communication awareness . . .

Followed far enough, this second awareness question leads to applied spirituality. I may dislike or disrespect your actions, and disagree with your values, and still genuinely honor and appreciate the innate worth and dignity of your spirit and soul as much as I honor my own. That's the ultimate =/= attitude that enables consistently effective internal and social communications. It may be truly said that one aspect of psychological and spiritual "maturity" is how far along you or I are on the path toward holding this attitude about our worst enemies. Skillful assertion allows us to *respectfully* confront such people when their actions displease, alarm, disparage, or harm us. Are you often able to do that, so far?

One of the interesting things that awareness and metatalk skills reveal is the R-messages embedded in (implied by) **common types of communication behavior**. See if you spot any of your favorites here . . .

Moralizing, preaching, or lecturing another (including kids), and giving unrequested advice ("being helpful"). The implication is "I know better than you, so I'm 1-up." Sometimes you *do* know better!

Blaming, criticizing, and attacking ("My values, actions, and judgment are *better than* yours.")

Monologing, rambling, obsessing, and "endlessly repeating." (Decoded meaning: "I'm filling *my* needs, and I don't care about yours now.")

Talking while doing something else ("Our conversation and your current needs are secondary to me, right now.")

Name-calling, threatening, ridiculing, ignoring, discounting, staring, sneering, sarcasm, and interrupting (R-message: "I'm *way* 1-up!")

Pleading, whining, hinting, complaining, acting helpless, over-apologizing, lying, and avoiding eye contact or confrontation all imply "I'm 1-down."

Prolonged or chronic silence, with or without eye contact, imply "I'm 1-up or 1-down."

Asking this second awareness question about your inner-family's R-messages is even more useful. Your subselves bellow, whine, interrupt, plead, lecture, complain, and reason with each other all the time. Your subselves are just as sensitive to disrespect as people are. For example, let's say your inner crew is debating whether you should call your mother now . . .

Rule Keeper *(subself): "We're responsible for Mom's happiness, and we're not supposed to question that responsibility."*

Historian *(Regular) and* **People Pleaser** *(Guardian subself): "It's been almost a week since I called, and Mom's probably starting to feel hurt, annoyed, and worried."*

Guilty Kid *and* **Shamed Kid** *(Vulnerable subselves): "Oh NO!"*

Adult *(subself): "Y'know, if Mom wants to talk, she can call. I have a million things to do. The phone works both ways. When I really need to talk to her, I will, instead of letting her guilt-trip me."*

Inner Critic *(sarcastically): "Oh, nice. Really nice. You get the Olympic gold medal for selfishness, you self-centered moron. Think of all she's done for you!"* (Implied R-message "I'm 1-up!")

Adult: *"Too bad all you can do is sling proclamations and insults, instead of making constructive suggestions."* ("No, I'm 1-up.")

Where do you think this inner communication sequence will wind up? Notice the absence of the Self, who is blended and paralyzed. Inner harmony depends partly on your subselves respecting each other, even when disagreeing. Do yours? If you have traits that you're ashamed of, your *Inner Critic* is surely sending "You're 1-down" messages to the subselves that bring you those traits . . .

Reflect. How often are you aware of the R(espect)-messages with you, and with others, in important conflicts and decisions? What might happen if you raised your awareness of them? You may wonder, *"If I'm aware that someone isn't getting an =/= R-message, or if I'm not sure what R-messages are being decoded in me or with others, what can I do?"* Chapters 5 (metatalk) and 7 (assertion) offer effective options.

Genuine self and mutual respect and empathy are essential for effective inner and interpersonal communications. Do you have "enough" of each of these with yourself and your key partners? If not, are you motivated to change that? Regularly noticing the R-messages within you, and between you and others, is the second of seven key awarenesses you can develop. The next one is . . .

Q3: "Do our communication needs match now?"

Recall our premise that we all communicate to reduce emotional, spiritual, and physical discomforts: i.e. to fill current true needs. Also recall that the **six basic communication needs** that motivate your and your partners' inner-family members are:

To feel respected (worthy) enough now (always present);

To give or get information, including gaining internal clarity [*"Why are you (a subself) bringing me this ache in my throat?"*];

To vent: express strong emotions and be empathically heard and accepted;

To cause action or change in another, including to regulating emotional and physical distance with others (intimacy). This surface need is *always* about reducing your own discomfort, in some way.

To cause excitement (end boredom); and . . .

To distract from (avoid) uncomfortable thoughts and/or feelings.

Since our need for respect is constant, you and any current

partner always have at least two of these needs. The more of these six needs you and I have together now, the harder it is for us to meet them all well enough, until we're both aware and can metatalk (Chapter 5). The tensions we each aim to reduce by communicating may conflict within us, between us, or both. Example:

Sue: *"So how* are *you? It's been too long!"* Communication needs: (1) get information, (2) avoid awkward silence (3) earn self-respect (*"I'm a sensitive, caring friend"*), and (4) cause several changes, including _ strengthen the friendship, and _ relieve some guilt and anxiety about not having called recently to say "Hi" (to express interest, concern, and respect).

Shelly (grinning): *"Well, I'm not sure you'll want to hear the full answer. Got about six hours?"* Possible concurrent needs: (1) earn self respect by responding genuinely and honestly; (2) give information: "I hear your question, and I respect it and you;" (3) get information, by asking indirectly "Can you tolerate my high need to vent?"; (4) cause change (strengthen our relationship); and (5) avoid the guilt of rude silence.

As they talk and listen, Sue and Shelly's mix of needs will shift dynamically, based on their emotional flux, their thoughts and inner images, and how they interpret each other's perceived behaviors. Over time (say a 25" conversation), some needs will predominate, and others will be secondary.

If Sue and Shelly's main current communication needs mesh, the friends may each fill them "enough." If their conversational needs don't match well enough, the effectiveness and satisfaction of their exchange will drop. Some non-respect needs can clash with others. In the table below, "!!!" means "create excitement, and "Avoid" means "avoid discomfort." "N" means clash; "?" means "may or may not match," and "Y" means "needs probably match."

Two-person Communication-needs Mixes
(Mutual needs for *respect* are omitted)

	Info	Vent	Act	"!!!"	Avoid
Info	?	?	N?	N?	Y
Vent	?	N	N?	?	Y
Act	N?	N?	?	Y?	?
"!!!"	N?	?	?	Y	Y
Avoid	Y	Y	?	Y	Y

If you and I both need to vent, or to get (different) information, then our communication needs will probably clash. If urgencies (and E-levels) are high, we probably need some negotiation (metatalk and problem solving). If you want to *vent* now and I want to *get information* and strengthen our relationship, our current mutual needs match. If either you or I don't feel respected enough by ourselves and each the other, *our other needs become secondary.* Other than that, it's hard to generalize here, because there are so many possible factors that shape your and a partner's internal and shared dynamics.

Reality check: Think of the last unpleasant vocal conversation you had. What *made* it unpleasant? Thoughtfully estimate what your and your partner's main communication needs were: _ respect and _ (what?). Next, honestly evaluate if each of you felt respected enough by _ yourselves and _ each other, during the exchange. If so, then use the table to see if maybe the "unpleasantness" was partly due to your other main communication needs clashing, without your being *aware* of that.

If your communications aren't working well with someone, pause to clarify what your and their main current _ inner and _ social *communication* needs are. If they don't match, use all seven mental/verbal skills to resolve the conflict. *Inner* need-conflicts are so common that Chapter 9 is devoted to exploring and resolving them.

Here, Sue says *"Great! Tell me all the juicy details."* Shelly complies by venting non-stop for 45". Sue's need for information (*"How are you?"*) is increasingly filled, she starts to feel flooded with too much information, and she increasingly needs to vent herself. Her body is also starting to need some movement.

If Sue is aware that her needs are starting to clash with Shelly's, she might assert respectfully: *"Shel, I'm starting to feel overloaded, and I'm having trouble staying focused on what you're telling me. Are you in a place to hear some things that are going on with me?"* Notice the implied mutual respect (=/ =) attitude woven into that question, assuming it's not spoken sarcastically ("I'm 1-up,") or timidly ("I'm 1-down.")

What if Shelly says, *"Of course! First, let me tell you what happened when I went to the doctor last week."* The implied R-message is *"My need to talk is more important to me than your need to speak. I'm 1-up"*) Chapters 6 (empathic listening) and 7 (assertion) offer some options on what Sue (or you) could do with that.

In addition to noting splitting, R-messages, and communication need-clashes, **a fourth communication factor you can learn to notice** is . . .

Q4: "What are we focused on now?"

Are you focused or distracted, right now? *Focus* can mean two things: _ Your ability to keep your awareness and thoughts ("consciousness") concentrated on one topic or objective (need), over time; and _ the current topic or subject. E.g. *"Our focus now is (discussing and deciding) whether you should bring your python to live in our house."*

In any brief or prolonged communication, you and your partner each fit somewhere on a continuum (line) between "very focused," and "very distracted." Your positions on that line can vary instantly, depending on inner and outer events. Effective communication partly depends on each partner staying internally and mutually focused, until each person's mix of current needs is satisfied well enough. I propose that if you're motivated, you can intentionally develop your awareness of focusing, and staying focused with a partner. Do you see benefits to doing that in your life? Have you ever considered doing so?

This section outlines seven useful factors you can coach yourself to become aware of in important communication situations. Before noting them, recall from Chapter 1: each emotion and some of the physical feelings you experience is brought to you, or carried by, one or more of your subselves. *Moods* are one or several subselves staying active, over time. Like members of a team or orchestra, each subself has its own perception of events, and its own reactions. If you burp unexpectedly in public, some parts will laugh, others will spasm in embarrassment, and others will yawn or doze. The same is true in any conversation you have, including imagined ones!

From this view, your or your partner's staying *focused* depends on the whether your subselves are quiet or excited, and what they each need now. People who are *spacey* and *can't concentrate* probably often have minor riots among their subselves, and a disabled Self. Self-motivated "parts work" (inner-family harmonizing) can improve this, over time.

Your subselves react fluidly to each other's behavior, to their perception of events outside your body, and to your body's functioning. If your inner team trusts your Self and key Regular subselves to handle things like airplane passengers trust their pilot and crew, you'll have no trouble being aware of distractions and staying focused. If your inner family is locally or often dominated by a false self, you're probably at risk of being easily distracted. This is true also of every communication partner, including kids.

As you develop awareness (1) above (*"Are our true Selves in charge now?"*) you can more easily assess the degree to which your internal and interpersonal communications are focused *enough*, if that's locally important.

Pause, and observe your thoughts now. Try sorting out which of your subselves is saying what. When you're ready, here's a buffet of **seven possible focus-awareness questions to assess**, in important situations:

Does anyone among us need to focus now?

Can we each focus now, or is someone distracted?

What topic are we focusing on?

Did we both feel finished with the last one?

Are we focused on *how* we're communicating, or something else?

Which do you or I focus more on: you, me, us (our relationship), or something else?

Here and/or over time, do we focus mostly on the past, the present, or the future?"

Here's brief perspective on each of these . . .

4a) Does anyone need to focus now?

In typical casual conversations, partners' E-levels are low. They (you) usually don't need a sustained topical focus. When one or more partners feels conflicted with another, or feels some pressure to get their communication needs met by a certain time, focus becomes key, or even vital. This is usually the case in business conversations, where "time is money," and spoken and assumed agendas are expected.

So this fourth awareness begins with building the habit of deciding "How important is focusing to each of us, now?" If you aren't sure and your comfort level would improve, *ask*! That might sound like *"Anything special you (or I) want to end up with here?"* This question also applies between your Self and any subselves who want to "talk" when you're alone or with another person. If you assume or learn there is an agenda (focus), the next awareness to grow is . . .

4b) Is someone distracted?

What kinds of things distract you from staying mentally and socially focused? The common answers are physical and emotional discomforts.

Physical Distractions: If you or a partner are too hungry or full, tired or "wired" (excited, keyed up), thirsty, hot or cold, itchy, ill, or sore, or your environment is too noisy, bright, hectic, smelly, or unsafe, it will be tough to get and stay focused. If you're in a situation like this, your options are to ignore it and "communicate anyway," or make your first focus easing your physical distractions, or improving your environment.

These require awareness and assertion skill. If you're controlled by fearful or shamed subselves, they may not want you to assert your need for more physical comfort, to avoid appearing "rude," "selfish," "picky," "wimpy," or "hypersensitive." For instance, you're in a friend's home, whose summer air conditioning is always set to reproduce midnight at the North Pole. You're freezing, and your host isn't noticing.

All your subselves: *"Aieee! Too COLD!"*

Adult/Self: *"Tell Jerry to turn down the air conditioner."*

Perfectionist/Editor: *"You mean ASK Jerry to turn it down, right?"*

Rule Keeper: *"Let's see, the 'shoulds' and 'oughts' here are, uh . . . here we go, (1) You shouldn't ask for what you want; (2) You have to be a polite, considerate, friendly guest, and never take charge of someone else's home; (3) Real men don't get cold, and (4) you must be a real man; (5) Hinting is better than confronting; (6) You shouldn't imply your friend is insensitive and embarrass him, so (7) avoid conflict, and keep* *it to yourself; and (8) If all else fails, make up a believable excuse and leave. Yeah, I think that's it . . ."*

Catastrophizer: *"We're obviously going to get pneumonia here, within the hour."*

Perfectionist: *". . . And you better not break any of those rules!"*

Shamed Kid: *"Well, I don't deserve comfort, anyway. I should suffer more. Jerry's comfort is more important than mine."*

Inner Critic (sarcastically): *"Oh, poor baby. Feeling sorry for ourselves again, are we?"*

Imagine several of these subselves talking over each other. This segment of inner-voice conflictual hubbub may look silly, but it's not. The point is: if you're physically uncomfortable in the presence of others, do you have solid internal permission to assert your needs, without undue guilt, shame, and anxiety? If your Self leads your inner family, you'll usually say *"Yes."* In this example, your Self would say, *"Jerry, no offense, but I'm cold, and that's distracting me. Would you turn the air conditioner down, or loan me a sweater please?"*

Otherwise, your false-self crew will keep you distracted and uncomfortable. If conversation is "light," then your defocusing from social chatting to your goose bumps may be acceptable. If the conversation turns "important," having a dominant false self will probably wreck chances for an effective win-win outcome. The same is true with the other class of communication focus-wreckers . . .

Emotional and "Mental" Distractions: When your or my subselves are highly activated, our E(motion)-level is "above the ears." That will usually distract our attention, so we can't hear our partners clearly or at all. Our conscious attention is deflected from the complex job of focusing on and perceiving our partner's behaviors, and thoughtfully decoding what they seem to mean. Remember the last time you couldn't listen well in an important conversation?

Besides feeling respected enough, a high-E person's main communication needs are usually to _ get clear information, or _ vent (release emotions, and be empathically heard and understood), and/or to _ cause immediate action. That's why trying to "reason with" a high-E person is like talking to a brick. If you intensely need to vent, the only communication needs that match in your partner are to (1) get information (*listen* to you), and (2) strengthen your relationship. Any other communication needs (e.g. persuade, vent, or give information) conflict with your needs, so your communication probably won't work well. Future chapters will show you how to manage such distractions effectively, after you're aware of them. Here's a preview:

If your partner seems diverted, check it out with metatalk. This might sound like . . .

"Nina, I feel you're not really with me right now. I wonder if something's bothering you."

If you need to focus elsewhere now, notice it (awareness), and say so (assert)! Doing this is a respectful gift to your subselves and your partner. It might sound like . . .

"I'm having a hard time staying with you, Jeff. I keep wondering if the tenant's check is in the mailbox. Let me look and come right back. Then I can really concentrate with you. OK?"

Trying to fake interest in a partner over time usually won't work: our subselves use subtle or obvious non-verbal signals to show what they feel and think ("leaking"). Your partner's inner crew will notice those, unless they're rioting or focused elsewhere.

When you notice significant physical and internal distractions, build the habit of acting to reduce those before trying important communications (including meditating and praying). Make the phone call, close the window, drink something, urinate, scan the mail, eat a snack, or whatever. Then return and resume. Any communicator denying significant emotional or physical distractions for long will dilute their real hearing, understanding, and communication effectiveness. We're reviewing seven focus options, within awareness question 4.

4c) What topic are we focusing on? and
4d) Did we finish the last one?

When my sister and I were young, Mom passed on a fun birthday-party tradition. She and a friend would patiently weave long lengths of cotton string into a "spider web" covering a whole room. The strings, one per child, were looped around table legs, lamps, and doorknobs, and each other. The "start" end of each had cardboard rectangle to wind the string around, and the other end was tied to a "mystery present" hidden under a cushion or in a drawer. When each child was poised, she'd grin and say, "OK . . .go! First one to finish gets an extra prize!" I think she had as at least as much fun as we did, watching us contort, laugh, scream, and unscramble our tangles.

Have you noticed that many communications, specially personal ones, tend to be like such spider webs? One strand connects to another, to another, to another, to . . . I have sat through thousands of business and therapy meetings where there was no agreed-upon focus, or there was one, but no one (including me) was able to keep us on it until everyone felt done. The outcome was usually one or more participants grumbling "What a waste of time" (i.e. *"I didn't get my needs met."*) Has this ever happened to you? In families and committed relationships, unprocessed old conflicts, hurts, and guilts increase the number of potential strands in the current (emotional/mental) web.

Besides being alert for physical and emotional distractions in key discussions, also become aware of what topic/s you're both focusing on. Then note whether either of you changes the subject, or ends, before the other person feels really done. A straightforward way of checking this is to ask:

"Nora, I notice we're changing the focus from your admission to the hospital tomorrow to your concern about your daughter. Are you feeling finished enough with your concerns about admission?"

If you're not finished, and your partner brings up a new topic, you may say something like:

"Before we talk about that, there's something else I need to say (or ask) about . . ."

An essential to effective problem solving, among your subselves and with another person, is to get and stay clear on *"What are we communicating about?"* I've witnessed hundreds of conflicted couples begin a therapy session with one problem, and within a few minutes bring up a new one, without noticing the topic change. They would regularly do this at home without being aware of it, and accuse each other of "not communicating." When this happens, the real culprit is usually that one or both people are controlled by conflicted, upset subselves. Nobody is aware of it.

Veteran relationship counselor Harville Hendrix offers a helpful way of learning if your partner has more to say before you move to a new topic. He suggests that when your partner has high energy on a topic, you build the habit of listening (empathically), and checking to see *"Is there more (you want me to know)?"* Said respectfully, vs. sarcastically or wearily, that helps your partner assess their own needs, and signals your true interest. Notice that you can also ask *yourself* that awareness question!

*4e) Are we focused on our **content**, or our **process**?*

When you and/or a partner have problems getting your true needs (Chapter 4) met well enough together, this focus-awareness question enables possible resolution. People hire skilled therapists to help them become aware of their inner and mutual communication processes, and/or to learn how to improve them.

You and your partners' having a clear definition of "innerpersonal and interpersonal communication" yields major benefits here. Recall: "Communication" (here) is anything you do, or don't do, that causes a physical, emotional, spiritual, and/or mental change in another person. It is a need-driven, cyclical cause > effect *process* in which each person _ expresses two or more un/conscious needs, _ decodes meanings from the other's perceived responses (behavior), _ experiences two or more needs from these meanings, and _ seeks to fill them un/ consciously by responding verbally and nonverbally.

Is this too complex? Relax. Unless you're a communication pro like a veteran therapist, you don't have to remember this definition. All you need to be aware of is, *"Are we focused now on how we're communicating, or something else?"* Notice the word *communicating*. It implies that even if partners are silent, you're still un/consciously decoding an array of meanings from your own inner dynamics (e.g. *"I'm really bored!"*) and the other's perceived behaviors.

The seven *awareness* questions you're learning here will often provide enough information to get you started identifying and resolving significant communication problems. If they don't, the metatalk summary (p. 382) shows you over 30 other process factors you can select from to do the job. There are many more in the Glossary (p. 418).

If you want to go for the *awareness* gold medal in your relationships, add two more focuses to notice. In typical conversations with your mate, your kids, your best friends, and your boss:

4f) Our focus patterns: You, Me, Us, or Other?

Think of the last satisfying adult conversation you had. I

suspect one of the reasons it was satisfying was that each of you had an "awareness bubble" that included both of you: you each were equally aware of, and respected, each other's needs and feelings. You each probably decoded =/= R-messages from the other.

Now think of an unsatisfying conversation, with a child, co-worker, or friend. On reflection, would you say that one or both of you had an "awareness bubble" that excluded yourself or your partner? Until they learn social skills (empathy and sharing), many kids and some adults are solely focused on *Me*. Healthy parents don't expect their young kids to have adult "consideration" for their needs until late adolescence. In low-nurturance relationships, parents demand that kids put the adults' needs first, and accuse kids who assert their needs of being "selfish." Such unaware parents are controlled by a false self and don't know it. This promotes their kids' developing a false self also, over time.

Some psychologically wounded people are very uncomfortable being aware of, or talking about, personal needs or feelings. Until in true emotional-spiritual recovery, their awareness bubble excludes themselves and most partners. These people usually focus on impersonal, non-intimate things like gossip, soap operas, sports, politics, fashions, pets, and the weather. If this is compassionately pointed out, their governing subselves will get anxious, guilty, and/or defensive. A shame-based and/or fear-based false self *always* dominates such burdened people.

If you have chronic problems communicating with another adult, assess the pattern of your "awareness (focus) bubbles." Exploring this honestly can unearth important things about one or both of you. For instance, if Guardian subselves like a *People Pleaser, Critic*, and *Catastrophizer* control you while trying to protect your *Shamed Child* from (further) rejection, you'll probably be used to focusing on other peoples' needs, and ignoring your own. This will be so familiar as to become normal;

i.e. "no (conscious) problem." It's characteristic of people burdened with the emotional-spiritual condition of "co-dependence," (relationship addiction). Intentionally putting your true Self in charge of your inner family, over time, can change this! Explore this Web resource: [sfhelp.org/02/a-bubble.htm].

4g) Our focus patterns: Past, Present, or Future?

Problems (need conflicts) exist *now*. One way distrustful false-selves avoid the discomfort of struggling with them is to unconsciously over-dwell on the past or the future. People who do this habitually are usually in self-protective denial of being controlled by a fear-based or guilt-based false self. The degree of their false-self control (low to high) can be estimated by the degree of their (subselves) resistance to focusing appropriately on the present, and their denial or defense of this.

Reality check: Reflect on several of your most important (vs. most satisfying) current adult and child relationships. How would you describe your normal patterns of focusing on me-you-us, and past-now-future? What does that mean? Option: use your communication journal to explore this. This is about *awareness,* not self-blame.

So: four key awarenesses you can build are who's leading your inner families, and communication R-messages, needs, and focuses. Here's another:

Q5: "Which skill should I use now?"

People *feeling* intensely often can't hear partners well, or at all. Their awareness (focus) bubble automatically shrinks to include only themselves. To pick the most effective communication skill in important situations, you need to become aware of which of **four E(motion)-level situations** you're in now. Note that "E-level" refers to emotional *intensity*, not just fear, hurt, anger, or frustration. Adults and kids who are elated, sexually excited, terrified, overwhelmed, traumatically injured, and intensely ashamed have towering E-levels.

1) My E-level and yours are both low. This is an easy one: use "normal conversation skills," and keep comfortably alert to see if your or your partner's E-level goes up as you converse. Also stay calmly aware of the other six awareness factors you're learning about here,

2) My E-level is low, and yours is high. If you notice that you're calm, and your partner is locally distracted by intense emotions, you have choices like these:

Ignore this, and assert your needs and feelings anyway. Unless you need to avoid their intensity (intimacy), this will usually leave you frustrated, because *your partner can't hear you*. It will probably leave your partner feeling ignored (unheard), unimportant, and disrespected. Sadly, this is often the case with overburdened (unaware, split) parents, and seriously upset kids. Or you can . . .

Automatically allow your *Inner Critic* (subself) to command your vocal cords, and say something like *"Calm down," "Get a grip,"* or *"Stop being so oversensitive (selfish, needy, childish . . .)."* Judgmental messages like these are really about your own discomfort, and send camouflaged "I'm 1-up" R-messages that hinder communicating. Or other options are . . .

. . . **make** im/polite excuses, and leave or hang up the phone (withdraw); or. . . .

. . . **fake interest**, and let your thoughts wander ("listen with half an ear.") Or you might . . .

. . . **empathically** accept without judgment that your partner's E-level is high, and they can't really hear you now. If you need them to, choose empathic listening skill (Chapter 6), based on an =/= (mutual respect) attitude. If you do this patiently and well, and have enough time, your partner's E-level will eventually fall "below their ears," and they'll regain their hearing. Or you can choose to . . .

. . . **wait for a pause**, and use an assertive metatalk comment like . . .

"You're E-level seems way over your ears now, and mine is starting to go up. I need (whatever)."

 # Reality check: Reflect on the last time you were with a child or adult who was really excited or "upset." Which of these six response-options did you choose? Was your choice unusual, or is it the way you usually react to High-E (excited) people? Were you aware of your response? How did it turn out: whose local needs got met?

Recall: this is the second of four E-level situations you encounter. We're focusing on your becoming *aware,* of which situation you're in now, and choosing which of the six other mental/verbal skills will best get your and your partner's true current needs met well enough. The third common situation is . . .

3) My E-level is high, and yours is low. Your E-level can be above your ears because _ you're upset with or for your communication partner, and you need to express something to them; or _ you're not upset with them, and need someone to hear you vent. Each can damage your relationship and self respect, until your Self becomes aware of your E-level and your communication choices. Let's look at each of these briefly.

Recall several situations in your life when you were hurt, angry, resentful, disappointed, or frustrated by the behavior of someone important to you. Someone breaks a promise or commitment to you. They lie to you, or ignore your needs and feelings. They embarrass you publicly, act disrespectfully, or use you to gain their own pleasure.

Can you remember other times when you were scared about the welfare of someone you loved, or you wanted to teach him or her something you thought would help them? Intense feelings of pain, anger, resentment, frustration, disappointment, sorrow, and fear all cause your subselves to activate, sending your E-level high "above your ears." If you (some subselves) feel guilty, ashamed, or anxious about your feeling or expressing these emotions, it goes even higher. What's your best communication-skill choice in a situation like this?

Recently the 16-year old daughter of a divorced client of mine ran away from home to stay with her non-custodial father. She blocked all her distraught Mom's attempts to communicate with her. Finally, she e-mailed her Mom ". . . *before I'll see you again, you must promise to keep your emotions under control.*" I asked the girl why she needed to assert this boundary. "*Because Mom gets hysterical any time I try to say what I need, and she can't hear me! When she goes ballistic, then I lose it.*" (Her false self takes over.)

This mom was paying a huge price because "her emotions got the better of her" (i.e. her subselves rioted and blended with her Self), and she knew no options. Her repeatedly "going ballistic" was really a symptom of (1) her intense love and concern for her daughter, and (2) her protective denial that she (the mom) was badly wounded because of severe childhood abuse and neglect. She needed more than just communication-skill knowledge.

If you're significantly upset with or for a child or adult, what are your **choices**?

Scream, threaten, name-call, monolog, blame, lecture, plead, whine, moralize, preach, manipulate, repress, punish, shun, play martyr, complain, etc. These responses may feel good short term, but often harm your relationship. People who choose these are usually unaware of being controlled by a false self, and of their options, as my client's mom was.

Say something vague like "*I am so upset with you!*" or "*You make me sick!*" and avoid further discussion and problem solving.

Get into an escalating blame > counter-blame festival with them.

Patiently use the seven mental/verbal skills to get your and your partner's true needs met, in a mutually respectful (=/ =) way. The general scheme is:

Calmly notice that your E-level is above your ears, so you can't problem solve with the other person/s until it comes down. If helpful, remind your subselves that they ("I") have a perfect right to feel their emotions!

Assess who's leading your inner family (Chapter 1). If your Self is, go ahead. If other subselves are, use "parts work" to fill their needs, put your Self in control, and then go ahead.

Meditate and identify what you feel, why, and what you need from your partner now. This might sound like "*I feel hurt and frustrated because my stepdaughter disdainfully refuses to cut the grass (and I feel disrespected), and I need to get her to agree to problem solve with me. I also need my mate to support me in this, and I need to preserve my own self respect.*"

Arrange an undistracted meeting with your communication partner, and use assertion (Chapter 7) to say clearly what you feel, why, and what you need. Expect resistance, and when you get it, use empathic listening (Chapter 6) to bring your partner's E-level down. Then calmly re-assert your true needs. Repeat this cycle until you run out of time, get credible agreement, or shift into problem solving. If your problem has to do with communication conflicts ("*I need you to stop interrupting me*"), use dig-down (Chapter 4) and metatalk (Chapter 5) skills to unearth your true needs.

Intentionally keep an =/= attitude as you do these steps ("*Sally's needs and dignity are as valid as mine.*") For a win-win outcome, your Self must keep distrustful Vulnerable and Guardian subselves from blending and taking you (your wise Self) over during these steps.

Reflect for a moment. Does this four-step scheme make sense to you? If your false self is controlling you now, the first step probably won't. Can you imagine being centered (unblended) enough and aware enough to do these steps with key people in your life? You really can learn to do so, if you *believe* you can, and commit to learning how. Listen to your self-talk for a while to see what your inner team is saying . . .

What if you're not upset with your partner, and you *really* need to vent about something. Your E-level is above your ears, and your partner's is low (below theirs). You need to feel respected, empathically heard, and validated, or accepted; i.e. you need your partner to *want* to listen and empathize. The wild card here is, your partner may need something else now. Your selectively using *awareness* and other communication skills here can raise your odds that you and your partner each get your respective needs met, and you protect your dignities and your relationship. **Choices**:

Check to see who's controlling your inner troupe. If your Self is, go ahead. If other subselves are, use parts work to fill their needs, put your Self in control, and then go ahead.

Use *awareness* to judge if your partner seems comfortable while you vent. If so, make no change. Note the implications that your awareness bubble includes them now, and you respect their needs as much as your own.

See if one or more of your subselves is anxious, and/or guilty about your high emotions, and maybe about "selfishly hogging the conversation," or "dumping my problems on (your partner)." If so, pause, focus inside, and ask the uneasy parts what they need. If your *Guilty Child* feels badly, you can mentally review your Bill of Personal Rights (p. 362) and affirm your right to experience and express your current true motions. You may also remind your inner crew of your partner's responsibility to fill his/her own needs, like feeling ignored, overwhelmed, or bored. This can take several seconds, and a steady focus. If some subselves are still uneasy, you can choose to . . .

Shift your focus to your communication process. Use metatalk to say something like . . .

"Jose, I know I'm really worked up, and I haven't been aware of what's going on with you. Are you OK if I get the rest of this out?"

Be prepared for Jose to say honestly some version of *"Not really, no."*

A freeing option here is to say . . .

"Jose, I'm worried that I may overwhelm, trouble, or bore you if I need to go on and on. Can I count on your telling me if you're having a hard time listening to me, or you need to say something?"

If you're genuine about this, vs. salving your guilt, this respectful invitation gives Jose full responsibility for himself, and (hopefully) lets your anxious subselves relax, unless they don't trust him to be honest.

If you need to vent and your partner isn't in a place to listen (needs something else now), you can choose to . . .

Negotiate a compromise together (*"Put up with me for another five minutes, and then let me tune in to you, OK?"*) or . . .

Quit for now, and you find another partner to listen to you; or . . .

Look for a hidden agenda together underneath your "venting," like thinking *"I hope by telling you how angry I am at my brother, you'll see I'm angry at you for the same reason, so I don't have to confront you and risk your attacking me."*

Another choice you have here is longer-range:

If you want perspective and your partner knows you well, you can choose to ask meta-questions like: *"Would you give me some feedback, please? Trust me: my ego isn't at stake. Do you see me getting this upset very often? Do you feel I over-react at times?"* Alternative: *"Do you think I'm in touch with (experience) my full range of emotions? How do you see me expressing my emotions; apologetically? Forcefully?"* And so on.

Such questions can help resolve communication conflicts, and aid your recovery (shifting inner-family leadership from a false self to your Self and Higher Power.)

Lastly, you can choose to use your high-E situational awareness to . . .

Do some "parts work." Identify which of your inner-family members are upset (needy), learn more about them, and assess whether they know of and trust your Self to validate their needs and help to fill them. If your partner knows parts work, perhaps s/he would help you do this.

We just explored your range of communication choices for situations where your E-level is high, and your partner's is low. Do you need to "do anything" (e.g. journal, discuss, meditate, plan) with the ideas you just read before continuing?

The last common communication situation is the most challenging. Your awareness of it can yield the biggest payoffs . . .

4) My E-level and yours are "above the ears." You both may share compatible excitements (no communication skills needed except comfortable awareness), or one or both of you may have inner conflicts among your subselves, and/or feuds between your two inner families. If so, *neither* of you may be able to hear each other well, or at all. In this complex situation, you can use all seven communication skills to help you each fill your true needs. **Your buffet of choices includes** . . .

Ignore your awareness bubbles, and try to get your surface needs met without caring much about your partner's needs. This will usually result in each of you decoding "I-m 1-up" R-messages from the other; feeling unheard, disrespected, discounted, and hurt; and either escalating your struggle fruitlessly ("arguing" or "fighting"), or one of you numbing and tuning out, or physically leaving. Or you can . . .

Proactively choose to use your communication skills like this . . .

Become non-judgmentally aware that your E-level is above your ears, so you can't problem solve with them until it comes down. If you need two-way dialog, you also need to invite your partner to lower their E-level and unblock their ears, as in situation 2 above. If helpful, remind your subselves that you all (including your partner's inner squad) have a perfect right to feel and express the full range of your emotions!

Check to see who's in charge of your inner family (Chapter 1). If your Self is, go ahead. If other subselves are controlling, use parts-work to fill their needs, and put your Self back in the lead. If this is a major project, you can _ try to finish exchanging now, and don't expect effective communications, and do parts work later; or else _ stop what you're doing, and shift your focus to reorganizing your inner family.

If your partner understands about subselves and inner families and you have common terminology, you can ask them to switch your shared focus to your communication *process*, and negotiate with them about what to do next . . .

"Miriam, I'm having an inner riot, and I need a time out to take care of it. I can't hear what you need until I do, OK?"

If a false self controls your partner, those subselves may not be willing to make this switch (*"See, there you go again, trying to weasel out of looking at your irresponsibility and insensitivity!"*). If you're aware of their false-self talking, you can choose to assert something like . . .

"I sense that some of your (personality) parts have taken over your Self. Neither of us is able to hear each other right now. How about if we each take a time out and get our true Selves back, and then try some problem-solving together?"

Another option is to use empathic listening:

"So you feel I'm trying to avoid acknowledging what you see as my faults, by claiming I need to work on myself." This is a non-judgmental observation, not a question.

Or you might say something like . . .

"You're not willing to take a time out now, despite my feeling we can't communicate well."

If your Self is in the lead, and you have a genuine =/= attitude, empathic listening responses like these will sound matter-of-fact, not sarcastic, whiney, anxious, or belligerent.

Stop reading now, breathe well, and take time to hear your subselves' reactions (self-talk). Can you imaging thinking and talking this way? Pretty odd, huh? Do you know anyone that "talks like this"? I'd be surprised if you do. Let's resume. If your best judgment is that you don't need to (or can't) do inner-family work, then . . .

Take a moment to center (*"Hang on a sec, please"*), and get clear what you feel, why, and what you need from your partner now. **Then** . . .

Estimate which of the six communication needs your partner has now, besides feeling respected. Can you name the other five? Option: use metatalk to reality-check your estimate: *"I think you need me to hear, understand, affirm, and maybe agree with you, right now; yes?"* Depending on what they say . . .

Take the steps in situation 2 above, to bring your partner's E-level down below their ears.

Take steps like those in situation 3 above to bring down your E-level so you can hear again, and then . . .

Invite your partner to use assertion, listening, and problem-solving skills to identify and fill both your needs well enough for now. If your partner doesn't know the skills, try your version, and see what happens. If you're skeptical or unclear what this means, wait until you've read through chapter 11.

If you choose this, _ keep all seven of the awarenesses in this chapter in mind, _ keep your Self in charge, and _ trust what s/he feels is appropriate, as your communication sequence unfolds.

How do these options compare to what you normally do when you and a partner are both significantly emotional and conflicted? Please don't shame yourself if you don't follow a scheme like this. The people who taught you to communicate probably were never aware of their options or the seven skills, so they didn't teach them to you. Few people know how to do "see," think, and talk like this. You can become one of them, if you (your Self) see the high benefits, and patiently leads your inner crew toward acquiring them.

We just explored your typical communication choices in the four common E-level situations between two people. The framework applies just as well if there are three or more people, though there's more to be aware of and balance. Your decisions on how to act, and which communication skills to choose, hinge on . . .

Your Self being in charge,
Your subselves feeling generally =/= (mutually respectful),
Your knowing the seven skills, and . . .

Your *awareness* of whether your and your partner's E(motion)-levels are above or below your respective ears.

Are any of your subselves overwhelmed by what you've just read? (Inner voice: *"This is WAY too complicated. We can never learn to do stuff like this!"* Discouraging thoughts like these typically come from a *Pessimist* or *Catastrophizer* subself protecting one or more overwhelmed, confused, anxious young Vulnerables. Please reassure your subselves: at first, many skills (piano playing, reading, car driving, playing bridge, speaking English) look complex and daunting. Think of some complex skills you're proficient at. Keep a patient, long-range attitude, and the open mind of a student: you *can* learn enough fluency these seven skills, over time, if your Self really wants to!

Now let's look at another key awareness question you can learn to ask. Its answer is essential in evaluating *"Was our communication effective?"*

Q6: *"What was our communication outcome?"*

Have you ever experienced communicating and getting what you want, but not feeling very good about how you did? (*"I harassed Ralph until he finally admitted he'd gone to the race track, and then lied to me about it."*) There are really two halves to this sixth awareness question:

"Did we each get our (two or more) key communication needs met well enough?" and . . .

"Did we each end up feeling good enough about _

ourselves (self respect), _ each other (partner respect), and _ our communication process?"

Premise: based on the two-part definition of effective communication in Chapter 1, any communication exchange between two people (or subselves) will have one of four need-fulfillment outcomes. Even if both partners each feel they met their needs well enough, there are four more possible *process* **outcomes**.

16 Possible Communication Outcomes

Our communication *Need* satisfactions		Our communication *Process* satisfactions	
MINE	YOURS	MINE	YOURS
met	**met**	**OK**	**OK**
met	unmet	OK	not OK
unmet	met	not OK	OK
unmet	unmet	not OK	not OK

Each of the four pairs of *need* outcomes can have four possible *process* outcomes. Only one of the 16 possible outcomes (met + met + OK + OK) yields each partner getting enough of their current needs met, and feeling good enough about themselves, their partner, and their communication process. So **the odds of truly effective communication in high-E situations are 1 in 16, or 6%!** With three or more agitated people, the odds are even lower. The good news: if all people _ have their true Selves leading their inner families, and _ know and use the seven mental/verbal skills well, the odds for shared communication success go way up!

This table and the gee-whiz 6% statistic are misleading, because they use black/white measures to illustrate the concept: The table says your needs are met or they aren't. In real life, most of us aren't clearly aware of what we *really* need (ref. Chapter 1), and may be unclear about whether our needs were met "enough." Add to that the complexity of having some subselves that feel "met," and others simultaneously fuming that their needs were "unmet." From many years' experience since childhood, we've learned to muffle or ignore *conscious* awareness of our needs and many of our communication outcomes.

Do you see the other 94% of outcomes as "bad," or as valuable chances to learn what went wrong (vs. *who* was wrong), and to what improve the next time? What's your philosophy about "making mistakes" in general? Which of your subselves is answering?

 # Reality check: Reflect . . . in each of your most important current relationships, what's your most common communication outcome in general, and in conflict? What would each of your partners say? Do you want to change something about this? Is it in your control? If so, what's in the way of your doing so now?

You and a partner can use this and the other awareness questions together over time (with the other skills), to identify and resolve communication problems inside (Chapter 9) and between you. You can model and teach this outcomes awareness to any kids in your life, and even make a learning-game or contest of it. You can apply this awareness where you work, live, study, or worship. You can ignore it, or defer: *"Yeah, this is a helpful idea. I'll start paying attention next week, after I . . ."*

Your choice, as with each of the six other awarenesses summarized here. Do you know which of your inner family members is making your choice? Here's the last of the seven main *awareness* questions you can learn to pay attention to . . .

Q7: "What are our sequences and patterns?"

A communication *sequence* is a behavioral series of (action > reaction > reaction > reaction . . .) between two people or subselves.

"Reaction" means the spontaneous mix of a partner's thoughts, emotions, perceptions, "decodings" of the other's behaviors, R-message, and needs. For two people in an ongoing relationship, any communication sequence has arbitrary start and endpoints. Here's a brief example of an (action > reaction) communication sequence: You approach me looking excited, and say:

"Hi! What are you writing?" (Action) I react like this:

I feel . . .
Glad to see you,
Curious about your excitement,
Irritated at being interrupted,
Guilty for feeling irritated, and . . .
That your current needs are as important as mine.

I need now to . . .
Respect you, and learn what you need,
Respect myself and keep writing, unless your need seems urgent; and to . . .
Protect and nurture our relationship.

I say . . .
"I'm doing more on my book about communication skills. I'm torn: I want to talk to you, and I also want to stay focused here. Could we get together in an hour or so, or do you need something from me now?" (Metatalk and problem solving).

I see (your reaction): you grin and give me good eye contact. Your face and body language seems calm, relaxed, and open.

I hear (your reaction): *"I know you don't like being distracted when you're dancing with your computer. I'll see you for lunch about noon, OK?"*

I feel (a reaction): respected enough (I decode your R-message as "=/="), appreciative, and relieved. My main current communication needs are met, and it seems like yours were too.

I say: *"Great! Thanks."* As I resume writing . . .

I think: "You have your own awareness impression of what just happened between us. I wonder if your sequence matches mine . . ."

This inner/outer communication sequence took less than 20 seconds. The full sequence would include what my partner needed, heard, saw, felt, and thought, too. This sequence concept enables you to use the powerful technique of mapping (p. 400). Mapping sequences can help you detect and correct habitual communication problems, when used with the seven skills, and an =/= attitude. Becoming aware of your communication sequences can reveal unexpected and useful things about your subselves, like their automatic assumptions, unconscious expectations, and hidden anxieties and guilts. Attending these improves communications and relationships!

 # Reality check: Think of an adult or child you have difficulty communicating with. Invest a few minutes exploring the (see-hear-think-feel-need-R-message) sequence you two usually go through, reaction by reaction, without judgment. What do you notice?

Communication Patterns

As your awareness expands, you'll confirm that we all repeat behavioral (communication) sequences with each other, with some variations, over time. We truly are "creatures of habit." A communication *pattern* is a series of behavioral sequences. For example, have you had the experience of "having the same conversation" with someone over and over again? Or the details may vary, but your emotions and thoughts at the end feel "familiar."

I have a friend 100 miles away who calls two or three times a year. Predictably, she (1) asks about my welfare, and (2) I summarize, and ask about her health. She (3) vents at length (complains and gossips) about that and some people we both know, and (4) I listen empathically, and comment in various ways. She (5) listens and responds, we share some laughter and affirmations, and then (6) we both vow to not let so much time go by before talking again. Then (7) five to seven months pass, and we don't talk. We have had this seven-step communication sequence for about six years. It satisfies both of us, and our relationship doesn't require any major variation.

Some patterns are relatively conflict free, like the one above. Veteran mates routinely exchange *"How was your day, dear?"* dialogs before or at dinner. Stockbrokers and clients have the same basic *"What's the market doing?"* exchange. Parents do with their kids (*"How was school today?"*) The details shift, but often the underlying sequences and pattern doesn't.

Other patterns are conflictual or toxic: one or both people feel dissatisfied or wounded. Ex mates complain, blame, and explain, over and over. A child longs to have their parent care and listen, and may repeatedly get phony interest, *"Not now, dear,"* or a lecture. A wife periodically tells her husband she longs for more intimacy, and re-experiences his predictable response as apathy, frustration, or hostility over and over again.

Awareness of the communication processes *inside* you (among your inner family members) and *between* you and a partner in this detail can clearly identify and explain most communication problems. The more *aware* you are of your communication sequences and patterns, the more options you'll have. That raises the odds that you'll fill your and your partner's main true needs enough, often enough.

Reality check*:* meditate on the pattern of your communication outcomes with several important adults or kids in your life. The four basic possibilities are win-win, win-lose, lose-win, and lose-lose. "Winning" is getting your or their main current needs met well enough, in a satisfying way. Include guessing how each of these people would rate your outcome pattern. If you're not sure, that probably means part of your pattern is to not talk about how you're communicating. That is, you're not using awareness and metatalk together.

We've covered a lot here, so let's review:

Awareness Recap

Awareness is the most fundamental of seven mental/verbal communication skills you and others can develop. During important situations, use it to objectively notice at least seven aspects of what's happening now inside yourself, inside your partner, between you two, and the environment around you both:

1) Is either of us blended (held hostage by a protective false-self group of distrustful personality parts)?   ˙

2) Are we each steadily getting credible =/= **R(espect) messages**? If not, don't expect effective communications. Option: switch your focus to your communication process, and use the other skills together to identify respect problems, and problem-solve them.

3) What do we each need here, besides feeling respected enough . . .

To give or get information; and/or . . .

To vent (be heard, understood, and accepted, vs. "fixed"); and/or . . .

To cause action, and feel potent; and/or . . .

To generate excitement (end boredom), or . . .

To avoid something unpleasant?

Once clearly known, do our present communication needs match?

4) Focuses: Do we need a common focus? Is anyone now emotionally or physically distracted so they can't focus on our conversation? Are we staying focused on each subject until we both feel done, or are we playing conversational "spider web" and generating "old baggage"?

5) Are your and my **E(motion)-levels above or below our ears?** (Can we each hear each other?) If I judge this conversation as "significant," what communication skills should I use now besides *awareness* and clear thinking?

6) What's our current **communication outcome?** Who got their needs met well enough? How do we each feel about our partner, ourselves, and the process we just shared?

7) What are the (action > reaction) **sequences and communication patterns** between us now, and over time? What is our pattern of communication outcomes?

As we end this chapter, try interviewing yourself in your communication journal:

Is your Self in charge of your inner family now, or some other subselves? How do you know? (See p. 74)

What do you know now that you didn't before you began reading?

On a scale of 1 to 10, how motivated are you to expand your communication *awareness* now?

What personal and relationship benefits might more awareness bring you, over time?

From what you just read, how *aware* have you usually been about typical and special communications (low > moderate > high)?

How *aware* have you been of the communication dynamics and sequences *inside* you? (little > some > very aware)

How aware of these seven factors would you say each of your main childhood caregivers were, or are? Your ex and/or present partner, if any?

If you're nurturing kids part time or full time, what have you taught them about communication (or global) *awareness* so far? Would you like to change that? Is anything in the way?

Your answers to awareness questions like the seven in this chapter are inputs to the fifth communication skill you can develop: metatalk.

Skill-building Options . . .

Browse these choices to expand your learning, before reading about the second communication skill. Add the pointers [..**/***.htm] to the base address [http://sfhelp.org/..] to get the full Web address of the referenced page [http://sfhelp.org/ **/***.htm] Omit the brackets.

Enjoy identifying your present communication *strengths* [..02/evc-strengths.htm]

Note the summary of this first mental/verbal skill (p. 367). Copy and use it as a portable reminder of the seven awareness questions, until they become a habit.

Find a partner, and use this practice exercise to help each other develop awareness of at least the seven basic factors described in this chapter: [..02/aware-practice.htm].

Review the ~30 communication factors in the metatalk summary (p. 382). See if there are some you want to add to the seven awarenesses highlighted in this chapter.

Use the worksheets in "Who's *Really* Running Your Life?" [Xlibris.com] or [..pop/assess.htm], practice noticing whether your Self is guiding your inner family in normal and high E-level (e.g. conflictual) situations. If s/he isn't, learn who *is*. Reflect on what that means about your ability to use the seven (or more) awareness questions. For example, if your false self is in charge in high E-level situations, you probably have trouble staying focused, and/or including your partner in your "awareness bubble." [..02/a-bubble.htm]

Develop a list of common personal and social situations, relationships, activities, and locations that tend to significantly *reduce* your communication awarenesses. Look for a pattern among them. Then use your findings and "parts (inner-family) work" to learn why those situations disrupt your inner-family harmony.

Identify some object (like your face in the mirror, or your dominant hand), a sound (e.g. the phone ringing), or feeling you have often in typical days (like thirst), and associate it with *awareness*. For a while, each time you see, hear, or feel it, say "*awareness*" or "*notice*" out loud.

Using tobacco products reduces the transmission of oxygen by your blood, which dulls (numbs) *awareness* of your senses and emotions. Quitting tobacco can help reduce physiological "numbness" that you aren't aware of.

Shallow breathing also numbs awareness, so intentionally practicing deeper breathing can help. Chronic or situational shallow breathing is often a clue to hidden false-self dominance. Another help is . . .

Choosing not to use various mind-altering chemicals, like ethyl alcohol. It is a poison that runs your car engine, distorts your perceptions, and kills irreplaceable liver and brain cells.

Meditating on your inner and outer experiences in a quiet environment can grow your *awareness*. The unpleasant or exciting reality is: if you're overloaded with responsibilities, tasks, or to do's and say "*I don't have time to meditate*," that's your (false self's?) choice. You are in charge of how you use each day's 24 hours. False selves who prize instant gratification and stimulation more than journaling or meditating unintentionally promote vagueness and numbness. Typical true Selves value the wholistic-health benefits of *awareness*, and choose ways to attain it.

Ideas and exercises in Julia Cameron's book "*The Artist's Way*" can help you grow aware. An anywhere/any time exercise is during various times of your day and night, practice thinking, writing, or saying the awarenesses on p. 70.

Add your own options . . .

Now that you're aware of your awareness, let's explore how you *think*. I assume you agree that how you think greatly affects how well you communicate and solve your problems. Reflect: among the many people you've known, have some been better *thinkers* than others? Why? Have you ever thought about how you think about your thinking? Do you think you can intentionally improve the way you think? Which of your subselves is *doing* most of your thinking, anyway? What would it mean to you if you could think more *effectively* more often? What are you teaching your kids about *thinking*?

Don your pith helmet, boots, and khaki shorts; bring a chocolate bar, bug spray, flashlight, and a notebook; and join me in exploring the mysterious, wonderful world of your *thoughts*. Ready?

Awarenesses: (or use your communication journal)

3) Clear Thinking

Besides breathing, can you think of a natural activity that you do more often than *think*? How would you rate the *effectiveness* of your thinking on a scale of one to 10: in general, and in inner and interpersonal conflicts? Generally, how aware are you of *how* you think?

This chapter proposes that you can learn to think more effectively, when you need to. Notice your self-talk now: is your *Inner Skeptic* proclaiming something like *"Well, I can't do anything about the way I think, no matter what this guy says?"* I respectfully disagree. Affectionately acknowledge your *Skeptic*, and explore with me . . .

I'm a veteran engineer, a "linear-thinking" man, a therapist, a clinical hypnotist, and communication-skill student, teacher, and facilitator. These roles have given me many reasons to study what goes on in our unconscious, semi-conscious, and conscious minds. Each of our three minds seems to have its own style of thinking, (processing information), which affects our feelings, goals, and behavior in different ways. Do you include your body (i.e. your nervous and endocrine (hormonal) systems, and/or your muscle cells) as parts of your "mind"? Do you think partly with your *body*?

From over 17,000 hours of listening to therapy clients, students, and others, I conclude that few kids or adults are aware of *how* they think. One result is that as we act to fill our daily needs, most of us (including me) suffer from gusts of "fuzzy thinking." The more frequent those gusts, the more our relationships, productivity, and self-esteem degrade. That lowers the nurturance levels of our families and social groups, and raises the odds that any kids involved will develop up to six psychological wounds (p. 37).

To lay the groundwork for improving the effectiveness of your thinking . . .

Your Thoughts on *Thinking* . . .

Here's a chance to learn what you know and believe about "thinking." There's no right or wrong here, just what the unique, amazing critter with your name thinks. Fill this out in an undistracted place and time, with the mind of a student. Option: use this questionnaire to interview someone else you want to know more about, like a child . . .

As I start this interview, I'm thinking . . .

1) I believe the purpose of thinking is . . .

2) I'm aware of *how* I'm thinking (vs. *what*): _ never _ rarely _ fairly often _ very often _ always

3) If a tourist from another galaxy asked me "What is this thing humans do called 'thinking'?", I'd say . . .

4) For me, the difference between a "thought" and a "feeling" is . . .

5) The difference between being "smart" and being "wise" is . . .

6) Some people I believe are or were specially effective thinkers are . . .

7) If I'm alone, I know I'm thinking effectively when . . .

8) *Thinking* and *knowledge* are very different things.
_ I agree _ I disagree _ I'm not sure _ I don't care

9) The factors that have had the greatest impact on shaping how I think are . . .

10) Some people that I feel are (or were) often fuzzy or muddled thinkers are . . .

11) Thinking is *fuzzy* or *ineffective* when it. . . .

12) I have an unconscious mind that is thinking something all the time: _ absolutely _ probably _ I don't know or care _ probably not _ no way!

13) When conflicted, my unconscious mind overrules my conscious thoughts: _ always _ often _ sometimes _ rarely _ never _ I don't know

14) I can think clearly without always being "logical."
_ I agree _ I disagree _ I'm not sure _ I don't care

15) I can learn to think more effectively if I want to.
_ I agree _ I disagree _ I'm not sure _ I don't care

16) If I began to focus on how I think, alone and with others, I'd probably learn . . .

17) Fuzzy thinking is very different than ignorance or stupidity:
_ I agree _ I disagree _ I'm not sure _ I don't care

18) I think "better" when . . .

19) The bigger my vocabulary is, the more effective my thinking will be: _ I agree _ I disagree _ I'm not sure _ I don't care.

20) Typical males and females tend to think *differently*:
_ I agree _ I disagree _ I'm not sure _ I don't care _ it depends on . . .

21) College graduates think more clearly and effectively than people with less education: _ true _ false _ I'm not sure _ that depends on . . .

22) *Thinking* is different than *believing*: _ I agree _ I disagree _ I'm not sure _ I don't care _ it depends on . . .

23) Conscious *awareness* is required for effective thinking: _ I agree _ I disagree _ I'm not sure _ I don't care _ it depends on . . .

24) I routinely hear different "inner voices"—i.e. there are different sources of the normal thought-streams within me: _ true _ false _ I/m not sure _ at certain times. (Which times?)

25) Some people are born "better thinkers" than others, so there's a limit to how well I can learn to think:
_ true _ false _ I'm not sure.

26) Anyone who really wants to can _ become aware of how they think, _ develop a clear concept of "clear or effective thinking", and _ improve gradually, via practice and feedback: _ I agree _ I disagree _ I'm not sure _ I don't care.

27) Some people in my life whose way of *thinking* (vs. way of communicating) causes me significant problems are . . .

28) Someone I'd pick as a "thinking hero/ine" (inspiring model) is . . .

29) The main differences between my *thinking* and my *values* are . . .

30) People who aren't *aware* of their thinking can still be highly effective communicators: _ I agree _ I disagree _ I'm not sure _ I don't care _ it depends on . . .

31) Recently, some things that have been more important to me than improving the effectiveness of my thinking are . . .

32) Relative to thinking *effectively*, what I'd most like to give the child/ren in my life is . . .

33) I believe that most people who know me fairly well would describe my way of thinking (vs. what I know) as . . .

34) If I could be objective, I'd describe my partner's (or another's) style and effectiveness of thinking as . . .

35) After reflection, my partner would probably describe her (his) general thinking effectiveness as being . . .

36) If my partner (or another significant person) and I chose to invest periodic times helping each other learn to think more clearly and effectively, then . . .

As I finish **this exploration, I'm aware of . . .**

Have you ever interviewed yourself like this before? Is there someone you'd like to show this to, or discuss these ideas with? Why (not)? Now that you've helped yourself to focus on your thinking about your thinking, see what other insights may appear by exploring . . .

What is *Effective* Thinking?

I propose that the purpose of our innate ability to think is to _ "make sense" (compute the meanings) of our current inner and outer environments, so we can _ consciously identify and understand our current true needs, and _ decide if and how to fill them.

So **effective thinking means** that your several minds coordinate to _ identify and decode meaning from your inner and outer environments accurately, and then _ process the meanings in a way that leads to _ filling your current true needs well enough. *Logic* may or may not always be *effective* thinking . . .

Fuzzy thinking distorts the meaning of your inner and outer environments, and/or processes your meanings in a way that doesn't meet your current true needs well enough. Human history is rich with hilarious and tragic *misunderstandings* where someone decodes the wrong meaning from their environments. Remember the last time that happened to you?

You think to "make sense" of your experiences, and build a data base (memory) of the things that form your internal and external environments. You learn that butterflies and broccoli are safe to touch, and that rattlesnakes and molten lava aren't. This ever-expanding database is the inner library your un/conscious minds use to "make sense" out of current perceptions and sensations, and make safe, useful decisions. Recent scans of living brains reveal that we naturally have several different physical brain areas that form a network of temporary, intermediate, and long-term "libraries."

One way of "making sense" is via conscious *thoughts*. These are (usually) coherent mental strings of words. Thinking can also include inner images "worth a thousand words." Some people have a greater capacity to image than other people. Are you a *visual* person? Can you image your favorite cartoon character now? Do you know someone who is "very visual"? Alternatives are being more *kinesthetic* (touch and movement oriented) or *auditory* (sound-oriented).

Our primitive unconscious mind bypasses conscious thinking. Instead of words, it uses a fluid mix of vaguely felt hunches, intuitions, instincts, fantasies or dreams, senses, (*"I sense you're angry now"*) or *knowings.* Our unconscious mind is a kind of backup system to help us survive when we're not consciously thinking "too well." It may be a "lizard-brain" (brain stem) inheritance from our earliest mammalian ancestors. Sometimes our unconscious mind/body can know what we need before our conscious mind makes sense of things. Do you ever experience that?

So your thinking is a _ semi-automatic mental + physical + spiritual + emotional *process* that _ uses information stored in your several mental "data bases" to _ consciously and unconsciously decode the immediate and long-term *meanings* of the ceaseless information from your five or six senses, to _ fill your immediate surface and underlying true needs. Whew.

"Semi-automatic" suggests that your conscious mind can control some of your thinking process, just as you can learn to change your breathing, sleeping, and eating habits. This implies that *you can learn to improve your thinking, within limits.* Do you agree?

If thinking serves to fill your true needs, then how often you feel "significantly stressed" is proportional to _ how *aware* you are of your true needs and your inner and outer environments, and _ how effective your thinking is. If you often feel worried, dissatisfied, anxious, sick, tired, lonely, or "upset," that suggests _ you're unaware of your true needs, and/or _ your thinking is ineffective (fuzzy).

What Causes Fuzzy Thinking?

I suspect at least four factors:

Emotional and physical insensitivity or numbness to what our inner and outer environments are telling us right now. This is like a radio with no antenna, so it doesn't receive many local signals. Numbness is reflexive: we grow numb to our numbness. Numbness to emotions and physical sensations is a symptom of significant psychological wounds (false-self dominance), which seem to come from a low-nurturance childhood. When you're numb or distracted, you can't discern what you *need* now. Another factor that hinders effective thinking is . . .

Unawareness **of the mental process you use** to translate the words, images, database information, and unconscious inputs into current meanings and needs. This is similar to unawareness of breathing, facial expressions, and social eye-contact habits. And fuzzy thinking comes from . . .

A lack of knowledge of at least three things:

What's possible. Most fuzzy thinkers don't know what their thinking-improvement options are, or see that these options would help fill more of their daily needs; and . . .

A greater vocabulary. Having a small vocabulary is like trying to paint a fine portrait with a 6" house-painting brush. And . . .

These seven mental/verbal skills, which empower anyone to define problems (needs) and alternatives clearly, and then act to fill current needs effectively. Restated, typical fuzzy thinkers don't know the information in this book, and they don't know they don't know.

A fourth factor that seems to promote ineffective thinking is . . .

Tolerating and creating constant distractions. Our culture is used to unawareness and fuzzy thinking, and unconsciously promotes it. The profit-minded people controlling our media and educational systems often focus on stimulation (entertainment) and information, not "effective thinking." Can you recall a recent radio or TV program, news article or coupon, billboard, local school program or course that focuses on how to *think* effectively? In all the years of education you've had, did you ever focus on this subject?

The ceaseless sensory stimulation our culture floods us with promotes personal and social numbness, and sensory overload. The stimulation ranges from hundreds of flickering cable-TV channels to racks of specialty magazines and newspapers to pocket-radio headphones, to advertising messages inside bottle caps to flickering Web page banners to junk mail to giant multimedia billboards, to . . .

Personal computers, the Internet, and the exploding wireless communication industry are adding new compound waves of choices and information to our lives. These greatly increase the speed of decision-making and social change. They all constantly distract us from quiet, focused awareness, and clear thinking.

Does it seem credible that these four factors divert you and others from thinking about thinking, and acting to improve yours? **The good news is** you can choose to reduce the impact of these factors and fill more of your true needs, if your dominant subselves want you to. Doing this requires you to want to change some key priorities and attitudes. You change when you feel enough discomfort, and/or when you see a safe, viable way to add comfort, safety, and pleasure to your life. Both of these require *awareness*. Numbness, habits, and sensory and mental distractions block your awareness.

Pause and listen in on the chatter that's going on in your mind/body now: your "self talk." What are your inner voices (subselves) saying? What are you feeling? Where are you focused? Which of your subselves are creating your thoughts, "senses," and images right now?

Five Goals

The hindrances above suggest these improvement targets:

Choose to **increase your** (physical + mental + emotional + spiritual) *awareness* (Chapter 2). This will enable you to identify your current true needs, and notice how you try to fill them, and how often you do.

Use your growing awareness to **learn *how* you're used to translating** (inner + outer events) into filling your current needs. Then intentionally improve your translation process òver time. Part of that can be choosing to note and reduce distractions in key internal and social communications.

Patiently **build your vocabulary**. The more words you're fluent with, the more accurately you can _ define and assert your needs, _ empathize and name your partner's thoughts and needs, and _ define your need-conflicts and resolution options (problem solve).

Become more aware of your spoken terms. Intentionally **avoid vague pronouns and _ ambivalent and _ emotionally-charged** "hand grenade" terms in key conversations.

Learn the seven communication skills, and practice using them with your *inner* family members. "Thinking" is your ruling and less active subselves communicating with each other.

How can you reach these goals?

Ways to Think More Clearly

If you value the current and long-term quality of your life, you'll want to create high-nurturance relationships among your subselves and with selected other people. Can you think of a more impactful way to do this than learning how to think and problem-solve more effectively? You really can, if your ruling subselves *want* to! You can also teach your kids and interested others to do the same. There are practical ways you can transform unawareness and fuzziness into more effective thinking, *if your Self is leading your inner family* (Chapter 1).

Put Your Self in Charge

Begin improving your thinking by becoming aware of **who's**

been running your life recently. Whoever is making your decisions will decide if, when, and how you experiment with more effective thinking. Is your reaction something like *"Well, duh. I am running my life now!"?* Do you know who "I" is?

Chapter 1 introduced you to the idea that young kids' personalities automatically adapt to inadequate nurturing by splitting into semi-independent subselves, or *parts*. These include an innately skilled leader, your true Self (capital "S"), and a group of other subselves called (here) your "false self." When your Self is disabled by other anxious, distrustful subselves, one result is fuzzy (jumbled, chaotic, unfocused, illogical) thinking. After 40 years' study, I believe that well over 80% of average adults and kids are ruled by a false self much of the time. They (you?) haven't a clue of that, what it means, or what to do about it. *Awareness* can change that for you.

Unless your subselves trust your Self to lead them, you may be thinking fuzzily much or all the time, and not know it.

Start improving your mental processing by checking yourself for significant false-self dominance. If you discover that you're often controlled by a well-meaning but reactive, narrowly-focused false self, your initial goal becomes intentionally freeing your true Self to lead your inner family ("recovery"). My companion book "Who's *Really* Running Your Life?" [xlibris.com] outlines ways and resources to do that. So do these Web pages: [http://sfhelp.org/pop/assess.htm] . My main motive is to alert you to what's possible about your and your loved ones' lives, not to sell books.

When you feel a mix of *calm, centered, energized, light, focused, resilient, up, grounded, relaxed, alert, serene, purposeful*, and *clear*, your true Self is probably leading your inner family of subselves. *Empowering your true Self, and choosing options from those below, will increase your conscious awareness of your current true (vs. surface) needs.* That and these skills will help you and those you care about fill them more often.

    # Reality check: if a protective false self controls you now, your well-meaning subselves will probably react like this:

    Defocusing you (*"Hey, what shall we eat tonight?"*)

    "Forgetting" what you just read.

    Making it "incomprehensible," and/or . . .

    Distracting you from acting on this today (*"But we have to take the cat to the vet right away!"*)

    And your protective Guardian subselves may produce persuasive thought streams like . . .

    "Ah, bunk! New Age garbage."

    "I can't do that."

    "I have too many other responsibilities."

    "Too much work. I'm OK enough as I am."

    "If I investigate my inner family, something really bad will happen!"

    or other discouraging thoughts . . .

    Your subselves are ceaselessly vigilant and protective. Their knowledge is limited, and often obsolete and *wrong*. Their perception of reality is often distorted, and their priorities are short range and skewed. Typical subselves view second-order (core attitude) life changes, like learning to think clearly, with high distrust and alarm. Their protective instinct is often to stubbornly resist change, unless they feel you're health or life is in immediate danger. That's why many of us repeatedly make frustrating, ineffective first-order (superficial) changes (*"Nuts! I've regained my 20 pounds, and added four more!"*). This can change when you get tired enough of your chronic discomfort to *want to* empower your true Self to lead your talented inner team of specialists.

    Pause, breathe from your belly, and become aware of what your inner voices are saying. Who is speaking them?

    Once your Self is guiding your inner team, what else can you do?

Other Pro-clarity Options

Here's a buffet of choices your inner team can select from to help you achieve the five clearer-thinking goals above. Option: use this section as a checklist to guide you toward actually working toward your goals. If a protective false self dominates you or you're in a true crisis, you probably won't (for now, anyway).

1) **"Raise your awareness"** is pretty vague. Specific options include _ reread Chapter 2 periodically, _ keep a journal of your thoughts and feelings, and noting how your awareness changes, over time; and _ periodically practice skill-building exercises like this: [...02/aware-practice.htm]. You (your Self) will see similar ways to grow your conscious and instinctual awareness. If you haven't *experienced* how greater awareness reduces fuzzy thinking and fills more of your daily needs, why should you want to do it? If you never tasted fudge before, why would you put it in your mouth? It's a faith walk.

2) _ **Evolve your own definition of** *effective* **thinking**, and _ coach yourself to *use* the definition to gauge your status and progress. How can you tell when your thinking is sharp and clear? Fertile places to spot fuzzy thinking are inner and interpersonal "problems" (unmet needs) that won't resolve permanently. Practicing with your dig-down skill (Chapter 4) will reveal a rich trove of fuzzinesses in you and your partners.

3) Coach yourself to notice your body, and develop your awareness of telltale feelings that signal _ false-self control (Chapter 1) and related _ fuzzy thinking. Conversely, notice how your *body* feels when your Self is guiding your inner family, and you're at your mental best. Is there a time of day, and a day of the week you think most clearly? Carol Orlock's fascinating book "Inner Time—the Science of Body Clocks and What Makes Us Tick" suggest there are probably regular windows of time you function (think) "best." Do you know when those times are?

4) Regard all your emotions as friendly, useful signals from your subselves that they need something now. If your *Inner Critic* labels emotions like anger, fear, and guilt as *bad* or *negative*, s/he is disregarding what other subselves are trying to communicate. That can shame them, which promotes blending and fuzzy thinking! Your accepting that all your emotions are *real* and potentially helpful, vs. *good* or *bad*, is a second-order attitude change. Such core changes often merit consciously grieving "the old way." A related option: _ coach yourself and key partners to distinguish between *feeling* emotions and *acting* on them: e.g. "*Yvonne, I support your* feeling *angry, and* (not "*but*") I *don't like the way you* expressed *it to me just now.*"

5) Coach yourself and those you love to _ **become "fuzzy word" and "hand grenade word" hunters.** In listening to hundreds of conflicted couples (i.e. their warring inner families), I observe that one or more partners or subselves aren't aware of using **vague, general words and terms** like *it, that, those, this, them, the problem, deal with, pretty soon,* and *work through* in talking about vital personal and relationship needs. For instance, "*We have to find a way to make it better.*" *i*s far less likely to promote effective communication and problem-solving than "*I need to understand specifically what you need from me now about my daughter's recent disrespectful behavior.*"

  You can _ build the habit of respectfully asking yourself and your communication partners "*What is 'it,' or 'that,' or 'the problem'? Who is 'they' or 'them'?*" Questions like these and in option 8) below will uncover an inadequate vocabulary, fuzzy thinking, and/or unseen false-self dominance and inner-family uproar.

You can also _ develop your skill and reflex to *listen* empathically (Chapter 6) in important situations. **Practice "hearing checks"** with your inner subselves and outer partners. They help to unearth misunderstandings over key words or phrases. For example, you say calmly "*So Martha, you're asking* *me for more intimacy, meaning better sex;"* and she replies *"No! Honey, I need more time just holding each other, and talking like we used to. I really need to know how you're feeling, and what you want. You never talk about those things, and I feel shut out, frustrated, and anxious. Our sex is fine, for me. I need more* intimacy.*"*

Another semantic cause of fuzzy thinking and ineffective communicating is **not being *aware* of using "hand grenade" words and phrases**. These carry specially powerful semi-conscious emotional "charges," and are usually decoded with an inflammatory *"I am* way *1-up here!"* R-message. Using explosive hand-grenade terms risks causing the listener to split and lose their true Self, blast their E-level into the sky, defocus, and replace listening and problem solving with explaining, defending, counterattacking, playing "yes, but . . .", numbing out, or fleeing.

Notice your emotional reaction to these common examples: *abuse* or *abuser*, *rape*, *addict(ed)* and *"your addiction"*, *irresponsible, stupid, dumb, thoughtless, insensitive, sexist, chauvinistic, childish, overreact, oversensitive, controlling, coward, bitch or bastard, nerd, mental case, weak, homo, manipulative, slut, whore, failure, selfish, liar, egotist, bigot, racist, self-centered, neglectful, brainless, arrogant, sick, wimp,* "real *wo/man* (husband / wife / partner / parent / . . .), *affair* (marital), *racist, perverted, lazy, pathetic, pitiful,* and *incest.*

For many people, **swearing** involves emotionally-charged words and non-verbal behaviors. Every family and culture adds unique hand grenade words and phrases to common ones like these. Are there other words that usually trigger your false self? What does your inner family do when you hear or say them?

Option*:* _ evolve a list of emotionally-charged terms and phrases that affect your key inner and outer relationships. Then _ consciously choose to avoid them, or confront them. Doing this will probably require your Self to confront your *Inner Critic, Judge, Bigot,* and/or *Warrior,* who rely on those words. _ Ask key partners to help you build and *use* your list. This is about more effective thinking and communicating, not *blame*!

Frequently using emotionally-explosive terms usually signals that _ a false self is in charge, and _ the speaker is unaware of their true current needs. For instance, a partner says *"Jeff, when it comes to confronting your ex wife, you turn into a spineless, yellow-bellied coward."* She may really mean *"Jeff I'm frustrated, split, and scared. I need to regain my respect for you, and my trust in you to help keep our relationship safe, by your* wanting *to be more assertive with your ex wife for your sake, not to please me."* Alert: this may be received as a "be spontaneous!" paradox (p. 425) and unintentionally *block* communication.

The more important and/or complex a situation is, the more benefit you'll get from being alert for vague or explosive terms, and for people (or subselves) having different interpretations of key words and phrases.

Status check: see where you stand on what you just read: T = true, F = false, and "?" = "I'm not sure."

I am _ usually aware of using emotionally-charged terms in my key relationships, including _ those among my subselves. (T F ?)

I am usually aware of my reaction to key other people using hand grenade terms with me or each other, including kids. (T F ?)

I _ **can** name at least five terms or phrases that provoke strong feelings in me, and _ I can describe my normal reactions to that. (T F ?)

I _ **know** how to assert my needs effectively with other people who use hand grenade words, *or* _ I'm now motivated to learn how. (See Chapter 7) (T F ?)

More options toward clearer thinking . . .

6) Build your vocabulary, over time. This may feel pretty vague and overwhelming. Our rich, evolving language is composed of tens of thousands of words and phrases. One do-able way to learn more of them is to focus on several classes of words and phrases. For instance, to reduce fuzzy thinking and speaking, expand your inventory of words that describe human . . .

Emotions. There are probably over 30 common terms (confused, curious, spacey, serious, annoyed . . .). How many can you name? How many do you use regularly?

True (personal) **needs**; e.g. "I need respect, security, appreciation, challenge, purpose, and stimulation." See the next chapter for more.

Communication basics, dynamics, and blocks. See Resources A and J.

Common _ family and _ relationship terms, including _ inner-family terms, and _ personality-splitting traits and symptoms (Chapter 1). The next book in this series has a glossary of these terms (*Stepfamily Courtship*; Xlibris, 2001)

Does building those special vocabularies feel more do-able than learning the whole dictionary? The communication/ relationship glossary (p. 418) can help you do this. Note that your intentionally breaking a big task into manageable chunks and prioritizing them is typical of a true Self in charge. Do you normally do this with important problems and relationships now?

7) Practice viewing *inner*personal and interpersonal "problems" as *need conflicts*. Then coach yourself and key partners to adopt the =/= attitude "*Your needs and mine are (usually) equally important to me.*" This becomes do-able if your Selves are guiding your respective inner squads. These steps will help you grow your dig-down skill (Chapter 4) to unearth your current *true* needs. That promotes this helpful clear-thinking option . . .

8) To avoid or resolve major conflicts, **learn to ask key questions.** _ Confirm that your Self is in charge, and then _ selectively ask your subselves and/or your partner questions like these:

"Specifically, what do you (or I) need right now; _ in general, and _ from me (or you)?"

"Specifically, what _ have you (or I) tried already, and _ what did you (or I) get?" and . . .

"Specifically, what do you (or I) feel is in the way of getting enough of what you (or I) need?"

Specifically invites you to avoid vague terms and phrases (5 above). This last question is not an invitation to blame someone, including yourself, any more than you'd blame a car tire for going flat. (*"Argh! What a stupid, insensitive tire!"*) This brings up another impactful option . . .

9) Coach yourself to **identify specifically what you *expect* from yourself and key partners**. My experience is that often, conflicted, over-busy, (split, unaware) adults and kids _ aren't clearly aware of what they expect from themselves and others, or _ haven't explained or confirmed their expectations; and/or _ haven't meditated and reality-checked to see if their expectations are realistic or appropriate under local circumstances.

Do these describe *you*? Note your options in critical situations to _ state your expectations of others clearly, and to _ ask respectfully *"What do you expect from me here?"*

10) Learn the seven mental/verbal skills in this book. Then use them and the special terms you learn in option 6) above to experiment with "mapping" the communication sequences between _ conflicted inner-family subselves (Chapter 9), and _ you and key other people. Focus your **mapping** on spotting situational or chronic fuzzy thinking in one or more of you (p. 400).

This is not about playing the shame-and-blame "Gotcha" game that some subselves delight in. It is about constructively identifying where one or more of you could improve your thinking and speaking (or writing) effectiveness. You can also use mapping to spot any of the common communication blocks (see option 7 above), and then use the seven skills to resolve them.

These seven skills and communication mapping can also

help illuminate how you alone, and with selected partners, decode inner and outer events into needs, and how you try to fill them. Popular vague shorthand for doing this socially is *talking together, talking "it" over, discussing "it," take a look at "it", dealing (or coping) with "this problem," working through "our problem,"* or *let's process this "thing."* Exactly what is *"it,"* and *"our problem"*?

11) Decide if you want to **develop your *Inner Observer's* talent for giving you factual feedback** on how you think, with certain people, situations (like conflict), or moods. Become familiar with the experiences of mind racing, or churning, and defocusing, and assess yourself for those nonjudgmentally.

One more way you can improve the clarity of your thinking is . . .

12) Work with a respectful, co-motivated partner towards clearer thinking. We can't avoid judging our thinking and behaving in biased (distorted, subjective) ways. This is specially true if we're controlled by a well-meaning false self. Exchanging clear supportive feedback with a respectful, unsplit, focused partner can safely expose and lower your (and their) distortions, and speed your work. It's also more fun! See these ideas on giving *effective* personal feedback: [...02/evc-feedback.htm].

 # Reality check: S - l - o - w d - o - w - n. Stop. Breathe easily. Close your eyes. Make a *comfort* sound, if you wish (*"Aaaahhhhhhh. . . ."*) Take a break from all this *thinking.* This is a lot of information! Relax, and enjoy letting your thoughts go where they may. Also enjoy knowing that the diligent, impressionable subselves who form your unconscious mind are taking good notes on which of these many ideas and options are specially relevant for you.

Reflect leisurely on the 12 choices you just reviewed. They're specific ways you can intentionally increase the clarity and effectiveness of your ceaseless *thinking*: making sense of "things." These options may suggest other useful choices to you. Notice: is your Self in charge of your inner family now? If not, who is, and what do they need?

Fuzzy Thinking in Action

To make these abstract ideas more real, here are several examples of fuzzy thinking. See if they bring anything to mind. True story: a couple remarried for 11 years hires me to help them "feel better about their relationship" (surface problem statement.) The twice-divorced, 50-something biodad/stepdad says earnestly, without eye contact . . .

"I'm absolutely committed to working this thing out."

His wife looks at him silently, without expression. I say . . .

"Bill, please help me understand what you mean by 'this thing'"

Bill struggles to get clear and articulate. Again without eye contact, he says . . .

"Well . . ." He went into a venting trance, and rambled for 10" about (1) his concern about losing his job, and related (2) money worries; (3) his guilt and defiance about not being emotionally available for his wife; (4) his unresolved guilt about the major (perceived) effects his divorce had on his older kids; (5) his indecision about whether or not to have their home open to all their (many) kids without restrictions; (6) his worry about his hospitalized father, (7) the painful effects of a recent hernia operation; (8) his semi-conscious fear of a third divorce; and (9) his shame as a "grown man" of not being able to master all these issues effectively.

I finally interrupted his (subselves') venting. This tormented, courageous college graduate seemed to be overwhelmed by a cluster of major inner and interpersonal stressors. I believe he was (usually) controlled by a false self, and wasn't aware of it. As a result, his leaderless, squabbling subselves were unable to focus on any one of these *nine* important sets of simultaneous unfilled *surface* needs. He could only express his composite interrelated "problems" by referring to them together as *"this thing."* Lack of eye contact like his often implies the (split) speaker's struggle to avoid visual awareness of the receiver's responses, and defocusing even more.

Another "fuzzy" example:

As a volunteer Website-management committee member, I say to the CEO of a national non-profit organization *"I don't think we're clear yet on who we're trying to serve."* She says diplomatically, *"Well, I may be missing something, but (I think we are.)"* I feel unheard, and list seven possible groups of people we *should* serve. She says soothingly, *"I think you have the right idea. We should focus on (three of the seven)."* I feel unsatisfied, mildly ignored, and unheard, and I'm not clear why.

Later reflection revealed my unawareness and related fuzzy thinking: What I was *really* trying to express was *"I'm frustrated and confused, because I feel our whole committee hasn't discussed or reached a consensus about the people that you feel our organization and Website should serve."* My subselves were doing an intricate approach-avoid dance between confronting the CEO, whom I respect and admire, and my honest values-conflict with her.

I was controlled by my false self, partially unaware of my true needs, and consequently fuzzy (ineffective) in my thinking and speaking. I did not get my true needs met then. My *awareness* of this now opens the possibility of discussing this more clearly with the committee and the CEO.

Another example: A resentful agnostic says in frustration to his fundamentalist Christian partner . . .

"I don't get it. As a bright, grown-up woman, how can you not see that your insinuating that you alone see the "one right way" of believing in some kind of God is elitist and arrogant? I feel totally put down by your insinuation, and you won't take responsibility for it! You're in class-A denial!"

The woman smiles wanly ("condescendingly", the man thinks), and says . . .

"No, no, you just don't understand! I'm not putting you down, or telling you what to believe, Honey. I'm offering you

a way to save your soul from burning in Hell, don't you see? I love you!"

This illustrates the potential multi-level complexity of communications. I believe both these people were controlled by false selves. They each had inner-family conflicts (Chapter 9), plus clashes between their two groups of subselves: i.e. three simultaneous battles. Neither was aware of any of this, or their communication process. Both were doing best-effort fuzzy thinking. They weren't aware of their option to dig down to and focus on their true needs (Chapter 4), and assess *how* they were talking (Chapters 1 and 5). Their two crews of subselves were in power struggle over who was "right," and several powerful subselves were ashamed and scared to admit that.

If the man's Self had been in charge, his thinking and speech might have said something like . . .

"Marcia, I'm venting. I need to feel that you want to understand and care about my feelings. I feel unheard, and disrespected by you implying my spiritual belief is wrong and inferior to yours. I'm not asking you to change your belief or adopt mine. I'm also frustrated at how hard talking with you about this feels. You're probably feeling put down by me, because I disagree with your belief. Are you?"

I suspect Marcia's inner conflict was among subselves who passionately felt a mix of . . .

"His Soul is in mortal danger, and he doesn't believe it!"

"Good Christians fight to save unredeemed sinners."

"God's commandment is that I should be a good Christian and should willingly and humbly obey. If I don't, I'll burn in Hell."

"I love this man, and don't want to offend or disrespect him."

"I feel he isn't able to understand me and receive God's Word, and is controlled by Satan."

"I want to be polite, respectful, and gentle."

"If I truly consider what he says, my whole life's religious beliefs might collapse. I can't face that!"

"I resent that _ he can't hear me, _ is so stubborn and arrogant, _ misjudges me, and _ is blind to his danger and my loving Christian concern for him."

What patterns do you see in these three real-life examples? I hope it's clear that "**fuzzy thinking**" doesn't happen in a vacuum. It **is a symptom of underlying problems like . . .**

Unseen false-self dominance; resulting in . . .

One or both partners feeling disrespected, ignored, and misunderstood; (Decoded R-messages: *"I feel you are definitely 1-down / inferior / wrong / bad"*); plus . . .

Unawareness of blending, communications, surface vs. true needs, and relationship basics; and mutual unawareness of these four factors in both people, and . . .

Mutual inability, and/or false-self unwillingness, to focus on these factors as =/= partners; vs. getting tangled up in a surface conflict over *"My needs and opinions are better/righter than yours, but I won't admit I feel that!"*

Have you ever been in frustrating situations like these? How likely is it that you and your adult or child partner were unaware of these four shaping your communications and outcomes?

Recap

You and the adults and kids in your life use *awareness* and *thinking* more than any other means to identify and fill your fluctuating current true needs. Thinking is the automatic decoding of *meanings* from current sensory information and stored experiences. All your communications are based on how your minds decode perceived (emotional + physical + spiritual + mental) sensations into meaning, and then relate those to your current surface and true needs.

This chapter provided _ an "interview yourself" worksheet to help you learn "What I think about how I think;" _ four proposed reasons that "fuzzy" (ineffective) thinking is the accepted norm in our culture, and _ 12 specific options your true Self has towards patiently accomplishing these **"clearer-thinking" goals**:

Intentionally raise your (physical + mental + emotional + spiritual) *awareness* (Chapter 2), so you can . . .

_ **Become nonjudgmentally aware** of *how* you're used to translating inner and outer events into meaning and current needs, and then _ intentionally improve your translation process (your thinking effectiveness), over time. This can include noting when you assume, generalize, defocus, ignore distractions and/ or hunches, use black/white decoding, intellectualize, and many more (Resource F). And. . . .

Patiently learn . . .

_ **A bigger** (more precise) **vocabulary**, and _ when to avoid vague pronouns and emotionally-charged "hand-grenade" words and phrases;

The seven communication skills, and what you can do with them inside and outside your skin; and . . .

To _ **dig down** to identify what you *really* need now (Chapter 4), and to _ brainstorm what your current options are, vs. doing black/white (bi-polar) thinking (Chapter 8).

To improve your thinking (*inner* communication), **an essential first step is** to assess *"Who's usually running my life: my wise Self, or a shortsighted, impulsive false self?"* Empowering your Self to take charge of your inner family, over time, will probably reduce fuzzy thinking (inner babbling, shouting, and arguing) significantly, by itself. Join me in wondering *"Which subselves are creating my thoughts right now?"*

Now let's shift gears and focus. Back away from all these details for a moment, and review the four major concepts we've explored so far:

False-self dominance and related wounds in your inner family of subselves.

A framework of communication premises and basics.

The learnable skill of *awareness*; and . . .

The related skill of *clear thinking*: decoding realistic, useful meanings from your current sensations and perceptions to help identify and fill your current true needs.

The next chapter explores how you can use awareness and clear thinking to "dig down" below your surface problems to identify _ what you and others *really* need now, and _ who's responsible for filling them. Before we go there, do you need a break? Would you benefit from journaling about what you've learned about fuzzy and clear thinking while the ideas are fresh?

Awarenesses here or in a communication journal:

4) Dig Down to *True* Needs

Grow "Level Four" Awareness Together

E ffective communication is about identifying and filling true, vs. surface, current needs. Unfilled needs are "problems." When you're significantly conflicted or uncomfortable, how often do you honestly get quiet and ponder . . .

"What do I really need right now?"

"Who is really responsible for filling my needs?"

This chapter uses *awareness* to illuminate four possible answers to those vital questions. Only one of them is consistently best at permanently resolving your most vexing problems and bringing *peace*. It is usually the most elusive and uncomfortable, for most of us. See if you agree . . .

"It's *Your* Fault!"

Were you taught as a child to worry about whether you were to *blame* for causing other people's problems? How often did a caregiver say something like "*You make me* so angry / scared / sick / worried / upset / tired . . .!" Implication: "*My discomfort is* your *fault (and I'm 1-up).*" Did you grow up among adults and kids who often argued about who was right or wrong, and good or bad? Did you play the "hot potato" (pass the blame) game with siblings and friends? ("*You jerk, you broke my toy!*"

"Well, mega-dork, you were stupid to leave it on the floor to be stepped on!") What did your caregivers model for you (vs. say) about taking responsibility for their own comfort, satisfaction, and "mistakes"?

In your first months of life, you instinctively felt *"Good* me!" and *"BAD* me!" from your perception of your caregivers' behaviors. Well before you could think and talk, you began experimenting with strategies for avoiding two searing *Bad-me* pains: primal *shame* (*"I'm a bad, unlovable person"*) and *guilt* (*"I do bad things."*) Over the years, many of us grew relentless *Perfectionist, Idealist,* and *Inner Critic* Guardian subselves. These continue the work of our critical caregivers, who unintentionally shamed us for being wrong, stupid, slow, clumsy, lazy, selfish, and weak. For those of us raised in low-nurturance homes, giving other people responsibility for our "mistakes" and "badness" became an unconscious reflex, like breathing. Our psychologically wounded, unaware caregivers often unconsciously strove for (modeled) the same hot-potato strategy, to avoid their own searing shame and guilt.

Reality check: take a moment to identify the current crop of life problems you want to solve. Mentally pick the three or four that cause you the most discomfort. Without judgment, notice whether you feel "other people" are causing each of these problems (spouse, child, boss, relative, politician, neighbor, co-worker, "someone," God . . .), or whether *you* are. For each "problem," identify honestly _ *"What do I really need right now?",* and _ *"Who's really responsible for filling my needs?"*

A **core premise** underlying this chapter and book is: ultimately, **only *you* can solve your problems** (fill your needs and reduce your discomforts.) The good news is: that gives you full control over solving your problems. You may ask, demand, and/or expect other people to fill your surface and underlying *true* needs along the way. They may or may not be able or willing to fill your surface needs, *and they can never fill your underlying true needs.* As long as your false self hangs on to the necessary childhood strategy of giving others responsibility for filling your true needs, you'll be often dissatisfied, anxious, and frustrated as an "independent" adult.

Restated: the **subselves who lead your inner family now are steadily responsible** for the quality and productivity of your life. Other adults' subselves are responsible for *their* lives. Dependent kids aren't wise, skilled, or able enough assume full responsibility for solving many of their problems. They need adult caregivers to increasingly award them that responsibility, while patiently teaching them the knowledge, skills, motivation, and self-confidence to master it on their own, and grow self-confidence.

Most of the marital, parental, workplace, and national "fighting" I've seen is struggling fruitlessly over whose *fault* someone's problem is: who is *wrong* and/or *bad*. Unaware, shame-based and insecure people, families, organizations, religions, and nations get snarled in blaming, defending, and counter-blaming, instead of focusing on . . .

What true needs each person or group needs to fill;

Agreeing who's *really* responsible for filling which needs;

Honoring all needs equally (an =/= attitude); and . . .

Brainstorming as partners, to find mutually acceptable compromises.

The "awareness bubbles" of typical fighters and arguers typically exclude their partners' needs and feelings. So their communication effectiveness plummets, until they become *aware* of what's happening. How recently has this happened to you?

This lose-lose "I'm right / better / more important / 1-up!" "No, *I* am!*" hot-potato battle regularly happens among your inner clan of subselves, too. Unless you're aware of that and get your Self to mediate, you wind up feeling *grumpy, unsure, irritable, distracted, tormented,* or *confused,* vs. *clear* and *serene.* Do you relate?

The combined effects of false-self dominance (reality

distortions, distrusts, anxieties, guilts, shame, and fuzzy thinking) can delude even the best "educated," most "mature" person into believing "*You* are causing my problem." Yes they may be, *and* YOU are responsible for identifying your true needs, owning them, asserting them clearly (Chapter 7), and enforcing clear limits (boundaries) respectfully and firmly if others can't or won't meet your needs.

I suspect the closing lines from William Henley's 19th century poem "Invictus" are often quoted because of their inherent universal truth: *"I am the master of my fate; I am the captain of my soul."*

Henley probably didn't know to differentiate whether "I" meant "my Self" or "my controlling other subselves." **If you're chronically ruled by a false self,** your subselves' excessive shame, guilt, and fear will block your taking full responsibility for your life quality. They'll protectively explain and defend your vehement justifications and denials of this to yourself and others. Notice your self-talk now. Do your subselves honestly agree with this premise about self-responsibility? If not, they'll probably be bored with, anxious about, or disagree with, what follows.

Reality check: breathe well, focus inside, and sense who is leading your inner family at this moment. If you feel *"I don't know,"* or *"I don't care,"* the odds are high that your false self is in the driver's seat. If so, don't expect to get or retain much from what follows. Option: Stop reading, get quiet and undistracted, go inside, and explore who has blended with your Self, and what those subselves' need now, to safely unblend.

This chapter adds a third powerful skill to your communication toolkit: the concept of "digging down" through several levels of superficial awareness to identify who has what specific unmet true needs. This skill aims to discern which needs you're responsible for filling now, and which needs belong to your partners. Applying this "dig down" skill with *awareness,* clear thinking, and a genuine =/= (mutual respect) attitude will help your Self avoid lose-lose power struggles and focusing fruitlessly on surface needs. That frees you to work cooperatively with your partner to fill your respective *true* needs. Working on *surface* relationship problems without digging down is like trying to fix a dripping faucet by painting it, or banishing termites by waxing the floor. Make sense?

To set the stage, let's review six key premises. Use your awareness and "mind of a (communication) student," to see how you feel now about these . . .

Key Ideas

Premise 1) You and all kids and adults act to fill emotional, physical, and spiritual *needs*: unconscious and conscious discomforts. Your needs regularly conflict concurrently _ within you; e.g. *"I need to sleep, and I also need to see how this TV show ends"*; and _ between you and your communication partners; e.g. *"George, I need you to discipline your son better. He has the table manners of a warthog in heat."*

Premise 2) Human relationship "problems" are *need* conflicts. Win-win problem solving, or conflict resolution, is about all people trying to fill each of their current needs well enough, long enough. Most people aren't taught to see "a problem" as "a need conflict." Were you? Therefore, they (you?) don't seek to discover *"What do I need and what do you need, now?"*

Premise 3) At any moment, all people have a fluctuating set of current conscious *surface* needs (*"I need some ice cream."*); and underlying *true* needs [*"I need a dose of sugar and fat to lower my semi-conscious anxieties* (discomfort).*"*] Until developing awareness (skill # 1), we're often unaware of our *true* needs.

 # Reality check*:* how often do you say something like: *"Hmm. You know, my problem isn't that you rudely interrupt me all the time (surface problem). It's that I feel disrespected* *and ignored by you, and I'm losing my self respect for not asserting my needs and limits. I need _ more respect, and _ to stop feeling like a victim; i.e. I need to feel _ impactful (powerful), _ more self-confidant, and _ more in charge of my own life. I really need to feel more secure and hopeful now."*

"Interrupting" and "rudeness" are value judgments and *surface* problems. They're symptoms of the unmet needs for *respect, potency,* and *security* below conscious awareness. Until you develop your awareness, you're often not conscious of fighting over who's needs are more important now, vs. identifying what you each really need, and teaming up to get everyone's needs met well enough. How often does your Self do the latter?

Premise 4) Any time you and another person communicate about a (conflict / dispute / disagreement / impasse / clash) there are always **four sets of needs that may not mesh** inside and between you two. You and your partner being *aware* of all four sets, and valuing them equally (=/=) give you two the best odds for lasting need fulfillment ("conflict resolution"). The four sets are: (1) my _ (two or more) *communication* needs, (Chapter 1) and _ my true needs that cause them now (below); and (2) your _ (two or more) communication needs, and _ your true needs that cause them now.

For lasting conflict-resolution, you each need to identify and match your communication needs before you can dig down (identify), and brainstorm filling your respective *true* needs as teammates. How many people do you know who do this in important situations, specially if their false self is running their show, and their E-levels are "above their ears"?

Premise 5) When two people . . .

1) are each guided by their true Selves, so they seldom do the "fuzzy thinking" that characterizes false selves in charge; and who . . .

2) genuinely feel their and their partners' needs are equally important now (have "=/=" attitudes); and who . . .

3) each *want* to include the other in their current "awareness bubble" (vs. having to do so out of duty, guilt, or anxiety); and . . .

4) *want* to help each other find out what the true needs under their surface problems; and . . .

5) know how to use the seven mental/verbal skills cooperatively, including digging down (this chapter);

then they are empowered to do consistently effective (win-win) _ internal and _ mutual problem solving. Restated: any two people who can usually do these five things together will often be able to help each other fill their respective *true* needs well enough, and really enjoy their relationship. "Two people" means any combination of adults and kids, or subselves. Notice that this is far different than saying they'll learn how to *avoid* internal and mutual need-conflicts. That beguiling concept is as illusory as the Tooth Fairy. Finally, see what you think about . . .

Premise 6) When relationship or household "**problems**" (need conflicts) **keep "coming back,"** or don't feel even temporarily resolved, that *guarantees* that the people in conflict aren't working together to develop these five factors and the seven skills. It also suggests that _ they're not *aware* of that option, and _ they're unaware of being dominated by a reactive, narrow-visioned false self.

Let's focus on premise 3 above. It's a powerful concept that greatly expands your options for *permanently* resolving key internal and interpersonal "problems."

Surface Needs and True Needs

Subselves, persons, poodles, eagles, and giraffes communicate to fill their current needs. It follows that we should know something about our and our partners' needs. If our touring space alien asked you to define a human "need," what would you say? Maybe *"Well, it's, uh, something a person wants."* And our persistent alien asks, "So what is a *want?*" After some mulling, you might offer, "*Well, it's about discomfort. It's something that doesn't feel good to us, emotionally, physically, or spiritually. Young and adult humans want to replace discomforts with things that feel good.*" For our purposes, wants and needs are the same.

Let's say that **a want or need is any kind of felt emotional, physical, or spiritual "tension,"** like a worry or fear, an ache, a longing, urge, thirst, yen, drive, hope, or hunger. Any of these can range from unconscious to excruciating and from silly to essential for our survival. Needing oxygen ranks higher than needing another cookie or knowing your checking-account balance.

Moment by moment, each communication partner's **needs can**:

Come in groups, though one or two may dominate for the moment.

Be conscious and/or unconscious.

Vary in intensity and priority. These can change instantly as our inner and outer environments shift. Normal differences between male and female need-priorities [..02/gender.htm] and books by Moir and Tannen (pp. 414, 417) can hinder clear communication. And our needs can . . .

Conflict within us, and/or between us, at the same time. This usually causes confusion, anxiety, and frustration.

As kids, we were often painfully taught that some of our natural human needs and feelings are *bad*. Getting angry; lusting; lying; hitting; stealing; being selfish, lazy, or rude; and cheating; are common ones. Driven by our anxious young need to be accepted, and lacking adult knowledge, we learn to deny, repress, project, or disguise such needs. We unconsciously numb, shame, or guilt-trip our subselves ("I'm 1-down") when such needs inexorably appear.

Feeling *needy* means we're human, not good or evil! The keys are whether we act on our needs, how, why, and with what effect. My momentary need to "kill you right now" can be acknowledged without shame, guilt, or harm. It surely stands for a deeper normal need like "I hurt, so a part of me wants to protect against repeat pain by wiping you out!" Try out believing **"All my and your true needs are legitimate and OK."** How does that feel? Do you buy it? Who would frown or scorn you if you adopted this view?

We usually have groups of overlapping physical, emotional, and spiritual needs at any moment. Some are conscious, and others unconscious. How, then, can we learn our true current needs, so we can decide when and how to assert them?

For instance, *"I want you to be on time"* is surface code (fuzzy thinking) for *"I need to feel respected, and that you see my time as valuable."* Likewise, *"I wish you'd stop smoking in the house"* may really mean *"I'm scared you'll get cancer, die, and I'll be left alone. I need you to respect me and my fear!"* If you battle over "smoking in the house," the *true* needs underneath stay unrecognized and unresolved.

Premise: We have unconscious, semi-conscious, and conscious minds, inhabited by a group of semi-independent personality subselves. At any moment, we can have _ conscious **(surface) needs, and _ underlying** semi-conscious or unconscious *true* **needs**.

We may fill our current surface needs by communicating, and leave the underlying needs unfilled because we're not aware of them. This can lead to a lot of personal and relationship frustration, self doubt, and distrust. This premise is pivotal in defining and achieving effective inner-family and interpersonal communication.

You regularly have several layers of needs. *"So how was your day?"* may cover two unspoken needs: (1) learning without seeming nosy, jealous, and insecure, if (2) you had lunch with your attractive coworker. These in turn mask the *real* needs: to reduce (3) insecurity and (4) abandonment fear, and avoid (5) guilt and (6) shame. This simple question illustrates a normal three-level, two-part need:

Spoken (conscious) need: get information *("How was your day?")*

Unspoken (semiconscious) needs: *"Did you spend time with Chris?"* (Don't think I don't trust you)

True (*unconscious*) **needs**: (1) *"I need reassurance you won't leave me,"* and (2) *"I need to be nice and respect my Self: nice people trust partners, and don't pry."*

Like emotional needs, concrete or resource ("thing") needs come in levels and clusters too. *"I need the car this afternoon"* really means *"I need a convenient, reliable way to get to the bank by 3 PM, and back here by 4:30."* In average situations, we don't need to analyze this, unless a major conflict erupts.

Each communication partner usually has several needs at once, including kids. Learning them all clearly, and comparing and ranking them cooperatively (=/=), can take time. Success at this requires shared commitment, patience, non-distracted time, and effective communication. We usually don't have to go below our surface needs in order to get "good enough" assertions and results. For major conflicts or decisions, delving deeper before asserting raises the chance of getting your true needs met.

Paper-clip this page, for you'll refer to it often in the coming chapters.

Typical True Needs

What are these universal true needs that only we can fill for ourselves? How about these:

Unconditional self-love, _ self-respect, and _ acceptance; vs. indifference, or self-abandonment and excessive guilt and shame.

Valuing and maintaining my mental + emotional + spiritual + physical (wholistic) health, vs. self-neglect.

Finding and keeping "enough" daily personal _ security and _ serenity, vs. anxiety and "stress."

Maintaining my drive to keep growing, despite obstacles and weariness; vs. depression, apathy, and hopelessness.

Clarifying my personal identity ("Who am I?"), vs. "identity confusion."

Enjoying _ myself and _ my life enough.

Finding and relating well to _ my Higher Power and _ my spiritual subself.

Learning and manifesting the main meaning (purpose, goal, mission) of my life.

Identifying, overcoming, and/or accepting my fears, confusions, and doubts.

Getting the nurturing _ physical, _ emotional, and _ spiritual comforts I need.

Recognizing, developing, and using my talents.

Recognizing, accepting, and adapting to my limitations.

Finding "enough" social acceptance, and reducing my loneliness.

Forgiving _ myself and _ others who disappoint or betray me.

Mourning my stream of losses (broken emotional bonds), and _ forming satisfying new attachments.

Balancing my daily and long-term work, play, and rest well enough currently and over time.

Identifying, asserting, and enforcing my personal boundaries.

Choosing and acting on my own short and long-term priorities.

Evolving a Bill of Personal (human) Rights and *acting* on them, despite resistance from other people. See p. 362.

Getting the love I want and need.

Satisfying and enjoying my sensual and sexual needs.

Add your own . . .

Would you agree that from time to time, each of these needs has caused a minor discomfort or high-intensity tension in you? If you reflect and answer *"No"* to some of these needs, could it be that they're there, but you're not yet aware of them? I propose that how happy and contented you are with your life now and over time are directly proportional to how consistently you have been able to fill your set of these underlying core needs.

Notice the words "you have." They imply that *you* are responsible for satisfying these underlying core needs in your life. If you expect your partner or others to be mainly responsible for filling them as you did as a child, you're setting yourself and them up for disappointment, frustration, hurt, anger, and resentment. This is specially true if they accept the responsibility!

A vital implication is that caregivers (vs. schools or "society") are inherently responsible for helping dependent kids learn to _ take full responsibility for identifying and filling their own true needs; and to _ ask for help in filling them, when needed, without excess guilt, shame, or anxiety. Are you doing that? Did your caregivers do that for you? Has anyone?

Another implication: *problems* and *conflicts* are mixes of unfilled needs. So resolving a problem or conflict means "identifying and filling your and my mixes of current true needs well enough, as judged by each of us." More about that when we study problem-solving skill in Chapter 8.

Now let's illustrate why this surface-need vs. true-need distinction is important to you and those you care about. See if these examples seem realistic:

Surface need: *"I need you to stop smoking."* Possible underlying (semi-conscious) true needs:

*"**I need to** reduce my fears of _ your getting cancer and slowly dying, _ my helplessness, sorrow, and anger; and _ being left alone and insecure in old age."*

*"**I love you**, and want the pleasure of seeing you live long*

and well. I need to avoid sorrowing over any pain, illness, and discomfort you feel."

*"**I need to** reduce my periodic discomfort over feeling powerless to get you to quit smoking, eat less fat and sugar, and exercise more often. And . . ."*

*"**I need to** reduce my guilt over semi-consciously disrespecting and resenting you for not valuing your own health, and causing me (and any kids) these discomforts."*

Surface need: *"I want you to do your homework"* may *really* mean:

*"**I need to** feel respected by myself (i.e. by my Inner Critic and other subselves) and important other people, as being a "good parent;" and . . .*

*"**I need to** reduce my anxieties about your school success, your self-esteem, and your being accepted at a good college;" and . . .*

*"**I need to** _ express my love and concern for you, and to feel satisfied with and proud of your achievements; or _ avoid the personal and empathic pain of your possible scholastic failure;" and . . .*

*"**I need to** reduce or eliminate the "stress" (inner-family criticism, resentment, and frustration) that I feel periodically from resenting that you seem too lazy and irresponsible (per my Inner Critic) to consistently do your schoolwork."*

Surface need: *"I need to get a haircut."* Possible underlying true needs:

*"**I need to** stop the annoyance of my Inner Critic and my Mother harping that I "look like something out of the jungle;" and . . .*

*"**I need to** end my anxiety ("worry") that my mate disrespects me, and is turned off by my shagginess;" and . . .*

*"**I need to** respect myself for setting a good grooming example for my kids."*

Surface need: "*Sal, I need the car this afternoon.*" Possible underlying needs:

"*I need a safe, dependable way to get to the dentist on time, and back home again.*"

And beneath that are the true needs: to . . .

"*Avoid the embarrassment and frustration of being late for my appointment again; and . . .*

"*End the soreness in my gums, and my anxiety about what's causing it; and . . .*

"*End my Inner Critic's yammering that I'm not taking good care of myself (and am a bad person), and end the pain that criticism is causing my Guilty Child.*"

Notice the pattern across all four examples. The surface need is simple, shallow, and "obvious" (conscious, "logical," and practical). The true needs underneath are elemental, multiple, simultaneous, in layers, and all aim at reducing various discomforts and/or gaining pleasure.

Breathe well, lean back, and defocus from this page for a moment. Take some time to notice what your inner voices are saying now, and any emotions you're feeling. Do you feel "Aha!", indifference (numbness), or some sort of anxiety or "unease"? Your crew of subselves may have a mosaic of thoughts and feelings.

Is this idea of surface and underlying true needs new to you? If it makes sense, do you see how using this concept selectively might improve your life? Here's the point: if effective communication depends on filling needs well enough, then it's helpful that you grow a habit of being *aware* (skill # 1) of your and others' underlying *true* needs. Otherwise you'll focus on surface needs, leaving unfilled true needs to resurface, and hindering effective problem solving inside you, and with other people.

 # Reality check: If you've glazed over from all these abstract ideas, take a breath, stretch, and try applying them to your own life. Note each of these that you (your dominant personality part/s) believe now:

I want to reframe the "problems" in my life as "need conflicts" (T F ?)

I'm generally aware of the difference between *surface* needs and *true* needs in _ myself, and _ my communication partners; specially _ kids and adults I don't respect, like, or trust. If I'm not generally aware of the difference, I'm _ very motivated to develop my awareness now. If I'm not, I'm _ motivated to find out *why* not. *A common root cause is that a covert, shame-based false self controls your inner team of subselves.* (T F ?)

I'm genuinely interested in learning more about "digging down," and then _ mulling how I might use this skill to improve the key relationships in my life, starting with those among my subselves. (T F ?)

I want to _ develop my ability to see which of my true needs I'm responsible for, and to _ give up the childhood urge to expect others to fill them for me. (T F ?)

I feel my true Self is answering these *awareness* questions right now. (p. 33)

Four Responsibility Levels

Keep the summary of common true needs above in mind as we explore four levels of problem ownership.

I first learned about problem ownership from Dr. Thomas Gordon, who founded Parent Effectiveness Training (PET). He invites each of us conflicted people to clarify, *"Is this my problem, or yours?"* That is, "Am *I* responsible for fixing this problem?" He aimed to raise co-parents' awareness of helping build their kids' self-confidence and self-reliance by selectively *not* helping: i.e. by lovingly avoiding taking responsibility for solving their kids' problems, within reason. **Enabling** is unintentionally promoting the self-limitations, toxic behaviors, and self-doubts of a needy person. You can choose to compassionately avoid enabling the uncertain kids, adults, and subselves you care about.

As you communication partners help each other dig down below your surface conflicts, your true needs and up to four responsibility levels may emerge:

Level 1: "I'm not psychologically wounded (controlled by a false self), and I don't have a problem." This is either true, or it's a false-self denial and repression of current emotions and needs. Couples, friends, or co-workers proudly proclaiming "We never fight." are usually unaware of promoting each other's splitting, and toxic level-one denials (reality distortions). Digging further may reveal . . .

Level 2: "I'm not wounded. I *do* have a problem (unmet need), and *someone else is responsible* for filling it. I need them to _ admit their responsibility, and _ *want* to change their attitudes, values, perceptions, and/or behaviors, to ease my discomfort."

Level 3a: "I'm not wounded, and *I'm* responsible for filling half of my needs in this situation. My partner (and perhaps others) is/are responsible for the other half. I need both/all of us to *want to* change, so that my discomfort goes down." A common variation for shame-based (wounded) people is . . .

Level 3b: "I'm not wounded, and I'm responsible for (causing and solving) my problems *and my partner's problems."* If your partner is a minor child or other dependent, this may be true. This is often the unconscious attitude of split people struggling with co-dependence (relationship addiction).

The toughest, most freeing "ownership" level to accept is . . .

Level 4: "I am _ controlled by a false self now, and *I* am fully responsible for _ empowering my true Self, and _ filling my own true needs. I can ask others for help, and expect them to honor any commitments they make. I retain ultimate responsibility for my own adult welfare, as they do for theirs." A closer look at this level reveals . . .

"I _ lack knowledge of key things (e.g. the ideas in this

book), and _ I'm responsible for learning and applying them."
And/or . . .

"My inner family is chaotic (split), because my Self has been disabled by anxious, needy, impulsive, distrustful subselves. I've been unaware of, or denying, _ **my inner-family discord and _ it's interactive impacts**:

Being periodically or often dominated by a false self, and living in denial of up to five other inner wounds (p. 37).

Often behaving impulsively, self-destructively, and ambivalently (sending double messages).

Picking equally split partners and low-nurturance (toxic) settings.

Self-neglect, including addictions; and not seeking or accepting relevant help.

Not setting and enforcing nurturing boundaries.

Living well below my great potential as a rare, worthy human being; and . . .

Denying all of these to others and myself, despite glaring evidence.

"I must change (learn of, become aware of, and harmonize my inner family via "parts work," or equivalent), to solve these hindrances, which cause or maintain most of my internal and social problem/s.

Level 4 option: "My partner _ *also* lacks knowledge, and/ or _ is often controlled by a false self. S/He and I have not known that, or known what to do about it. S/He is responsible for _ acknowledging that, and _ harmonizing her or his inner family. I am responsible for my half. We can be of great help to each other here!"

Do these four responsibility levels make sense to you? Honestly: which of them are you most comfortable in _ generally, and _ with the "difficult" (argumentative, arrogant, aggressive, selfish, insensitive, whiney, defensive . . .) people in your life? Most kids and many wounded adults operate mainly on levels 1 and 2: denial, repression, and blaming others.

"Mature" adults may operate between levels 2 and level 3 in peaceful or conflictual times. Major variables are whether they're wounded, how badly, and how often. Adults in true (vs. pseudo) recovery from inner wounds can increasingly achieve and master level 4 awareness: balanced self-responsibility for their own needs, and empathy for others' needs. This is *true* maturity.

Gaining level-4 awareness is hard, because most people aren't aware of their inner family of subselves. Even if they (you) are aware, distrustful and anxious subselves promote protective denials and distortions. Yet until you and your partners usually operate from level 4 in calm and conflictual times, your true needs often go unseen and unmet.

Alert: If upset Guardian and Vulnerable subselves often govern you, your Self probably can't tell accurately which responsibility level you're communicating on. Many of your subselves are well-intentioned masters of deception. As you develop your seven or more *awarenesses* (Resource C), you're more apt to get a clear reading. Option: use the Web worksheets in the book "Who's *Really* Running your Life?" [xlibris.com] or at [..pop/assess.htm] to self-assess for unseen false-self dominance.

Let's summarize what we just covered. In any conflictual situation, whoever leads your inner family may choose . . .

Responsibility level 1: *"I'm not wounded, and I don't have a problem."* This is either true, or your false self is denying uncomfortable reality.

Level 2: *"I'm not wounded, and my problem is caused by someone else. S/He is responsible for reducing my discomfort, whether s/he agrees or not."*

Level 3: *"I'm not wounded, and I'm responsible for at least half of each of my current problems. Other people are responsible for the other half,* if they've agreed to help fill my needs." Or . . .

Level 4: *"I am governed by a false self. I am fully responsible for _ healing that, and _ identifying and resolving* *all my unmet true needs. Each of my adult partners bears equal responsibilities for healing their wounds, and filling their needs. Each of us can ask for help in doing this.*"

Reality-check your understanding of this by explaining these levels to several people who know you pretty well. Then ask them to honestly rate your average responsibility levels in general, and in conflictual situations. If you're ambivalent or reluctant to do this, and/or if you reject others' honest feedback, your Self is probably disabled. That means in (at least) conflictual situations, you're probably operating in responsibility levels 1 or 2. If so, that means you have minimal chances for awareness and clear thinking, and fully effective communications. *That* means you regularly have trouble filling your true needs.

Do your dominant subselves accept _ the six premises that began this chapter, and _ the concepts of true vs. surface needs, and four responsibility levels? If so, you're ready to learn how you and your partners can work to resolve your significant *surface* problems. Compare the three examples below to how you and your key partners usually try for conflict resolution now. You may also compare these examples to how you remember your childhood caregivers reacting to conflicts. Though these examples illustrate common stepfamily conflicts, the principles apply to any inner-family and interpersonal situations and relationships.

Example 1) Surface *Loyalty* Conflicts

Can you describe a "loyalty conflict"? They're a special kind of personal *values* conflict. If you're in a stepfamily, I'd be startled if you haven't struggled with versions of a problem like this:

Stepfather **Jack** finally has had too much. He's well past level-1 ("I have no problem") denial. He storms to his wife Meg *"I am SO sick of your kid ignoring me! I knock myself* *out month after month, driving her to school, paying her dentist, providing the roof over her head, and being pleasant. I say 'Hi, Jan.' She grunts and walks by with no eye contact. 'How was your day?' More grunts. She treats our dog better than me, and you don't seem to care. All you do is make excuses for her, and say sarcastically 'After all, Jack, you're supposed to be the adult here.'"*

In this divisive loyalty conflict, biomom Meg feels impossibly torn between pleasing her husband, her own integrity, and her beloved custodial biodaughter Jan. If Meg must choose (can't compromise), who comes first? Choosing not to choose is not an option. Typical stepfamily members experience conflicts like these for years after re/wedding. If co-parents (stepparents and bioparents) can't spot and resolve them, their re/marriage is at increasingly high risk.

Notice that conflicts like these are always toxic PVR (Persecutor-Victim-Rescuer) relationship triangles (p. 330).

Here Jack feels victimized, sees stepdaughter Jan as the Persecutor, and expects Meg to rescue him. Meg sees Jan and herself as co-victims, Jack as the persecutor, and wants to rescue her daughter. None of them see these triangles, or know how to dissolve them. See [..09/triangles.htm].

All relationships, including those between your subselves, have values and loyalty clashes. Can you think of any in your life or inner family now? What would "digging down" look like here, if Jack and Meg had increasing awarenesses, knowledge, and motivation to do it? Imagine that like most people, they've never seen the ideas in this book.

Level 2: Surface *Problems and Blames*

Jack's false self: *"My stepdaughter Jan is rude, selfish, and insensitive (says his Inner Critic subself.) After all I've done for her, that really hurts! Meg sides with Jan, and seems to value her daughter's needs and feelings more than mine. Meg* *denies this when I confront her. I need her to agree that this isn't fair, is her fault, and that she should change her attitude and discipline Jan."*

Jack's false self focuses on his surface needs, and holds Jan and wife Meg responsible for causing and reducing his discomforts. This guarantees implied *"I'm 1-up!"* R-messages any time Jack communicates with either partner. That will probably raise their (subselves') anxieties and E-levels, impair their hearing, and block problem solving.

Meg's false self: *"Jack is oversensitive and childish at times, and his expectations are unrealistic (says her Inner Critic). I really resent his criticizing Jan, and implying that I'm a bad Mom and an uncaring wife. If Jack really loved me and was a grown man, he wouldn't make me choose between Jan and him. I need him to accept that, and stop complaining and criticizing."*

Meg's Guardian subselves (*Critic, Perfectionist,* and *Idealist*) _ blame Jack for her and Jan's discomforts, and _ hazily identify some surface needs about Jack changing. Meg's Guardians instinctively defend her daughter from her husband's scorn and criticism, partly to ward off her own unhealed post-divorce guilt (*Guilty Girl* subself).

In level-2 situations, neither partner is *aware* of their false selves, the seven skills, awareness bubbles, their true needs, their resolution options, or their inner and mutual communication basics and processes. Their primary communication needs are . . .

To feel respected and valued enough,

To vent and be respectfully *heard* and accepted by their mate and other supporters, and . . .

To cause action: i.e. to get their ("persecuting") partner to own their responsibility, and (want to) change.

Until in true recovery, most psychologically wounded people operate on levels 1 (denial) and 2 (blaming others). Such people direct typical low-nurturance families, companies, schools, churches, committees, and nations. It's our national norm, so far.

With more knowledge and awareness, Jack and Meg might sound like this . . .

Level-3 Needs and Attitudes

Jack's Self: *"I need to feel genuinely heard, respected, and appreciated as a person, a husband, and a committed stepfather by Meg and Jan. And I need my wife to validate these needs as legitimate and important. These are my needs, and I don't see how to fill them by myself."*

Meg's Self: *"I'm scared and confused. If I side with Jack, I'll betray Jan again, (after failing at my marriage) and I'll lose my integrity. If I side with Jan, I'm scared Jack will detach from me, over time. I need to find a way to balance these. This is my problem, not Jack's, and I need his genuine empathy, understanding, patience, love, and support."*

If both mates had read, discussed, and worked to implement the ideas in this book, they might have . . .

Level 4 Awarenesses

Jack's Self: *"I'm pretty wounded. That, and this conflict with Meg and Jan, are my problems to solve. When Jan needs to ignore me, my other subselves activate and take me over. They doubt my own worth and competence as a man, a mate, and a stepdad. Those subselves look for reassurance outside of me that I'm OK. Other subselves feel guilty and embarrassed to admit that to Meg or myself. My* Inner Critic *wants me to believe that virile men aren't weak and needy, and that I'm 'bad' and to blame here. He's wrong about that. I am needy, and that's normal and healthy.*

"I need to respect myself from inside me, not from what other people think. I'm ashamed of feeling ashamed, and I need relief from this 'stress' (guilt, shame, and anxiety.) I need to get

my doubting subselves to trust my Self. I really need Meg's help here. I know she has her own wounds, and that both she and Jan are struggling too. I need reasons to hope that we can find a lasting solution to this!"

Meg's Self: *"Some of my inner family members desperately need to feel competent as a woman, a wife, and a mother, so I can feel like a worthy person. Parts of me are terrified that I'm doing something wrong here, that Jan will be hurt even more, and that I'll be abandoned to die a lonely, unloved old woman. This is my inner-family problem, not Jack's fault. I see that his personality parts are struggling with self-doubts, anxieties, and shame just like mine.*

"I need my inner crew to feel safe and self-confident, and to trust my Self to find a solution with Jack and Jan. I also need to feel that Jan's OK and safe enough now and in the future, too. Some young parts of me feel scared, guilty, and ashamed to admit some of this to anyone. My whole inner gang needs hope that this pain and confusion will go away soon, and I need a viable plan. I need Jack's help, and I see that he needs mine."

Both mates (i.e. their Selves) now see and accept their core needs, and their personal responsibility to fill them. The mutual blaming is replaced by an honest appreciation that both mates are controlled by false selves, and both need help to fix that. Jack and Meg's true Selves have overcome Guardian subselves who want to play the Victim in this pair of relationship triangles.

They've stopped *blaming* the other (seeing them in the Persecutor role). That frees all three people from their strangling relationship triangle, and opens up the chance for real =/= problem solving. In some relationship triangles like this, the Guardian subselves of the person in the Victim role promote an addiction, an affair, a "depression," or using the court system, to avoid admitting their false-self dominance and taking full responsibility for fixing it.

If Jack did *inner* family therapy with a competent clinician, he'd probably discover a *Shamed Boy*, a *Perfectionist*, an *Anxious/Guilty Boy*, a *Magician* (reality distorter), an *Inner Critic* (Blamer), an *Idealist*, a *Doubter*, a *Stoic*, a *Rager*, a *Thinker/Analyzer*, and an *Achiever* (Workaholic). These squabbling subselves don't yet trust Jack's true Self to fill their needs. They aren't aware of this, or of Meg's being similarly split. Jack's deepest need is to harmonize his inner family (personality) under the leadership of his true Self. In level 4, he and some of his subselves know that. And . . .

If Meg did her own parts work, she would find four Vulnerables reacting to Jack's complaints: *a Shamed Girl, a Guilty Girl, a Terrified Girl, and a Good (obedient, nice) Girl. Guarding this needy group are a Catastrophizer ("No surprises here: we'll divorce again, and die alone!"), a Worrier ("How are we ever going to unscramble this? Did I make a mistake marrying again?"); a Good Mom, a Procrastinator, ("Let's do some parts work—later . . ."); an Adult Woman, an Inner Judge, a Paralyzer/Numb-er, a (food) Addict; an Illusionist (reality distorter); and an Amazon ("I'm strong enough to handle this. Too bad Jack isn't").*

These subselves distrust or don't know her true Self and/or her Higher Power. They aren't aware of her and Jack's being wounded, ignorant, and unaware. Like her husband, Meg's core need is to harmonize her inner family (personality) under the guidance of her true Self.

Most Jacks and Megs are unaware of typical stepfamily realities. One is that typical post-divorce stepkids need to *test*, over and over again, to see if their custodial parent is going to abandon them like their other parent did. Such (unconscious) testing often takes the form of "disrespecting" the stepparent, to see whether these adults will split up. (*True* need: "Am I *safe* in this new family?")

A second normal need, specially for teens, is to research "How much post-remarriage *power* do I have (in my new family)?" A third reality Jack and Meg need to learn is that stepfamily loyalty conflicts are normal, inevitable, and resolvable *if* the adults agree that if viable compromises don't appear, their integrities come first, their remarriage second, and everything else third. Real life U.S. stepparents often get caught up in numbing (level 1) and reciprocal finger-pointing (level 2). Studies suggest that well over half eventually divorce, emotionally or legally.

Stepdaughter Jan is probably totally bewildered and overwhelmed by all of this (vs. "rude.") She has her own complex set of surface and underlying true needs. Her inner family is controlled by a group of Vulnerables and Guardians also, at least around her stepdad Jack. As Meg and Jack become aware of their own inner conflicts, they can help Jan to see and solve her own. Ideally, Jan's biofather Philip would also understand inner-family concepts, and join in helping each other work toward inner harmonies.

Key themes in this example are . . .

Both adults consciously choose to stop playing "Hot Potato," and shift from blaming other people for their discomfort (level 2) to inner-family awareness and non-shamefully charging *themselves* with responsibility to fill their own needs (level 4 awareness). This example presumed both adults had broken through level-1 denials and repressions, to consciously and socially admit their respective discomforts.

Both adults intentionally shift from vague awareness of what they need, to identifying *surface* needs ("*I need Jan to grow up,*") to owning their true underlying needs ["*I need to (1) harmonize my inner family, and (2) build mutual respect among my subselves. I also need to (3) earn Self-respect by asserting my need for respect to Jan and Meg, and by learning what they need from me.*"]

These shifts allow the mates to break free from the unseen crippling Persecutor-Victim-Rescuer triangle that was promoting lose-lose (attack > defend > counterattack) cycles. These cycles were blocking cooperative family problem solving.

This "de-triangling" creates the option that if Jack and Meg learn and apply the seven communication skills as true teammates, they and Jan are much more likely to get all their true needs met, over time. There are parallel issues that need solutions, too, like _ Jan's fear of abandonment, and mastering a complex group of stepfamily adjustment tasks; and _ Meg and Philip's reducing their residual post-divorce guilts and shame. The mates need to sort out and prioritize their (many) concurrent true problems, get appropriate help, and work patiently at staying focused on improving them one or two at a time.

For brevity, this example omits similar summaries of Jan's and her biodad Philip's true needs, and what help Jan needs from all three of her co-parents.

Pause and reflect: have you ever seen relationship problem-solving premises and ideas like these before? Does this four-layer problem-ownership scheme seem realistic and credible to you? If not, why? What are your inner voices saying? Who among your inner-family members is "speaking"? Is it your true Self? How can you tell? I'd be surprised if you (your Self) weren't hearing a lot of skepticism, doubt, or even ridicule from your alarmed Guardians and Vulnerables.

Have you experienced (surface) loyalty conflicts and PVC relationship triangles like this in your family? The subjects and details vary widely, but the underlying true needs to feel respected, worthy, acknowledged, competent and hopeful are universal among adults and kids. Our cultural need is to build inner-family and communication knowledge, self and mutual awareness, and self and mutual empathy and compassion . . .

Before exploring some practical suggestions, here are two more examples of digging down below typical surface "problems" to identify co-parents' and kids' underlying true needs.

Example 2) Typical Ex-mate Conflicts

As the millennium begins, almost half of American spouses legally divorce. An unknown number live every day with *psychological* divorce. Over 65% have one or more dependent kids. Among typical divorced families and stepfamilies, the variations of "awful-ex-mate conflicts" are beyond listing. See this Web page for some: [..Rx/menu-nf.htm]. Here's an example of typical surface problems, and the true unfilled needs beneath them:

Mark divorced Sherrie, and re/married Linda. Mark's two pre-teen sons live with Sherrie, and sleep over at their "other home" every other weekend. Mark and Sherrie's divorce was "messy," bitter, expensive, and "took forever." Stepmom Linda has grown resentful and "upset" over almost three years of "endless" intrusions and "problems" that Sherrie persists in causing her and Mark. She is trying to learn her alien new stepmom role, and is finding that raising boys part time is "a lot different" than raising her own live-in, pre-teen daughter Marilee. Linda and Mark have never really talked about being "a stepfamily," and have never read or discussed anything about them.

For brevity, this example doesn't include biomom Sherrie's set of surface conflicts and underlying true needs. We'll assume here that the co-parents have broken any Level-1 denials, and admit "We have a problem here." Notice the vague language (fuzzy thinking).

Level 2: The Ex-Mate Is "The Problem"

Stepmom Linda's false self: "*Sherrie is unreliable, rude, selfish, intrusive, vindictive, and a mediocre, inconsistent mother*" (says her dedicated *Inner Critic*). "*She treats her sons' father (Mark) like dirt, and poisons the boys' minds against him and me. Then she denies doing that, and blames us! She causes most of our problems. I'm getting real irritated and* *resentful that Mark keeps giving in, and letting her dictate our lives."*

Linda isn't aware of her false-self's control, and doesn't clearly define what she needs. She (her false self) labels Sherrie as the main Persecutor in their relationships, and her and Mark as co-Victims. She's starting to develop a different triangle with Mark as a Persecutor, and herself as the Victim. If she complains about Sherrie or Mark to her Mom, sister, or close friends, they may all become Rescuers in several interlocked relationship triangles.

Biodad Mark's false self: *"Sherrie is impossible to reason with. She initiated our divorce, and now claims that I left her. She's so moody, erratic, and volatile that I'm scared for (biological sons) Kevin's and Brian's mental health. But if I went for custody, she'd fight mean and dirty, and seek endless revenge. With college expenses looming, we can't afford big legal bills. Sherrie is the biggest problem Lin and I have."*

Mark doesn't yet define his specific surface needs, though several are implied. He, too, casts his ex mate as the Persecutor, and includes his sons as co-victims. There's no sign that this good man acknowledges he or Linda are each causing part of this complex stepfamily family conflict. With more awareness and knowledge, this couple might sound like this . . .

Level 3: Mates Blame Each Other and the Ex mate

Linda's false self: *"I'm getting real tired of Mark's not listening to* (i.e. not agreeing with) *me, making excuses for Sherrie, giving in to her, and putting off confronting her as he's repeatedly said he would. I'm starting to lose patience and respect for him. I need him to (want to) confront Sherrie. If he really loves me, he should want to do that without my asking* (reality distortion).

"My trust in Mark's promises and resolve is slipping, too. If he's not committed to enforcing our home and marital

boundaries, what else is he going to cave in on? This isn't what I signed on for! Mark and Sherrie are (my) problem, and I need him to own that, and fix it!"

Mark's false self: *"I'm getting pretty fed up with feeling like I'm supposed to solve everything here, and Linda thinking I'm a wimp for not being Attila the Hun with Sherrie. I can't help it if Sherrie is a mental case! I feel caught between two wildcats.*

"Lin just doesn't understand how impossible it is to get through to Sherrie, and she won't talk to Sherrie directly. I need Linda to see the good things we have, understand my side of this, and just accept that this is how it is, for now. It'll get better as the boys get older. I need my wife to adapt, and Sherrie to get healthy and sane."

So far, neither mate . . .

Knows _ they're controlled by distrustful subselves; _ about surface vs. true needs, _ relationship triangles, or _ the seven communication skills you're studying.

Tries to see Sherrie as a wounded person of equal dignity and worth (=/=).

Sees that the disrespect and distrust they broadcast to Sherrie are inflaming her (subselves') resentments, distrusts, hurt, anger, frustration, and causing reciprocal disrespect; and neither partner . . .

Is *aware* **of** the communication sequences inside them, with their mate, and between them and Sherrie.

If Mark and Linda helped each other apply the ideas in this book, their descriptions of their "problems" would sound quite different:

*Transition toward Level 4: "*I'm *Half of the Problem . . ."*

Linda's True Self: *"I've often been split in our two-home stepfamily. I have subselves that feel guilty and ashamed that I can't be more loving and patient with Mark, and more forgiving* *of Sherrie. They wonder "Is something wrong with me?" I don't like who I'm becoming! My subselves feel less and less safe as this mess with Sherrie and the boys keeps grinding on us."*

"I need to feel real hope and confidence, and to have some plan to make things better for us. Because I'm blended, I feel I'm being a bad Mom and Stepmom somehow. I can't seem to get clear and stay clear on what I need. My mind keeps jumping around, and we go nowhere. Part of me is scared I made a wrong choice marrying Mark, Sherrie, and their boys! Maybe I'm the problem!" [Implied needs: _ calm self doubts and worries about future divorce; and _ grow clear, focused thinking: harmonize her inner family.]

Mark's True Self: *"I need to stop the battles inside of me, and coach my team (of subselves) toward a clear action plan. Part of me wants to get tough and enforce some limits with Sherrie, and another part is afraid to. Part of me wants to confront Sherrie to please Linda, and another part says, 'Uh uh, wrong reason.' Part of me wants to run away, and part of me is afraid to.*

"Man, I hate this! I never expected any of this (conflict and confusion) when I remarried. Why didn't I see this coming?

"And I'm torn between what's best for the boys, and what's best for Linda and me. Part of me believes this'll all work out, and another part of me really thinks we'll divorce again. I need to sort all these battles out, and find a way to resolve them. I wish (need to have) someone understood how I feel. I don't think my wife does . . ."

Notice that as they "dig down," both partners shift from outer blame to acknowledging their own feelings, and some specific personal needs under the surface. Mark is starting to acknowledge his major concurrent *inner* conflicts, and his own responsibility to solve them.

What would this look like if both mates knew about their inner families (Chapter 1), and wanted to apply those concepts to themselves and each other?

Level 4) Awarenesses and Realities

Linda's Self: *"I am really torn here! I need my (inner) clan to feel much more (1) daily emotional serenity; (2) mental clarity, focus, and direction; and (3) self respect, as a woman, a wife, and a child caregiver. My crew needs more (4) self-confidence, and (5) to feel truly partnered (heard, empathized, accepted, and loved) by a loving, respectful, respectable friend, companion, and lover, and a caring Higher Power.*

"I deeply need to express and manifest the love I feel for (biodaughter) Marilee, Mark, and others, and to love myself. *For all our sakes, I need to grow my compassion for Sherrie as a badly wounded woman, instead of following my Inner Critic's bias that she's a selfish shrew, lousy Mom, and a vindictive bitch."*

"I need communion with Mark, and to acknowledge that he's struggling with similar inner battles. I guess I, or we, should find a counselor to help us work on separating and solving these problems inside of him and me while we balance our other daily roles. I need to find out how Mark feels about this and what he needs."

Mark's Self: *"My inner crew is riding off in all directions. They go nuts when Sherrie's false self acts out, and when I sense that Linda's false self is blaming me. I . . . no, my inner crew, needs to feel (1) more inner peace and contentment (freedom from anxiety); (2) like I'm a worthy person, man, husband, and father; who is (3) potent and competent; and my subselves all need to feel (4) clear on the purpose and direction of my life, and (5) more confident that I'm growing wiser, stronger, and clearer. Those won't happen as long as some of my inner kids and Guardian parts don't trust my Self to accomplish these things, with some help.*

We (subselves) also need (6) to feel companioned by Lin as I work to fill these needs. I need to fill the emptiness *I've felt my whole life. I'm sure Linda's pretty wounded, too. I* know

Sherrie is. I need to talk all this over with Linda, and learn what she thinks and needs."

If Linda does patient, Self-directed inner-family work, she may come to see who comprises her active false self when Sherrie's behaviors are troublesome:

Three inner kids (Vulnerables): a *Guilty Girl*, an *Abandoned/Scared Girl*, and a *Shamed* Girl;

Several Guardians: her *Magician* (reality distorter), *Pleaser, Inner Critic, Pessimist,* a *Blamer (of others)*, a *Nagger*, a *Defocuser*, an *Idealist,* a *Rager*, and an *(Exercise) Addict.* Most of these don't solidly trust her Self yet, or feel like a team; and . . .

Her Regulars: her Nurturer (Good Mom), Historian, Observer, Adult Woman, Wise One (Crone), Spiritual One, Achiever, and her Self.

The shortsighted, reactive Vulnerables and Guardians usually don't trust Linda's true Self to lead and problem-solve (fill their needs) yet. They aren't aware of, or care little about, her, Mark's, and Sherrie's *ignorances* (knowledge deficits about the ideas in this book and stepfamily realities) or their personality anarchy and inner conflicts. They want comfort *now!*

With some inner-family exploration, **Mark can become aware of his energetic false-self crew**:

Vulnerables: Shamed Boy, Guilty Boy, Orphan (lonely, sad) Boy, and Good Boy-Pleaser;

Guardians: Critic (Inner Shamer), Worrier, Procrastinator, Loner-Fugitive, Judge (Blamer), Denier-Justifier (reality distorter), and an aggressive Warrior; and his . . .

Regulars: Analyzer, Observer, Good Dad, Adult Man, Responsible Guy, Fixer, Spiritual One, Achiever ("Get going!"), and his true Self.

Both mates' dominant subselves distrust their Self's wisdom and leadership skill, and they aren't aware of the three adults' being wounded, unaware, and uninformed. Neither co-parent knows what you're reading about here. Ex-wife Sherrie is a shame-based woman from a low-nurturance childhood, in protective denial. She's often controlled by a false self. She isn't aware of that, Linda's and Mark's similar splits and blendings, or the concepts in this book.

None of the friends, relatives, and therapists trying to support Linda and Mark know any of this. Neither do the kids involved, or their teachers. They don't know what they don't know, so they aren't motivated to learn anything. All of this promotes confusion, anxiety, guilt, and mutual blaming. To break this communication pattern, Linda and Mark need to learn about false-self dominance and harmonizing their inner teams, and the seven communication skills.

Doing so can free them to start empowering their Selves, and increasing their options from *blaming* to effective inner-family and mutual problem solving (Chapter 8). Applying these learnings, and making some needed second order (core attitude) changes, will set the stage for real lasting resolution with their struggles with Sherrie and each other. The two boys depend on their three co-parents to do these things for them, though they won't know this for many years.

The same options are available to Sherrie, and her Self must elect them. If Mark learns all these things and tries to "show her the light," her false self will interpret that as a discount (*"Oh, Mr. Know-it-all stoops to tell me how I should run my life, eh?"*), and will make things *worse*.

A better alternative is for Linda and Mark to compassionately see Sherrie as a badly wounded, unaware person, terribly burdened by shame, guilt, anxieties, and angers that she didn't cause, and doesn't (yet) understand. Then their assertions and limit-settings can become *respectful* and *empathic,* and her false self's defensiveness and hostility may gradually wane. Until that happens, Mark and Sherrie need to use the Serenity Prayer (p. 495), and turn over what they can't control to their Higher Power/s.

Digging down further to the fourth layer of needs and

responsibilities discloses some well-camouflaged inner-family conflicts inside each co-parent. These are scary to admit and accept, because of painful old combined (false self) feelings of . . .

Shame ("I'm a bad, worthless, unlovable person);"

Guilt ("I break many 'rules': shoulds, oughts, and musts);" and . . .

Fears (anxieties): _ "I'll never deserve or get the love I need; _ I'll never be able to be a competent parent and mate, so I'll ultimately have to live and die alone (primal terror of 'abandonment'); and _ There is nothing I can do to prevent this. I'm totally helpless." Linda's version is "I can only pray for God to help me here." Mark lacks the spiritual faith and experience to do this, which is part of his *emptiness.*

Again, **the deepest (fourth, semi-conscious) layer of true needs and personal responsibility is usually the hardest to reach** for average people like Mark and Linda, and probably *you.* I believe that's because . . .

. . . **our** national leaders and legislators now _ deny that low-nurturance parenting and psychological wounding is our society's norm and biggest problem; and they _ are ignorant of splitting, recovery, and these seven communication skills; and . . .

. . . **shame-based** false selves' strategic determination to blame others, vs. taking courageous self responsibility for filling true needs; plus . . .

. . . **the ceaseless** hubbub and responsibilities of fast-paced outer and inner life, as relentlessly promoted by our mega-billion dollar instant-gratification media engine; plus . . .

. . . **widespread** _ **ignorance** of the concepts and vocabulary needed to identify true needs; and the motivation, practice, and _ encouragement to identify and help each other fill them.

Pause for a moment to digest what you've just read and experienced. Take some time to sort out what this "dig down" concept means in your life situation. What responsibility-level are you and your partner/s usually operating on?

Let's see what happens if we apply the "dig-down" technique on a widespread source of marital and family stress . . .

Example 3) Digging Down With "Money" Conflicts

The first year and a half after remarrying with high hopes, Myra and Manuel ("Manny") didn't acknowledge they had any serious disagreements about money (level 1 denials). As time passed, each began to "grumble," and came to openly acknowledge that they were having trouble with a group of "money problems" and some others like those above.

Level 2: My Mate and My Ex Cause My Problems

Biofather Manny's false self: "*Myra insists on spending too much, on things we don't need and can't afford. She's a true shopaholic. Periodically, she starts world war three because I forget to tell her of getting ATM cash. Then she nags me to do something because (my ex wife) Lupe hassles me about being a day late with sending child support.*

"*And Myra constantly bitches at Lupe for spending the child support on Gucci boots and bags instead of kid clothes and cereal. Somehow, I'm supposed to fix that. And Myra's after me to make a will. We're healthy and under 40, so why pay some lawyer an arm and a leg until we're older?*

"*Also, Myra rags me about putting her name on my house and car titles. She doesn't hear my side of it. Oh, and we both agree Lupe should split the premium for the kids' dental insurance, but my ex just whines and plays 'poor me' . . .*"

Stepmom Myra's false self: "*Manny doesn't appreciate having fine things in our home. He grew up poor, and has to hoard money. We both work, and we have enough! It drives me nuts that he hands over his check, wants me to pay the bills, and then won't help me keep the checkbook balanced!*

"My biggest aggravation is about child support. To keep the peace with his teenybopper ex, Manuel agreed to pay way more than our state's guidelines. Then he accuses me of spending money we don't have! And I seem to have married an ex wife who is about 15, max.

"All she wants is for us to pay her regularly so she can play, flirt, and party, while her kids go to school in rags. It's a crime, and Manny just shrugs! At times, I think I married a big kid, not a man. Despite all his macho talk, he won't draw the line with Lupe. So I have to do it, and I'm getting tired! I didn't say 'I do' to Lupe!"

Neither mate has begun to dig down to see what they and the other two adults *really* need, so no real problem solving can happen, so far. Both are blaming the other two adults for their problems. If Myra and Manny grew aware enough to look under their surface "problems," then . . .

Level 3: Blaming *Shifts to Identifying True Needs*

Manny's Self: *"I need to feel genuinely heard, respected, and appreciated as a man, a husband, and a committed father; first by Myra, then Lupe. I need to feel my wife is my partner, not a nag, critic, and an enemy.* "I'd feel a lot better if I felt on top of this mess (fuzzy thinking). *At times, I just feel overwhelmed. Was I wrong to pick Myra?* "I'm beginning to worry that this (marriage) isn't going to work out either, and I'd be a two-time loser! I need to stop badmouthing Myra and my ex after I've had a few drinks. That doesn't feel good."

Myra's Self: *"I need to find a new way to talk to (problem solve with) Manny. Any time something about money comes up, we both get frustrated and angry. I expect him to not hear me, get defensive or whiney or surly, and run away. I'm mad before I even open my mouth. I know that's not fair to him, but I can't find a different way!*

"I realize I'm feeling out of control and unsafe here. I want

(need) more control and security! I also realize I'm starting to distrust Manny's judgment; at least about practical things. I hate to say it, but I'm losing respect for him, and at times, for myself!

As this couple becomes more aware, honest, and motivated, they can learn about subselves, communicating, and stepfamily norms. That knowledge and *awareness* could promote a . . .

Transition toward Level 4

Manny's Self: *"I'm starting to see that 'money' and Myra aren't the real problems here. I need to (1) lower my guilt, and regain my (2) self control, (3) my self-confidence, and (4) self-respect. And I need (5) a credible plan as to how Myra and I are going to stop fighting and start problem solving together. And I also need (6) us both to agree to stop focusing on the past, blaming each other, name calling, and complaining, and focus on solving one problem at a time, together!"*

Myra's Self: *"I need to learn how to control my expectations and temper with Manny, at least on money issues. And I need to find a way to feel more secure in this family. I must admit that I'm scaring myself. I need to find a new way of looking at and discussing all these problems so Manny and I can start solving them. And I need to regain my senses of self-confidence and hope that these conflicts are going to dwindle. I have to (need to) stop worrying about this all the time!"*

Increasing knowledge of false-self dominance, stepfamily realities, and communication dynamics would reveal the true problems underlying Myra and Manny's surface "money problems":

Level 4: "I Cause Half of My Problems, and I Need Help!"

Manny's Self: *"I haven't seen before that I've been controlled by . . .*

My Vulnerables: a sad Orphan Boy ("Manuelito"), an Anxious/Guilty Boy, a Shamed Kid, and a raging two-year-old;

Their Guardians: my Magician (reality distorter), Critic (Blamer), Weasel, Salesman, Doubter, my Macho Man, my Proud Guy ("I need no help here!"), and my Friendly Guy; and . . .

My Regulars: my Philosopher, a Thinker/ Analyzer, a Good Dad, a Child of God, and a Worker (achiever).

"These subselves haven't learned to trust my Self, God, and Myra, so far. Myra and Lupe are both pretty wounded too. We all need help to get our inner crews acting like true teams, and we all need to work at learning and using better communication skills. Now I see that "my" money problems really are our stepfamily's problems, and we three adults are mutually responsible for solving them. I have to work on my part of this, and I need help!"

Myra's Self: *"Now I see that our money conflicts have kept my false-self troops in control, because they don't trust Manny or my Self."*

My Shamed Girl (*"I'm not lovable, and I don't deserve a good life!"*), my Scared Girl (*"We'll never pay our bills, and I'll always be poor."*); Guilty Girl (*"I shouldn't be so jealous and critical!"*); and a Jealous Girl (*"I want the freedoms and good things that Lupe has!"*); and their Protector subselves:

My Catastrophizer (*"Manny won't stand up to Lupe, because in his heart he still loves her. He'll eventually leave me for her, without a doubt, and I'll be left to die alone and unloved."*),

Playgirl (*"I admire Lupe. She's a woman who knows how to have fun!"*);

Critic (*"You married a loser. Stupid, stupid decision!"*);

A **Worrier** (*"Oh! How are we ever going to solve all these problems?"*);

A **Cynic/Pessimist** (*"This 'false-self' junk won't help. Neither will these supposed communication skills. We're all in way over our heads, here."*);

My **Idealist/Perfectionist** (*"Keep the faith! Love really can conquer all these problems!"*);

My **Distorter** (*"I am* not *responsible for these problems!"*); and . . .

My **Whiner/Shrew** (*"Lupe is just a selfish little bitch, and she has Manny hooked. Why can't he treat me better? I get the shaft again!"*)

Some of these subselves don't know of Myra's true Self. Others know her, but don't trust her as a competent leader yet. Manuel and Myra are beginning to see their false-selves' control and recovery options, some new relationship basics (like mutual respect and true needs, and de-triangling); and some new communication choices, based on the seven skills. As their awareness of these grow and their Selves take more charge, they feel more like teammates and less like antagonists. The mates realize they have some basic core attitude (second order) changes to make together over many months, to nourish their wound-recoveries, their remarriage, and their stepfamily.

Ex-wife Lupe has her own complex set of surface and underlying true needs. Like the re/wedded couple, her inner family is often controlled by a group of subselves, and she's not aware of that.

Pause again, and notice your thoughts, feelings, images, and body sensations: your "self-talk." How does your inner team feel about this dig-down concept, what it might mean about discovering the true needs and responsibilities in *your* life and family?

Though the details above probably differ from your situation, look for common themes. Each of these three examples is simplified, to illustrate the dig-down concept. In real life, each person has a dynamic group of simultaneous surface conflicts and underlying true needs and priorities that shape their fluctuating perceptions, feelings, and behaviors.

 # Reality check: with these examples in mind, get quiet and focused, identify several current "problems," in your life, and practice identifying mentally or on paper your (inner family's) specific expectations about who is responsible for solving each problem, one at a time. Use the summary of true needs above, or your own list, to try to identify what you and other people *really* need, in each situation. You don't have to do this perfectly. The experience of *trying* this dig-down skill is more important than the results, for now.

How can you evolve your own way of seeing below your surface "problems" to your and your partners' true (level 3 and 4) needs? Not doing so risks your major need-conflicts staying unresolved and stressful, like endlessly clipping off weed-tops, vs. pulling out their roots.

Keys to "Digging Down" Effectively

Effective dig-down skill requires forming some firm beliefs, and then following some simple steps. The keys below presume your Self is guiding your inner team. Option: use these guidelines as a checklist to clarify what you or someone else believe now. Use "?" if you feel unsure or ambivalent, or " * " if you want to develop the belief or reflex. If you *don't* believe versions of these, see if you can sense which of your subselves brings you the different belief, and what they fear would happen if they adopted the belief below.

Key Beliefs (Attitudes)

1) Human *needs* are normal, universal, and acceptable. Challenge any old belief that "neediness is weakness," specially in males. Baloney. Neediness is as natural as your heartbeat and breathing. Clarifying and asserting your needs *respectfully* is wholistically-healthy self-care. Repressing or ignoring your needs, or feeling ambivalent, guilty, and/or ashamed of them, is self-neglect. That's usually a symptom of a shame-based ancestry, a low-nurturance childhood, and a disabled true Self. Not noticing or honoring *other* people's needs (including kids) with equal respect promotes conflict, and strangles relationships, intimacy, and love. Those foster loneliness, isolation, and despair.

What do your inner voices say now about honoring your own mental, spiritual, emotional, and physical needs? What does your Self say? How would each of your main childhood caregivers responded to this premise: "*All* needs and related emotions are healthy and OK. What counts is how you choose to act on them"? Note that adopting and acting from a new belief about asserting your needs without guilt, shame, or anxiety, is a second-order (core attitude) change.

2) Most of my personal and interpersonal "problems" are surface *symptoms* of underlying true needs (discomforts). See how your inner crew and key others in your life feel about this premise:

"To act effectively in high-E(motion) situations, I need to know what you and I really need. Our first impressions are probably only symptoms, and we need to take the time to help each other dig down to learn our respective true needs."

Really *believing* this may require a second-level change for you, like quitting junk food or smoking. Review the list of universal human true needs on p. 149, and edit it to fit your view of the world.

3) I am responsible for _ discovering and _ filling my true needs, and other adults are responsible for theirs. I can ask for (vs. demand) help in filling my needs, but I remain responsible. Unless another adult is disabled, my taking responsibility for filling their true needs (e.g. "find my life purpose, and inner peace") is probably *enabling*: unintentionally blocking them from developing their own self-sufficiency, self confidence, and contentment.

4) To get clear on who's *really* responsible for filling your and my true needs, we may pass through four levels:

Level 1: you and/or I feel "I have no unfilled needs. I don't have a 'problem' right now." This may be true, or it may be our false selves guarding one or both of us from discomfort (pain) by denying, repressing or distracting our bodily senses and consciousness from current true needs.

Level 2: "I'm not blended (controlled by a false self), and I do have a problem now. It's not my fault, and someone else is responsible for fixing my problem (filling my needs.)"

Level 3: "I'm not blended, and I'm at least half responsible for filling the true needs under my surface problems. Someone else is responsible for the other half."

Level 4: "I am controlled by a false self, and I own *full* responsibility for _ empowering my Self, and then _ identifying and filling *all* of my true needs. I respectfully give other adults the same responsibility for their needs, without guilt, shame, or anxiety. I can choose to help others do this or not, and ask for help with mine, or not."

Interpersonal problems are often fueled by unrealistic expectations of other people and/or ourselves; e.g. "*I expect myself to love my arrogant stepchild, and I expect her to love me, and appreciate the sacrifices I make.*" A more realistic expectation would be "*I expect myself to see the inherent dignity in my stepchild, and remember that she is wounded, searching, and unsure. I also expect myself to set firm limits about my stepchild's behaviors, and to act respectfully and consistently when she tests by exceeding my limits. Further, I expect my stepchild to frequently put her needs ahead of mine, because she's immature, impulsive, and wounded, not disrespectful. I don't expect her to love me or openly thank me for my sacrifices now. She may some years from now.*"

More key beliefs and awarenesses that promote successful "digging down":

5) I understand the difference between first-order (superficial) changes and second-order (core attitude) changes.

Help your subselves and other people accept that first-order changes are cosmetic (temporary), and usually don't fill true needs permanently. They're false-self strategies for trying to change without changing. For example, "trying a new diet" is a first-order change which usually results in the pounds returning, along with guilt, frustration, and self-doubt. First-order changes are strong symptoms of denied false-self dominance.

Choosing to _ *really* value your wholistic health; _ consistently eat less fat, salt, sugar, bulk, and more organic fruits and vegetables; and to _ exercise regularly; is an applied second-order change. That usually signals a true Self guiding your other subselves. Applying this awareness promotes clear thinking and effective communication, and is essential for you and others to fill your *true* needs.

6) When my Self identifies my true needs, I can learn to use these seven skills with a genuine =/= attitude to fill them. Reading these beliefs means little. *Applying* them by thinking and communicating effectively will help you fill your (and others') needs "well enough." If you weren't taught these beliefs and skills, you'll benefit from some version of this last belief:

7) There is high value for me in adopting a patient, long-term view, as I develop and apply these beliefs about digging down and owning my responsibilities.

In a very real sense, taking full charge of your own life and using your talents well and wisely is what "adult maturity" is about. Like the old saying "nine women can't have a baby in a month," evolving your awareness, knowledge, and communication and relationship skills takes its own time. Celebrate short-term successes, learn from your trial mistakes without anxiety, and keep an appreciative wide-angle view of your evolution. Working patiently and creatively to empower your Self is probably the most productive way of doing this, over time.

A "Dig-down" Technique

In High-E(motion) situations like major conflicts or threats, experiment with these steps. Reduce distractions, and **use** *awareness* **to confirm** . . .

_ my Self is in charge of my team of subselves,
_ my E(motion) level is "below my ears,"

_ I have a stable, two-person awareness bubble, and . . .

_ a solid =/= (mutual respect) attitude; and. . . .

_ I believe respectful digging down will probably benefit everyone.

Then ask your subselves and/or your partner . . .

"What do you need right now?"

When they answer, **use empathic listening** to make sure your Self hears them clearly. Then ask . . .

"OK, why do you need that?" or *"And you need that now in order to . . .?"*

After s/he answers, ask . . .

"If you don't get that, then what might happen?" and then . . .

"If that (bad thing) happened, what would that mean to you?"

Keep digging down nonjudgmentally with each answer you get, using empathic listening to stay in synch. Avoid commenting, agreeing, judging (*"What a stupid idea!"*), sympathizing, or digressing. As you dig down, calmly expect some anxiety and confusion. When people first try this technique, they often reach a point where the momentary answer is *"I don't know (what I need or feel or fear)."* Practicing breathing-awareness, meditation, journaling, respectful silence, and *listening to* or *sensing* your mind-body-spirit usually dissolves the not knowing.

Here's how digging down might sound with our last couple.

Myra's false self says to Manuel *"Do you have early Alzheimer's? How many times do I have to ask you to tell me if you withdraw ATM cash?"*

This is a level-2 surface problem: Myra is unaware of her true needs, and that her false self (*Scared Girl, Magician,* and *Critic*) sees Manuel as causing her problem.

Manny's normal (**false self**) reactions might include some mix of . . .

Explaining (*"Look, I didn't tell you because . . ."*);

Defending (*"I couldn't tell you, because . . ."*);

Asking for examples, and *then* defending or explaining;

Whining (*"I know I should, Myra, but I just can't remember . . ."*)

Playing "*Yes, but . . .*", and counterattacking (*"Well how 'bout you remembering where you leave the car keys, Bright Eyes? Do you know how aggravated I get with that?"*)

Changing the subject (diverting) *"Wait. Did you make that appointment for Angel's dental surgery?"*

With awareness, mutual dig-down knowledge, and Manny's Self in charge, here's a different scenario . . .

Manuel's Self (sincerely): *"You're really frustrated when I forget to tell you about my withdrawals (empathic listening). Myra nods. "Let's dig some, here. Why do you need me to do that?"*

Myra's false self (feels heard and respected, and her E(motion)-level starts to drop): *"So I can balance our checkbook and stay on top of our money."*

Manny's Self (digging down): *"OK, and why do you need to do that?"*

Myra's false self (thoughtfully): *"Well, because I get frustrated if the checkbook doesn't balance, and I don't like not knowing how much money we have."*

Manny's Self (still respectful): *"All right, why do you need to know how much money we have?"* Here's where it gets interesting . . .

Myra's false self (sarcastically): *"Duh! Because . . . because if I don't, we could get into trouble."* (Fuzzy thinking.)

Manny's Self (respectfully, true Self in charge): *"What kind of trouble are you worried about?"*

Myra's false self: *"You know, Manny, not being able to pay our bills."* (More fuzzy thinking.)

Manny's Self (patiently): *"Uh huh. So what do you feel might happen if we don't pay our bills?"*

Myra's *Sarcastic Teen* **subself:** *"Oh, minor stuff like our* *home and car being dispossessed, and our credit rating disappearing."*

Manny's Self (doesn't blend or get hooked): *"And if those happened, what would it mean to you?"*

Myra's false self (exasperated): *"We couldn't live, Manny! (I'm afraid) we'd be homeless street people, and the kids'd starve in rags!"* (This sounds like her *Catastrophizer* subself doing her protective job enthusiastically.)

Manny's Self: *"So you're ragging me to . . . sorry. You're asking me to tell you about ATM withdrawals seems to be about your fear of us and the kids being homeless."*

The couple has clarified a key true need of Myra's, but she's still ruled by a false self who's at level 2, expecting Manny to be responsible for reducing her fear. The situation could develop from here in many ways. Their mutual priorities, constraints, *awareness*, and knowledge of subselves and the seven skills, will shape their joint decision among options like these:

The couple could change focus, and try digging down to learn Manny's true needs. (*"What do you feel would happen if you remembered to tell me about your withdrawals?"*) What might emerge is that he doesn't like to tell Myra about withdrawals, because he (his *Guilty Boy*) feels guilty about not earning more, because his *Perfectionist* and *Inner Critic* relentlessly demand that Manny *"be a real man"* (and provide well). His subselves also decode Myra's behavior as disapproving and scornful, when "money" or his job comes up. Manny's (subselves') true need is to avoid *feeling* guilty, inept, and ashamed. That empathic awareness of this could lead to problem solving those discomforts together (Chapter 8).

Another option the couple has is to stop "digging" here, and try problem solving with what they know so far. For instance, if Myra could regain her Self, she might ask, *"Is there something I'm doing that makes it hard for you to tell me about the ATM?"*

If they knew about inner families, these mates could

cooperatively switch focus, and explore whether both their Selves were present. On finding that Myra's wasn't, they could team up on exploring what would help her *Critic*, *Magician*, and *Scared Girl* relax and trust her Self to improve her young Vulnerable part's security. Another option they have is to . . .

Cooperatively focus on mapping (p. 400) and changing their shared communication pattern (repeating sequences) each time Myra initiates her complaint about Manny not remembering to tell her about withdrawals. When communication mappers know about inner families, this option can illuminate where to _ better use the seven skills, and/or improve their _ E-level management and/or _ their =/= attitudes. Those in turn can lead toward better understanding their respective _ true needs, and _ the subselves who have those discomforts. Doing those steps allows getting clearer on who is responsible for filling what true needs. Whew!

There's more to this than the example shows. For instance, another core need Myra has is to feel *respected* (worthy) by herself and her husband. If he ignores ("forgets") her need to know of his cash withdrawals, she (i.e. various subselves) feels disrespected, then resentful, then critical and disrespectful of Manny. The disrespect activates various members of her inner family (e.g. her *Adult Woman* and *Shamed Girl* subselves). If not noted and corrected, it also chokes their chances for effective problem solving.

These risk her subselves activating and overwhelming her Self (blending), and her behaving "impulsively," like name calling, discounting Manny's needs, or withholding sex as a punishment. If Myra and Manny don't know the seven mental/ verbal skills or who's running their inner families, the odds that each of can fill their true needs via effective =/= problem-solving are low to zero.

For interesting perspective on how your and other people's inner families interact, read "*Embracing Each Other*," by Hal Stone and Sidra Winkleman-Stone. The Stones also give us

"Embracing Your Inner Critic" My bias is that every High School senior and adult, specially co-parents, should study both books (and this one)! A final dig-down resource you can tailor and use . . .

Helpful Dig-down Questions and Statements

You can build a set of mental/verbal tools to help you and any partner dig down to your respective true needs. These work best when your Self is leading your inner squad, and you have a genuine =/= attitude about your communication partners. The tools' effectiveness rises if you omit any wordy explanations, preambles, and apologies, and if you use comfortable direct eye contact. These tools are based on your *awareness* skill, and work well with your metatalk vocabulary (p. 384). If you choose to build and use a meaningful Bill of Personal (human) Rights (p. 362), your Self will have no ambivalence or hesitance about asking or saying things like . . .

"What do you need from me now?" (Then *listen!*)

"What I need from you here is . . ."

"I'm not clear on what you need from me now."

"So you need me to . . ."

"What do you think I need from you right now?"

"Who do you expect to fill that need (of yours)?"

"That's your need, not mine."

"So you're asking my help in filling your need." (Implication: you are responsible for filling it.)

"Whose needs feel more important to you right now, yours or mine?" This is an "=/=" (mutual respect) attitude check. The best answer is *"Our needs are of equal value to me now."*

"That feels like a surface need to me. Let's do some digging."

"I think I am (you are) blended now. I need to get my (your) Self back in charge."

"Which of your inner crew needs to feel heard, right now?"

or *"Which of your subselves needs (whatever)?"* For this one, both partners need to know the inner-family concept, and have a sense of their respective subself "rosters."

"Why are we communicating right now?" This works best if both people know the six communication needs (p. 46), and are developing their awareness and metatalk skills. If someone responds, *"I don't know,"* summarize the six reasons, and/or check for false-self dominance. Can you do that yet?

Notice the simplicity, clarity, and directness of these questions and statements, and the thinking behind them. In my experience, few adults or couples, and no kids think and talk like this in high-E(motion) situations. Do you? If not, what do you think might happen if you intentionally built and *respectfully* used dig-down tools like these? How would the key people in your life respond to them? How would the lives of any kids in your life be affected?

 # Reality check (revisited): *try* these dig-down concepts again. Think of a current or recent conflict in your life. In the spirit of discovery, not blame, mull . . .

Is each partner's true Self in charge here? If not, what are our options?

What does each of us need, on the surface? Can you write them down?

Who, specifically, is each of us expecting to fill those surface needs?

Are we conflicted over that?

If we dug-down to our respective underlying *true* needs, what would they be specifically? If I'm not sure, what's in the way of me answering?

Who do I feel is responsible for filling these *true* needs?

What could happen if we all _ learned, and _ used the four levels and dig-down tools in this chapter for key discussions—as =/= teammates, vs. opponents?

Option: journal about your experience. What are you aware of, as you try digging?

Recap

You and others you live and work with may have trouble permanently solving relationship "problems" because you're _ unaware of focusing on surface needs ("conflicts"), rather than the true needs underneath them; and _ unconsciously or consciously expecting others to fill your true needs, vs. accepting personal responsibility for them. These suggest that a false self is locally or chronically controlling your inner family of subselves. *These seven relationship skills, including digging down, won't fill your needs consistently until you harmonize your inner team under your Self's expert leadership.*

This chapter offers three examples of couples using their first communication skill (Chapter 2) to dig down through **four levels of awareness**:

1) "*I have no problem*;" (protective false-self denial and repression).

2) "*I'm not blended (ruled by a false self). I do have a problem, and it's someone else's fault*;" (blame).

3) "*I'm not blended, and I'm* half *responsible for solving my problem*;" and . . .

4) "*I am controlled by a false self. I'm fully responsible for _ enabling my Self, and _ identifying and filling my true needs, now and every day.*"

The chapter suggests and illustrates a dig-down technique to help explore below your surface (level 2) problems (symptoms) to get clear on *true* needs, and affirm who's responsible for filling each of them. The usefulness of this dig-down skill in your life depends on your _ intentionally empowering your true Self; and choosing to grow your proficiency with _ *awareness* and _ clear thinking, over time. Together, these three empower you to learn and use the other four skills to get more of your needs met, and to help others (like your kids) do the same.

Notice your thoughts and emotions now ("self talk"). What

are your subselves saying about these ideas and your life-quality? Reflect on how (or if) you want to experiment with digging down this week, and whether there's anyone you want to discuss this with. Do you know any kids who might like to become true-need "treasure hunters"? How do you think your childhood caregivers would react to the ideas in this chapter? Option: if they're living, *ask* them!

When you've reflected and refreshed, don your pith helmet and backpack, regain the "mind of a student," and we'll explore the fourth communication skill you can learn: *metatalk*. Based on *awareness* and clear thinking, learning how and when to metatalk will allow you to clarify and describe inner and interpersonal communication problems. That's the first step toward solving them.

5) Metatalk: Talking About Communicating

If you're a parent, and/or you have a paid job, have you developed a special language to use in these activities? People in most occupations (chimney sweep, brain surgeon, car salesperson, postal clerk, hobo . . .) evolve a special set of terms to promote common understanding with associates, clients, and peers. In the same way, people who live or work together need a special language to discuss and resolve their *communication* problems. The skill you can learn to help you do that is called (here) "metatalk."

Metawriting is writing about writing. Metasinging is singing about singing. Metatalk is talking about communicating. This fourth communication skill puts the results of *awareness*, clear thinking, and digging down, into words. Metatalk is mutually respectful (=/=) dialog between partners about their inner-family and interpersonal communication processes. Rather than talking about "our fight last night," metatalk focuses on *"how we're talking now* about our fight last night." Have you heard of *metatalk* before? If not, you have a lot of company. If so, do you use it regularly?

Put this powerful skill to work with these steps:

You partners _ learn the communication basics in Chapter 1, and _ some or all of the communication concepts and terms in the Glossary (p. 418). Then . . .

Use these and your *awareness* skill (Chapter 2) to notice when the communication *process* between _ you and a partner or _ between your inner-family members isn't working well. That will help you to . . .

Use respectful "meta-comments" and empathic listening to identify what the problems are, so you can . . .

Use your other communication skills to resolve them together.

Take a look at the terms on p. 384 and return here. Could you teach someone clearly what each of these 33 concepts means? Do your key communication partners know them? See the Glossary for descriptions, and other useful relationship terms. The more of these concepts you understand and use with a shared =/= (mutual respect) attitude, the more communication and other needs you can fill!

What Does Metatalk Sound Like?

You'll develop your own style and vocabulary with this skill, but the theme remains constant: clear, nonjudgmental descriptions of your communication *awarenesses*.

Imagine you're talking with someone and you notice that they interrupt you repeatedly. You realize you're feeling put down, unheard, and increasingly irritated. You then consciously decide to make a meta-comment about your inner and mutual communication process. You say:

"Sylvia, I notice that pretty often, you start to talk before I'm finished. I'm not feeling heard by you, and I'm starting to get frustrated." You could stop there, or you might add *"Were you aware of doing that?"* or *"I'd like you to let me finish my thoughts."*

Another scenario: your partner laughs and says:

"I just had the most unbelievable fight with my sister. It was awful!"

You feel confused (awareness), and say *"I just got a double message from you, Burt, and I'm not sure what you're really feeling. Your words were: 'the fight was awful', but you chuckled and smiled."*

Notice how the meaning of this message would change if it was said sarcastically or blamefully (embedded R-message: "I-m 1-up") or apologetically ("I'm 1-down").

Guidelines for Effective Metatalk

Once you _ grasp the metatalk concept, _ learn key communication factors, and _ become aware of your option to focus on your communication *process*, how can you maximize your effectiveness with this fourth skill? These suggestions assume your Self is leading your inner family:

Use this skill any time you're *aware* you have a significant internal or interpersonal communication problem.

Mutually-respectful metatalk improves communications with adults and kids! Metatalk delivered timidly or as pleading (R-message: "I'm 1-down"), or harshly, critically, condescendingly, or sarcastically ("I'm 1-up"), will probably make your situation *worse*. If your partner gets defensive from, or upset about your meta-comments, one option is ask them what R(espect)-message they're decoding from you now.

Another is to listen empathically (briefly say back their response without judgment), so they feel heard. When their emotions come down, their ears can re-open, and they can hear you better. Then restate your meta-comment. A third possibility is that their shame-based false self can't trust that you're not attacking (criticizing) them, despite your assurances.

Check your partner's E(motion)-level, before metatalking. If it's "above their ears," use empathic listening first (Chapter 6).

The point of any meta-comment is to help you both get more of your current needs met. So offering such =/= feedback is a potential gift, not a criticism, complaint, or attack. Develop the reflex of clearly knowing *why* you're making a meta-comment. If a false self controls you, s/he may have a hidden agenda for metatalking. That risks *increasing* your conflicts.

Using your partner's name occasionally in your meta-comment (or in general) affirms them, and may make it easier for them to hear you clearly.

Make your meta-comments as brief, factual, and specific as you can. This minimizes possible misunderstandings, and getting lured off onto other subjects. One way to do this is to describe specific environmental conditions, feelings, and behaviors of your partner that could be recorded on film or tape, rather than personality traits. "*I notice you start to stutter (a behavior), whenever we talk about sex.*" vs. "*You get nervous (a judgment) when we start to get intimate.*"

In high-E(motion) situations, be aware of any expectations about your partner's response to your meta-comment. If you expect them to (ultimately) reject or ignore your statement, or attack you for it, or if you feel unjustified or ambivalent in making it, your odds for being *heard* drop.

As with other respectful assertions (Chapter 7), it helps to expect "resistance" to your meta-comments. If your partner isn't used to metatalk from you, their first reaction to statements like these may be to have their false self defend or explain themselves. Point out the difference between reporting and criticizing, if their E-levels are below their ears. If not, switch to empathic listening (Chapter 6) until their hearing returns. If your partner can hear and accept your meta-comment, and if their needs or perceptions conflict with yours, often the next best step is win-win problem solving together (Chapter 8).

For major or volatile communication problems, plan your meta-comment in advance, and practice it alone or with an objective partner until it becomes more natural and spontaneous.

Encourage yourself to experiment with metatalk. Evolve your own style and skill, rather than trying to be perfect at it (despite your *Inner Critic* and *Perfectionist* subselves). This skill doesn't always work, but it does raise the odds you and any partner will get more of your needs met, in a mutually satisfying way.

Practice remembering that every spoken or written communication has a *content* half (what we're communicating about: our topic, or focus), and a *process* half (*how* we're communicating _ now and _ over time). Metatalk focuses on your inner and interpersonal processes, so meta-comments are sometimes called *process* comments.

Now let's see this skill in action. Notice your reaction as you read over these metatalk examples. If they seem weird, awkward, or strange, that's a normal signal that they're a new kind of communication choice that you're not used to. Give the skill a try, be patient, and be aware of the evolving (pleasant) results! The examples below show possibilities, rather than absolutes.

Whichever meta-comment you choose, successful communication-problem resolution hinges on each partner wanting to include the other in their awareness bubble (p. 425), and genuinely feeling that the other's current true needs are just as important as their own (an =/= attitude).

Sample Meta-comments

Here's a set of common conflictual (high E-level) communication situations, and typical meta-comments you might use. **There is no right or best one** for a situation, but your choice needs to contain an embedded =/= R-message to be effective. As you review each of these, compare the meta-comment to how you would normally respond. Consider which response would probably fill your respective current communication needs best. Have some fun here!

Option: check any situations below that you specially want to improve. "Name" is the name you use for your current communication partner:

1) You aren't sure if your partner is willing to receive a meta-comment now:

"(Name), are you open to some feedback about how we're talking now?" What if they aren't?

2) Something feels wrong between you and your partner, but you don't know what:

"(Name), I need to be quiet for a bit. Something's not feeling right about us to me, and it's making it hard for me to listen to you now. Can you wait with me while I try to get clearer?" Their answer may be "No."

3) You feel 1-up or 1-down (vs. =/=) toward your partner, in terms of your dignity, worth, or role:

"I want to own that I'm feeling critical of (1-up on) you now, and it's getting in my way"; or *"I don't know why, but I feel intimidated by (1-down to) you now. Would you be willing to shift (from the present subject) now and take a look at that with me?"*

4) You're not sure what your partner's communication goal is:

"I'm confused, (name). What do you need from me in our discussion now?"

5) Your communication goal doesn't seem to match your partner's:

"I sense that our communication needs are clashing. I need to _____. What do you need from me now?"

6) You're bothered (distracted) by something, and can't focus on your partner:

"I'm sorry. I'm feeling really distracted by _____. Could I take care of that and resume with you at (a specific time)?"

7) You want to express anger at your partner safely:

"I am REALLY irritated and frustrated with you because (specific recordable behavior)! Are you in a place to hear me on this? If you're not, I need to agree on a time when we can work on this! I'm so mad so I can't hear your side of it right now." See p. 244.

8) You want to express gratitude or praise to your partner and be heard, vs. discounted:

"(Name), when you (specific recordable behavior), I feel really (grateful / proud of you / appreciative . . .), because (of a specific positive effect on your life). Thanks / Nice job!"

9) You don't feel safe to truth-tell or talk intimately with your partner:

"I'm pretty nervous about saying this . . . (Name), I can't be really honest with you about (specific subject). I'm scared that (specific reason). I'm informing you, not blaming (if true)! Will you problem-solve with me on this?"

10) You don't understand your partner's current thoughts:

"I'm confused. Could you make your point another way?" Or *"Could you recap your ideas in a few sentences?" I want to be clearer on what you mean."*

Another option here is to use empathic listening. *("So you think / feel / want / believe . . .")*

11) You're bored by your partner:

"(Name), I confess I'm having a hard time staying interested in (their topic) right now. Maybe I can hear you better another time."

12) Your partner seems 1-up: i.e. you currently feel disrespected and unvalued because they _ constantly interrupt you, or _ talk non-stop, or _ change your subject before you're done, or _ ignore or deride your ideas, or _ name-call, or _ work while you talk, or _ are sarcastic, or _ avoid your eyes, etc.

"When you (describe their specific current behavior, factually and objectively), I feel my needs aren't very important to you. I feel ignored and really hurt!" (". . . and I want you to stop doing that.")

Be careful with that last part, if you use it: asking or demanding someone to want to value you more can be a self-defeating "Be spontaneous!" paradox. A productive option is to explore whether you (your inner family) value yourself!

13) Your partner seems 1-down: e.g. they discount their own current feelings, needs, or thoughts.

"(Name), when you say 'I'm probably wrong again' (or other specific behavior), I feel you put your Self down. I get very uneasy / uncomfortable / _____."

14) Your partner is (now or often) uncomfortably curt or silent:

"Looks like you need to be brief / quiet now." Option: "Am I doing anything that stops you from saying what you're thinking or feeling?" Or *"What do you need from me now?"*

15) Your partner (often?) leaves before you're finished talking:

"When you take off before I finish our (talk / issue), I feel unimportant, frustrated, and put down! I need to know if I'm doing something that blocks your talking with me. Will you work on that with me?" (What if they won't?)

16) Your partner currently or frequently won't look at you:

"When you avoid my eyes so much, I feel uneasy and distracted from what you're saying." ("Do you have some problem with me right now?") Note that shame-based people are often uncomfortable with direct eye contact.

17) Your partner brings up an old conflict (again?) you thought was ended:

"(Name), I get REALLY frustrated when you bring up (a specific old issue) again and again! I feel punished, attacked, and weary! What do you need from me so you could let go of (this specific issue)?" If they don't know, or aren't willing to find out, what are your options?

18) Your partner rambles on and on, and you feel *flooded*:

"Whoa (fingers in ears)! I feel swamped. You're saying so much! When you need to do that, it gets hard for me to hear you, after a while." ("You don't really need any input from me right now, yes?") Or *"(Name), when you talk on and on without asking for my response, or asking about me, I feel increasingly used, hurt, and resentful. Can we talk about this?"* Or *"(Name),*

I need you to know I'm nearing my limit of being able to hear you, as you vent."

19) You decode a double message from your partner's behavior: (e.g. their words don't match their body / face / tone): *"Please stop, (Name), I feel confused. Your face looks (specific emotion: sad / angry / bored . . .), but you say you're not. What gives?"*

Recall that double messages are usually a symptom of local false self-dominance.

20) Your partner makes (wrong) assumptions about you; e.g. they finish your sentences, and/or tell you what you're thinking, feeling, wanting, or really meaning: *"(Name), I'm starting to resent you're making assumptions about me. When you tell me what I'm 'really' feeling or thinking, I feel disrespected and ignored by you. I feel like I'm the kid, and you're the adult. (. . . And I'm going to call you on it when I notice you 'mind-reading' me, because I really need you to stop it.)"*

21) Your partner says you're playing communication or mind games: *"So you feel manipulated or conned by me just now . . ."* (Wait for a response . . .) If "Yes": *"I'm pretty frustrated that you feel that way. I'm trying to tell you honestly what I (think / feel / want), and to clearly hear what you need."* Options: *"What is it I'm doing that makes you feel that way?"* or *"If you need me to change something, what is it?"*

22) Your partner uses personal information you've shared to attack or criticize you: *"Name, I feel really betrayed. I trusted you with (specific information), and I'm feeling like you're using it against me. I'm feeling (resentful / hurt / angry), and a lot less safe in confiding in you!"*

Pause, and notice your self-talk. Go back and review any of these situations you're having "second thoughts" about. When you're ready and these ideas are fresh, try them out in your own life. Easy does it: you don't have to hit the bulls-eye on your first try!

Reality check: Try designing some meta-comments for your own conflictual communication (relationship) situations:
Situation:

Possible meta-comment:

Situation:

Possible meta-comment:

Situation: '

Possible meta-comment:

Three key steps to growing your metatalk comfort and effectiveness, over time:

Check to see if your Self is leading your inner team. *S/He* probably is, if you're feeling some mix of *calm, centered, energized, light, focused, resilient, up, grounded, relaxed, alert, serene, purposeful,* and *clear.*

Intentionally build your communication vocabulary: Learn at least the seven *awareness* factors in the last chapter, and the 33 concepts in the Metatalk summary (p. 382). Option: become clear and fluent with all the concepts and terms in the Glossary. **As your awareness and vocabulary increase . . .**

Use **them**. Build the habit of spotting these internal and social process factors in troublesome communications, and describing them and their effects to your partner/s in clear, factual, objective, specific terms, with an =/= attitude.

Options

While these metatalk ideas are fresh, see if any of these choices appeal to your inner crew . . .

Read about giving effective feedback [http://sfhelp.org/02/evc-feedback.htm]. All meta-comments are a kind of feedback that focuses on your internal and shared communication causes, dynamics, and outcomes.

List the key communication factors you'd like to start noticing, like eye contact, R-messages, E-levels, and double messages. Then mentally use the list to notice the factors in your and others' conversations today. This is about building your *awareness*, not criticizing!

At the end of your day, spend some quiet time recalling key solo (inner) or social communications. Evaluate each of them for the communication factors on your list (above). Easy does it: don't try to get all the factors at once!

Try out one or two meta-comments with trusted partners. Option: explain what you're doing, and why. If a partner shares your interest, you can practice with each other safely, as fellow students. A related option is to teach kids in your life about metatalking, over time.

If you have a partner, tell him or her that you're experimenting with these concepts and skills to improve your communications. See if s/he's interested in joining you.

Add your own . . .

Status check: see where you stand on what you just read:

I can _ clearly describe _ *metatalk* to other people now, and _ when to use it. (T F ?)

I believe _ I'm capable of learning to use this skill well, and that _ my life and relationships will improve if I do so, over time. (T F ?)

I can _ name several guidelines to help me raise my metatalk skill, and _ I know two sources (in this book) of metatalk terms. (T F ?)

I see major benefits to modeling and teaching this skill to the young people in my life. (T F ?)

My Self is answering these questions. (T F ?)

Awarenesses . . .

When you're ready, let's move on to the powerful skill of listening with your *heart*. To prepare, use a scale of 1 to 10 to grade yourself on these aspects of the art and skill of listening. "1" is "very poor," and "10" is "among the best."

In non-conflictual work or school situations, I'd rate my general listening effectiveness as a __

In non-conflictual personal and family situations, I'd rate my general listening effectiveness as a __

In conflictual work or school situations, I'd rate my general listening effectiveness as a __

In conflictual personal and family situations, I'd rate my general listening effectiveness as a __

Overall, I'd rate my general ability to listen well to other people as a __.

Notice your self-talk. Have you ever assessed your *listening* skill before? Have you ever studied how to listen well? Do you think you could listen "better" if you tried? Is anything stopping you from trying? If you did try, what would you probably get? Will I ever stop pestering you with questions?

6) Empathic Listening

Hearing with Your *Heart*

After 20 years' clinical experience with hundreds of troubled couples, parents, and kids, I can generalize that most of the adults, even if "well educated," and "mature," averaged about 2 to 4 with each other on an effective-listening scale of 1 to 10. Many of the adults would sheepishly or defiantly agree, and would have no clue how to improve that. Many mates, specially wives and ex mates, complained that their present or former partners rarely *heard* them. Many clients semi-consciously confused *listening* with *agreeing*. When alone with me, many kids tearfully or angrily said they felt *unheard* by their parents, and/or some relatives and siblings.

A paradoxical pattern emerged among my hundreds of communication-class students over the years: they spontaneously said it was much easier to listen at work, or even to strangers, than at home. Is that true in your life? Do you have a credible explanation?" Think of the people you most wish relationship harmony with. I'll bet you're living with them, unless they're your parents, or wish you were. Because the emotional stakes are the highest with them (possible loss of respect, love, and emotional or physical rejection, disapproval, and abandonment), *listening* to them empathically is often the hardest.

Many books and articles have been written about why listening is vital, and how to do it well. **You'll find some helpful new wrinkles in this chapter**: E(motion)-levels, R(espect)-messages, and false selves. Before exploring them, invite some mental partners to join us. Thoughtfully identify and image a person in your past or present life whom you have experienced as "a really good listener." Then identify one or several kids or adults you'd judge as "poor listeners." Include yourself as a candidate in each group. Mull for a moment why you picked each of these models, without anxiety or guilt. If you're brave, imagine how each of them would rank *you* as a listener. Bring them along, as you read . . .

What Does "I *Hear You*" Mean?

You *listen* to other people to accurately experience and decode the meaning of what they're trying to send you: to "understand" what they mean. Do you agree? Recall the premise that *meaning* comes from decoding and combining up to four concurrent messages from a communication partner:

"You think . . ."
"You need . . ."
"You feel . . ." and . . .
"You see me now as 1-up, 1-down, or just as worthy as you are."

Fully *understanding* another person, then, is accurately deducing each of these four things from their behavior, not just their spoken or written words. This implies that in the best case, we want to listen to each other with our ears, eyes, and our empathic hearts. Remember the last time someone heard your words without understanding what you *felt* or *meant*? From this four-message view, does it make sense that truly effective listening requires willing, undistracted focus on your partner, and clear, objective *awareness* of their verbal and non-verbal behaviors?

A frustrated parent says *"For ignoring curfew again, you're grounded."* Their child yells *"I hate you!"* What the child is trying to convey is *far* more than just three words. How about . . .

"I feel disrespected, distrusted, and rejected by you, now (or over time);" and . . .

"I feel really guilty and ashamed that I've disappointed you;" and . . .

"I'm really angry at myself for displeasing you, and ignoring the rule;" and . . .

"I feel stupid, inept, and unlovable, right now;" and . . .

"I think your curfew rules are unfair and too strict, but I don't know how to negotiate;" plus . . .

"I'm hurt and feeling powerless, so I want to (feel powerful and) hurt you back;" and also . . .

"I'm frustrated, because I can't sort out all these feelings, and put them to words we both can understand;" and . . .

"I hate having to obey stupid rules that I didn't make, which limit my freedom;" and . . .

"I feel discouraged, because from past (communication) experience, I believe you won't be able to understand that I mean all these things, accept them, and help me with them;" and also . . .

"I feel guilty for feeling all these things, and for disliking "you" (your rules, consequences, and behavior, and all these bad feelings.)"

Does this collage of simultaneous meanings make more sense if you imagine that they come from a group of the child's semi-independent subselves? These probably include her or his *Guilty Child, Shamed Child, Fearful Child, Helpless Child, Inner Critic, Perfectionist,* and protective *Rebel.* So *"I hate you!"* is really a mixed chorus, not one sentence from one person. How likely is it that an average hard-working parent, who has no concept of "subselves," is going to accurately decode and accept all these meanings (messages) from their child's "defiant" three-word statement?

If the parent's inner family is guided by their Self, s/he may decode their child's statement as meaning *"I feel guilty, frustrated, and angry at you for confronting (criticizing) me and enforcing the rules, but I really don't 'hate' you."* If the parent is shame-based (disrespectful of themselves as a person and/or as a competent parent), their false self might decode their child's message as something like, *"I think you're a rotten, uncaring parent, and I really don't like you or living with you!"*

What if the parent sees their child *smiling* (vs. *smirking* or *glowering*) as s/he yells, *"I hate you!"*? The implied meaning of their multi-level message now includes *"You know I'm kidding, don't you?"* This is why effective listening requires us to use our eyes, where possible.

Besides listening with your ears and eyes, you may or may not use your "heart." That's a metaphor for listening intently to others with genuine attitudes of interest, acceptance, respect, and compassion, rather than indifference, scorn, criticism, and disrespect. Part of "listening with your heart" aims to sense without judgment what you're partner is *feeling* as they communicate. This requires you to empathize. If you don't, your hearing is limited to *intellectual* understanding, which is only one of the four messages your partner is sending.

I credit Stephen Covey ("Seven Habits of Highly Effective People") for the term *"empathic* listening." How would you describe **empathy**? The essence is the ability to "sense" accurately and nonjudgmentally what your partner is feeling and what they need, whether they describe those or not.

Have you experienced times when you "didn't know" what you felt or needed? This is pretty common for most of us, specially for psychologically wounded people who are influenced by a protective *Numb-er* (feeling blocker) or *Distracter*. Do you know anyone who *represses* or *denies* certain feelings, specially hurt, shame, fear, and anger? Empathy can help you sense the feelings and needs that they aren't fully aware of.

Note the big difference between *empathizing* **and** *assuming*, here. True respectful (uncritical) empathy allows you to sense your partner's emotions and motives whatever they are. Assuming is *computing* what you think the other person feels and needs, based on your own biased experience, current needs, and personality.

 # Reality check: Recall the "really good listener," and "poor listener" you identified earlier. Would you say that the former often cared about, sensed, and accepted the feelings and needs of their partners? Did the "poor" listener? Who would you say was more empathic? How empathic do you think they would judge *you* to be?

To strengthen your listening effectiveness, **here are some key points to know:**

The purpose of *listening* is to accurately sense the current (fluctuating) thoughts, feelings, needs, and respect-attitude of your partner. Decoded and combined, these four messages yield *understanding* what your partner's dominant subselves *mean*.

Hearing (the words and surface meanings) is not always *listening* (understanding). In important conversation, Hearing (decoding) fewer than four messages is partial listening.

Sometimes your partner isn't clear on what they think, feel, need, and believe, so what they say and/or do is not what they *mean*. They may or may not be aware of this, or admit it.

If several uncoordinated subselves (a false self) control your partner, s/he can have multiple *conflicting* thoughts, emotions, motives, and respect attitudes. S/He may or may not be aware or admit this. This often results in experiencing double messages from your partner now and/or over time, and feeling confused and "uneasy."

Identify the most important relationships in your life. How often would you say you have these five factors present as you communicate in key situations with each of your partners? How often do they have the factors with you? Do they *know* about these factors? Do you ever (meta)talk about them?

What Is *Empathic* Listening?

It is perceiving your partner's behavior, decoding it, and briefly telling them your sense of what they're thinking, feeling, and needing now *without judgment. Empathic* implies that your communication aim is to hear all four of their expressed and implied messages clearly and fully. In other words, you want to (vs. *have* to) sense as well as you can what it's like to *be* your partner now. "Reflecting back" their behavior like a mirror is a respectful way of checking to see if you're sensing them accurately, as they communicate.

Stay clear that you're not "giving in," or giving up your own feelings, thoughts, values, and needs by doing this. *Listening empathically does not necessarily mean that you agree with your partner!*

Sincere (=/=) vs. manipulative (1-up) **empathic listening benefits all participants:**

It signals your respect for, and interest in, the speaker, so . . .

. . . **they're** more apt to keep talking. That builds trust, intimacy, and relationships.

Unless a false self controls them, your partner is also more likely to listen well to you . . . later!

Unlike saying "I hear you," empathic listening *demonstrates* whether you truly comprehend what the speaker perceives, thinks, feels, and needs. This . . .

. . . **minimizes** misunderstandings, and promotes win-win outcomes. And empathic listening . . .

. . . **may** help your partner clarify their ideas, emotions, and needs, as they hear your nonjudgmental summaries of what they're trying to express. Communication professionals Robert and Dorothy Bolton teach that this skill evokes the "Fy sisters": Clara (clarify) and Vera (verify).

Based on communication knowledge, mutual respect, and awareness, effective empathic listening helps you to define and clarify current true needs. Those are the key ingredients for win-win *inner*personal and interpersonal problem solving. As you know, you can't permanently resolve conflicts without *listening* well!

When Is This Skill Useful?

Listening can range from casual (partial, intellectual) to full (four-message). Choose to use full empathic listening skill when you're aware of these conditions:

Your Self is leading your inner family; and . . .

. . . **your** partner's E(motion)-level is "above their ears" and they can't really hear you now; and . . .

. . . **you** now feel of equal worth and dignity with your partner (=/=); and . . .

. . . **you're** truly, vs. dutifully or fearfully, interested in them, and . . .

. . . **you're** able to focus on them now; i.e. you're not too distracted by the environment or your own current needs.

When you don't meet these five conditions, use all seven skills to get your mutual needs met. Note that you don't have to use empathic listening all the time. Awareness will alert you: "*My partner's E-level is above their ears. I can choose to listen now, or . . . (another option)*!" A helpful guideline: **any time you're aware of feeling conflicted about or with a partner,** *listen*! Stephen Covey suggests "Seek first to understand, *then* to be understood." False selves have trouble doing that, because they seek instant gratification ("*My* needs come first!") Note that empathic listening is just as useful when your Self wants to understand an excited subself as it is with "upset" (high E-level) people. Do you listen with empathy to your inner family members now?

How Do I Listen With My heart?

Consciously select from these steps, until practice makes this skill automatic:

1) Mentally reaffirm "Genuine listening is _ a gift to us both, and _ it's not necessarily agreeing!"

2) Temporarily set your own opinions and non-communication needs aside, and . . .

3) Focus *nonjudgmentally* and empathically on your partner: **watch** their face, eyes, body, and hands. Note postures, motions, expressions, and gestures, or the lack of these; and . . .

. . . **listen** to their _ words and _ speech dynamics to estimate their main thoughts, feelings, needs, and R(espect) attitude; and . . .

. . . **stay comfortably aware** of your own _ feelings and _ E-level, as you do these.

4) From time to time, tell your partner the essence of what you sense they're _ thinking, _ feeling (emotionally and/or physically), and _ needing . . .

. . . **briefly** . . . (use a few words or a phrase, at most);

. . . **in your own words** . . . (don't parrot theirs);

. . . *without questions, comments, or suggestions.*

Note the difference between *interjecting* brief feedback when your partner pauses, and *interrupting* them with a comment, question, vignette, or a judgmental response ("*Why on Earth would you ever think that?*") Effective interjections are like inserting a knife parallel to moving water: no splash. Interruptions are like turning the knife sideways, disrupting the flow.

5) Use attentive posture; comfortable eye contact; and gestures, expressions, and intensity that match the speaker's. When you're truly focused, centered, and empathic, these will happen automatically.

6) Watch and listen to your partner's reaction. S/He will indicate agreement (a nod, "*Uh huh,*" or "*Yeah, and . . .*") or say something like *"No, more like . . ."* Either way, you both get clearer. Win-win!

What's your self-talk now? Are any of your subselves feeling overwhelmed, skeptical, or pessimistic? (*"No way. We can't remember all these steps!"*) When you were young, the prospect of *reading* a grown-up book was "impossible." Now you do it without thinking. How did you learn that amazing ability? Learning empathic listening skill is no different. Keep the great benefits in mind, take small steps, practice patiently, and stay willing to learn from your mistakes without guilt or anxiety. Over time, these *will* bring you proficiency.

This interpersonal skill has been called *active* **listening**, because it involves concentration, awarenesses, and periodic commenting by the listener, not just "sitting there nodding and grunting." Empathic listening is also called *reflective* **listening and** *mirroring*, because the listener returns only the gist of what s/he perceives, (ideally) adding or subtracting nothing.

Empathic Listening In Action

Here are some typical beginnings to empathic-listening comments:

"So you think that . . ."
"It seemed to you that . . ."
"You're really feeling . . ."
"What you need now is . . ."
"Pretty tough, huh?"
"So you were up against . . ."
"You're anxious about . . ."
"Really mystifying" (to you)
"Now you look really . . ."
"Seems you were unsure of . . ."
"You were furious with me!"
"They totally missed your point!"
"Wow! Really confusing!"

"Miraculous!" (you thought)

These are spoken with friendly eye contact, and *with emotions matching the speaker's.* Note the absence of our favorite word "I." *"You're wondering about . . ."* is usually a more effective empathic listening choice than *"I think you're wondering about . . ."* because it's briefer, less distracting, and it focuses *only* on your partner.

Note that these are statements, not questions. Some communication coaches feel that listening effectiveness drops if you raise the inflection of your last feedback words, as in *"You were stunned?"* vs. *"You were stunned."* This is a matter of style, so experiment and see what fits best for you.

Reflect for a moment. How often in casual or conflictual conversations do you use responses that start like these? Don't berate yourself if you say *"Not often."* Until people consciously choose to develop their listening skill, few adults and no kids think and respond like this!

If you were on the receiving end of this communication, imagine how you'd respond . . .

Mom on the phone: *"You know, I wish we talked more. I sure like knowing what you and Pat and the kids are up to. It puzzles me that you won't call me more often. I know you're busy, but are you really so jammed up you can't say 'hello' for five minutes, every couple of days? I really don't think that's too much to ask, but you always have some excuse. You make me feel . . ."*

Grown child (respectfully): *"It really frustrates you that I don't choose to call you more often, and you see no reason for that."*

Notice several things: the child _ interjected with Mom, because she may have gone on and on. She _ did *not* argue, explain, whine, apologize, counterattack, change the subject, or get huffy, angry, or defensive, or use the word "I"; and she _ made a brief statement, not a question.

How do you think Mom would react to an empathic listening statement like that?

Alternatives to Listening

See if you spot your normal response to talkative or upset people among these common (false self) favorites:

Preaching, Instructing, Advising, and **Lecturing**: *"Now Sol, what you should do in a case like this is . . ."* Harried, anxious, or unaware parents can do this one too much, or too soon, without *really* hearing what their child is thinking, feeling, and needing.

Moralizing: *"You know that lying is always wrong, period."* Ditto.

Criticizing or blaming: *"How could you do a dumb thing like that?"* Ditto.

Arguing, disagreeing, or denying: *"I never said that!"*

Explaining: *"Wait a minute. You don't understand what was going on with me . . ."*

Monologing or changing the subject: *"Ah, that reminds me of an interesting thing that happened when I was in Nova Scotia."* (blah, blah, blah)

Intellectualizing and analyzing: *"Now Miriam, let's take a look at what your reasons were, and the outcomes of your choices here. First of all . . ."*

Generalizing: *"You know as well as I do that people in your situation always wind up wishing they hadn't done that."*

Interrogating or questioning: *"So let me understand. Had you gotten a good sleep the night before? What did you have for breakfast?"*

Prolonged silence, which may leave the speaker unsure you're really hearing them.

Threatening: *"If you don't stop slandering Margie, I'm going to . . ."*

Reassuring or comforting: *"I'm sure you'll feel better after you apologize, Ned."*

"**Overreacting**" (responding with inappropriate emotions): "*Oh, my GOD! Your socks didn't match at the meeting? How unbelievably devastating!*"

Withdrawing emotionally or physically: "*Hey, look at the time! Gotta go . . .*"

Refocusing on you: "*How could you do such a thing to me?*"

Joking, or changing the mood: "*Man, you were as nervous as a long-tailed cat in a room full of rocking chairs!*"

Minimizing or trivializing: "*That really wasn't such a big deal. Why were you in such an uproar?*"

Pretending: "*Oh how awful! (You are such a jerk.)*"

Did you realize what an amazing inventory of responses we all have to each other's venting? Each of these reactions has its place, but will usually get in the way if your partner needs you to respect and *hear* them without judgment. Typically, each of these verbal reactions and their non-verbal versions (e.g. a disapproving glance and eye-roll) convey an embedded "I'm 1-up" R-message. They yank the conversational focus away from the speaker to you and your agenda. Is it clearer now why focused empathic listening is a challenge?

If you unconsciously do several of these alternatives regularly with other people who need you to *listen*, your partners will come to semi-consciously expect that you won't hear them. They may start to withhold or withdraw. That's specially toxic in intimate and caregiving relationships. When you were upset as a child and needed to vent, how did each of your parents usually respond? What was the effect of their behavior on yourself-respect and your relationship with them? How would your own child/ren answer that?

 # Reality check: think of the last time you were with an adult or child whose E(motion)-level was high, and who needed to vent with you. Review the list of alternatives to empathic listening above, and see if you see your responses. This is not about blaming you, it's about raising your awareness! Now think of several important people in your life, and see if you find their normal responses to you in the list. What do you notice?

Empathic Listening Tips

Caution: using empathic listening to avoid conflict and *pretend* you respect and care about your communication partner will probably backfire over time. Adults and even young kids usually have the innate ability to notice tiny cues in others' behaviors. If all your subselves don't genuinely respect your communication partner as a dignified person, s/he will probably sense that unconsciously or consciously. The result will be a mix of "unease," mistrust, or resentment that you're being dishonest, no matter what your motive. This is specially true if s/he confronts you (*"George, I don't think you* really *care about my rash."*), and your false self denies your reality.

Note that you can choose to listen empathically for 40 seconds or three hours. Again: using this skill does *not* mean you agree with your partner. It means you want to understand their opinions, feelings, and needs. You can switch from listening to assertion or problem solving any time, specially if *your* E-level goes up. Empathic listening aims to fill your current needs for self-respect, information about your partner, and to nurture your relationship.

Expect some awkwardness and doubt as you try your "empathy ears." You'll develop this and the other six skills over time, rather than be a star your first time at bat. Also, watch for people who know you reacting warily, if they don't know you're trying to "listen differently." Insecure partners may feel "uneasy" or suspicious that you're trying to "pull something" on them if they don't understand what you're doing and why. If _ you have a truly respectful attitude and _ your Self is in charge, eventually they'll regain or raise their trust, even in major conflicts.

Notice your self-talk now . . .

Hearing Checks

In key relationships, a useful application of empathic listening can be called a "hearing check." A partner decides that the current communication is important, and asks: *"Alice, could you give me a hearing check* (tell me what you think I just said and meant)?"

This works best when both partners view this as a signal that the requester wants mutually effective communication, not to disparage or intimidate the listener. It can also mean that the sender isn't sure that they've expressed themselves clearly. Note the difference between requesting or inviting a hearing check (R-message: =/=), and *demanding* one (implication: "I'm 1-up!")

Recall that empathic listening works with your subselves who need to vent, just as with physical adults and kids. The next time you feel a strong emotion, try thinking to the subself who brings you that feeling *"You're really angry / sad / scared / guilty (or whatever)!"* Note the difference between that and *"I feel angry / sad / scared / guilty."* The latter fits when your unblended Self is in charge, since s/he has a full range of emotions too.

Recap and Options

This chapter describes the fourth of seven communication skills you can learn: *empathic* listening. It differs from "regular" listening in that you _ consciously put your own values and opinions aside for the moment, and _ focus entirely on your partner. You use your awareness and empathy skills to estimate *nonjudgmentally* what s/he _ thinks, _ feels, and _ needs moment-to-moment, and over time. Then periodically interject (summarize) those respectfully, to see if you understand them well enough.

One payoff for choosing this skill when your partner's E(motion)-level is "above their ears" is as s/he feels genuinely respected and *heard*, his or her E-level will inevitably drop and restore the ability to hear *you*. The second payoff from honing this skill is that you nurture your own self-respect, and your relationships. Helping your partner to lower their E-level is essential before you assert your own opinions and needs. Identifying and asserting what _ you and _ your partner *need* is one third of what you need for effective internal and interpersonal problem solving.

Most people won't listen empathically in high-E situations until they're *aware* of _ their communication process and _ these seven skills. They'll automatically preach, moralize, interrupt, intellectualize, analyze, interrogate, advise, criticize, pretend, assume, defocus, monolog, explain, attack, tune out, or leave. If habitual, these responses invite hurt, distrust, frustration, and shrinking intimacy; specially if partners don't use metatalk together (Chapter 5).

Now you have an overview of true and false subselves, communication basics, and four of the seven skills. Before exploring the powerful art and skill of assertion, see if any of these would be useful now.

Show this chapter (or the book) to one or more special people, and discuss it with them.

Ask special people how they experience you as a listener: generally, and in conflicts.

Use a reminder like a sticky note, or some symbolic object to try empathic listening. Put it where you can see it on an average morning at home, school, or work.

Redo the listening quiz at the end of the last chapter to see if your opinion has shifted.

Learn about giving effective feedback [http://sfhelp.org/02/evc-feedback.htm], and decide if you want to tell a special person about the way you experience them listening. If you do, get clear on who needs that (your Self?), why you need to do that, and watch your R-messages!

Read the interesting reprint "Why Listening Is Good For

You," by James J. Lynch, and perhaps share it another person you care about. [..02/listen-lynch.htm].

Use the listening inventory at [..02/listen-inventory.htm] to raise your awareness of your normal listening responses to key people, and their responses to you.

Use the practice exercise [..02/listen-practice.htm] with a partner, to help each other build this vital skill.

Identify an empathic-listening "hero/ine": someone you respect and admire, and could use as an inspiring model. When you experience challenging communication situations, try imagining how they would respond. Mull whether you think they're controlled by their true Self or not, per the criteria in Chapter 1. Note their names here, if you wish. Also note your option to express your verbal or written admiration to them.

If there are kids in your life, meditate or journal about your listening habits with them generally, and when either of you is conflicted and/or "upset" (controlled by a false self). A related option is to ask them for (constructive) feedback on how often they feel *heard well* enough by you, on certain topics, or when you disagree. Another option is to teach your kids about E-levels, and how to give and ask for hearing checks. Model these for them, and encourage them to develop their own style.

In important inner-family and interpersonal exchanges, experiment with asking *"Do you feel heard / understood well enough by me now?"* Be ready for *"Not really."* Also note the reverse option, using awareness to make a meta-comment like *"I'm not feeling heard clearly by you now."* Note how different that sounds than *"You're not listening to me!"* That's a blameful *you* message containing an embedded disrespectful "I'm 1-up" R-message. That raises your partner's E-level, and makes it *harder* for them to hear you!

Your growing fluency in awareness, clear thinking, digging down, metatalk, and empathic listening will increase your effectiveness with your sixth mental/verbal skill: assertion.

Would you like to be a more *effective* asserter in general, and in conflicts? The next chapter shows you how to use empathic listening and other resources to greatly boost your effectiveness. Note with affection how your inner team feels now about that possibility . . .

Notes / Thoughts . . .

7) Effective Assertion

Yesterday a client was expressing her pain because her grown daughter stoutly denied her husband's active alcoholism. The daughter of an alcoholic herself, this slender divorced grandmother of nine was anguishing over the effects of her son-in-law's addiction on her cherished grandkids. I asked if she had expressed her concern to her daughter. *"Oh, I couldn't do that,"* the white-haired woman said quietly. *"I can't hurt anyone's feelings, you know."*

In early old age, I suspect this troubled woman had lived most of her life with chronic anxiety and guilt. It was her daily "normal." She didn't know that fear-based subselves chronically controlled her, or that she could learn a new attitude and a set of verbal steps that could help her assert her concern effectively to her kids. Her grandchildren's risk of inheriting six psychological wounds (p. 37) was higher because of these two correctable ignorances.

Every day, you communicate within yourself and with others to try to fill your current needs (reduce current discomforts). The last time you needed something from a person you live or work with, did you *express* your need? Did you get the response you wanted?

Effective *assertion* is the learnable ability to state your needs and opinions in a way that can be clearly heard and accepted.

Skill at respectful assertion is essential for effective win-win problem solving. In my adult communication classes, students have consistently rated this skill as the most difficult of the seven. Most also say that asserting with mates and relatives is often harder than with co-workers. Would you agree with these two opinions?

Have you known an adult or child that you feel is an effective *asserter*? What is it about them that earns your opinion? Would you describe each of your childhood caregivers as *assertive* people? If not, what were they? What did they and other key teachers show you about if, how, and when to express your needs to other people? On our scale of one to 10, how highly would you rank your present ability to assert *effectively* with other people now, in calm and conflictual situations?

This chapter builds on what you've learned in the prior ones. It will show you a set of attitudes and simple communication steps you can take which *will* increase your getting your needs met with other people in a satisfying way. If you aren't a gold-medal asserter yet, learning these attitudes and steps will require you to make a second-order (core attitude) change. Based on new information and awareness, you'll have to shift some familiar old beliefs to "get the gold": the rich benefits this powerful skill can earn. My client grandmother would have to shift to genuinely believing that "hurting (her daughter's) feelings" was less important than trying her best to protect her vulnerable grandchildren and her own priceless integrity.

Is there someone you interact with now who often causes your ruling subselves to feel intimidated, anxious, timid, or submissive? Can you imagine learning a way to relate to this person confidently and calmly, as a person of equal worth? Listen to your inner voices now. Any cynics piping up?

Well used, this sixth communication skill will empower you to nourish your self-respect, comfort, and satisfactions by . . .

Preventing future conflicts;

Telling your true feelings and needs to (confronting) kids and adults who frustrate, hurt, or disrespect you, and . . .

Praising subselves or people in a way they can't deflect or minimize.

Do these sound interesting? Respectful assertion fits midway between timid *submission* ("I'm 1-down") and selfish *aggression* ("I'm 1-up"). It's the preferred language of healthy worry, frustration, hurt, and anger. Respectful ($=\neq$) assertion builds self-esteem, and promotes honest, solid relationships. This skill is easiest to use with partners whose inner family is usually led by their Self. The real challenge here is learning to assert respectfully with everyone else, including your distrustful subselves.

Why Assert?

Assertions range from spontaneous and small (*"Please turn the radio down, OK?"*) to preplanned, life-pivoting ones (*"I need you to stop gambling for good or get qualified addiction counseling by May first. If you choose not to, I need you to move out."*) Success at major assertions requires up to nine conscious steps. Minor assertions don't need them all. Before exploring the steps, note what *effective* **assertion aims to do**:

Get _ your and _ my current _ *true* (vs. surface) needs met well enough, _ in a mutually satisfying way; and _ **nurture** our relationship, if that's what we each want.

How does this compare to your definition? See if you can intuit which two of those five factors most self-help books and articles never mention.

How would you describe the difference between an assertion and a verbal or written *attack*? Shame-based people who aren't aware of their false self's control risk misinterpreting a respectful assertion as criticism or blame. They're apt to attack back, with an exploding E(motion)-level. The steps below and the prior five skills offer a potent way for Self-led people to respond.

See how these steps compare to how you usually express your needs . . .

Nine Effective-Assertion Steps

1) Check to see if your Self is leading your inner family. If not, correct that via "parts work" (See "Who's *Really* Running Your Life?"). Otherwise, expect ineffective assertion and go ahead. Either way, guesstimate if your partner's Self will be in charge when you assert. If you suspect it won't, review your options and decide how to communicate respectfully with their false self.

2) Consciously *choose* **to assert** (do these steps), until they become automatic:

3) Get clear on _ what you feel, _ why, and _ dig down to identify specifically what you *really* need from your partner right now (p. 140). Then _ assess whether your partner can *fill* your need, because some core needs (like self respect) can only be filled by *you*. If you're not sure of these things and time allows, clarify them before you assert.

4) Make four quick attitude checks on how your subselves all honestly feel about . . .

Your partner's needs. If your inner-family consensus is *"His / Her needs are as important as ours,"* then check your awareness bubble (p. 425). If you can include your assertion partner in it, go ahead. If not, lower your expectations about the assertion outcome, or explore which of your subselves are blocking an =/= (mutually respectful) attitude.

Your right to ask or demand. If you solidly feel *"I have a right to say, ask, or demand this,"* go ahead. If your *Inner Critic* is running the show, s/he'll decree *"I'm being selfish / pushy / greedy / demanding / controlling . . ."* Unchallenged, beliefs like these cause your voice, face, and body to broadcast "I'm 1-down," which will probably defeat your assertion. Building a Bill of Personal Rights (p. 362) really helps here. And check your attitude about . . .

Your ability to calmly handle your partner's reactions, like anger, rejection, disagreement, and attack. If you feel confident enough, go ahead. If not, work with your inner family to explore and heal subselves' ignorances and fears (mistrusts). Finally, get clear on . . .

Your expectations about the outcome of your assertion. If you feel "My partner and I can each get our needs met, and we'll probably feel OK about our exchange," go for it. If you (some subselves) believe *"This assertion won't work,"* it probably won't.

5) State your need simply and directly, with steady eye contact.

6) Nonjudgmentally, **expect resistance**. It's a normal human response, not a weakness or wrong! When it happens . . .

7) Use =/= empathic listening, until your partner's E-level comes down and their ears open up; then . . .

8) Recycle steps 5-7 as needed. Keep re-stating your needs clearly and directly, and using empathic listening with each new resistance, until you . . .

. . . get _ a clear agreement, _ an acceptable compromise or refusal, or _ new information that changes your needs or priorities; or . . .

. . . you're interrupted or run out of time. In major assertions, arrange lots of time . . .

9) Note the outcome of your assertion. If you and your partner/s each got your main needs met, thank them and appreciate yourself! If someone didn't get all they needed, use *awareness* and digging down to discover what would work better the next time.

Could you assert in important situations and leave any of these steps out? Pause for a moment and tune in to your self-talk. What are your subselves saying about these nine steps? Do they feel these steps would really work for you all? If not, why?

Let's explore each of them for perspective and ideas . . .

Step 1) Are Your Selves in Charge?

Like most people in her generation and yours, my client grandmother wasn't aware of the inner-family concept. She never questioned the ancient one-body, one-brain, one-personality myth that caregivers and society taught her. Therefore, this vital first assertion step would have no intuitive meaning for her. If you read Chapter 1 for meaning, you have at least an initial understanding about true and false selves, and can see why this question is relevant.

The blunt premise here is (again): if your and/or your partner's false self is in charge when you assert, the odds of your communication being *effective*, as judged by both of you, drop sharply. That's due to the traits that being ruled by a false self usually brings: excessive shame, guilts, and fears; reality distortions (e.g. denials and repressions); and impaired abilities to bond (emotionally attach) and genuinely empathize with others.

Recall: if your and your partner's true Selves are present, you'll each feel a mix of *grounded, clear, upbeat, focused, light, compassionate, aware, alive, centered, purposeful, alert, resilient, balanced, open, and confident.* The alternatives are other clusters of emotions like anxious ("worried"), spacey, "off," defensive, "heavy," hostile, bored, numb, frustrated, empty, hopeless, disrespectful, aggressive, intellectual, and pessimistic.

"Who's *Really* Running Your Life?" [Xlibris.com] shows you how to assess for false-self dominance and how to harmonize your inner family under the leadership of your Self and Higher Power. "Project 1" at the Web site [http://sfhelp.org/01/project01.htm] offers a comprehensive overview of this vital relationship project.

Step 2) Consciously Choose to Assert

One of seven core communication *awarenesses* you can build (pp. 367-70) is that of your and any partner's E(motion)-

level. If you note that yours is "above your ears," that can signal you *"Time to assert!"* If your partner's E-level is above their ears, and your Self is in charge, use =/= empathic listening to help them regain their ability to hear you. When they do, then consciously coach yourself to select from these nine assertion steps.

If you haven't got all the steps down, recall three keys:

My needs, feelings, and opinions are legitimate, *even if my partner disagrees*;

Respectful (=/=) assertion is a gift, not an attack or imposition; and . . .

Nonjudgmentally *expect* **your partner to "resist,"** and respond to that with =/= empathic listening. Then calmly re-assert your need.

As with most skills, the more you practice awareness, empathic listening, and assertion, the more automatic they'll become. Do you trust that? For a way to practice, see [..02/ assert-practice.htm].

Step 3) Identify What You Really Need

Recall the premise that what we *think* we need is often a surface symptom of our semi-conscious true needs. In important assertions, your odds for success rise if you first dig below your surface needs to see what discomforts your inner family *really* wants to reduce. This step is important if you want to make a permanent change in recurring problems. If you change the surface conflicts and settle for a first-order (cosmetic) change, the underlying needs go unmet and your discomfort is likely to return.

Until you get the hang of it, "digging down" to your real needs (Chapter 4) can feel alien, confusing, and time-consuming. If you're a shame-based (wounded) person, digging down may be scary and uncomfortable, for you'll probably confront the part of you that believes *"I don't deserve to get my needs met!"* and *"I'm bad if I seek to fill them!"*

Example 1

Surface need: Denise thinks, "I am so tired of my brother's sarcasm. Every time I try to show him consideration, he discounts and belittles me. I need to confront him about that, and get him to stop (speaking sarcastically)." Some reflection may lead to "I need my brother to respect me." This is a trap, for it gives her brother responsibility for something only Denise can give to herself: respect.

True **needs** (plural): "I *really* need to . . .

. . . **respect** *myself* by asserting my feelings and needs;

. . . **heal** my guilt about causing my brother (and others) discomfort; and . . .

. . . **build** my confidence and reduce my anxiety about personal confrontations and conflict; and . . .

. . . **express** my love for my brother by no longer *enabling* his disrespectful behavior, and feeling badly about blocking him from confronting himself; and I need to . . .

. . . **raise** my serenity and security by *experiencing* that I have mutually respectful options here, and I don't have to accept living like a victim." (Chapter 10)

Planned assertion: When his E-level seems low, Denise says *"Roy, I've noticed that often when I try to support you, you respond with a sarcastic tone of voice. That hurts and frustrates me, and I feel like I'm gradually pulling away from you. I need you to work with me to reverse the trend here. Will you do that?"*

Example 2

Surface Need: Phillip thinks, *"I have to tell my wife I'm concerned about her chronic trouble sleeping, and her irritability. Her short fuse and snapping at me and the kids all the time is really getting to me."*

True Needs: *"I really need to . . .*

. . . lower my growing resentment at Sylvia's behavior, and the inner conflicts it's causing me and the kids; and . . .

. . . regain my self respect (lower my shame at not stepping up to the plate and 'being a man') by confronting her, and lower my growing guilt at not being a good Dad; and . . .

. . . confront my fear that she'll feel attacked, rather than supported, and pull away from me (possible sub-basement fear: abandonment); *and I need to . . .*

. . . overcome my fears of discovering that something serious is wrong with her or us, and that it's getting worse by my not asserting."

Planned assertion: *"Honey, I need some help. I'm nervous about bringing this up. I've noticed over the last several months you sleep poorly, and the next day you seem really irritable and short-tempered. The boys have told me they're worried about you, and I'm getting concerned. I'm starting to resent your snapping at the kids and me all the time. I need you to tell me if something's wrong for you in our home, or inside you. If you don't want to talk to me, I need you to get some competent medical help or therapy. I can't just ignore this any more. Can we talk about this?"*

The purpose of digging down like this is to learn whether you're (fruitlessly) asserting to try and get someone else to fill a need that only *you* can fill. The implacable reality here is that *you* are responsible for your own happiness and security, not your partner, your child, your parent, the Republicans, the Baptists, or God. It often turns out that the act of asserting really fills your true needs (e.g. for self respect and personal potency), rather than the thing you're asserting for . . .

Once your true needs are uncovered enough, the second assertion clarity to seek is whether your partner is able (vs. willing) to fill them. Other people may or may not have the resources or abilities to reduce our tensions. *"Could you scratch my back?"* or *"May I borrow your lawn mower?"* are easy enough. Review the set of true needs that only you can fill (p. 149).

Other people can support and encourage you as you seek

to fill these deep needs. Expecting, requesting, or demanding your partners to reduce such tensions will surely create anxiety, frustration, anger, and resentment. Getting clear on your true needs without guilt or shame, and taking responsibility for satisfying them, builds self and mutual respect. Do you agree?

Once you're clear on *what* you need, and *who's* responsible for filling it, you're in a much better place to decide . . .

What Response Do I Need Here From My Partner?

This important awareness allows you to decide afterward if your assertion "worked" or not. Your options are clear and simple:

I'm venting: I need you to respect, hear, and accept me now. I don't need action or agreement; or . . .

I'm *requesting*: I need action. I can live with a compromise, or even a refusal right now (get clear on which). The action I need can be a behavior change in you, or your agreement to problem-solve a mutual conflict with me; or . . .

I'm DEMANDING! You must commit to taking specific actions, by a certain time and/or in a particular way. Compromises, exceptions, or refusal are *not* acceptable to me here.

Your choice of acceptable response may change as your assertion-exchange progresses. Stay aware of your inner and mutual processes! If your subselves want to you to assert in order to get something else from your partner, like . . .

. . . **an apology** ("You're 1-down!");

. . . **remorse** and an admission of guilt ("Admit it: you we're wrong / bad / thoughtless / insensitive / irresponsible / selfish . . ."); or . . .

. . . **suffering** (pain), to "pay for" hurting, betraying, or burdening you . . .

then your false self is setting you and your partner up for disappointment, guilt, and regret. All goals like these are inherently *aggressions* ("I'm 1-up"), not =/= assertions.

Notice what your subselves are saying now. Do they think you could (or should) learn to dig down and identify what you *really* need for important assertions? If you have protective *Saboteur* and/or *Procrastinator* subselves, how would they probably get you to avoid learning to dig down? What does your Self feel is the best thing for you to do with this assertion step, now that you're aware of it? Note that you'll meet this same step in the next chapter, when we focus on problem-solving skill.

Reality check: Think of a recent conflict you've had with an important child or adult. Take time to reflect and think or write about what your surface needs were. Then dig down below each of them (Chapter 4) to uncover your underlying *true* needs. Then try to empathize with the other person, and repeat the exercise to unearth *their* probable true needs. See if doing this shifts your attitude about your surface conflict, and how you two tried to deal with it. If it's useful, use the list of common true needs on p. 149 as a resource.

The real struggle and prize for working to grow effective communication skills is getting to know your self (i.e. your inner family) intimately and honestly. Are you up for that now? Who's responding?

OK, you've checked whether your Self is guiding you, you've consciously decided to follow these nine steps, and you're relatively clear on what you want, and why. The next step in a planned (important) assertion is to . . .

Step 4) Check Key Attitudes

Once you're clear on what you need, your assertion may still "fail" because your key *attitudes* and *expectations* are unclear, conflictual, or unhelpful. *Awareness* can empower you to get clear on your attitudes, if your Self wishes to. Here's some brief perspective on **four key questions . . .**

A) Do I Really Have An =/= Attitude Now?

You can start answering this by noticing your awareness bubble (p. 425). If you're truly concerned with your partner's needs as well as your own, your bubble will steadily include both of you. Once it does, see if you have mutual respect.

If your ruling subselves really feel 1-up (superior) or 1-down (inferior) to your partner/s, assertion won't work well. Arrogant, "self centered" asserters care more about their own comfort than their partner's. They aggress, rather than assert. Timid false selves don't believe their needs are legitimate, and/ or fear some painful consequence from asserting them. Such people plead, hint, or whine, rather than assert confidently. Aggression and pleading are usually symptoms of unseen false-self dominance. If your dominant personality parts are arrogant, you need to rebalance toward empathy and compassion. If your false self is timid, you need to build those subselves' trust in your Self and your innate human rights (p. 362).

Obviously you can't make either of these core personality adjustments quickly, and you'll need to assert anyway. Work toward objective *awareness* of what's going on inside and between each of you, and the outcome you two get.

B) Do I Have the Right to Ask For This?

If your inner team feels that your needs are silly, invalid, weird, or shameful, your voice and body dynamics will broadcast, "*I'm 1-down*" when you assert. How can you tell if you're doing this? Avoiding direct eye contact is a major clue. Frequent "ums" and "uhs" and incomplete sentences are others. So are choices of vague, indirect, negative, or mild terms. Reflexive apologizing, and using "we need" rather than "I need" are other signs of a 1-down mindset. The implied message here is *"You probably won't agree or give me what I'm asking for. Oh well, I tried . . ."*

If you're tired of being chronically timid about asserting

your needs, four effective **ways to promote your Self to equal over time are . . .**

Commit to doing some form of inner-family or "parts work," to replace old core shame with genuine self-respect and self-love, over time. Pay special attention to retraining your diligent *Inner Critic, Perfectionist, and Pessimist* (subself), and nurturing your *Shamed Child.* This work usually becomes spiritual. See "Who's *Really* Running Your Life?"

Develop a Bill of Personal Rights that you really believe in, and experiment with using it. If your inner leader/s truly see your communication partners as equally worthy persons, your Bill of Rights will apply to them as well.

Read and apply "The New Peoplemaking," by Virginia Satir (Science and Behavior Books, 1988); and "Healing the Shame That Binds You," by John Bradshaw; (Health communications, Inc., 1994). Try out the healing exercises in the latter book.

Learn to spot any demeaning self-talk: self-criticisms and put-downs. Develop and use affirmations that convert these messages to positive statements you really believe. Compassionately, notice your thoughts now. Anything like . . .

"Oh, I can't do that."
"That won't work."
"Too hard; too much work."
"But I don't know how."
"I have other things to do."
"They'd laugh, if I did."
"That's really stupid."
"I don't do stuff like that."
"I'm not interested."
"The plants need watering."
"I will, pretty soon . . ."
"Books are boring."

Such discouraging, pessimistic self-talk is a way distrustful Guardian subselves protect anxious your young Vulnerables from getting hurt from scary new behaviors. While keeping us (your Vulnerables) "safe," beliefs like these often stunt or block your growth. Their main message is *"Don't risk change!"* Until you listen for them, such inhibiting comments are often unconscious. They're whispers behind your thoughts that control you like iron shackles. Do you relate?

Reality check: If Your Self is in charge, negotiate with your other subselves to give you *encouraging* self-talk like this . . .

"My Bill of Rights will help me!"

"Affirmations work for me."

"I can do each of these, now!"

"I'm finding the way!"

"I'm learning how to do these!"

"This makes sense to me!"

"I'll respect me if I do these!"

"I will start, right now*!"*

"I am the only person in charge of meeting my needs."

In building affirmations that really work, motivation experts suggest:

Keep them simple, clear, and specific.

Focus on what you *can* do: e.g. *"I'm growing calm and confident with upset people,"* vs. *"I'll stop being so scared of angry people."*

Use the present tense (*"I'm getting / doing / learning . . ."*) vs. the future tense (*"I'm going to . . . / I will . . ."*)

If you're visual, picture yourself doing each affirmation successfully, *often.* Imagine vividly how this *feels.*

Say each one aloud, often. Option: look in a mirror, with steady eye contact.

Write your affirmations out and post them where you'll see them regularly, like your car dashboard, desktop, phone, bathroom mirror, PC, refrigerator, night stand, bulletin board . . .

As you promote your Self to equal, **expect insecure other people to resist and sabotage** your changing. Respect their fear and need to control, and don't comply! They're responsible for managing their fear, not you!

What if you feel your present needs *are* more pressing than your partner's? For instance, easing your current dental pain *is* more pressing than your partner's to review vacation photos. If your needs seem to come first most of the time, however, look for a hidden anxiety-based (false self) compulsion to *control* situations. These seven relationship skills won't work consistently well until you heal fear and shame-based "Me first" or "Me *last*" attitudes. Either of these implies a protective false self is covertly running your life. Note that this is about wanting to reorganizing your inner family (a second-order change), not *logic*!

Regardless of the intensity of your needs, your and others' dignities and worth as unique persons are always equal. If you often feel entitled to more than those around you, you'll broadcast that. Partners who regularly tolerate such a 1-up attitude are usually shamed, guilty, and fear abandonment, and may be co-dependent. A 1-up / 1-down partnership may be stable, but is usually unfulfilling and stressful for at least one partner. Important communications are seldom really effective.

The third attitude check before making an important assertion skill is . . .

C) Can I Handle My Partner's Responses?

If you're not used to asserting clearly and directly, or your experience is "*Asserting usually doesn't work for me,*" you'll enjoy growing new confidence from this "secret": an =/= attitude, patience, and genuine (vs. manipulative) empathic listening will *always* disarm the majority of resistances you'll get from any partner when you assert! Exception: your partner's ruling subselves are really panicked and hysterical for reasons beyond you.

Which of these responses from others usually give you the most anxiety and loss of calm focus?

_ Irritation, anger, or rage;
_ Subservient apologizing and whining;
_ Ridicule and scorn (shaming);
_ Withdrawing emotionally or physically;
_ Blame and criticism (attacking you).
_ Evading or avoiding, like changing the subject;
_ Vagueness and indecision ("*I'll think about it.*");
_ Indifference, trivializing, or minimizing your feelings and needs (discounting);

Practice will affirm that when your Self is enabled, *awareness* and respectful empathic listening (step 7) will neutralize every one of these responses. In other words, your partner is very likely to feel respected and heard (vs. agreed with). Then their E-levels will come down, and you can re-assert (step 8).

Reading this probably won't dissolve any skepticism you have. *Trying* empathic listening will grow your confidence. The more you do it, the more you'll believe in its predictable power in situations where your partner's inner family is not hysterical.

Until it's automatic, review your confidence level in staying calm, focused, and firm in receiving your partner's reactions to major, conflictual assertions. If you choose not to, you risk your voice, face, and body broadcasting "*I'm 1-down.*" This often will *unconsciously* encourage your partner to resist, minimize, or ignore your assertion, specially if s/he's governed by a false self.

Here's a second confidence builder: unless your partner withdraws, you'll usually get one of three things from your well-planned assertion:

A credible **agreement** (success),

A "*Maybe*," a **refusal**, or a **postponement** (a new problem), or . . .

New information that changes your needs and communication goals.

In the last two of these, you can calmly _ re-assert; _ act on a consequence you've asserted *("If you choose not to change, I'll ____ ");* or _ shift from assertion to cooperative problem solving.

In other words *you never run out of viable communication options!*
As your experience with these skills grows, so will your confidence
in this premise. This nets out to: no matter how your partner chooses
to react, you can *always* (eventually) find a win-win response,
though some may be scary or painful.

So this third attitude check is: *How confident am I that I
can handle my partner's responses well enough?* The last check
before making important assertions is . . .

D) Do I Expect This Assertion To Succeed?

Recall: successful or *effective* assertions (1) get _ your and
_ your partner's true needs filled "well enough," and (2) nurture
your _ mutual respect and _ your relationship. If you expect
this outcome before you assert, you're more likely to get it. If
you're new to the inner-family concept and these seven skills,
I assume you feel some skepticism. There's nothing wrong with
that, unless you let it stop you from trying. Just be *aware* of
your protective, narrow-viewed *Inner Skeptic* or *Cynic*, and
affirm and negotiate with her or him as you experiment.

Try polling your subselves, and see how confidant they are
before making an important assertion. If your false-self crew is
controlling your assertion process, those subselves will capture
your body, and broadcast your skepticism. Over time, your
commitment to gaining competence with the seven mental/
verbal skills, and practicing them patiently over time, will yield
solid assertion confidence. You can choose an attitude that
promotes this is: *"My 'failures' are valuable chances to learn."*
How does this compare with your attitude about assertion?
Notice your self-talk now . . .

These four preliminary steps prepare you well for . . .

Step 5) State your need, with good eye contact.

Your best odds for an effective assertion are when you
express your needs respectfully and unambiguously.

Respectfully occurs by itself, when you see your partner as an equal in worth and dignity. *Unambiguously* depends on your simplicity, directness, and choice of words.

The value of being simple and direct (vs. hinting) is obvious. A **simplicity check:** can I phrase my need in no more than three sentences? One is even better. The more words you use to express your needs, the higher the chance for confusion, misunderstanding, and resistance.

Since words and phrases mean different things to each of us, well-prepared assertions may fail from misunderstandings (assumptions). *"Be on time"* may mean *"No more than five minutes early or late"* to you, and *"Within half an hour"* to your partner. Asserting with simple, concrete, specific words and phrases, and perhaps respectfully asking your partner for a hearing check (p. 216) can really help here.

If your partner's actions bother you, can you describe their irritating behavior factually and objectively? Imagine capturing their disruptive actions on audio or videotape: you can record a specific tone of voice, expression, gesture, etc. You can't record feelings or opinions like *idiotic*, *abusive*, *thoughtless*, *wimpy*, *insensitive*, *inconsiderate*, *nerdy*, and the like.

Limit describing your partner's behavior and changes that you need to things you could record. Asking, *"Please lower your voice"* is do-able. *"Stop being so angry!"* demands a major attitude shift, and is self-defeating because of its implicit "1-up" R-message. Are you appreciating how vital your *awareness* of _ what you want to say, and _ how you say it are?

A helpful assertion format is called an "I" message:

"I" Messages vs. "You" Messages

Before learning these seven skills, typical communicators with high E-levels automatically use *you* messages. These are kinds of blaming statements that imply or say, *"You are wrong or bad. My problem is* your *fault* (so I'm not responsible)."

Remember the last time you felt blamed, accused, judged, or attacked by an adult or child? How did you feel and respond? What happened to your E-level, and your ability to really hear your partner? Did you two have effective communication?

"I" messages come from taking responsibility for identifying and filling your own needs, and genuine =/= mutual respect. They optimize the clarity and impact of your assertions, and raise the chance your partner will be able to hear you. These assertions have two or three parts:

"**When you** (specific recordable behavior), . . .

. . . **I** (specific effect on your life), . . ."

(optional assertion): ". . . **and I need you to** (take a specific action)."

For example:

"Al, when you bring the car back 45" after you say you will (specific behavior) . . .

". . . I get frustrated and angry because then I'm late for my bowling league." (The concrete effect of Al's behavior on your life).

An optional ending is:

"If you'll be more than 10" late, I need you to call me, so I can arrange a ride. Will you do that?" (Asking for a commitment to change).

Delaying the third part gives your partner the dignity of offering his or her own solution. If s/he chooses not to, assert your need, and calmly *expect resistance*, without blame! Respond with awareness and empathic listening.

This I-message assertion is clearer and more respectful (=/ =) than . . .

"It really bugs me when you're so incredibly selfish with the car, you jerk! From now on, be a grown up, and be on time!" (Embedded R-message: "I'm way 1-up")

If your partner's behavior isn't bothering you and you need something from them, describe clearly what, how, and when. For instance, compare . . .

"Jean, I need you to vacuum the living room by 5:30 tonight, including under the end tables and behind the aquarium. OK?" with . . .

"Hey! Clean up the front room later, Jean."

For important needs, get clear acknowledgment from your partner that _ they understand you, and _ are willing and _ able to comply. Option: ask for a hearing check.

Steps 6–8) Listen Empathically and Re-assert

Expecting resistance and responding this way is the key to effective assertions. My experience is that when the idea is presented to people, most say, *"Yeah, makes sense,"* yet few *do* it before studying these skills. If that's true for you, I hope you don't beat yourself up. You have *lots* of company!

Remember the last time someone asserted something that you didn't want to hear? How did you feel and react? Did you resist by arguing, questioning, attacking, changing the subject, pretending, and/or withdrawing? These are normal (instinctive) responses, specially if your false self is in the driver's seat. So you can help you and your partners by growing the empathic attitude that resistance to assertion is *normal*, not *wrong, childish, wimpy, weak, irresponsible,* or *bad.* How does your inner team (specially your *Inner Critic*) react to that idea?

When you _ *expect* your partner to resist and _ feel confident in your empathic listening skill, your E-level will probably stay down. If you paraphrase their resistance *respectfully*, your partner will usually acknowledge your response like *"Yeah,"* or *"You got that right," "Uh huh,"* and/or a nod. Because empathic listening doesn't mean you *agree*, you're free now to re-assert, unless you got new information that changes your needs. After you re-assert, calmly expect your partner to resist again. Keep patiently listening and re-asserting until you . . .

. . . get a credible agreement (success), or . . .

. . . get a solid refusal or postponement (a new problem), or . . .

. . . get new information that changes your needs and communication goals, or you . . .

. . . run out of time or get distracted.

 # Reality check: Pause and recall the last time you asserted your needs to an adult or child. What was your surface need? What did your assertion sound like? Did you have an =/= attitude? What did your partner need then? Did s/he resist? How did you respond to the resistance? What happened? If you were to try an empathic listening statement, what would it sound like?

In my experience, people who aren't aware of these nine steps and seven skills usually get into a power struggle here. Person A has a need, and asserts, often with an implied "I'm 1-up" voice tone or body language. Person B feels disrespected and attacked, and denies, argues, counterattacks, or changes the subject. Person A gives a *you* (blaming) message, and B fights back. Unaware couples can spend hours battling about who is *right* (vs. filling true needs) with increasing frustration and escalating E-levels. This is a guaranteed lose-lose sequence.

The last step for important and practice assertions is to . . .

Step 9) Note the Outcome

Reflect: what's your definition of an *effective* or *successful* assertion? Mine is: a communication exchange which ends with each person feeling they _ got their main *true* needs met well enough, _ in a way that they both feel _ preserved or improved their mutual respects and _ their relationship.

Until they're communication students, most people won't have a clear assertion-success criterion. Can you recall anyone you know discussing how *effective* an assertion was? The rationale for this ninth step is obvious: if you don't evaluate how you did, you'll not affirm the benefits of this skill, or spot ways to improve. The wry observation of therapists Steve and Carol Lankton applies here:

"If you always do what you've always done . . .
You'll always get what you've always got."

Now let's get a flavor of what this skill sounds like.

Assertion in Action: Examples

You're in a movie, and someone near you keeps talking loudly to their seatmate. You feel irritated, decide to assert, and do a silent inner-family and attitude check. You acknowledge the other persons' rights to communicate and to see the movie, and your right to not be distracted by them (=/= attitude). Assertion has worked for you before, so you feel confident enough in it and your skill at it.

You decide you want the other people to either stop talking, or change seats. If they won't, or if they make too big a conflict, you'll move to another seat. *Expecting resistance*, you quietly and briefly assert to the talkers:

"Excuse me. It's hard for me to enjoy the show (effect on you) *when you both keep talking* (specific behavior). *I'd appreciate it if you'd wait 'til the show's over."*

They may apologize and/or stop talking (you get your needs met, and thank them), or they may get defensive or aggressive, like (belligerently): *"If you don't like it, find another seat. We paid our money, just like you!"* (What's the R-message here?)

You're not surprised or offended by this resistance, which lets you avoid a win-lose power struggle. *Awareness* discloses two main choices: repeat your request or demand, or do respectful empathic listening. That would sound like (calmly):

"You feel you've a right to talk here." (This doesn't mean you agree!)

If their response is *"Yeah!"*, then firmly restate your request:

"And I (and my partner) have a right to watch without distraction. Please talk later, or move."

They could comply, or become more combative, like (loudly) . . .

"And YOU'RE disturbing everyone else around here, big-mouth, so practice what you preach!" (Either more resistance or a refusal).

Decide if it's important enough to you to continue listening and re-asserting, or if it would be better to let go, move, and enjoy the show without guilt or shame.

You can't control the other person's responses, but you can *affect* them by your choices of attitude and language. Consider the example above with one change: you state your request sarcastically. Your voice tone and body language might be decoded as:

"I see you as inconsiderate jerks, and my needs are more important than yours (I'm 1-up)."

The odds for angry refusal would surely rise, and you'd be distracted from the show both by moving and your own irritation.

A third possibility: the same situation, but you skip the attitude checks. Your tone of voice is apologetic. A scared or protective subself gives you this thought/feeling . . .

"My needs aren't that important, and I shouldn't cause trouble. They probably won't agree, anyway."

The talkers will probably sense that you expect or will tolerate a refusal, and will give it to you.

This is an example of an unexpected incident. Assertion skill is also useful in . . .

Preventing Problems

Imagine that you're expecting to be picked up for a dinner party by a friend who's often late. You know the hosts value timeliness, and you want to respect that. Here you have more time to do attitude checks, and to plan how and when to assert. You choose to call your friend in the morning, and say something like:

"Barb, the Masons are really bothered by people coming late to their home. It's important to me that you pick me up no later than 5:45 tonight. Can I count on that?"

Notice: no apologetic qualifications (*"I don't want to hurt your feelings, but . . ."*), and no beating around the bush (*"Hey, uh, no big deal, but I kinda wanted to ask you if you'd mind considering . . ."*).

You could get either *"Sure, no problem!"* here, or some expected defensiveness like (irritably) *"You don't trust me?"* or *"Well, it's really hard to predict the traffic between my house and yours . . ."*

You can reassert, or use empathic listening first. Your need is to get a clear commitment from Barb that she'll be prompt. You're clear that a compromise is *not* OK here, so you're making a demand, not a request.

If she is on time, you may give assertive thanks, like this: *"Hi, Barb! I'm really grateful that you're here at 5:40* (specific behavior). *Now I don't have to walk into the Mason's house feeling anxious and guilty, and I can enjoy being there with you!"* (specific benefit).

Asserting Praise

This last example illustrates the third satisfying way you can use your assertion skill: to declare appreciation for someone in a way that they can't deflect, discount, or "wiggle out of." Have you ever had that experience? How do you feel when you need to compliment someone, and they discount you, using something like these dodges:

"Oh I was just lucky"
"Anyone could have done it."
"It was no big deal."
"(someone else) should really get the credit."
"I don't take compliments very well."
"Yeah, but (some mistake or shortcoming)."

(Embarrassed silence or a mumble, with no eye contact.

If you take a moment and use the "I"-message format to frame your assertion, and if it's genuine (=/=) vs. polite, dutiful, or manipulative, you'll have a much better chance of delivering your praise in a way your partner can't avoid. The format is:

Factually describe something your partner did that could be recorded on tape; and . . .

. . . **describe** the specific benefit on your or someone else's life realistically, not gushily or with exaggerations and theatrics; and then . . .

. . . **nonjudgmentally** *expect resistance!*

If your partner's false self uses one of the ploys above, you may accept that, or use empathic listening (*"So you feel you really don't deserve special credit here."*) When they agree, then, with good eye contact, firmly re-assert your admiration or praise. This may sound like a game, but it isn't. Most people like to praise each other because it *feels* good. Praising others usually nurtures your own self-respect, and makes it more likely the other will return the gift sometime. Win-win!

Let's use these steps and ideas to master a subject that gives many kids and adult trouble . . .

Asserting Anger Constructively

How would you rate your ability to _ feel and _ express anger constructively, on a scale of 1 (very poor) to 10 (consistently constructive)? What were the main rules about feeling and expressing anger in your childhood years? If you're co-parenting, how would the child/ren in your life answer this?

Were you taught to view anger as "negative"? Anger is a natural, primal emotion, like all others. Well expressed *by your Self*, its energy empowers you to defend yourself and/or set personal boundaries against present or future harm. The first step in asserting anger constructively is to separate *feeling* the emotion from the effects of *expressing* it. You may need a second-order change here: well-directed anger helps "put out fires," like a blasting fire hose in professional hands. Anger-energy is potentially useful, not *bad*! Note, for example, that constructive guilt-free expression of anger is a vital ingredient of healthy grieving, for infants, kids, and adults like *you*.

Do you know anyone who . . .

. . . represses ("stuffs," or numbs) their anger often? How do you feel about them? Do you sense that's healthy for them and their relationships?

. . . expresses their anger constructively?

. . . expresses their anger in a way that harms _ themselves (reduced self respect), _ the receiver/s (inner-family uproar and take-overs), and/or _ their relationship (increased distrust and disrespect)?

What makes the difference? Here are some ideas:

Constructive **expression of anger** _ raises the self-esteem of the expresser, and _ adds appropriate emphasis to the need they're asserting; _ without shaming or scaring their partner. *Destructive* (aggressive, 1-up) expression of anger usually omits the receiver from the sender's awareness bubble ("*I don't care how you feel about this!*"), and delivers a clear "*I'm 1-up!*" R-message. This can be expressed by words (swearing, name calling), voice dynamics (sarcasm, sneering, threats,) and/or non-verbals (contorted face, clenched fists, glaring, threatening posture . . .) I can't think of any instance where physical violence was a constructive way to express frustration or anger; can you?

The destructive or toxic expression of anger often causes guilt, shame, anxiety, and remorse (later) in the sender. It also increases distrust, disrespect, anxiety, defensiveness, and perhaps shame and guilt in the receiver. These often lower self-confidence and self respect, specially in insecure kids and shame-based adults. Constructively expressed anger builds relationships and intimacy, and destructive anger erodes them. Note that if you (or someone) feels anger is "negative" because you or they *lose control*. The real issues are false-self dominance, ignorance, and *unawareness*; not *anger*!

Constructive Anger: Guidelines

Some keys to raising the effectiveness of your expressing anger are . . .

1) Intentionally choose the beliefs that . . .

. . . well used, feeling and expressing anger is *not* "negative." It can *help* me and those I care about, if I'm aware and take responsibility for how I express it;

. . . as a worthy person, **I have a right to *feel* and respectfully *express*** my natural anger when I'm frustrated, hurt, or scared, *no matter what my partner believes*; and . . .

. . . with these seven skills and patient practice, **I *can* learn to express my anger** without _ my false self taking over, and/or _ unintentionally wounding my partner or _ damaging our relationship.

2) It will help me to express major anger only when my Self leads my inner family. Otherwise, I'm at risk of expressing my anger aggressively ("I'm 1-up") or timidly ("I'm 1-down").

3) It will help me to use "I"-message assertions (p. 237) in expressing my anger, with appropriate eye contact. For example . . .

"Mario, when you read the paper when I'm trying to discuss this issue with you, I feel hurt, frustrated, and angry! It feels like the paper is more important to you than I am, and I feel discounted and disrespected. I need you to (want to) put the paper down, and discuss this with me." Alert: this can be a "Be spontaneous!" paradox! (p. 425)

4) It will help me to remember that if my partner is controlled by a false self, *I am not responsible* for causing or healing that (unless s/he's your child). If her or his subselves are intimidated by my anger, I can compassionately acknowledge that, and not sacrifice my needs because of *their* problem. I need not feel anxiety, guilt, or shame, for another adult's inner wounds. I can offer encouragement to them to recover, and I am not responsible for their choice.

5) I will make "=/=" my motto. My emotions, needs, dignity, and opinions are just as valid as anyone else's, regardless of their age, gender, role, authority, religion, wealth, education, or nationality.

6) I will remind my inner crew that every other person has the same tights to express their anger *respectfully* to me. If they choose to express it disrespectfully, I may confront them on that, without undue guilt, anxiety, or shame. I can request or demand what I need from them, but cannot control their response. I am ultimately responsible for whether I tolerate destructive anger expression or not.

7) I can use awareness, metatalk, and empathic listening to work with my key partners toward improving our ability to feel and express our situational angers constructively and safely.

8) I'll remember that expressing anger may be part of healthy grieving, and try to notice when that's true. See [http://sfhelp.org/05/grief-intro.htm].

9) I can stay aware that often, anger automatically follows emotional *hurt*, *frustration*, and *overload*. I use this awareness to learn what caused the pain, and whether I need to do anything about it.

10) I can choose to help the kids in my life adapt these anger-guidelines to fit their values and personalities, over time.

11) I (my Self) can use these same constructive-anger guidelines to improve the relationships between my team of subselves.

Notice your self-talk now. Option: Star or hilight guidelines you want to change or strengthen, and consider how you'll do that, over time. From your history, imagine how protective subselves or people close to you might try to sabotage you, and how you want to respond to that.

 # Status check: see where you stand now . . .

I can now explain to another person what *effective* assertion is. (T F ?)

I'm clear on the difference between assertion and aggression. (T F ?)

I'm very satisfied with the way I assert with _ my partner, _ family members, _ friends, and _ co-workers now. (T F ?)

I believe practicing my version of the nine steps in this chapter can significantly improve the effectiveness of my assertions. (T F ?)

I'm really motivated to improve my assertion skill now. (T F ?)

I have an assertion "hero/ine" who inspires me. (T F ?)

I· _ now have a good idea of how to express anger constructively, and _ I'm motivated to improve the way I do that. (T F ?)

My Self is answering these questions. (T F ?)

Recap

Assertion **is the learned skill** of choosing to say what you think or need to someone in a way that they can hear you clearly, vs. *agree* with you. Effective assertion is based on _ a set of attitudes, and _ fluency with a set of steps with many choice points. Assertion skill is essential for effective win-win problem solving. Alternatives to asserting are submission (lose-win) and aggression (win-lose). Effective assertion requires _ *awareness* and focus on your mutual _ true needs and _ process, _ patience, _ empathic listening skill, _ confidence, *and _ genuinely equal respect for yourself and your partner/s.* When this skill works, everyone gets their main true needs met, and feels good enough about how that happened. When it doesn't work, use the other six skills to learn why, avoid blame, and correct that next time.

Effective =/= assertions can be spontaneous or planned. They can . . .

. . . **prevent** anticipated conflicts,

. . . **respond constructively** when someone's behavior hurts one or more of your subselves, or endangers someone you care about; and . . .

. . . **give "dodge-proof" praise** to an adult or child. They work equally with people and your inner-family members (subselves).

Assertions range from small to life-changing. The more important the assertion, the more valuable using all nine steps above. **The keys to assertions that *work* are** _ your Self is in charge, _ you have a clear =/= (mutual respect) attitude, _ you know and validate what you *really* need, _ you **expect resistance** *without blame*, _ you use awareness and empathic listening when you get it; and _ you're patient and confident.

Does assertion seem complex? Relax: you only need all nine steps in major situations. As the importance of your needs rise, so does the value of your feeling equal, clear, and confident in preparing and delivering an effective assertion.

Options

Before studying problem-solving skill, review the assertion-building choices below and follow those that appeal to you. Take your time!

Read the companion volume "Who's *Really* Running Your Life?" (xlibris.com) to assess whether a shame-based or fear-based false self often governs you. If so, use the "parts work" scheme and resources outlined there to reorganize and harmonize your inner family under your true Self, over time. This is probably the single most rewarding project you can invest in to raise your communication effectiveness.

Copy the summary of assertion skill (p. 391) to give you a portable reminder of the key points in this chapter.

Give a copy of this chapter or its summary to a partner who shares your interest in building your communication skills. See [http://sfhelp.org/02/assert.htm]

Keep practicing the prior five skills. Your assertion success is directly proportional to your fluency with them

Read Dr. Nathaniel Brandon's book, "The Six Pillars of Self Esteem," (1995); and "Healing the Shame that Binds you," by John Bradshaw; (1996). Though written for Adult Children of Alcoholics (ACoAs), the latter book has exercises and encouragements for anyone who was significantly shamed as a child. Shame blocks effective communication. See [..01/shame.htm]

Review the sample "Bill of Personal Rights" (p. 362). Edit it, or evolve a similar declaration of your own. Then copy and refer to it any time you doubt your right to assert. If your false self is leading, your Bill will probably generate ambivalence, hesitance, double messages, and anxiety.

Show your Bill of Rights to any kids in your life. Explain it to them, and help them apply it in conflicts and confusions. Help them understand that everyone has the same rights *and personal responsibilities.*

Use the "I"-Message worksheet at [..02/I-msg-wks.htm] to help you build the habit of using this assertion tool. Also use the worksheet to help any young people you care about learn to assert effectively.

Take several recent conflicts you were part of, and **use the communication-sequence mapping technique** in the problem-solving summary (p. 400) to learn more about how you handle general and special assertions. Extend the mapping to discern whether you and your partner each seemed to get your needs met. Try replaying the sequence using appropriate assertion steps, and see if you think the outcome would improve.

Use the assertion profile worksheet on the Web at [..02/assert-profile.htm] to grow clearer on your present style of asserting, and identify ways you can improve your effectiveness. Option: ask trusted people you know how they see you as an asserter, and any suggestions they have for improvement.

Option: ask if they want feedback from you on *their* assertion style and effectiveness.

Pick a trusted partner and ask them to practice with you. Use this: [..02/assert-practice.htm]. List the people and situations you'd like to build your assertion effectiveness with, and do so!

Pick an assertion hero/ine from the people you know: someone whose assertion style and skill you admire. Use that person as an inspiration in times you're unsure about if, when, and how to assert.

With the mind of a student, **watch other live or media characters in conflict**. Practice your awareness of how they assert (or don't), and what results they get. Record or explore on what you observe in your communication journal. Assess whether you think their Self is in charge, and what R-messages they're sending and receiving. Notice how they handle their partner's resistances.

Practice giving assertive praise to people you care about and strangers. Notice how it feels, and how the other person reacts. See if a pattern emerges. Teach your kids how to do assertive =/= praise, and praise them for doing it well. Enjoy!

Reread this chapter regularly to see if it's meaning and usefulness change. There's a *lot* to experiment with and become aware of!

Several evenings a week, review any important recent assertions and how they turned out. Note if your Self was leading, or other subselves. Option: record your observations in your communication journal. Work to keep a glass-half-full attitude, and enjoy your progress!

Look for chances to affirm and appreciate people who assert with you in mutually respectful ways, including your Self.

Coach yourself to remember: *"Progress, not Perfection."* Patience, patience . . .

Use the Serenity Prayer to keep you clear on what you can assert for (change), and what you can't (p. 495).

Reflect neutrally: are there obstacles to your developing your assertion skill? If so, what are they, and what's needed to overcome or remove them one at a time?

While these ideas are fresh in mind, record anything you want to remember or do about assertion in your communication journal.

Since you started this book, we've journeyed far. Do you recall why you began reading? The basics (Chapter 1) and the six prior mental/verbal skills (Chapters 2 through 7) now set the stage for the payoff: learning win-win problem-solving (conflict-reduction) skill. Few of my therapy clients and conflicted friends (or subselves) were taught as kids *or* adults how to do this essential relationship and life skill. I never was. Were you?

Awarenesses / Notes . . .

8) Problem Solving (conflict resolution)

K ids and adults all have daily *problems* . . .

"My husband never listens to me!"

"My stepmother is a witch!"

"My ex mate is a psychopath! She is doing everything she can to turn our kids against me."

"I need to change jobs, but I can't."

"My girlfriend is pregnant, and we're torn over what to do!"

"I just filed for bankruptcy, and my parents have disowned me."

"My daughter is flunking out of school, and she won't accept help!"

"My wife is a harping, controlling bitch. She never apologizes, admits she's wrong, or gives in!"

"I was raped when I was 14, and now I can't enjoy sex with my husband."

"My partner is a compulsive gambler, and refuses to admit it."

"My boss is an arrogant, egotistical, political weasel. I have no respect for him, but I need this job."

"My brother is talking suicide. I don't know what to do!"

As a psychotherapist, I've listened for 20 years to over 1,000 average men, women, and some kids describe anguishing personal and relationship problems like these. They sought help to fill unmet needs, because they didn't know how to do so. Some didn't *want* to know. *Not one of them* knew the seven skills in this book, or the basic relationship factors in Chapter 10. Most of them had no clue that a shortsighted, reactive false self often controlled them and the people who troubled them. Most of them were in stressful marriages or post-divorce struggles with ex mates. Many were having "stepfamily problems."

These typical people, and hundreds of students in my communication and stepfamily classes, described a rich kaleidoscope of strategies to reduce their personal discomforts which weren't working. A minority described strategies that *did* work well enough—temporarily. I'm confident that for every one of these people, there are millions of others with similar inner wounds, problems, and ignorances who don't seek help. They tough it out alone, too proud, shamed, poor, or scared to share their struggle with a counselor. Other thousands go to counselors who *are* dedicated helpers, but don't know what you're reading here.

This chapter outlines a seventh powerful mental/verbal skill: win-win problem solving. It uses all six of the other communication skills to help unravel and resolve minor to major personal and relationship "problems" like those above. When used by your true Self, this learnable skill is a *far* more effective strategy than fighting, arguing, avoiding, postponing, repressing, whining, aggressing, or withdrawing! The theme of this skill is clear and simple, yet most people can't describe it. I suspect if you were fluent in this skill, you wouldn't be reading this. If so, that's no cause for shame.

To raise your motivation and curiosity, think of several "problems" you're currently experiencing. By the end of this chapter, I hope you will see a practical new way of reducing or resolving each of them. I expect your *Cynic* or *Skeptic* Guardian subselves to deride this proposal. That's their job! Acknowledge skeptical thoughts, regain the open mind of a student, and let's start at the beginning . . .

What Are "Problems" and "Conflicts"?

If our touring space alien asked you "What is this thing you Earthlings call *problems*? And please, what is a *conflict*?" what would you say? Here, we'll say . . .

"A *problem* is anything that causes you or another person significant discomfort right now." Problems are always unfilled needs, but not always *conflicts.*

"A conflict or dispute is a dynamic situation where two subselves, or two inner families (personalities), have values, goals, perceptions, and/or needs that don't mesh or harmonize now, in someone's opinion." The former is an inner conflict, and the latter an interpersonal conflict. The Latin root of conflict means, "To strike together." An *impasse* (p. 457) is a special kind of conflict.

This chapter builds on all that you've learned about inner families, *awareness*, metatalk, clear thinking, true needs, empathic listening, and assertion. We'll add some key attitudes, and eight steps you can use selectively to assess and resolve *any* life-problem. Chapter 9 offers ideas and suggestions on using all these skills and resources to resolve *inner*personal problems. Chapter 10 offers foundation premises toward resolving "problems" and building high-nurturance relationships.

Prerequisites

To become effective at problem-solving over time, you'll need to develop _ chronic inner-family harmony, _ a set of primary beliefs and values, and _ fluency in the prior six skills. Doing these three things will surely require you to make some second-order (core attitude) changes, which some of your subselves won't believe are safe or useful. Let's explore each of these three challenges:

Inner-family Harmony

In almost 40 years' lay and professional study of relationship and communication dynamics, I've never encountered any writing or theory that builds on the *multiplicity* idea you learned in Chapter 1. If you don't _ understand and _ accept that concept, and _ apply it seriously to your life, these chapters will have little practical value for you. Meeting and harmonizing your inner family under the leadership of your Self is essential to harvest the full benefits of these seven relationship skills. The companion volume, "Who's *Really* Running Your Life?" (Xlibris, 2000), offers an experience-based framework to help you do that.

Here's a quick recap. The *multiplicity* concept says that every human personality, including yours, comes from the combined functioning a group of interrelated brain regions called (here) "subselves" or "personality parts." These parts constantly interact with each other and your glands and muscles in response to the outer environment, physiological events (like hunger), and each other. Most of this interaction is unconscious, until you choose to become *aware* of it.

Conceptually, these subselves form an *inner* family, or team. Like members of an orchestra or athletic team, individual subselves each have their own goals, roles, perceptions, values, talents, limitations, and strategies. "Thinking" can be seen as the ongoing conversations or arguments among your subselves. Many times a day, subselves conflict *within* you, causing *inner*personal problems (discomforts). Most people are only vaguely aware of this.

Premise: most (all?) major *inter*personal "problems" are three concurrent conflicts: _ inside you (your inner family), _ inside your partner, and _ between your two groups of subselves. Effective problem solving requires you to be *aware* (skill # 1) of all three. Does this make sense?

Like human groups, *inner* families range between "*very*

chaotic and conflictual" to "*very* peaceful and harmonious." They are led either by a wise subself whose innate talent is excellent leadership, the Self (capital "S"), or by one or more other subselves who are specialists, but not as inner-family leaders. Here, locally-dominant subselves other than your Self are collectively called your "false self."

Premise: your effectiveness at resolving problems within you and with other people depends on how often your Self is guiding your decisions and communications. The nature and outcome of your social problems are greatly affected by whether your respective communication partners are dominated by a false self or not. I believe most people are significantly *split* and *blended*, at least in major conflicts. Their wise Selves are disabled by distrustful false selves, and they don't know it.

 # Status check: Reflect and get clear on your current status with this *multiplicity* and inner-family concept:

I now accept these concepts and (Chapter 1) premises without any doubts or qualifications. (T F ?)

I feel _ ambivalent, doubtful, and unclear about the multiplicity and inner-family ideas now; and _ I want to study and experiment more before I make up my mind; *or* _ I'm really not motivated to learn more about these ideas now. (T F ?)

I reject some or all of these premises as absolutely untrue, and/or _ I believe they don't apply to my life. (T F ?)

There is zero chance that I'm often controlled by a short-sighted, reactive, well-meaning false self. (T F ?)

If I haven't already, I'm very motivated to _ read "Who's *Really* Running Your Life?" or _ study the Web pages at [..01/project01.htm] to verify who's controlling my relationships and daily contentment . . . (T F ?)

Notice how you feel. Who do you sense answered those questions, your Self, or someone else? How can you tell? What if it was a well-intentioned, protective false self?

Effective problem-solving starts with some . . .

Key Attitudes

We adults and our kids all base our daily decisions on current *knowledge*, and _ good-bad, right-wrong *attitudes* (values), plus _ *beliefs* about what's true and false about the world, plus _ our *expectations* about how people and events will act and turn out. Do you agree?

Your *attitudes* came from what key mentors taught you, and what experience has shown you. As life unfolds, some of your attitudes change, and new ones emerge. On an inner-family level, that shows that your individual subselves can and do change their attitudes and beliefs when they get new information.

These core attitudes are like the foundation of a building. I believe you'll need them for consistent problem-solving success. I'm not proposing that these beliefs are "better" than yours, but that they to predictably help people reduce their discomforts. Option: use this section as a checklist to identify where your inner family stands with each of these ideas. **If you don't believe these attitudes,** notice what you *do* believe:

1) awareness: I *can* grow my awareness of the factors in this book, starting with sensing whether my true Self is leading my inner family.

2) Mutual (=/=) respect: My personal dignity and human worth is no greater *and no less* than any other person I interact with. While each of us has a different set of skills, knowledge, values, and beliefs, every child and adult is a person of equal worth and dignity. My needs and my partners' needs are usually of equal importance to me, except in emergencies.

3) Personal rights: Like every other person, I have a set of rights that form the basis for my asserting my current needs. If I don't yet have a clear Bill of Personal Rights, I can commit to building and *using* one today. See p. 362 for an example.

4) Self-responsibility: I solidly accept that the ultimate responsibility for resolving the problems and conflicts inside me and with other people lies with my inner family. I can ask other people to share the responsibility, but ultimately the outcome is up to me and my Higher Power. I can request, but not demand, that others fulfill my expectations. I am not obligated to fulfill *their* expectations unless I've committed to do so. I am responsible for the outcome if I don't. I am *not* a bad or immoral person if I give ultimate responsibility to other potentially *competent* adults for filling their own needs. I can choose whose needs, and which needs, to help them fill, and others can choose to do that for me.

More basic problem-solving attitudes:

5) Realistic optimism: I firmly believe that if I commit to doing so, I (my governing subselves) can _ grow these attitudes and _ learn fluency in these skills, to better fill my own needs and other people. I can strive for an attitude of realistic optimism, vs. pessimism, cynicism, or unrealistic idealism.

6) Long-range view: I accept that harmonizing my inner family, and learning fluency in relationship and communication skills, will take *years*. I'm comfortable enough with this, and enjoy knowing that the benefits of doing this patiently will start to accrue soon, and will accelerate over time.

7) Perfection: I can't communicate *perfectly*, no matter how I try. I *can* fill my needs, and others' selected needs, well *enough* now, and over time. I choose a motto like *"Progress, not Perfection"* to guide and support me, as I learn and grow.

8) Experiential learning, and "mistakes": I understand that problem-solving fluency will only come from *trying* these skills, and learning from the results. I believe that unless they hurt or hinder other people, my "mistakes" help me learn what *not* to do. I am not a bad person because I make mistakes, and neither is anyone else. I see no value in allowing my *Inner Critic* to shame me for "failing" in these complex and challenging personal-growth quests.

9) Individuality: I can adapt these attitudes, skills, and techniques to fit who I am as a unique human in Earth's history.

I _ may or may not accept these inner-family and communication ideas as presented, or at all; and I _ can apply them in ways that make best sense to me, without guilt, shame, or anxiety. Others are free to do the same.

10) Preaching: I feel that trying to fix ("help") other adults by "showing them the light," (about their inner family and these skills) is inherently disrespectful (R-message: "I'm 1-up!"). If they *ask* me about these ideas, I can tell them as a co-equal. I _ believe there's priceless value in modeling and teaching my version of these concepts to kids in my life, over time.

11) Pacing: I grant myself solid permission to work at inner-family harmonizing, and learning these seven skills, at my own pace. I can work, pause, and rest in the way that feels best to me at any time. I also grant myself permission to *not* harmonize or learn these skills. I'm OK either way. I may change my mind at any time.

12) Your own key attitude . . .

Pause. Breathe well. Notice with interest what your subselves are "saying" now. If you wish to adjust one or more of your attitudes to enhance your communication effectiveness, which ones? Is anything in the way of your shifting your attitude? Use *awareness* and "parts work" to find out . . .

Besides key attitudes, **another prerequisite for problem-solving effectiveness** is . . .

Fluency in the Other Six Communication Skills

What are you *fluent* at? Fluency is unconscious proficiency at something, as judged by someone. You may have gained fluency in feeding yourself a relatively healthy diet every day. Fluency at a language, raising kids, or writing poetry grows from motivation, awareness, and practice. It also draws on innate skills. The seven prior chapters offer you a mosaic of concepts to help you build your awareness of *what* to practice, toward becoming fluent at resolving need conflicts. This chapter adds to the mosaic by outlining a framework for your seventh mental/verbal skill: problem solving. This skill might also be called *need filling*.

Recall the premise that **to be *effective*, communication between two subselves or two people (inner families) must result in . . .**

. . . all participants genuinely feeling that they got enough of their current *true* needs filled, . . .

. . . in a way that leaves them feeling good enough about _ themselves, _ their partner/s, and _ the processes (communication sequences) in and between them.

Problem-solving skill focuses the impacts of your other six skills to help fill your respective current needs. Here's a framework for how to problem-solve with two or more people or subselves. Contrast these steps to *arguing, avoiding,* and *fighting.* As with the nine assertion steps, you don't need all these steps in every situation.

Problem-solving Steps

The basic problem-solving process offers you many choice-points:

1) Acknowledge that you have conflicting or unfilled needs, without guilt, anxiety, or shame. Common false-self alternatives are denial (*"What problem?"*), minimizing (*"It's not that big a deal,"*), whining and complaining, (*"It·burns me up that . . ."*), and avoiding (*"I'll tackle it later"*). Which do you usually do, with challenging life problems?

2) Check to see if your Self is guiding your inner family. If *"Yes,"* go ahead. If *"No,"* or *"I'm not sure,"* invest time in identifying which of your subselves think you have a problem, and what they each need now. If you're not familiar with working with your subselves, see the companion book "Who's *Really*

Running Your Life?" When you feel some mix of *calm, centered, energized, light, focused, resilient, up, grounded, relaxed, alert, aware, serene, purposeful*, and *clear*, your true Self is probably leading your inner family of subselves.

3) If your *Self* feels you have a problem, decide how serious it is. Options range from "minor" to "crisis." For minor problems, decide when and how you want to resolve them, and move on. For "significant" needs or conflicts (in your Self's judgment) . . .

4) Decide what level and type of problem you have, because they're each solved differently:

A conflict among your *inner*-family members (Chapter 9); and/or . . .

. . . conflict with another person. If so, is your stress (need) over a . . .

. . . **communication** mismatch like "I need to vent, but you need to persuade";

. . . **an *abstract* values or preference** conflict ("I think abortion is humane and OK, and you abhor it.");

. . . a **concrete resource** conflict ("*You and I each need the car now*");

. . . **another kind** of conflict; e.g. roles (responsibilities), expectations, relationship priorities, perceptions, or something else; or . . .

. . . **a combination** of these. If so, prioritize them, and pick one to focus on.

**5) With the focal problem, _ *make* time to decide "who owns this problem: whose discomfort is it, and who's responsible for fixing it? Then _ "dig down" below your surface needs to clarify your *true* needs (p. 149). Once you're clear enough, review your options; e.g. _ do internal problem solving first, _ accept what *is*, _ get more information, _ clarify or verify something, _ assert to someone, or _ problem solve.

If your inner crew decides you need to assert or problem-solve now or later with another person, decide whether you need to *plan* before doing so. Note that so far, you haven't contacted another person. When you're ready . . .

6) To *assert* with a partner, follow some or all of the steps on p. 392. That may fill your current need, or it may lead you to . . .

7) *Problem-solve.* Select the appropriate steps from these:

Reaffirm that you're clear on _ your true need/s, and _ specifically what you want from this partner. Common initial needs are genuine _ respect, and sincere _ agreement to problem solve with you as partners, vs. opponents; or . . .

If you're definitions differ, _ **agree with your partner what "problem solving is."** (*"We're brainstorming to get your and my true needs met well enough."*) If s/he doesn't trust that you care about her or his needs equally, _ consider adding, "Rebuild trust" to your goals (needs);

Do E-level, respect, and attitude checks. If _ no one's E-level is above their ears, and _ each partner seems to feel =/= (mutually respectful) now, and _ all of you expect problem solving to probably work, then go ahead. Otherwise, _ use empathic listening to bring E-levels down, and/or make achieving _ mutual respect (=/= attitudes) and _ realistically-optimistic attitudes your first shared problem solving goal/s. Both require all six other skills; and/or . . .

. . . **Agree out loud to problem-solve** as partners, and _ use *awareness* to spot and reduce any major distractions; and/or . . .

Cooperatively, use *awareness*, empathic listening, and assertion to **explore below your or their surface needs** to find the true discomforts driving each of you (p. 149). Help each other spot slipping into 1-up or 1-down attitudes. They both mean someone has blended (lost their Self, or *center*); and/or . . .

Use empathic listening to confirm that you and your partner each clearly understand the others' real needs, and values them equally.

Agree on what type of problem you're working on together: **If it's a communication problem**, use metatalk and the other skills to focus on your inner and mutual processes, and _ identify and _ separate multiple problems. Then prioritize them, and brainstorm them one at a time. Start by assessing if your current communication *needs* match (p. 46). Then use *mapping* and the Internet resources listed in the problem-solving summary (p. 395) to help. Also see the checklist of communication blocks on p. 405.

If your clash is abstract (differing opinions, perceptions, or values, like "*I like fish; you prefer red meat,*") aim to either _ compromise, or _ agree to disagree (=/=). Trying to convert your partner to agree with you implies "*My way is better: you're 1-down.*" If your or their response to this is "*Yes but . . .*" dig down further (Chapter 4) for one or more hidden true needs.

If you disagree over a *concrete* resource, like both needing the car at the same time, seek your true needs underneath, and creatively brainstorm and pool all possible solutions, no matter how weird. Nutty ideas can lead unexpectedly to win-win outcomes. This step is not a contest. It can be fun and even hilarious, if E-levels are down and nobody feels overly 1-down or anxious.

Pick the best-fit option, and see if each of you is really satisfied enough. If not, avoid blaming yourself or another, and recheck your attitudes and expectations. Consider recycling these steps if time, energy, and patience allow.

8) If problem solving works for everyone, appreciate each other and yourself. Option: explore together *why* it worked well for you. If your process "sort of" succeeded, or didn't work, avoid criticizing. Agree on how to try it differently the next time. Recall: "*Progress, not perfection.*"

Do all these steps and options seem complex and confusing? You'll find that the more you practice them, the more natural and unconscious they become. If you identified all the steps you go through to drive your car to the grocery store, it would probably boggle your mind, yet you do it routinely, with little thought. Some of these steps take less time to do than the time it took you to read them.

These eight problem-solving steps net out to these questions:

What do I really need to reduce my current discomfort?

If I need something from another person, _ who and _ what?

What do they need now, _ in general and _ from me?

What are our options, as co-equal partners?

How do these eight problem-solving steps compare with your normal response to personal and social conflict? **Check which of these are new to you:**

_ The concepts of subselves, and true and false selves (*multiplicity*) (Chapter 1);

_ Noticing E(motion)-levels and _ R(espect)-messages (Chapter 1);

_ Using the seven skills together to fit varying E-level mixes (Chapter 1);

_ The four types of conflicts: *inner* family, communication, abstract, and concrete resource; and . . .

_ Being *aware* of all these factors and your communication choices (Chapter 2), as your and your partner's Selves negotiate to get your respective true needs met well enough.

_ Options to improve the clarity of your thinking (Chapter 3);

_ Digging down below surface needs to identify your *true* needs (Chapter 4);

_ Identifying and solving your *internal* conflicts before your interpersonal ones (Chapter 9);

These concepts offer you powerful new options toward communicating more effectively. Do you agree? Take comfort knowing that only the most complex, vital problems require all of these many awarenesses, options, and steps. The summary you just read is "industrial strength" problem solving.

Recall our core premise: your Self-led communication skills, including the way you think (*inner* communication), are probably the most powerful assets you have to fill your daily needs. Filling your physical, emotional, and spiritual needs determines how satisfied, comfortable, productive, and "happy" you are each day. If you have minor kids, they're depending on you to help them learn fluency in these life skills to become self-sufficient adults.

Reality check: recall why you decided to read this book. What did you need? Was it something general like "to communicate better," or something more specific? Now that you're almost done reviewing the basic concepts, have you found what you sought yet? If not, what are you looking for now? Which subselves are responding now?

Example: Problem Solving In Action

Here's a brief sample of problem solving at work, between Beth and Tony. They know the seven skills, and have used problem solving before with mixed success. They accept the inner-family concept, and have practiced detecting false selves at work, and empowering their true Selves. **Beth begins**:

"I am really fed up, Tony! I need something to change, now!" (General assertion)

Tony unconscious decides *"We (vs. 'I') have a significant problem, and I want to work on it now."* He senses that his Self is in charge, and he's not distracted by anything major right now. He holds comfortable eye contact with her, and says *"You're pot's really boiling, and you need something to shift."* (Empathic listening)

Beth: Nods. *"Yes!"* Her E-level comes down, as she feels acknowledged, respected, and *heard*. Notice the many options Tony didn't take: e.g. he might have complained (*"You're always upset about something."*), been silent (implied R-message: *"You're 1-down"*); unconsciously let an anxious subself blend with his Self (*"My God, Hon, what's wrong!?"*), faked interest he didn't feel *("Yeah?");* or kept his awareness bubble around himself (*"You think you got problems? Listen to what happened to me today."*) Instead, he says . . .

Tony: *"Are you in a place to try some problem solving?"*

Beth: *"Yeah. I'd like to try it."*

Tony: *"You feel your Self is running your show?"*

Beth: Pauses, breathes, and says, "Yeah, *She's here now."*

Tony: *"OK. So, what do you need?"*

Beth: *"It's about our nights. I need . . . more cooperation with dinners during the week."* (Surface need)

Tony: *"If you don't get more help, what'll happen?"*

Beth: *"Well . . . I'm just so tired most nights after work. I get irritated and short tempered if I can't get a breather when I get home. You know, I snap at you and the kids, and then I feel really guilty. It's getting to the point part of me dreads coming home. I hate that!"*

Tony: *"So you need to recharge when you get home so you don't say things you regret to me and the kids."* (Empathic listening, and true needs);

Beth: *"Yeah, Tony, that's it exactly."* (Implication: *"I feel well understood by you now."*)

In real life, reaching this clarity might take longer, with more exploration and empathic listening responses. At this point, Tony has unconsciously judged this to be a moderate problem, so he can bypass many of the nine problem-solving steps. He understands implicitly that this is not an internal problem (a conflict between Beth's subselves), a communication problem, or a concrete resources conflict. Tony senses Beth needs to lower her discomfort by *rebalancing* their time and responsibility mix. Her asking his help as a partner feels legitimate (*"This is our problem"*), rather then her dumping "a Beth problem" on him.

Tony: *"Uh, You need recharges like starting right away, huh?"* (Affirmation, and seeking information)

Beth: *"I really do! I feel at the end of my rope. I hate* *bickering at the dinner table. It's the only time we're all together, and I want it to be nice. I need you to help!"*

Tony, smiling: *"Whoa. That's a solution, not a need. Hang on to that."* (Awareness and metatalk.) At this point, typical males unconsciously assume responsibility for "fixing" their partner's problem. See "You Just Don't Understand," by Deborah Tannen.

Beth: *"OK, you're right.* (Silence). *Well, what* d'you *need?"* (Her awareness bubble encloses both of them, and she feels mutually respectful: =/=.)

Tony: *"I don't want to jump right into dinner when I get home either. I work my tail off too, you know, here and at work!"*

Beth: *"You work just as hard as I do, and you need some quiet time after you get home, too . . ."* (Genuinely empathic, vs. dutiful or intellectual, listening.)

Tony: *"Yeah. And I need to not feel guilty that you're overloaded, and not to get into hassles with the kids over eating, too."* (Assertion)

Beth: *"So you don't want to feel responsible for me . . ."* (Acknowledges a key true need)

Tony: *"Uh huh . . ."* (Feels heard and respected)

Beth: *". . . and, uh . . . you don't want the kids complaining a lot."* (More empathic listening)

Tony: *"That's it.* (Pause) *Well, let's play with this. What are our choices?"*

In the next 10 minutes, Tony and Beth brainstorm as =/= teammates. They focus on their current needs ("problems'), not on each other's traits, past history, deficits, or other stressors. They harvest these possibilities before judging them:

Start dinner half an hour later.

Pre-cook more meals.

Eat out more, within budget limits.

Hire a part-time cook—maybe a foreign exchange student.

Pay the older kids to cook.

Trade responsibilities for dinners (1 week "on," one week "off").

Simplify the menus.

See if they could start and finish work earlier.

Get Tony's bachelor uncle to cook some nights.

Eat bigger lunches.

Order out some nights.

Everyone cook for themselves.

Ask the kids for ideas.

One of them changing to part-time work.

Trade with the neighbors in cooking for both families together two nights a week. And . . .

Move closer to Tony and Beth's jobs to shorten their commutes.

Many of these ideas weren't practical enough. After some experimenting, the best solution turned out to be a combination of several less extreme options. This process of defining their respective needs, and then brainstorming options, left both people feeling heard, respected, and closer to each other. They're motivated to use problem solving again, and have modeled it for their children. They invested about 35 minutes in this process, and strengthened their marriage and their self and mutual respects.

Can you imagine you and a partner handling problems like this? What would have to change? Notice your self-talk now: is an inner voice really skeptical or negative? If so, do you want to change anything?

Ineffective Problem-solving Strategies

If two adults, or parents and kids, don't use a set of steps like those you just read, what do they do? What do *you* and your key partners usually do? My clients and others have demonstrated a rich array of alternatives.

From habit and unawareness, governing subselves select one or more of the responses below to innerpersonal and interpersonal conflicts. Until you become fluent in the learnable skill of *awareness*, your subselves' responses will probably stay largely unconscious and automatic. You'll also only be hazily aware of the outcomes, and of your communication sequences and patterns, over time.

Your and your partner's unconscious minds (false selves) are probably dominating your comfort levels and your relationship. How does that idea feel? Scan the overview of **common ineffective communication strategies** below, and add any others you know. Seen all together, our buffet of possible responses to inner-family and interpersonal conflict is pretty amazing, isn't it? Consider that we (you) never "studied" any of these, but became experts anyway!

_ **Denying** your thoughts, feelings, needs, and/or current reality to your Self and/or your communication partner

_ **Avoiding** (lying, omitting, "forgetting", and "walking out" fit here).

_ **Intellectualizing**, rationalizing, analyzing, over-explaining, and/or lecturing.

_ **Gunnysacking**, and re-living (bringing up and rehashing old unfinished issues).

_ **Minimizing** (the conflict, and/or its importance).

_ **Deferring**, not following up, and/or procrastinating.

_ **Giving in**, giving up, and/or choosing a *martyr* or *victim* mind-set.

_ **Defending** (justifying beliefs, opinions, behaviors)

_ **Never forgetting** or forgiving yourself and/or your partner.

_ **Deflecting**, distracting, and/or confusing.

_ **Numbing** or spacing out (defocusing), or silence ("clamming up").

_ **Complaining**, whining, nagging, and hinting (vs. asserting).

_ **Catastrophizing**, exaggerating, and over-dramatizing.

_ **Getting sick**, hysterical, depressed, or enraged.

_ **"Mind reading,"** assuming, second-guessing, and/or predicting.

_ **"Time-traveling"** (over-focusing on the past or the future).

_ **Threatening**, demanding (vs. requesting), intimidating, and/or bullying.

_ **Attacking**, blaming, shaming ("guilt trips"), and/or "getting even."

_ **Discounting** (minimizing) your Self and/or your partner's worth, opinions, feelings, and/or needs.

_ **Pretending**, faking, and/or disguising (like laughing when anxious or hurting).

_ **Previewing** your response, while your partner talks.

_ **Interrupting**, and/or over-talking (vs. genuine listening).

_ **Confusing** *fighting* and/or *arguing* with problem-solving.

_ **Competing**: equating "problem solving" with *winning* (being 1-up).

_ **Generalizing** (*"You always . . .; You never . . ."*).

_ **Preaching** and/or moralizing (*"You're bad / good / wrong / right / when you . . ."*)

_ **Rambling** (talking on and on with no clear point).

_ **Rehearsing** (reacting now to an event that hasn't happened yet).

_ **Psychologically blending** (disassociating): losing one's true Self, or center.

_ **Denying** responsibility for one's own part in the conflict

_ **Flooding**: venting a stream of gripes, and not pausing to let your partner respond.

_ **Dictating**, ordering, commanding, and/or threatening. All these imply *"I'm 1-up here!"*

_ **Name-calling**, swearing, yelling, and/or throwing things.

_ **Punishing**, by withholding something of value, or intentionally bringing up something painful.

_ **"Dodging"** (responsibility): using "we" or "you" instead of "I;" or saying *"I was only joking."*

_ **Avoiding** eye contact.

_ **Playing** "*Yes, but . . .*" (a covert *control* or entertainment game).

_ **Collapsing**: controlling the situation by being helpless.
Add your favorites:

What Do These Strategies Sound Like?

Here's an example of what some of these *ineffective* communication strategies sound like. A custodial biofather, **Jim, declares** in exasperation to his new (second) wife Rae: "*You're all first with me! No one comes in second! Why can't you get that, Rae!?*"

His response came after the couple had been "talking" (i.e. arguing) in their bedroom for almost 10 minutes. The "talk" began when Jim got home from work, and Rae immediately began to complain to him that his pre-teen daughter Georgia had *again* ignored Rae's requests to pick up her clothes from the living room floor. The example below omits some repetitions, and nets out their attempt to resolve their shared tensions. *Reactive false selves control both people, and neither one knows it.*

Rae: "*Why won't you ever get after her about picking up her messes? You never miss a chance to rag Nickie (Rae's biological son) about not putting his dishes in the sink—but hassle or put reasonable limits on your princess daughter? Never! Clearly, your daughter remains far more important to you than I am. I'm sick of this!*"

Communication blocks: _ generalizing; _ playing "I'm helpless;" _ sarcasm, which implies "*You're 1-down*"; _ attacking (blaming) Jim, vs. problem solving; _ not focusing on her own needs; and _ complaining. Rae starts to _ *flood* Jim with three different problems at once.

Jim: (Grimacing, sighing, not looking at his wife) *"Rae, I've had a really long day. Gimme a break, for once. We'll talk about this later."*

Blocks: _ unawareness; _ avoiding eye contact. Rae unconsciously decodes this as *"You think I'm not important now—i.e. I'm 1-down"*; _ attacking by implication; _ dictating; _ avoiding; and _deferring.

Rae (sarcastically): *"Yeah, sure. That's what you always say, Jim, only later never comes. And why am I always the one who has to bring up these problems? You don't! For you, everything's always la-la fine."*

Blocks: _ distrusting; _ discounting; _ sarcasm; _ blaming and shaming; _ attacking; _ exaggerating; _ generalizing; _ de-focusing; and _bringing up a new problem. Whew!

Jim: *"Well how come when I ask you to get Nick to turn his boom-box down after dinner, you always give me 'the look', and tell me I'm (sarcastic falsetto mimicry) 'just being too picky'? Your son has the sensitivity of a tree stump."*

Blocks: _ not listening; _ defending; _ counterattacking (sarcastically: "I'm 1-up"); and _ deflecting the focus to yet another problem.

Rae (shaking her head, snorting): *"You seem to have gotten us off the main problem again. OK, I'll try it one more time. I want you to act like a father for a change and talk to Georgia. Get her to show a little responsibility in this house by picking up her litter around here. I am getting really tired of being just the maid here, and coming in last with you, behind your job, your daughter, and Nina (Jim's ex wife)! This isn't what I signed on for, Jim. I never thought . . ."*

Blocks: _ blaming, vs. problem solving; _ not *hearing* Jim (solo awareness bubble); _ deflecting responsibility back again (see "level 2" in Chapter 3); _ assuming the Victim role in a relationship triangle (Chapter 10); _ discounting Jim's dignity and needs, via words, voice tone, and body language; _implication: *'You're* way *1-down'*; _ attacking Georgia (adding *another* problem); _ implied vague threat; _ generalizing; _ exaggerating; _ dramatizing; and _ flooding. These all happen in *less than 30 seconds.*

Jim: (glaring): *"Read my lips, Rae: You - are - ALL - first - with - me! No one comes in second! Why can't you get that!?"*
   Main blocks: _ false selves in charge, _ no awareness, and _ arguing: i.e. _ interrupting (not listening), _ not focusing, _ defending (explaining), and _ counterattacking, vs. problem-solving. Overall implications: _ *"You're* wrong," and _ *"I'm 1-up."*

Rae (Overwhelmed and frustrated, she shakes her head, and sighs loudly): *"Oh, I give up! I can never get through to you."* She turns angrily and walks out of the bedroom.
   Blocks: _ blaming; _ generalizing; _ complaining; _ giving up (overwhelmed); and _ unawareness of _ her false self and _ his, and _ their communication process.

Jim: looks after her, and shakes his head in irritation, weariness, anxiety, and frustration.
   Blocks: _ avoiding; _ giving up (overwhelmed too); _ silent blaming; and _ denial.

This communication sequence took less than five minutes. It raised Jim and Rae's frustrations and resentments, and lowered their respect and trust in their shared ability to solve family (relationship) problems, and their intimacy and partnership. **Both people were controlled by reactive false selves, and were totally unaware** of their communication blocks and options.

Notice what you're thinking and feeling now. Anything sound familiar here? This is a classic stepfamily loyalty conflict, where the bioparent feels in caught the middle of a frustrating, impossible lose-lose situation, and the stepparent feels painfully second best (i.e. disrespected and unimportant), and guilty for "forcing" her mate to choose. Did you identify with Rae and/ or Jim here, or neither? Why? Did either of these good people get their *true* needs met?

Though this bit of typical (lose-lose) co-parenting dialog is brief, it illustrates a lot:

Neither mate was aware of the process inside or between them.

Neither identified what they really needed, or stuck to it, though Rae tried.

Neither false self really tried to *hear* the other person non-judgmentally, as an =/= (mutually respected) partner. One result was that their E-levels stayed well "above their ears."

Neither Jim nor Rae thought to change their focus to *how* they were trying to problem-solve. As they each felt increasingly un-heard and frustrated, they got more and more tangled in a growing knot of unmet needs ("problems").

During the exchange, **neither mate felt respected** by the other: they each decoded "1-down" R(espect) messages from the other. Thus, their communication process *added* to their unmet true needs, vs. reducing them.

Each mate unconsciously **used many ineffective resolution strategies** to re-create a predictable communication sequence, including it's lose-lose outcomes:

Neither dug down to identify and assert their true needs, so they didn't get met.

They **diminished their mutual trust** that "talking" together (on this loyalty-conflict issue) would "work." Their expectations of "communicating well about the kids" dropped, so the next time they try, they'll expect it won't work. That rapidly becomes self-fulfilling, with unaware, unskilled co-parents and co-workers . . .

Jim and Rae both unconsciously **added this incident to their respective "gunnysacks"** of "unfinished re/marital business" (old hurts and resentments).

They each repressed their angry frustration, which "leaked out" later in their relations with Nickie and Georgia, adding to their kids' unspoken stepfamily anxieties. And finally . . .

Rae and Jim's re/marital relationship received another "wound."

As such wounds accumulate, hope, respect, trust, compassion, and intimacy wither. That promotes emotional or legal re/divorce. This also applies to conflicted parents and kids, friends, neighbors, and co-workers. Does this seem reasonable to you? Do you know people who have experienced this erosion?

From ignorance, unawareness, psychological wounds, and unconscious habits, this normal stepfamily couple each tended to find fault with their partner, rather than agreeing *"Let's do some win-win problem-solving together soon, when we're both up for it."* Both these good people are moderately shame-based, so their dominant subselves perceive feedback (information) as *criticism*. Their false selves reflexively defend and counter-blame, rather then saying objectively *"How can we make this better together as partners?"*

As their process unfolded, each became more focused on their own feelings and needs. their awareness bubbles shrank and excluded each other, and they weren't aware of that. Also notice the compounding effect: each partner created a group of communication blocks, which provoked more blocks from the other. The accumulated effect of all these blocks overwhelmed Rea (i.e. her inner family), so she had to withdraw or "lose it."

Are you wondering *"What would this have sounded like if they did problem-solve effectively?"* Let's take a look . . .

Replay, Using the Seven Skills

Jim comes home from work, tired, and goes to their bedroom to change clothes. Rae joins him there, greatly frustrated about her stepdaughter's messing up the bathroom and ignoring Rae *again*. In this example, both mates have worked for months to help each other become aware of _ their inner families, _ stepfamily loyalty conflicts, and _ their conflict-resolution style. They're now used to switching between *what* is bugging one or both of them (the topic), and using awareness, digging down, and metatalk together to identify their true inner and mutual needs. Neither co-parent did these before their remarriage, nor did their ex mates or any of their parents.

Rae: *"You look beat, Hon"* (=/=, empathic acknowledgement.)

Jim: nods and snorts, *"Yeah. They seem to have put more hours in this day than usual. I am tired! How're you?"* (He feels acknowledged, and gives genuinely concerned, =/= feedback. The partners include each other in their awareness bubbles.)

Rae: grimaces, and says with humorous sarcasm: *"Well, brace your Self, dear. I'm really upset* again. *It's replay 118 of our favorite stepfamily loyalty conflict, starring us and Georgia."* (Rae vents, and returns an "=/=" message. Her Self is in charge, and her empathic humor helps both of them from overreacting. If Rae had said with cutting sarcasm "starring . . . your *daughter*," or ". . . my *wonderful* stepdaughter," Jim probably would have immediately felt attacked and defensive.)

Jim: rolls his eyes, and groans wearily. *"Aaggh! Rae. What now?"* He listens with genuine concern, despite weariness and a little apprehension. Implied =/= message to Rae: *"Your feelings are truly important to me right now, and my Self is in charge of my inner crew."*

Rae: *"I really need to talk with you about it, Jim. Are you up for that now, or do you need some time to unwind?"* She's aware of their options and his needs (=/=). She is willing to wait (vs. aggressing, or giving in or up), based on her experience-based trust that Jim will willingly focus with her on their loyalty conflict when he feels less distracted by work issues and weariness.

Jim is silent for a moment. *"Thanks, Rae. I think I'd be a better player if I took a breather before we talk. How 'bout we take a walk after dinner, maybe over to the park?"* Guilt-free self-care in action, based on self respect, and trust that Rae is genuinely willing to defer her need to talk, out of respect for his needs. He also trusts that if she can't wait, she'll say so now.

Also, Jim gives a credible reassurance by proposing a specific (kid-free) time, rather than a vague *"Let's talk about it later, OK?"* The implication she decoded is, *"I will work with you on this tonight."*

Rae nods thoughtfully, unsmiling. *"OK, Hon, that works for me. But I really need something to change here, Jim!"* She flexes co-operatively on filling her need for immediate discussion, and re-asserts her general needs to vent and get action.

Jim looks into her eyes, and nods. *"Yeah, well . . . let's take another swing at it after dinner. Do you need some help with feeding the tribe now?"* He makes a non-defensive acknowledgment, and shifts clearly to other present co-parenting needs, with light humor.

Rae nods, and sighs. *"Yeah, I do. That'd be nice."* She moves close and they hug wordlessly for a moment, exchanging mutual non-verbal affirmation and support as teammates, not opponents. (Nice, huh?)

After dinner and clean up, Rae and Jim see that the kids are into their homework. They tell Nick and Georgia they're going to walk their spaniel Raquel to the park. Jim adds, *"We're working on another loyalty conflict, guys, so stay tuned. We're probably gonna need your help. We'll be back in about 30 minutes or so."*

The couple firmly deflects questions from the kids about this and other issues. Their kids know what a loyalty conflict is, from prior talks. The couple models co-parenting teamwork and remarital priority. Their eye contact, light tone, and simple informative statement demonstrate:

Respect for the kids' needs to know what's going on, and to feel included: an =/= adult-child attitude;

. . . **staying focused** on "adult stuff," rather than defocusing on kid's needs; and . . .

. . . **demonstrating** to the kids that their remarriage is a mutual high priority now. That's reassuring to the kids, whose biofamilies broke up.

They leave, Raquel pulling eagerly on her leash. After walking in silence, **Jim** says: *"OK, Lady R. What's up . . . or down?"* He invites problem solving (indirectly), and makes good on his promise to work with Rae tonight. He doesn't pre-judge, and genuinely wants to *listen.*

Rae sighs, reviewing her day. *"You can guess. I am really ticked with Georgia again. She left her towel on the bathroom floor, her breakfast dishes all over the kitchen, and after school she managed to deposit half her wardrobe all over the living room. Nickie sees her doing this, and I . . ."* She vents, factually (vs. dramatically) reporting the source of her present frustration. Then she starts to dramatize, exaggerate, and de-focus.

Jim raises his free hand. *"Whoa, whoa! I think you're bringing up a second problem. Sounds like you're real frustrated again that Georgia messed up our house, and you need something from me about that."* He looks at Rae's profile, as the streetlights come on. [Strengths: awareness, and staying focused on one issue. He uses empathic (=/=) listening by restating objectively what he hears, and what's *implied* about Rae's current surface need.]

Rae (wearily): *"Thanks, Jim. I was starting to confuse our issue. My inner crew is so worked up about this! And yes, I do need something from you about Georgia. We've struggled with this so often, Honey, I'm feeling really discouraged."* Rae owns her own process and feelings, affirms she needs something from her partner, and vents a main emotion as a teammate, not an opponent. Because her Self is leading, she factually owns her current surface need and feelings, vs. denying and/or attacking Jim, his daughter, or his ex mate.

Jim: *"You're weary of this old hassle, Rae, and you don't see a good way out, for now . . ."* More patient, respectful empathic listening. Implied message: *"I understand, value, and accept your feelings and needs here, Rae, and I don't feel attacked."*

Rae nods, looking away. She feels respected and heard by her husband, vs. agreed with.

Jim: *"So let's problem-solve, OK?"* Rae nods again. *"Can you say what you need from me, here?"* He invites their shared resolution process, and consciously avoids an instinctive male response to take responsibility for fixing "her problem" immediately. Had he done so, the implication would have been *"I believe you can't solve this, and I can and should, so I'm 1-up."*

Rae: *"I'll try. It's hard, Jim. There seems to be so many pieces to this . . . Uh, I need . . . to find some way of motivating Georgia to respect my need for order and neatness in my home space. As her stepmom, I don't feel right imposing a lot of consequences on her yet. It's so different with Nickie . . ."* Rae uses "I need" (ownership) vs. *"you* need . . .", which is 1-up mind-reading and dictating. She struggles to get clear on her surface need ("order and neatness in my home . . ."); and begins to describe two other problems: co-parent role confusion, and feeling powerless . . .

Jim nods, having heard versions of this before. They pause, while Raquel explores a bush. *"So basically, Hon, you're feeling disrespected and ignored again by my daughter; and, um . . . real frustrated, and powerless . . . because you're not Georgia's Biomom."*

He consciously uses *awareness* to avoid _ getting de-focused on the two new problems, and _ acting on his instinctive urges to defend Georgia and himself, blame Rae, and start offering explanations and/or solutions. He empathically (=/=) estimates Rae's true needs, which are to feel *"I have some power and choices here, and that I don't have to be a victim in my family and my home."*

Rae looks at Jim, and nods. *"Yeah, Hon, that's good. That feels real close."* Her E-level falls below her ears, because she feels clearly heard and accepted by (i.e. respected, and important to) her husband. Her voice is softer and less intense, which relieves some of Jim's anxious subselves.

Jim (genuinely interested): *"So is there more?"* He again intentionally defers his growing need to vent his side, because from prior experience, he trusts Rae to listen to him soon.

Rae: *"Well, yes. Yes there is! Jim, it really bothers me that you don't get as upset as I do about this. I feel like the Queen Grinch all the time. Another part of the problem is that when Georgia's with her Mom, anything goes. There are no rules! I mean Georgia's being taught that it's perfectly normal to hang your underwear from the ceiling light, and leave a can of peaches to rot on the kitchen counter. I dread every time Georgia gets ready to visit . . ."*

She feels heard, safe, and respected, and stays focused on describing her surface needs vs. defending or attacking Jim. Then her emotions rise, her awareness bubble shrinks to enclose only her, and Rae's false self takes over. Several passionate (needy) subselves begin to _ gunnysack, (bring up a cluster of related unresolved problems, without focusing); _ flood (non-stop self-focused venting); _ blame; and _ complain about Georgia's biomom Nina.

Jim's voice gets firm. *"Rae, stop. Slow down! It feels like we've got about four problems on deck, now, and the list is growing. Let's go back to what you need from me about Georgia's not respecting you, OK?"* He asserts as a co-equal teammate; confronts (asserts) Rae's "flooding" respectfully; and refocuses them both, without shaming her.

Rae clutches her head and shakes it, laughing. *"Awright, awright, Dr. Freud. I was getting a little carried away there. But those other problems are real, too, Jim. I need some problem-solving with you on Georgia's visitations, and on me feeling more and more like the wicked witch of the West, too. And, uh, also on my worry that Nickie's picking up bad habits from Georgia and her Mom."*

She non-defensively acknowledges Jim's invitation to focus and continue, and restates three other problems. Rae re-asserts their significance to her too, and defers, not giving in.

Jim crouches and talks to their spaniel, who looks startled.

"Well, girl, I hope you're in shape. Looks like we're gonna be taking a lot of walks together . . ." His humor re-grounds them both, and implies *"I'm OK with you and this complex problem now."*

Rae smiles, and strokes Jim's shoulder. *"I am so glad you're willing to listen to me about all this stuff, Hon. It makes it a lot easier for me. When we talk, I don't feel so . . . alone."* Their eyes meet for a long moment. *"Do you think there's some way out of all this?"* Spontaneous, loving affirmation, from Rae's heart. Jim's problem-solving patience and motivation are acknowledged and nourished. This is verbal and non-verbal intimacy, strengthening their mutual feeling of partnership.

Jim: *"I dunno, Babe. But if not, it sure won't be for lack of us trying! It's . . . hard for me, too. Uh, are you in a place to hear my reactions, or d'you need to spew some more?"* Strengths: remarital commitment, =/= communication-process awareness, patience, and co-leading their resolution process. Jim starts to assert his feelings and needs, testing Rae's current "done-ness" with awareness and metatalk.

Rae: *"Well, I feel pretty well heard, for now, Jim. I want to know what you need, now. About Georgia's ignoring me. Uh, no; I mean about my feeling ignored by her."* She grinned. She implies this is a shared "we" problem, and takes responsibility for her part, vs. blaming Jim and/or her stepdaughter.

Jim: *"I feel a lot of stuff, Rae . . . Frustration that we haven't found a way through this yet, and sympathy for you. I know Georgia can be pretty self-centered at times. But she's just a normal kid, and a good one! Any teeny-bopper's going to leave a litter trail, you know? I mean last Tuesday, Nickie . . ."*

He consciously avoids blaming, counterattacking, and defending; empathizes with Rae's feelings; and begins to defend his daughter and "normalize" (even out) Rae's reaction to Georgia by starting to focus on "equal" littering by Rae's son. This is defocusing, and starting to bring in a new "problem."

Rae snorts. *"Hey, Jim, now you're bringing in another issue. Stay on track, OK? I feel your main points just now were that you're frustrated with our loyalty conflict, too, and you feel Georgia's a normal, good, pre-teen kid."* Communication strengths: _ =/= assertion; _ guiding the resolution process by refocusing; and _ empathic listening: restating Jim's point concisely, without rebuttal or comment.

So far, this couple has just begun to get mutually clear on what Rae's *true* (vs. surface) needs are . . .

_ **to feel** respected by stepdaughter Georgia, husband Jim, and herself;

_ **to feel** she has some power and control in her own home and life, vs. feeling helpless,

_ **to protect** her remarriage (protect her and her son's securities, and avoid old-age aloneness), and . . .

_ **to evolve** some credible plan of action with her partner, with hope of getting her other three needs met "soon enough."

The couple has just started on the next step: getting mutually clear on what *Jim's* true needs are.

Notice your reactions to all this: anything like . . .

"This seems like a lot of work!"

"These steps are too complicated."

"This is a farce: couples just don't talk like this!" (Yep. Why?)

"We sure don't sound like this!"

"We could never do this . . ."

"The example doesn't bring in what the girl's biofather wants." *(True, for brevity's sake.)*

If your inner chatter sounds anything like this, ask yourself "what would have to happen for me to start thinking like . . .

"We can learn to do our version of this problem-solving process, over time."

"Our kids are depending on us to develop an effective way of resolving conflicts, and we can!"

"I want to learn how to resolve our family conflicts better, and I'm willing to experiment and change some."

"Effective (win-win-win) problem solving really begins with our basic attitudes and expectations!"

Let's continue, to see where Rae and Jim's resolution-process takes them . . .

Jim: *"Thanks, Rae. I was starting to defocus."* He sits quietly for some moments, trying to get clearer on what he needs. He hears Rae non-defensively, and affirms her. The man takes genuine (vs. strategic) responsibility for his behavior, and authorizes himself to take time to clarify.

"Well, first of all, I want you and Georgia to be happy. So I need to work out a compromise here with you and her so that we all feel OK enough. And, uh . . . I need to find a way to stop resenting you both when I feel stuck in between you two." Jim articulates a fundamental surface need, and a generic solution. Then he takes responsibility for a second problem, and avoids a blameful "you" message: *"I feel stuck,"* vs. *"When you two stick me in the middle."*

Jim continues: *"You need Georgia to take more responsibility about . . . No. You need Georgia to respect your need for order in our home."* **Rae** nods. He says *"I'm used to her messes, so they don't really bother me as much as they do you. I grew up in a messy house, and so has she."* He refocuses himself, restates his perception of what Rae needs, and clearly states a values conflict between him and Rae *non-defensively*.

Jim pauses thoughtfully again. *"I think my biggest need now is for more info. I need the three of us talk together soon about this lousy loyalty conflict. I'd like to be with you when you tell Georgie what you need, and have us both learn what she needs. Then I think we'll all be in a better place to all try for a win-win compromise."*

A plane drones by overhead, and a cool breeze stirs the park foliage around them. Rae's husband defines a current *true* need; and proposes a trial solution, honestly expressing his frustration and weariness. He acknowledges that Georgia has needs, and proposes respecting them, too (=/=). Jim uses *awareness* to consciously avoid making a black/white demand of his daughter to please his wife, or punishing his daughter for being "disrespectful."

Rae: "*Mm. I wouldn't have thought of that, Hon. I'm feeling so hurt and frustrated, all I could think of was getting even, or having you side with me and really landing on her hard to get through to her*!" She acknowledges her self-focus (awareness bubble excluding Georgia), without guilt or shame (Self affirmation); and implies _ affirmation of Jim's need for information and compromise, and _ openness to his trial solution.

Both: "*So when should we meet?*" They chuckle and smile at each other in the dark. Raquel yawns, lifts her head, and stares at her people, ears alert. The couple is focused on action, thinking and speaking like =/= teammates, vs. opponents. They each feel clear enough, and heard well enough, and exchange non-verbal appreciation, affection, and affirmation.

Jim: "*One option is to include Georgie on that decision. We can tell her tonight that we need another three-way, because we have a loyalty conflict to fix . . .*" Rae chortles sarcastically "*She'll be thrilled*!" He grimaces. "*Yeah, really.*" Jim starts to brainstorm a concrete group problem (picking a mutually-good time to meet). They've all done this before. Rae's resentment is still alive and well, and though empathic, Jim consciously chooses to not feel responsible for it.

Rae: "*So, what if she says she won't?*" She starts planning for a potential problem; and invites Jim to strategize with her. This promotes both of them feeling calm, prepared, and centered in making a conflictual assertion.

Jim: "*I think we should tell her we need her help, which is true! If that doesn't work, I'll have to pull rank and make it a demand.*" He _ proposes an =/= assertion as a couple, with a less desirable backup plan; and _ supports Rae by taking responsibility for his daughter's attendance.

Rae: "*Yeah, I agree.*" She brushes a wisp of hair from her eyes. *"Then I guess I should use an 'I' message about . . . uh . . . how her leaving the towel on the floor, and dishes not rinsed makes me really angry."* The stepmom begins to draft her part in their three-way meeting, and uses awareness and metatalk to propose her communication action.

Jim: *"Would it fit OK to say those things make you resentful? I worry that 'angry' would hook her defensiveness, her E-level would go outa sight, and her hearing'd turn off."*

Rae nods. *"Yeah, that'd be better."* Both take their time as co-parenting partners, and seek the best way to achieve a win-win-win compromise. They focus on their unmet needs and their resolution (communication) process, not on attacking the girl, each other, or themselves.

Rae: *"By the way, I think we need to explain to Nickie that this loyalty conflict really doesn't involve him. You don't need him at this meeting, right?"* She honors both Jim's and her son's needs, and tests another family option: whether her son's presence would hinder or help their resolution meeting.

Jim: *"No. I think you're right, Hon. He'd probably distract Georgie by getting a giant smug attack."* Rae grimaces and smiles. *"So let's get back to the 'I' message. How will you say what you want from her?"* Rae feels heard and affectionately affirmed as an equal partner. He refocuses on their shared resolution process, and leaves Rae responsible for stating her need to Georgia.

Rae: *"OK, I say . . . 'Georgia, when you leave your wet towel on the floor, and the washcloth on the sink, I feel that our bathroom's a mess. I don't like that, so I feel I have to pick up after you, or nag you. Either way, I start to resent you. I don't like that, either. I want to find a way to solve this with you without it turning into Desert Storm II."*

Rae looks at Jim. *"How's that sound?"* She shows her experience at assertion by _ picking one incident at a time, and _ factually describing both _ Georgia's behavior, and _ how it affects her (Rae). She doesn't plan to force a solution on Georgia, blame her, or punish her. Instead, she visions inviting the girl to brainstorm some (unknown) solution with her, trying to respect her stepdaughter's needs equally (an =/= attitude).

Jim puts his arm around his wife and hugs her. *"I like how that feels: like respectful of her and you together. How'd I get so lucky, eh?"* Rae feels acknowledged, competent, and loved. Her husband avoids becoming the "fixer," and implies he'll support Rae's lead here.

Rae: *"We're not done yet. If Georgia does her normal 'I don't know . . .' or 'well, I don't have any ideas' numbers, I can't brainstorm with a non-partner . . ."* Again, using history and a little sarcasm, Rae forecasts possible paths their meeting might take, and invites brainstorming.

Jim: *"OK. Two things: first, that's when we use empathic listening, and then you repeat your I-message"* (metatalk). Rae nods. *"Then if she doesn't pitch in, I'll say I also need her to be considerate of the three of us in picking up after herself. Maybe we need a hamper in the corner . . ."* He proposes using two of the seven communication skills (empathic listening and assertion) if Georgia resists Rae as they both expect. Jim affirms his support for his wife, and jumps ahead in the resolution process, seeking a solution that would work for everyone.

Rae: *"And who's job would it be to empty this hamper so we don't get mildewy?"* She begins to lose focus and forecast a different problem.

Jim: *"Whoa, Hon. One thing at a time, OK? I guess I'm jumping the gun, too."* He looks at his watch. *"Let's stick to just planning our loyalty-conflict meeting. It's getting late."* He refocuses, owns his own responsibility, and avoids trying to predict or control the meeting's outcome. He also begins to shift to fill unspoken surface needs: *"Let's see that the kids are OK, and have done their homework."*

Rae: *"How time flies, huh? You know, I feel pretty weary now, Jim. I don't think we should talk to Georgia tonight. If she is willing to problem-solve, I'd rather be more alert. How 'bout* *we ask her now to meet with us right after dinner tomorrow?"* She factually acknowledges her distraction, (weariness), and proposes a specific alternate time (vs. "let's meet soon") when their meeting has a better chance of succeeding. Rae indirectly re-asserts her need for a clear plan (lowering her true anxiety: fear of conflict); and respectfully suggests a specific alternative, rather than dictating or imposing one.

Jim: *"Good call. Oh, but Rae, I think she has Drama Club after dinner tomorrow."* He joins her in trying to pick a suitable time for all three of them.

For brevity, we'll stop observing Jim and Rae's process here. **Here are some key points** about their conflict resolution process:

Unlike the first example, each of these partners appeared to be guided by their true Selves.

Each acted as an =/= teammate, and neither of them put themselves 1-down.

Each *affirmed* (respected) the other, and helped them to identify and stay focused on, one problem at a time.

The couple acknowledged and respected their kids' needs, as well as their own.

They implicitly agreed to stay focused on the present, vs. dredging up past gripes or forecasting future ones.

They knew and *used* the seven mental/verbal communication skills. Their shared awarenesses and =/= attitudes helped them avoid many of the clusters of communication blocks the "unaware" Jim and Rae got snarled in (p. 273).

The mates chose to invest a lot of non-distracted couple time to work together toward a win-win resolution of their stepfamily loyalty conflict. Not dedicating a block of time like this for relatively modest problem is a widespread communication blocker. This couple's doing so implies the high priority they each give to their self-respects and their marital and family harmony.

The couple verbally and non-verbally affirmed and

confronted each other dynamically, as they worked toward clarity and resolution.

They planned for some possible "what if" scenarios together, to raise their confidences; and . . .

The couple acknowledged each other's needs as equally important. Rae's surface need is keeping their bathroom neat. Her *true* needs beneath that are to feel _ *respected* by her Self, her stepdaughter, and her husband; _ *heard* and supported by her husband; and _ in charge of her own life and home. Rae also needs to _ guard against her son's feeling ignored and unimportant, and _ to reassure him clearly this loyalty conflict doesn't involve him (so far).

Jim's *surface* need is to "fix" the conflict between his wife and his daughter, without damaging any of their three relationships. His underlying true needs include _ keeping his Self respect, partially by asserting his own needs and boundaries in this situation; _ reducing his anxiety and some misplaced guilt about this loyalty conflict; and _ staying balanced and grounded; i.e. working on it with other current personal, stepfamily, and work goals and tensions in mind.

Notice that each partner here has a group of current true needs, not just one. Effective communication works toward acknowledging and filling each of the needs "well enough."

Re-read the first Rae and Jim example now, to increase your awareness of the differences between ineffective and effective problem solving. Review the eight problem-solving steps, and identify if and when each step appeared in the second example. Note that we didn't go far enough to see if everyone (including Georgia and Nickie) got their core needs met.

The basic relationship skill of *awareness*, plus knowledge of communication basics, allows us to evaluate *how* this couple was talking. If these observations had been spoken, they would be metatalk. What could you learn if you and a partner tried out non-judgmentally assessing a recent conflict-process between you in the same way? A more thorough way of assessing communication processes is using sequence *mapping* (p. 400).

Recap

This chapter defines a *problem* or a *conflict* as unmet or opposed *needs*: emotional, physical and/or spiritual discomforts. A core premise is that needs, problems, and conflicts are natural and inevitable, not *bad.* The chapter outlines and illustrates the seventh mental/verbal skill you can choose to develop to get more of your daily needs met: win-win problem solving. It illustrates typical communication blocks, and all seven skills at work, in an average interpersonal situation. The next chapter illustrates how problem-solving can work among members of your *inner* family.

Your problem-solving success is directly proportional to _ who's leading your inner family, _ your confidence in, and fluency with, all seven mental/verbal skills; and _ your dominant subselves holding a genuinely respectful, =/= attitude about every communication partner.

You've read _ a set of foundation attitudes that promote problem-solving success, and _ an outline of eight steps you can tailor to meet any type and level of internal or interpersonal conflict. These steps propose **four kinds of universal conflicts**, which each merit different responses:

Internal **clashes** between inner-family members, which requires some kind of Self-motivated "parts work": *inner*-family negotiating and harmonizing.

Communication process **problems**: e.g. _ mismatched communication needs (p. 46); and _ the other common blocks on p. 405. Solving communication problems requires all seven of these relationship skills.

Abstract conflicts over values, roles, expectations, perceptions, responsibilities, goals, and strategies. These may require partners to respectfully accept your differences and agree to disagree, vs. trying to "win" and convert your partner to agree with you; and . . .

Clashes over concrete resources (e.g. *"You and I want different TV channels now."*) These are *always* surface conflicts over underlying true needs. They may require cooperatively digging down and brainstorming options to fill each partner's needs well enough.

This chapter identifies common ineffective problem-solving strategies, and illustrates ineffective and effective attempts to problem-solve a stepfamily loyalty conflict. The illustrations could have just as well focused on need-clashes between an adult and a child, two kids, co-workers, neighbors, relatives, service-provider and client, or between relative strangers. With some tailoring, the steps apply to organizations, religions, and nations.

The next chapter offers practical suggestions on how you can apply these attitudes and communication skills to resolve need conflicts *within* you. A core premise is that most "conflicts" between two or more people are often simultaneous with minor to major conflicts inside each partner, between their teams of subselves. Notice your self-talk about that idea.

Have you still got the "mind of a student"? Do you need to stretch and reduce any discomforts now?

Awarenesses / Notes . . .

9) Resolve Your *Inner* Conflicts

Have you ever felt *confused, indecisive, doubtful,* or *torn?* Have you said *"Part of me wants to . . .";* or *"On the one hand, and on the other . . ."* Have you ever had trouble *making up your mind?* Have you done things you knew were *wrong?* The unarguable proof of your *inner* family's reality is the conversations, debates, and screaming matches that go on daily inside your head like this:

"You should visit Jack in the hospital today!"

Another "voice" (thought stream) quickly says . . .

"But I need to wash the windows, balance my check-book, and get my hair cut. I don't have time today. Go see him later. He won't mind."

Perhaps a third voice sneers . . .

"You spineless, selfish wimp. Never can make your mind up, can you? Always thinking of yourself first. It's a wonder your brother even speaks to you. He's in pain, and you want to get your hair cut. You're pathetic."

Does it make sense that arguments like these cause you emotional and sometimes physical stress? Can you imagine finding an effective way to mediate these hassles? If allowed to, your talented inner leader, your Self, can do exactly that. That means you can choose to proactively reduce some of your daily stress without getting out of your chair. Notice your reaction to (i.e. thoughts about) that idea. Does your *Skeptic* subself pipe up? What would your life be like if you could really resolve many or most of these inner battles effectively?

This chapter uses all that you've read to outline a practical way to resolve *inner* conflicts. To better understand it, re-scan the inner-family basics in Chapter 1. That introduces the three or four kinds of normal subselves that comprise your *inner* family, or personality: Regulars, young Vulnerables, and their vigilant Guardians. How do you feel about having such subselves? If your Self is leading yours now, you'll probably feel interested and open to exploring the inner-family concept, vs. dismissing it. If your false self is dominating, you'll probably experience this chapter as *silly, boring, ridiculous, too intellectual, far-fetched, nutty,* or *New Age tripe.*

Status check: as a baseline, clarify what you believe now. T = true, F = false, ? = "I'm not sure," or "it depends on (what?)":

I now believe and accept that _ I have a group of personality subselves, including _ a wise, reliable, competent true Self; and that _ I am not crazy or weird in any way. (T F ?)

I believe that my subselves can react, argue, and disagree, just like people; and that _ they cause my thoughts, emotions ("moods"), and (some) bodily reactions like headaches, all the time. (T F ?)

I experience conflicts among these subselves every day, and I _ know that at times, these disputes cause me significant anxiety ("worry"), confusion, and stress. (T F ?)

I believe that I _ can grow the ability to avoid and resolve these conflicts effectively, with patience, awareness, and commitment. I also believe that _ I can significantly raise my inner peace by doing so. (T F ?)

I believe that learning to resolve my *inner* conflicts will definitely help me resolve my disagreements with other people more effectively. (T F ?)

Pause and notice your thoughts (inner voices) now. Are there several? This chapter will be useful and practical for you if you can honestly check each item above. If not, read it anyway, and see what happens!

I write this book to your true Self. See what s/he thinks about these basic ideas:

You are separate from each of your other personality parts. You (Self) can have interactive conversations with your other subselves just as you do with other people. The conversations are an interactive sequence of thoughts and feelings, which your *Observer* subself can describe. Pause, and imagine writing down exactly what you are thinking and feeling at this moment, as an objective reporter would. Can you do that?

Many adults and most kids can *image* their subselves, which can make these inner conversations more real and interesting. Try these simple steps to see if you're such a "visual" person:

Picture your favorite cartoon character. Imagine the face of your mother, father, or best friend. Can you "see" them in your "mind's eye"?

Try imagining a blue cat in a party outfit riding on a giraffe, trotting through the business section of your community. If you can do that, then you'll have no trouble with this:

Pick a favorite trait that describes (part of) you, like "I'm passionate / stubborn / analytic / creative / judgmental / solitary / impatient / a worrier / responsible / carefree / good natured . . ."

Imagine that trait to be brought to you by one of your subselves.

Invite an image that represents that subself to form in your mind. If you hear an inner voice (thought fragment) like *"This is ridiculous!"*, respond empathically to that protective subself (*"You feel this makes no sense at all."*) and go ahead. You could also take an interesting side path, and ask, *"Are you, or is some other subself, afraid of something here?"*

Trust the first thing you "see." Don't edit your image, and don't evaluate whether it's *good*, or *makes sense*. It's not your subself, but a symbol of it, like a mask or a photograph of someone. Images can be anything: faces real or fictional people, cartoon figures, abstract forms, real or fanciful animals, or objects. Subselves will often choose a preferred image to represent them. If they don't, you can assign one, if it helps your communication.

Did you get an image of the subself who brings you the trait you chose? If so, use this imaging ability to make conversations with your subselves more real. If you didn't get an image, that's OK. You can build your ability to recognize each subself's "voice," and use that to differentiate among your inner troop. ("Ah, that's my *Scared Kid* talking.") Some people come to recognize individual subselves by a *feeling*, or a *sense*.

Your inner *Observer's* talent is to factually note what's going on now and over time, *without judgment*, like a reporter or scientist. Do you know that part of yourself? Do you have an image of her / him / it? If you were able to stand 10 feet from yourself, and write an objective description of what you're doing now, that's your *Observer* at work. Your other subselves can observe also, but they're more apt to be judgmental and biased, and distort or miss details.

Who's In Charge Now?

An essential first step in resolving any conflict is assessing whether your Self is solidly in charge of your other subselves now. Do you remember the mix of emotions you feel when this is true? They include any of these: *peaceful, serene, alive, alert, aware, calm, grounded, purposeful, clear, patient, compassionate, focused, resilient, centered, confident, "up,"* and *strong.*

Typical; alternative emotions that indicate a false self is in charge are *anxious, nervous, or worried; irritated, angry, or enraged; frustrated; "out of touch;" distracted, spacey, or scattered; despairing or hopeless; resentful; revengeful; upset or bothered; high or hyper (manic); apathetic, low, or depressed; numb, or blocked; confused or torn; bored or unmotivated; and "uneasy," which stands for a combination of these.*

Reality check: pause, breathe comfortably, close your eyes, and describe what you're *feeling* right now. What do you notice? On a scale of 1 (not at all) to 10 (all the time), how aware of your current emotions and your breathing are you? What subself is answering?

If your Self is not in charge, you can _ use "parts work" (inner-family harmonizing) to change that, or _ try inner-conflict resolution anyway, and lower your expectations. The companion volume "Who's *Really* Running Your Life?" [xlibris.com] outlines how to do parts work. It augments this chapter on how to resolve your inner conflicts.

Remember the lilting music "Getting to Know You," from Anna and the King of Siam? (Can you *image* who sang it?) It's great background music for your next step . . .

Meet Your Selves

Remember what it felt like to be part of a team, committee, or family that had disagreements? Each person had their own values, perceptions, opinions, and *needs*, and probably tried to explain, persuade, or force their way on the others. If your group had a leader who tried to resolve the conflict, s/he probably tried to clarify who was conflicted over what, and to negotiate a compromise. If none appeared, your coach or leader used authority to dictate a solution, and move on toward the group's local goals. If the other people respected and trusted, or feared, the leader, that may have "worked" without resolving the true conflict of needs or opinions.

Handling your *internal* conflicts is exactly the same process. So one of the most helpful things you can do, over time, is to clarify *who comprises my inner team?* Who is it that's clashing, and what do they each value, believe, and need now? To do that, choose an undistracted block of time, bring writing materials, and try this safe "personnel roster" exercise. Give yourself lots of permission to feel strange and weird doing this . . .

Re-read or scan "Inner Family Basics," (p. 29) if you need to. For more perspective, read the Web pages at [http://sfhelp.org/01/innerfam1.htm].

Using the set of emotions above, decide if your Self seems to be in charge now. If not, guess which of your personality parts is. There may be several. _ Without good-bad judgments, ask your *Observer* to list as many qualities as you can that describe you as a unique person, like intelligent, creative, timid, curious, brave, resourceful, compassionate, selfish, dis/organized, drifting, humorous, etc. Have some fun with this! Try to avoid making positive or negative judgments about your traits (i.e. request your *Inner Critic* to bite her or his tongue for now.) I'd be surprised if you don't come up with 15 or more.

Imagine that each trait you identify is a separate subself. The trait is the special gift or talent that s/he brings to your inner family (personality). _ Put an "R" (Regular), "V" (Vulnerable) or "G" (Guardian) by each trait/subself. If you identify a spiritual part, label it "S" or another symbol you prefer. _ Mull the lists of common subselves on p. 35 or [..01/innerfam2.htm], and add any relevant ones to your own roster. If you skip this, you risk avoiding or "missing" subselves you're not delighted to have on your team. They are often vigorously involved in your inner conflicts, whether you like that or not!

See if you've included "my Self" or equivalent title among your Regulars. Many people initially forget their leader and/or their sexual and spiritual subselves, for several reasons. For each trait/subself, one at a time, try to sense a fitting image, and his / her / its _ approximate developmental age, _ name or nickname, and _ gender, if any.

Note these on your roster. It's normal to have one or several parts of the opposite gender, or some that seem genderless.

Try to identify which young Vulnerable subself each of your Guardians is devoted to comforting and protecting. For instance, "My *Procrastinator* seems to care most about my *Scared Kid* and my *Shamed Kid*. An interesting option is to *ask* each Guardian "Which ones are you protecting?", and then *trust the first response you get*, even if you don't like it, or can't understand it.

See what term feels best to describe your whole group of subselves. Your *inner* family, troop, troupe, gang, squad, team, bunch, company, clan, circle, tribe, board, council, mob, committee, cast . . .? Note that "my personality" now refers to all these subselves together, and probably several that you're not aware of yet. Notice the new meaning of the normal social greeting "*How* are *you (all)*?" If we weren't a collection of subselves, we English speakers would ask, "*How* is *you*?"

Review: You'll probably have at least a dozen inner family members; four or more of each of the three types of subselves. If you don't, that's OK for now. The more you work with your inner conflicts, the more subselves will emerge as distinct members of your crew. My experience is that most kids and adults can have 15 to 25 parts, some of which activate only in very special situations. Some subselves bring you more than just one trait.

Finally, see if you can identify and star (*) _ which subselves are the most influential in your daily life, and _ which are the most often distrustful of or opposed to each other. For example, you may have an *Adventurer* (Regular or Vulnerable) who wants you to get out in the world, risk, travel, explore, and try new things; and a *Bookworm* or *Couch Potato*, who would much rather curl up with a novel, crossword puzzle, or good TV movie.

 # Reality check: You've just done some basic "parts work": working with your personality parts. Notice your emotions and thoughts, and journal about them, if you wish. If you do, try to sense which subselves are "speaking." If subselves are scared of this exercise, a common Guardian is a *Blocker* or *Numb-er* who will protectively blank out your mind and emotions.

Does the question "Who's *really* running your life?" take on new meaning? Who among all your subselves is making most of your un/conscious decisions? Do the concepts of *inner communications* (talking among your subselves), *inner conflicts*, and *inner council meeting* seem more real? Because these talented parts of your personality are semi-independent and play different roles, they *must* disagree with each other over various things, as your needs vary, and you age and grow. Note that the words "I" and "you" can mean one, several, or all of your subselves, with or without including your body, so be aware of your terminology.

Focus on one or more of the key people in your life. Imagine that they also have a set of Regular, Vulnerable, and Guardian subselves like, and different than, yours. Do the ideas of *arguing* or *fighting*, *negotiating*, and "getting along with each other" take on new meaning? Recall the premise that major interpersonal conflicts are often simultaneous conflicts within _ you and _ within your partner, and _ between your inner crews. Complex, huh?

Now that you have an initial sense of "*Who's in there*," let's see how the ideas in the prior chapters can help your subselves to get along better together. If you want a more detailed scheme to reorganize and harmonize them over time, read "Who's *Really* Running Your Life?" This chapter is a summary introduction.

Resolve Your *Inner*-family Conflicts

What do your subselves argue about? Psychologist John Rowan summarizes types of inner conflicts most of us have. See if you experience these . . .

Caring for others vs. caring for your self.
Wanting change, vs. wanting the safety of no-change.
Being practical, vs. serving high ideals.
Being free and independent, vs. dependent.

Being reasoned, thoughtful and "sensible," vs. being impulsive, playful, and spontaneous.

Being honest, vs. being safe.

See your favorites here? Can you add to this list? How about "wanting to achieve and accomplish, vs. wanting to rest and relax?; and "Wanting pleasure *now*, vs. delayed gratification"

Recall a conflict with another person where you were able to reach an acceptable compromise together. How did you do that? Here's an overview of how it can work with your conflicted subselves. As you read this, note that the one doing the action steps is your Self (capital "S"): your skilled inner coach, CEO, conductor, quarterback, captain, chief, chairperson, or director. First, try out these foundation premises. They come from clinical training and 12 years' experience doing inner-family systems therapy with scores of clients, and my own inner crew.

Inner-conflict Baselines

You have no *bad* or *evil* subselves. In their unique ways, they each mean to help you, though at times their actions hurt you or others badly. They don't see or trust other options.

Your subselves communicate all the time, via thoughts, hunches, dreams, "intuitions," visions, images, and bodily sensations. Very young subselves may be pre-verbal, and can only use *feelings* to express their needs. Some are often silent, others raucous. Each part has its own style of reasoning and logic, which may make no sense to other parts, including your Self, or other people.

If s/he feels safe, any subself will "talk to" your Self: i.e. give information; answer and ask questions; disclose their feelings, goals, and fears; and *listen*. With new information and awareness, your parts can change their minds, values, goals, and roles "just like people." Practice at having dialogs between your Self and unconflicted subselves will strengthen your ability to resolve inner disputes.

Your Guardian subselves exist solely to protect certain young Vulnerables. Guardians' loyalty, focus, and priorities are fiercely and narrowly focused on the (psychological) welfare of one or several young parts, *not* on you as a whole person, or anyone else. If they're in charge, they proudly cause "selfish" behavior.

Each of your subselves has her or his unique _ needs, values, feelings, perceptions of the world (e.g. safe or unsafe), _ ways of decoding meaning from events, and _ style of expression. Some may use humor, others exaggeration, and others imagery, hunches, metaphors, or "logic."

Each subself may or may not know or trust your Self and/ or your other personality parts. As in your early years (before your Self developed), they don't trust your Self *now* to make good decisions, so such subselves "blend" and take your Self over. Then you (the person) think, feel, and see what that "false self" does.

A subself may know other subselves or not. They can meet and "get to know" each other just like distant relatives can build a new relationship.

Some of your subselves, specially inner kids (Vulnerables), **may be living in the past.** That means they have a distorted perception of what's *real* now. When this is so, there was usually some major ongoing or sudden childhood trauma that happened to you. They truly do not know you're an adult living in the current calendar year. *Inner* family therapy offers effective ways to bring them safely into the present. *Logic* is ineffective here.

Generally, any chronic illness, pain, mood (e.g. "depression), or unusually strong emotion indicates there's a conflict between two or more of your subselves. These symptoms usually mean that one or more have taken over (blended with) your Self, like mutinous crewmembers overwhelming their nautical captain. And . . .

Your Self can intentionally use the seven communication skills to manage and resolve conflicts between your subselves, just like s/he can with disputes with other people. Each of your subselves has the same six core communication needs (p. 46), specially the need for *respect*. Each has E(motion)-levels that vary, just like people. In fact, your subselves' emotional changes *cause* your and other peoples' E-levels to fluctuate.

Again, we've covered a lot of (alien?) ideas in a short time. Pause, stretch, breathe, be *aware* of what your inner crew feels, thinks, and needs now. Your Self will know what you need to do, if anything, before continuing. Note whether overall, these premises are believable to you, so far. If they don't, what follows may be of little practical use.

Guidelines for Resolving Inner Conflicts

Recall: a *conflict,* or *problem,* is two or more opposing needs, perceptions, or values. Can you think of the last significant inner conflict you had? Do you have any right *now*? [*"Keep reading."* *"No! We should do (something else)!"*] If your parts are disagreeing, try applying the framework below. Use some or all of the eight problem-solving steps on p. 262 with these differences:

Identify and accept that *"I have an inner conflict, and that's OK."* At first, some subselves may feel uneasy, scared, or defensive about admitting this. (*"I must be nuts!"*)

Authorize yourself to make enough time to "go within" (meditate), and reduce any physical or environmental distractions. If it's helpful, have a written roster of inner family members with you, until you know them.

Refresh your Self's attitude that each of your personality parts has dignity, worth, value, and legitimate needs, no matter how "unfair" or "wrong" they may seem now. Inner communications work best when your subselves exchange genuine =/= attitudes. Recall: you have no *bad* parts. You often *may* have misinformed, distrustful scared, angry, needy, and hurting subselves who will (eventually) respond to compassion and respectful suggestions.

Trust that you (your unblended Self) can find a workable compromise to any inner hassle, given time, focus, an =/= attitude, the seven skills, and opportunity.

Identify the specific subselves that are arguing by image and/or voice, and sort them out. There are often more than two. Tell each part that you (your Self) are there to help them get their needs met safely. Initially, expect disbelief or pessimism in some Guardians. Ask them to try trusting you, and seeing what happens. Trust your first reactions, without analyzing.

If you identify a conflicted subself and notice that you're feeling angry at it, or scornful, contemptuous, embarrassed, fearful, or disgusted by it, know that a subself has taken charge. Respectfully ask the judgmental or frightened part who's taken your Self over to step aside, so you can resolve the problem. If s/he won't, refocus on what *that* subself needs and feels, right now. Use empathic listening. Can you see why this work takes a lot of patience, until your team of personality parts is well harmonized?

If things are too heated, ask the warring parts to separate for now. Work with them one at a time, assuring the others they'll get their turn (then follow up!). Ask each what it wants, specifically, and *listen* empathically (Chapter 6)! Repeat back concisely, without judgment or comment, what you hear. Like people, overexcited parts will start to calm down (their E-levels will drop) when they feel your Self accepts and respects them, and *wants to hear* them without judging.

Note your option to have an *inner* council meeting, chaired by your Self. Some options:

Invite the Vulnerable/s who activate your Guardian parts to the council, to express their own feelings and needs about the conflict directly.

Invite subselves not involved in the current inner conflict to join you as consultants, like your *Historian, Analyzer,* and *Adult* ("common sense").

Block your *Perfectionist, Critic, Skeptic,* or *Catastrophizer*

Guardians from controlling the process. If present, acknowledge their concerns respectfully, and ask them to stand down and trust you (your Self) to negotiate a solution. If they won't, you have some harmonizing to do.

Invite your Spiritual subself to participate, and ask for its guidance ("still small voice"); and/or . . .

Get relevant information from any other humans related to the conflict (*"Brian, I need to know if you're angry with me now."*), and bring the results to your inner council.

Be alert for your parts' true needs "beneath" their stated needs. As with people, one way of identifying these is to ask *"What do you feel will happen if you don't get (your surface need) filled right now?"*

In this chapter's opening wrangle over going to the hospital or not, the *People Pleaser* part might say . . .

"Well, that's obvious. If you don't go see your brother, people will think you're selfish and insensitive, specially Jackie. If you're ever in the hospital, they won't come to see you, and you'd be all alone. I don't want that to happen."

A *Nurturer* part might say . . .

"You'd really feel good going to see him. You know how much it would mean to him. And we really do care about your brother . . ."

Your *Driver-Achiever* (Regular) subself might break in with . . .

"Don't you see that if you don't get your hair cut, people will start to think you're sloppy and unattractive? That could lead to all kinds of rejection and trouble! And you know what happens when you put off balancing the checkbook: checks start to bounce, your credit rating drops, and the phone starts to ring. Forget the hospital. Jack's in good hands now. He'll understand!" and finally . . .

Choose to mediate, brainstorm all options, and seek a win-win compromise among all conflicted subselves. In this example, your Self might propose:

"OK, how about this: The checkbook should only take about 15"-20", so we'll do that now. Then I'll go to the hospital for an hour or two. I can get a haircut tomorrow, with a little juggling, and I'll ask Ted tonight if he'll help with the windows this weekend. Can you all live with that?"

As each of your personality parts experience your Self's natural abilities to _ hear and care about their current true needs, and _ balance them fairly with other parts' needs, their trust in his/her motivation, judgment, and leadership will rise. A nice spin-off: as you develop this inner conflict-resolution process, you'll probably find yourself mediating selected conflicts with people around you in the same effective win-win way.

Notice your reactions now. Do you think these steps will work for you? Are you willing to try them out? If *"No"* or *"Not now"*, who (inside) is reluctant? What are they afraid of?

Inner-conflict Resolution Tips

Many inner struggles aren't as neat as the example above. **Here are some suggestions** your Self can select from to raise your resolution success rate. Most of these apply to interpersonal conflicts too . . .

Stay focused on the current conflict. Avoid getting diverted by other current or past issues. One problem at a time!

Stay clear on what aspects of the current situation you can impact or control, and which you can't. If a subself fears that global warming or the Ebola virus will kill you soon, empathically _ acknowledge their fear, and underlying wish to protect you; and _ respectfully assert that there's really nothing you can do about that, so you (your Self) are choosing to work on filling other current needs.

Watch out for a protective *Catastrophizer* part warning about dire worst-case crises and threats. Stay focused on current realities and needs. And yes, sometimes, your Catastrophizer really *is* on target (*"If you keep ignoring the IRS, you're going to get a really awful letter, one day soon."*)

Avoid assuming that past experiences are always valid guides for the present. You've never done parts work before, so your inner and interpersonal resolution results may pleasantly surprise your crew!

Avoid the black-and-white thinking that a *Controller* subself promotes (*"Do it, or don't*!) Usually there are *many* possible solutions to a conflict, not just two!

If one or more of the conflicted parts are young Vulnerables who can't understand realistic practicalities, consider having a nurturing or companion subself stay with them for reassurance while you negotiate with other subselves. Your inner kids need your Self and inner *Nurturer* to be compassionate, decisive leaders, not buddies. They'll usually feel better knowing someone's in charge of setting and following (enforcing) safe limits, even if they don't like them.

More inner-conflict resolution suggestions:

If it helps, agree on a signal that anxious or distrusting parts can use to get your Self's or another part's attention along the way. That might be an image, a thought stream, or a physical sensation like tingling, warmth, a yawn, or a muscle ache or "twinge." If you pick one, practice it so it can become a reflex.

When any inner kids (Vulnerables) are scared of an impending event, consider inviting them to "go play," or "hang out in your safe place" while your older, wiser parts handle the real-world situation. Help your young ones trust without guilt that *they* don't have to handle your inner or outer conflicts. Their important job (role) is to be curious, contribute their priceless energies, emotions, views, and gifts; and to experience and learn, over time.

Learn the special talents and abilities that each inner team member brings you, and use them! Delegate responsibility for aspects of a current conflict solution to subselves with relevant abilities, rather than feeling you (your Self) has to "do it all."

Those of us from low-nurturance childhoods often need persistent encouragement to ask for, and accept, help, without great guilt and anxiety.

As you experiment with this concept, notice and grow what works for you. Affectionately acknowledge, and don't agree with, your inner *Perfectionist's* need to have conflict resolution work exactly, every time. Focus on learning from those times that aren't "perfect" or "totally successful." Aim for compromise and meeting each part's needs enough for now.

To clarify and sort out complex conflicts, **use a log, journal, or "lab notebook"** to write down what each involved subself needs, and why. A client's Self taught me to make a three column worksheet that lists _ each subself involved in a conflict; _ their main inner-family role, or job, as *they* see it; and _ *what activates them*: i.e. what they want or fear, and are trying to guard you or a Vulnerable part from.

Expect these many steps and guidelines to become routine (semi-conscious) habits, with patient practice and experimenting, just like the enormously complex business of driving a car safely or balancing your daily responsibilities has.

Add your own guidelines . . .

 # Reality check: These are just ink stains on paper, until you *try* the ideas they represent. Are you motivated to do that right *now*? Listen with interest to your self-talk: are there several voices (thought streams)? What do they each say about pausing your reading to *try* these steps on a real conflict among your inner selves now? To confirm that you have more than two choices here (e.g. *"Try inner resolution now!"* / *"No, don't!"*); **consider these options** . . .

Wait until you're sure your Self is in charge, before trying inner resolution. Can you name the emotional clues that suggest your Self is leading?

Identify one or more of your subselves now, and experience having an inner "hello" conversation with her / him / it. See what that *feels* like. Include asking a question, and trusting the first response you sense. (*"How old are you? What's your job; what are you trying to do for me? What makes your job hard? What do you need now? How does it feel to have me talk with you?"*)

Do the same, and practice using empathic listening (Chapter 6) with one or several subselves.

Continue reading, and try inner problem solving in the next several days, when it "feels right."

Reread the eight steps of problem solving in Chapter 8 to raise your confidence and clarity on how to intentionally resolve conflict among your subselves, and what your options are.

Experiment with identifying a subself's surface need, and then digging down to their *true* underlying need, but stop short of conflict resolution.

Try these ideas for experience, without feeling you *must* resolve the conflict.

Take a small conflict, and practice with it. Pay as much attention to how this inner process *feels* as to the outcome.

Experiment with trying resolution when other subselves are in control, and see what that feels like.

Ask someone you trust to help you try your first inner resolution, perhaps by reading the steps to you, and coaching you as you go. Caution: adding another person may bias or distract some subselves . . .

Trust your Self to pick the right option among these and others that s/he sees, and act on that right now.

Recap

This chapter outlines a framework of ideas to help you apply all that you learned in prior chapters to successfully resolving disputes among your *inner* family members (subselves). Growing proficient at this can be an important strength in doing Project 1—harmonizing your inner team.

These are the key ideas to remember:

You're personality is naturally composed of three or four groups of subselves who *will* constantly argue over their differing values, perceptions, roles, and motives. These inevitable *inner* conflicts drain your energy, distract your focus, affect your mood and body, and slow or block your growth and self-actualization. The same is true of your partner and others important to you. Until you develop your *awareness*, many of these conflicts are semi-conscious or unconscious. Until your Self proactively reorganizes your inner team and earns the other subselves' trust and confidence, their conflicts can cause frequent or even chronic blending, disabling your true Self. If that happens often, it will feel "normal" to you, and you'll see no reason to change.

Your Self can communicate with other subselves, as they do with each other. Therefore you can negotiate with them, just as you can with physical people. Using the seven skills, and core attitudes behind them (like mutual respect for all subselves), your Self can learn to use the eight problem solving steps (p. 396) to usually fill the needs of your battling subselves well enough, in a way that feels good enough to all your inner parts.

This chapter invites you to _ inventory your subselves, _ sense who usually leads them in calm and conflictual times, and _ experiment with communicating and problem solving with them. The chapter concludes with guidelines and tips that can raise your *inner* conflict-resolution success, with practice and time.

What are you *aware* of, right now? Some **options:**

Discuss these *inner* conflict ideas with another person you trust.

Journal about your reactions to these ideas and their implications in your life.

Meditate and identify chronic inner conflicts that bother you. See each one as a candidate for the resolution process outlined in this chapter. Enjoy imagining vividly how your life would be if you could *really* resolve each of them. Firmly block your inner *Pessimist, Saboteur,* or *Cynic* from derailing or discouraging you . . .

 # Status check: before exploring high-nurturance relationships, see where you stand with the key ideas in this chapter:

I accept that I have an "inner family" of subselves which disagree (T F ?)

I have _ honestly evaluated whether I have symptoms of the six psychological wounds (p. 37) *or* _ I'm strongly motivated to do so in the next several weeks (T F ?).

I accept that disputes with other people often involve significant inner disputes too. (T F ?)

I believe I have a true Self who can use the seven skills to help resolve my inner disputes (T F ?)

I'm motivated now to try the seven skills and problem-solving steps with selected inner disputes to see what happens. (T F ?)

I'm confident that my Self is answering these questions. (T F ?) see p. 33.

For a full perspective on resolving inner conflicts, read "Who's *Really* Running Your Life?" [xlibris.com].

Besides attending bodily health and comfort, some of our highest-priority daily needs are *relating* well to other people. Even fluency in the seven skills doesn't guarantee successful relationships. The next chapter explores what it takes to build high-nurturance relationship between two people or subselves. **To prepare, try jotting down your answers to these questions** . . .

_ What true needs do I seek to fill by having "relationships" with other people?

_ Specifically, why are some relationships more satisfying and enjoyable than others?

_ What's my definition of a *nurturing* or *healthy* relationship?

_ How can I tell if a relationship is *toxic*?

_ What's the difference between dependent, independent, and interdependent relationships, and which of these is best for me?

_ Specifically, what's the difference between a *friend* and an *acquaintance*?

_ What are the five most important factors that determine how satisfying a relationship is for me?

_ How would I describe my relationship with *myself*? With a Higher Power?

_ How do I know if I'm in a *co-dependent* relationship?

_ How am I feeling, as I consider these questions?

_ Is my Self answering these questions? If not, who is?

Bring your thoughts, feelings, curiosity, and journal, and let's explore some key ideas about the relationships inside you and with other people.

Awarenesses / Notes . . .

10) High-nurturance Relationships

How many *important* relationships do you have in your life right now? How many *casual* relationships? More than a hundred? If you send year-end greeting cards, how many did you send last season? On our scale of 1 to 10, how high would you rank the *effectiveness* of each of your important relationships, and the satisfaction (need fulfillment) they usually bring you, over time? Are you interested in increasing your satisfaction, in a way that respects each of these people, and empowers them to feel more satisfied too? You can do that, if you get clear on some basic beliefs, put your Self in charge, and creatively apply the seven skills you're learning here.

This chapter offers you 24 ways to become aware of what you believe about _ yourself, _ human relationships, _ personal and interpersonal "problems" or "conflicts," and _ how your communication skill relates to solving your relationship problems. Clarity on these can help you resolve "relationship problems" and proactively build high-nurturance relationships.

This chapter might be titled "A Relationship Owner's Guide." Use the ideas here to become more aware of yourself and the key beliefs that shape your personal and business relationships. Hilight or star ideas here you want to clarify, change, challenge, or apply. Let's start with a "silly" question:

why do we all instinctively seek and form human relationships? What *needs* do your relationships fill?

Hierarchy of Needs

Two generations ago, psychologist Abraham Maslow proposed that kids and adults in every era and culture behave to fill a hierarchy of five primal needs: See if these apply to you, in order:

First, we need **to raise current physical and emotional *comfort* to "tolerable"**: i.e. reduce hunger, thirst, fatigue, or pain *now*. When this need is temporarily filled enough, we then need . . .

To feel *secure* that our physical and emotional comforts and safety are assured in the near future. Maslow proposed that when this discomfort is eased enough, most people strive . . .

To *belong* to a respected group of other people, vs. feeling isolated, disconnected, alienated, and alone. When we're able to do this, then we need . . .

To *be* noticed *and appreciated* as a worthy, unique individual in that group. If and when we satisfy all four of these needs, then we yearn . . .

To be "self actualized": i.e. to have the freedom to develop and productively use our unique personal talents in ways we feel are valuable and meaningful.

Maslow proposed that you can't effectively focus on fulfilling any of these needs until you fill the preceding ones well enough. As a pundit says, *"If you're up to your neck in alligators, it's hard to focus on draining the swamp."*

Recall the Chapter-4 idea **that you have *true* needs below your surface needs**. These five are such true needs, and are often semi-conscious. Reflect for a moment on this motivational hierarchy, and decide what level you're at now today and in general. If you've satisfied the first two, then this chapter may be relevant to your next two needs: being steadily accepted by a group of other people, and then becoming known, respected, and appreciated among them. Each of these requires that you intentionally build and maintain a set of healthy *relationships*, with intimacies (trusts) ranging from low to high. Many people, including me, believe that for ongoing wholistic health, these must include a primary *spiritual* relationship with a credible, nurturing Higher Power.

In this book, *healthy, functional,* or *high nurturance* relationships are characterized by both people feeling their primary true needs (p. 149) are satisfied *enough,* with acceptable investment of time, energy, and risk. *Toxic, low nurturance,* or *dysfunctional* relationships often block wholistic needs from being satisfied. They're characterized by one or both people feeling significant guilt, shame, anxiety, confusion, ambiguity, pain, frustration, and anger with themselves and/or each other.

Recall: *nurturance* relates to the process of filling someone's short and long-term emotional, physical, mental, and spiritual *needs*: lowering their discomforts, and raising their satisfactions and pleasures. We communicate within ourselves and with each other to try to fill our current emotional, physical, and spiritual needs. This chapter suggests how to apply your communication skills toward building satisfying, high-nurturance relationships. Let's start with some basics:

Premises about *You*, Relationships, and "Problems"

The clearer you are on your basic life premises, then the clearer _ your thinking and "reasoning," and _ the more effective your communication, need fulfillment, and relationships will be. Do you agree? Can you articulate your primary premises about *healthy relationships*? To help answer that, see how these proposals and definitions compare with yours. Use this as a checklist, and consider hilighting, making margin notes, and/or journaling any reactions your inner family members have as you review these. Some of these repeat what you've read before. If you're clear on them, move on to the next. If these are new ideas to you, they probably bear repeating.

Premise 1) The clearer you are on your set of basic life premises (core beliefs and attitudes), the more often you'll feel truly centered, clear, serene, calm, decisive and productive in any life situation. Being centered promotes making the best short and long-term decisions. So choose to *develop your awareness* (Chapter 2). This chapter aims to grow your awareness of your beliefs about relationships, and solving relationship "problems."

Let's start with proposals about the most interesting subject: *you.* You may or may not agree with them. I invite you to thoughtfully learn what *you* believe, as you read these.

About Extraordinary You

Premise 2) You are a truly unique, talented, worthwhile person, virtually without past, present or future equal. Each other person in your life was and is just as unique and worthy, in their special way. You have an intrinsic *potential* value, as judged by yourself, others, and the universe. Anyone who needs to label you as "worthless" probably feels that about themselves (i.e. some subselves do), but can't see and accept that yet.

Your innate worth comes from your natural capacity to promote wholistic health and growth, peace, safety, and love in and among living things, starting with yourself and those who depend on you. Your human worth does not depend on whether you make other people "happy" or "comfortable," no matter what others say or imply. Each of us is ultimately responsible for our own periods of "happiness," though we can help each other find, enjoy, and extend them. We *do* need each other for comfort and support!

Premise 3) Being unique means that **you have priceless talents and abilities,** or gifts, which you may or may not recognize, develop, and use. Your doing these brings you periods of fulfillment and satisfaction, or "happiness," over time

(Maslow's "self actualization"). Other people have different (vs. better) gifts than you do. We have no control over what talents we're born with. We (you) do have total control over what we do with them.

Premise 4) You have inherent neuro-chemical and genetic limitations and unawarenesses, vs. "weaknesses" or "defects." You didn't cause them, and may not be able to change the former. You can _ calmly acknowledge and accept your limits, and adapt to them. Alternatively, you can _ feel guilty, ashamed, despairing, frustrated, or angry about your limitations, and maybe _ pretend they don't exist, by minimizing, projecting, and/or denying them.

The latter reactions are signs of being ruled by a reactive false self, and probably living in a low-nurturance environment. Those reactions never promote lasting true serenity, health, productivity, and joy. Awareness, respectful feedback, and the Serenity Prayer can help you identify and accept your limitations, and your Self can identify where you can reduce or compensate for them.

If your natural limitations cause a problem for others, that's *their* problem to resolve, not yours, unless you *consciously* choose to base your serenity on theirs. This may not be true in some dependent relationships (e.g. parent-child), compared to genuinely interdependent or independent ones (premise 19 below). This is not meant to promote your being indifferent or insensitive to the needs and feelings of others. It is meant to encourage you to empathically allow others responsibility for their comfort, while you attend your own.

Premise 5) You are a spiritual being. "Spirit" comes to us from the Latin *spiritus*, which means "breath." You are a person with *breath*. Your spirituality means that you have an intangible spirit or soul, which affects your serenity, behavior, and communication all the time. It also means you have the innate capacity to experience or sense guidance, support, and power, beyond your five or six bodily senses: hunches, intuitions, and "knowings."

If you accept and value these two points, you can choose to develop your spiritual *awareness*, over time, which is a vital part of communication skill # 1. If your false self disbelieves or ignores your spirit/soul and spiritual ability, those subselves will strangle or block your spirituality by ceaselessly focusing on logic, practicality, and instant gratification or relief. Your protective subselves can overrule your spirit and Self to insist on endless activities, responsibilities, and sensory stimulations, like headphones, PCs, cell phones and pagers, eating, "working out," and home media systems.

Choosing spiritual awareness means you can learn to get quiet and attentive, and sense the "still small voice within": your Guardian Angel, "Wise One," "the voice of God," or your *conscience* made visual as Walt Disney's *Jiminy Cricket*. When you're faced with a complex, difficult decisions, access to this sense and the courage to trust it can be of enormous help in guiding you to do "the next right thing" in your busy life. This includes making complex, impactful communication (behavior) decisions (*"Should I tell Max I don't love him any more?"*)

Do you believe you have a Soul, and/or a spiritual subself who mentors your inner family? If so, what do you believe its purpose and talent is? Do you listen to it at important times? If so, what happens when you do? How do you *feel*? How do the other members of your inner team feel about this spiritual "part" of you? How does your spiritual part affect your communication effectiveness with key people in you life? Have you ever experienced a "soul mate"?

Premise 6) Because your brain processes information in multiple regions at once, **your personality is formed of a dynamic cluster of semi-autonomous *subselves*, or *"parts."*** Each part has unique goals, roles, opinions, values, and talents. Among these, your true Self is a skilled leader, which can be disabled (taken over) by other distrustful parts. When this happens, you are "blended" and governed by a reactive, shortsighted "false self" that often makes low-nurturance or toxic decisions. "Parts work" is a way of correcting this, over time (Chapters 1 and 9, and "Who's *Really* Running Your Life?")

Premise 7) You're a masterpiece in process. You're constantly changing, physically, emotionally, mentally, and spiritually. You can consciously affect some of this changing (*"I'm starting to practice Tai Chi Chuan"*) or "growth," but you can't fully control it. One implication is that you can learn new knowledge, and adopt different attitudes, behaviors, and choices. This enables you to become a more effective communicator, *if your governing subselves choose to.*

These seven foundation beliefs are about *you* and every communication partner, including people who cause you the most stress. Pause for a moment, and reflect on how you feel about each of these premises, and all of them together. Option: journal now about what your inner family is saying about these seven beliefs and what they *mean* to you. Add any other beliefs about *you* that feel important to you.

Now let's focus on a second set of core beliefs that shape your communication outcomes . . .

About Relationships

Premise 8) A human *relationship* exists when one or both people are significantly affected emotionally, physically, or spiritually, and/or mentally, by the other's perceived well-being and/or behaviors. Each day, you are the supreme judge of what "significantly" means. Your subselves may disagree (*"Julie is important! No she isn't!"*) From this viewpoint, you have hundreds, if not thousands, of current relationships, including people who are dead, unseen for many years, and/or living across the world. "Out of sight" is not necessarily "out of your unconscious and conscious minds!"

Premise 9) Right now and over time, each of your relationships can range between "*very* toxic" and "*very* nurturing." Toxic relationships block filling your true current wholistic needs, and nurturing ones promote filling them. In the same way, families and other human groups (book clubs, congregations, schools, political parties, corporations, neighborhoods, and nations) can be judged between toxic and nurturing for individuals or all members. Kids have unique developmental needs that powerfully shape whether their nuclear and extended families are *very* toxic to *very* nurturing. Alternative adjectives are "very low nurturance" to "very high nurturance." "Low nurturance" may feel less shaming than *dysfunctional*. Adults can consciously choose whether to have nurturing or toxic relationships, or none.

Premise 10) Regardless of age, gender, and setting, mutually-satisfying (nurturing) relationships usually have most of the ingredients below. This checklist is meant as a thought-provoker and discussion starter, not as absolute truth. Use it to help you and key partners discuss and clarify your respective truths about what it takes to build and keep a "healthy-enough" (high nurturance) relationship. "Partners" means any mix of two adults, kids, or infants.

Mentally focus on a special adult or child partner, and check each factor below that you feel you each have enough of. For those that you don't, star any that you're intentionally working to develop. This is not about anyone being good or bad, or right or wrong!

For a wholistically healthy, high nurturance relationship, **each partner needs to have . . .**

___ 1) A **harmonious inner family** of subselves, led primarily by their true Self. That promotes all these other factors:

___ 2) **Self trust,** _ Self **respect, and** _ Self **love.** These promote consistent self-nurturance, vs. self-neglect and abandonment.

___ 3) A evolving, nurturing (vs. toxic) **spiritual faith** in a benign Higher Power.

__ 4) An accurate **awareness** of self and others, and _ the ability to expand their awareness "bubble" to include others without losing self-awareness.

__ 5) The **ability to *bond*** with (emotionally attach to and care about) other people.

__ 6) The **ability to grieve** broken bonds, mentally, emotionally, and spiritually.

__ 7) **empathy**: the ability to nonjudgmentally and accurately sense what others are thinking, feeling, and needing.

__ 8) The **ability to balance** work, play, and rest, as daily environments change.

__ 9) A _ clear, congruent personal **identity and** _ **effective** personal **boundaries**.

__ 10) A realistic, vs. idealistic, **optimism**: a glass-half-full attitude about life.

__ 11) Generally **effective thinking** and reasoning (Chapter 3).

__ 12) Enough current emotional, spiritual, and physical **securities** (Maslow's levels 1 and 2).

__ 13) An emerging **life purpose** and meaning: "This is why I'm on Earth."

__ 14) **Willingness** to _ initiate change, _ to risk, and _ to fail (learn).

__ 15) A **tolerance** for environmental change, and _ the ability to adapt to it, without undue anxiety.

__ 16) "Enough" _ **knowledge** of these factors, **and** _ **motivation** to learn more.

__ 17) Spiritual and social **supports** other than their mate and child(ren): friends.

And to have a high-nurturance relationship, both partners need to have . . .

__ 18) Reciprocal **trusts**, and the _ shared desires and _ abilities to repair them, if broken.

__ 19) Genuine, stable **respect** for each other vs. "I'm 1-up" or "I'm 1-down."

__ 20) Genuine **commitment** to each other and your relationship, based on love, caring, and trust, not fear, guilt, or duty.

__ 21) **Compatible-enough** _ core beliefs, _ values, _ priorities, _ interests, and _ goals (dreams), as judged by each partner. Married mates also need _ compatible-enough sexual desires, values, cycles, and boundaries.

__ 22) A **shared prizing** of the relationship, and _ a conscious desire to nurture it. This fosters the mutual desire to _ make (vs. "find") enough time to communicate, problem-solve, and experience things together.

__ 23) The desire and ability to **flex and balance** between focusing on _ my needs, _ your needs, and _ our needs.

__ 24) Innerpersonal and interpersonal **fluency in the seven communication skills** in this book. This allows partners (including kids!) to think clearly, discuss each of these ingredients as =/= teammates, and to problem solve effectively together.

Add your own . . .

Reflect: What are you thinking and feeling right now? **Where do you think people with these traits and abilities get them?** I feel that most come from being raised in a wholistically healthy, high-nurturance family [..01/health.htm], by caregivers who got these traits from *their* ancestors and society. The flourishing mega-billion dollar U.S. divorce epidemic and industry, and drug, crime, addiction, and abortion institutions witnesses how rare this is, as we begin the newest Christian Millennium.

Reality check: Identify your most successful, nourishing relationships, and reflect: were or are most or all of the ingredients above consistently present? Now think of past or

present relationships that cause you and/or your partner "considerable" stress. How many of these ingredients were missing "too much, too often" in your opinion? Was either of you aware of this? How did you respond?

If you're married now or hope to be, note that the exhilarating, romantically-idealized courtship phase of your relationship is apt to distort your clear, subjective assessment of these relationship ingredients. Serious distortions are guaranteed if either of you are dominated by a false self. Recently, almost half of typical American mates wind up realizing that their false selves committed to the wrong *people* (including in-laws), for the wrong *reasons*, at the wrong *time*. Paradoxically, over half of "older and wiser" American *re*marriers divorce at a higher rate, and millions of middle-aged others choose to endure emotional divorce, in numbness or depression and despair.

Consider which of these relationship ingredients you can and can't control. For instance, you can't *make* a partner trust, respect, like, bond with, or love you. Once aware, motivated, and self-responsible, you *can* help each other develop some missing or weak ingredients, over time, like trust, respect, and appreciation. Do you believe that?

Recall: we're reviewing a set of basic premises about building and maintaining healthy relationships. Whether you're aware of them or not, you and each partner have a set of premises (inner rules, or beliefs) like these. Your version of these premises will shape how effective the seven communication skills are in resolving your *inner*personal and interpersonal need-conflicts, or "problems."

More relationship premises . . .

Premise 11) All relationships have some things in common, like the need for mutual respect, trust, and empathy. Business and personal relationships differ in some key ways. Being aware of these differences can help keep relationship expectations clear and realistic, and avoid some relationship problems. How would you describe the key differences? How about some of these:

Certain behaviors and personal communication topics are "inappropriate" in typical business relationships. If partners don't define or agree on these limitations, or one exceeds the other's "should (not)s" and "must (not)s," relationship conflicts occur.

Expectations of each other are shaped by assumed or declared codes of professional conduct and ethics. For instance, your dentist is "supposed to" keep her or his hands and attention focused above your neck.

The risk of dislike, misunderstanding, disagreement, and rejection is usually much higher in prized personal relationships. If you have these too intensely, too often, with a co-worker, you risk changing or losing your job. If you have these with a mate or child, you risk losing a key *love* relationship, and part of your security and identity. Bosses, co-workers, and jobs can be replaced, but a parent, child, sibling, or beloved partner or friend can't. This is why we (you) have more trouble *listening* to family members than to co-workers or strangers. The stakes are far higher!

Compared to personal relationships, business and professional relationships have a narrower set of roles that partners need to agree on. A *role* is a set of responsibilities and behaviors that (ideally) each partner understands, and agrees to fill for the other. Your dentist chooses the *role* of competently helping you maintain oral health. You choose the role of "patient," which entails caring enough about your mouth to bring it in for maintenance, following the dentist's instructions, keeping your hands to yourself, dressing "appropriately," and paying their fee. You don't expect her or him to be your spiritual advisor, give you a backrub, or evaluate your stock portfolio . . . or do you?

Friends, children, and lovers expect their relationship-partner to share (some) personal information; give respectful personal feedback (*"Did you realize your socks don't match?"*); and to care genuinely and consistently about your wholistic welfare. Within some bounds, physical contact is expected and exchanged in personal relationships, but little or none in most professional ones.

In both personal and professional ("impersonal") relationships, **a source of stress can be *role* conflicts**. These happen when two people (including adults and kids) . . .

. . . aren't clear on, or disagree over, what responsibilities and behaviors are expected of the other person, in their relationship (*"You're* supposed *to call me if you're going to be late."*). This includes either person having *inner* conflicts ("confusion") over their role responsibilities, priorities, and rules of conduct.); or . . .

. . . one or both can't or won't meet the other person's expectations about their role behaviors and responsibilities, and the other person can't accept that.

Premise 12) Your relationships with friends, relatives, acquaintances, strangers, adults and kids range from minor through ambivalent to close to primary. One way of ranking each relationship is how intensely the other person's actions and well-being affects you, over time. Your ranking of each relationship may be based on your exchange of emotional/ spiritual respect, liking (enjoying), and caring (bonding) i.e. *love.* As you know, relationship rankings vary, as you, your partner, and the world majestically evolve.

Your version of these five premises shape your choosing, evaluating, and maintaining your relationships, whether you're aware of them or not. *Awareness* brings you the possibility of conscious choices and needs-negotiation (problem solving).

How are your subselves doing with these abstract ideas? Some of your inner crew may be bored, numb, or distracted. If you need a mind or stretch break, take one! When you can regain your "mind of a student," let's combine and apply these premises about *you* and *relationships* to raise your daily satisfactions . . .

About Relationship Problems

Premise 13) The word *problem* means "one or more unmet needs." A *need* is a minor to major current physical, emotional, or spiritual discomfort. We kids and adults semi-consciously seek to get and keep personal balance and peace by acting to fill enough of our dynamic current needs. We form and try to maintain *relationships* to fill a set of core true needs.

Premise 14) All human relationships are dynamic multi-level processes powered by each subself and each partner concurrently trying to fill their main current *needs* well enough. So permanently solving your *inner*personal and interpersonal relationship problems hinges on all partners knowing their *true* (vs. surface) needs well enough (p. 149).

Premise 15) Your and my needs are . . .

Neither good nor bad by themselves, like our eye color or fingerprints. The way we act to satisfy our needs can be "good" or "bad," if our choices cause pain or block health and growth in ourselves and/or others. Many of us were taught to shame others or ourselves for being "too needy." That's like labeling a person *bad* or *weak* for needing to breathe, eat, or sleep.

And your needs are . . .

Conscious, semi-conscious, and unconscious. Your and others' needs are usually on the "surface" of our awareness. There are usually (always?) semi-conscious and unconscious true needs underneath them (lower in consciousness). And our needs . . .

Come in complex clusters. At any moment, you and others have sets of minor to major _ emotional, _ physical, and _ spiritual surface and true needs that constantly shift and interact. They . . .

Are dynamically interactive. That is, my emotional, physical, and spiritual needs cause and affect yours, and vice versa. They change moment to moment, day and night, face to face, and across time and the globe.

Our needs are **satisfied temporarily** at best; then they usually recur. And they . . .

Follow a natural emotional ranking, or hierarchy, like Abraham Maslow's. We semi-consciously judge some needs as more urgent or morally worthier than others. Some of our rankings change, with age, wisdom, and circumstance.

Premise 16) Three key factors in any relationship problem you have are . . .

. . . what each person's current *true* (vs. surface) needs are (premise 19 below),

. . . how each person ranks their and their partner's needs, and . . .

. . . how *aware* each person is of their own and their partner's current true needs.

Inner and mutual harmony may happen when all subselves and partners genuinely believe **"Your and my needs are of equal importance to me, now."** Here and in companion books, this is called an equal/equal ("=/="), mutual-respect attitude. Most conflicts, and most emotional and legal divorces, happen because partners aren't able to genuinely rank their needs, values, or human *worth* as co-equal, over time. When true, that usually implies that one or both partners are often dominated by a false self, and aren't aware of that.

Implication: a primary childcare task is to patiently, lovingly guide minor kids to change their natural "*My needs come first*" instincts to "*Your and my needs (usually) rank equally now.*" The latter attitude is one trait of true maturity. Do you think most co-parents are aware of this vital goal?

Pause for a minute, and *breathe*. Back away from the details here, and notice what your subselves are saying. If this is getting too philosophical or intellectual for some of them, note your option to stop reading and do something else for a while or until your priorities change. When you're ready, here are some more ways of learning about your basic premises about relationship "problems" . . .

Premise 17) Most significant relationship "problems" have four parts: Jack's _ surface need/s and _ underlying *true* needs, and Jill's _ surface need/s and _ underlying *true* needs.

Unless Jack and Jill _ are consistently guided by their true Selves, _ are clearly aware of all four of these, and _ agree to brainstorm with _ mutual respect, filling their respective *true* needs effective long-term problem-solving is unlikely.

For example: if Jack says "*You never listen to me,*" and Jill (dutifully or anxiously) tries to improve her listening, Jack may remain dissatisfied because his real unspoken need is to feel more valued and respected. Filling that need would take spontaneous (vs. requested or demanded) new behaviors from Jill. It also might take Jack healing his old *shame* wound, which has nothing to do with Jill. .

In my experience, most partners are unaware of their or their partner's underlying true needs (p. 149), and aren't used to assessing or discussing them ("*I need to feel more trusted and respected by you.*") This leaves partners focused on surface needs, or worse, attacking each other as persons ("arguing"), vs. helping each other identify and fill their respective true current needs. Does this make sense? Does it *happen* to you?

Premise 18) Needs can conflict concurrently within us and between us. One implication of this is inner "fights." One inner-family subself may want their person to act (e.g. thought stream: "*Come on, come on, pick up the phone and call Mildred!*"), and one or more other subselves may urge "*No, No! You'll probably get lectured at and rejected, which will hurt. Don't call!*" Ring any bells? For most of us, these inner squabbles are so common we're not even aware of them. They distract and defocus us, and use up lots of energy ("*Why am I so tired all the time?*")

As you develop inner-family and communication *awareness*, you'll start to recognize these semi-conscious inner struggles. In recovery from false-self dominance, you can quiet and sort out all the inner voices, and invoke the skill and wisdom of your true Self to mediate and reach acceptable inner compromises. That paves the way for effective interpersonal negotiation and compromise (Chapter 9).

A sobering implication of this premise is that a "problem" between mates (or any two people) can really be a whole cluster of simultaneous inner and mutual conflicts (1) several concurrent conflicts within *you*, plus (2) several concurrent conflicts among *your partner's* inner family, and (3) several conflicts between some of your subselves, and some of your partner's subselves.

This is why it's vital to have your respective true Selves in charge of your two personality teams, to sort all these out and promote some structure and order to resolving the most pressing conflicts first. Adults and kids who focus on resolving their inner personal need-conflicts first (Chapter 9) are best able to resolve current interpersonal problems. If you agree, is that what you usually do?

Here's a tough one for many of us "adults:"

Premise 19) *You* are responsible for identifying and filling your true needs! If you expect your partner or others to be mainly responsible for filling *true* needs like these below, you're setting yourself and them up for disappointment, frustration, hurt, anger, and resentment. This is specially true if s/he accepts the responsibility! All human *motivation* comes from our conscious and unconscious drives to ease our concurrent physical and spiritual discomforts, and fill primal emotional needs like the ones in Chapter 4.

We're the first generation to popularly acknowledge the harmful relationship dynamic of *co-dependence*. If out of kindness, compassion, or misplaced guilt I take on too much responsibility for your problems (unfilled needs), I unwittingly block you from learning how to master them. Thus *enabling* is the opposite of *empowering*, which is what wholistically-healthy co-parents want to do for their dependent kids and each other. Remember this ancestral wisdom?

"Teaching a hungry person how to fish is more helpful than giving them a fish."

A major implication is that co-parents are responsible for teaching their kids how to "fish:" i.e. helping them learn to _ accept full responsibility for identifying and filling their own true needs, and to _ ask for help in filling them, when needed, without excessive guilt, shame, or anxiety. Are you doing that? Did your caregivers do that for you? Has anyone? Co-parents can start to help each other learn effective problem solving, and model and teach it to their young people and others, at any time.

See if you agree with this proposal about relationship problems:

Premise 20) "My *integrity* is _ knowing my core beliefs, values, rights, *and true needs*; and _ acting on them consistently *without undue shame or guilt*, despite resistance or criticism from others." Have you ever clearly defined your integrity? It comes from the Latin root *integer*, meaning *whole* or *complete*. Do you know what it feels like to honor, live by, and preserve your integrity? Doing so is the source of self-respect and dignity, which underlie all effective communication. People who "walk their talk" (live their core values) most of the time despite conflict with others, are usually guided by their true Self and Higher Power. Relationships require a balancing of two personal integrities as inner and outer worlds ceaselessly change.

Premise 21) Relationship problems often involve a vexing, stressful dynamic described by psychiatrist Dr. Murray Bowen as **"triangling."** The basic idea is that "problems" apparently between two people often involve a third person, in a way that keeps the problem going or growing Solving such problems requires nonjudgmental awareness of who's needs create and maintain the (Persecutor-Victim-Rescuer) triangle, and filling their needs another way.

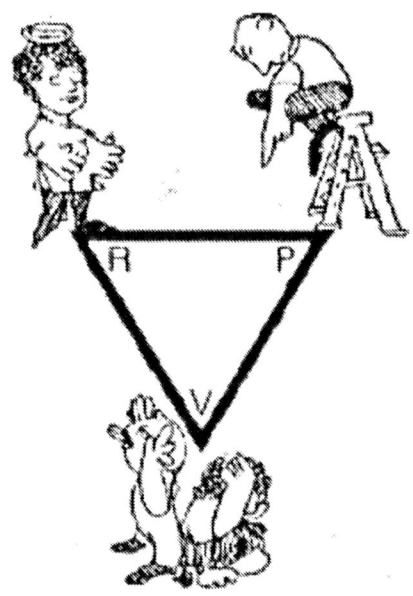

The problem with "PVR" relationship triangles is that they promote "1-up" and "1-down" R-messages. These activate shame-based false selves and disable true Selves, which *always* hinders attempts to communicate. Communication inside and among triangled people is rarely effective. If triangles aren't noticed and respectfully dismantled via awareness, metatalk, and personal healing, they relentlessly block people from filling their and each other's needs. Inner-family and social triangles cause increasing distrust, hurt, resentment, disrespect, anger, and emotional detachment: toxic relationships.

Triangles often multiply and interlock. Someone in one triangle's Victim role (e.g. older brother) plays the Persecutor in another triangle (Victim = younger sister.) Respectful awareness, metatalk, listening, and assertion are specially potent in "de-triangling" kids and/or adults in personal, business, and spiritual relationships.

Premise 22) There are three kinds of relationship dependencies.

An **interdependent** adult relationship is one in which both partners genuinely feel "I choose to be with you, and I can live well enough without you if I have to." Social surveys steadily report this feels best to most people, and lasts the longest, compared to . . .

A **dependent or enmeshed** relationship in which one or both partners gives their power and personal responsibility to the other, believing "*I can't live without you.*" Such people often usually badly wounded and living from a false self. They are often fear-based and/or shame-based, until choosing true (vs. pseudo) personal recovery; or . . .

An **independent** relationship, where neither partner really needs much from the other, and has a weak or no emotional/spiritual bond with them. They may pretend otherwise to themselves and/or other people for various reasons.

Awareness can reveal which of these three relationship types is the most satisfying to your inner family, and why. If your subselves disagree on this, your Self has an important inner conflict to resolve.

How are you doing with these three sets of premises? If your false self is in charge, those subselves are probably urging you to blank or numb out, skip ahead, defocus on something more interesting, or to feel increasingly overwhelmed or bummed out. If your Self is guiding your reading, s/he will urge patient attention, consideration, and pacing. My Self wants to reassure all your inner troops: **getting clear on *your* versions of these premises will help you all get your needs met more often**! If you were building a house, these are the foundations on which everything else rests. You wouldn't skip those, would you? Do any young subselves say, "*Sure would!*"? Hang in there: we're in the home stretch!

About Relationships and Communication Skills

Premise 23) If you're controlled by a distrustful false self, and/or if you're not aware of your version of these relationship premises, you'll unconsciously try to fill your surface and true needs by mixes of the ineffective strategies on p. 270. *None* of these strategies will fill your current true needs well enough, for long, starting with the need for respect. People who use them are not *bad*, they're uninformed, psychologically wounded, and unaware!

Here's the bottom line:

Premise 24) Any day, you can decide to start building fluency in the seven learnable relationship skills and a related set of attitudes outlined in this book. *Any Self-led adult or child who knows and uses these skills and premises with a genuine =/= attitude, can resolve any need conflict ("problem") in their inner and outer relationships.* If you take full responsibility for your life quality, and use the Serenity Prayer with =/= compassion, *this will be true whether a false self dominates your partner or not.* I suspect that few parents or schools currently teach these skills, so you and your family members all probably can benefit from learning them together.

Do you believe this? I'd be startled if some of your subselves weren't pretty skeptical. I suspect that you've never known anyone who _ was consistently lead by their Self, _ was fluent in these seven mental/verbal skills, and _ *used* them within your vision and hearing, so you could _ see the results, and _ compare them to your normal communication choices and behaviors. Am I right?

This is a little like a primitive person raised in a jungle confronting their first chocolate sundae, and being urged *"Put that in your mouth. You'll like it!"* My respectful guess is that if you commit to at least trying to put your Self in charge, and to experiment with these skills with open mind, you'll like the results! Moderate skepticism (your *Inner Skeptic, Pessimist,* or *Cynic*) protectively urges caution: *"Take very small steps, and evaluate them, don't just jump in with both feet and closed eyes!"*

Your *Cynic, Pessimist, Distracter, Doubter, Numb-er, Scared Child,* and/or *Catastrophizer* Guardian subselves may overwhelm your Self here. Their combined strategies to protect your Vulnerable parts will block you from trying these skills, and "loving" the results. If you're a shame-based person, you'll be invited to believe *"I don't deserve to get these benefits (high nurturance relationships), so don't bother trying these skills."*

A third possibility is that a fear-based false self controls you. Those subselves will give you persuasive thoughts like *"I know I can't do these skills well," "I know I'll fail,"* and *"Other people won't like me if I try these new ideas and behaviors."* Your enabled Self will say something like *"These ideas seem realistic and useful. I'm confident I can find a way to learn and use these skills to solve my relationship problems. Let's go!"*

So who is (which subselves are) *really* running your life today?

Our unremarked U.S. divorce and redivorce epidemic, and our social welfare industry, bulging prisons, and "drug culture," all imply that the denied norm in our U.S. society is psychologically wounded parents, and low-nurturance marriages and childcare. Hidden low childhood nurturance seems to pass significant false-self wounds on to the next generation. That means that a high percentage of the adults and kids in your life are probably governed by a false self, and don't know it. The checklists in "Who's *Really* Running Your Life?" and on the Web at [http://sfhelp.org/pop/assess.htm] list common traits of such people. What are your choices if you *want*, or *must* have, a non-toxic relationship with a person whose Self is often disabled, and who doesn't know it?

Relating to Psychologically-Wounded Partners

I hope you'd agree that your first and best option is to _ assess *yourself* for significant psychological wounding, and _ commit to true personal recovery (harmonizing your inner family), if it's warranted. The next best option is to for your Self to assess any minor or independent kids you have for symptoms of the **five traits of false-self dominance:**

Excessive **shame and guilt**.

Excessive **fears** of rejection, emotional overwhelm, conflict, failure, success, and the unknown.

Often **trusting others too much or too little**, including your Self and a benign Higher Power.

Major **reality distortions**, like denials, repressions, idealizations, projections, illusions, exaggerations, and minimizings; and from all these . . .

Difficulty bonding (attaching and exchanging love, commitment, and intimacy) with selected or all others.

If you conclude that one or more key adults or kids in your life have these symptoms "too much," what are your choices?

Perhaps the most impactful one is to let go of any strong need to save, heal, or fix wounded partners. In my experience, you *cannot*, with the possible exception of a young dependent child. Manipulating, hinting, or demanding that a wounded person "get help," or "work on yourself," no matter how well meant, is inherently insulting ("I'm 1-up!") Such communications will usually increase anxiety, shame, and resistance in the other person's governing subselves. The Serenity Prayer offers the Way here.

Another gift you can give yourself and split people is to let go of hoping for a really healthy, high nurturance relationship (and effective communications) with them. You can have a relationship, but unhealed false-self dominance will limit how satisfying and nurturing it can be. Fixating on trying to help or heal a split person *if they don't want help* is usually a sign of co-dependence (false-self dominance) in *you*.

A major gift you can give each psychologically wounded person in your life, including your living or dead childhood caregivers, **is *compassion***. The alternative is to revile, scorn, despise, ignore, or reject them as "bad" persons. Because the high majority of split people aren't aware of their false selves, this is like judging someone with leukemia or baldness as a "bad" person. If you overfocus on condemning a person's frustrating or hurtful behaviors and ignore the source of their behaviors (inherited ignorance, psychological wounds, and protective denials), you'll promote ongoing conflict within yourself and them, and between you. This doesn't mean that you don't assert and enforce firm boundaries with them. It means you do so with *compassion* and respect for yourself and them, rather than disdain, bitterness, revenge, scorn, or indifference.

 # Reality check: Think of someone in your life that often stresses you. Where do you judge this person now on the line between '"very bad person" and "very good person," when they're vexing you? If you're significantly governed by a false self), your *Inner Critic* will judge them toward the "bad" pole, and other Guardians like your *Moralizer* and *Rationalizer* will defend this (*"S/He deserves it, no matter what you say about inner wounds!"*). If *you* are wounded, what attitudes do you need from other people in your life? I'd be startled if your inner voices didn't say *"understanding, acceptance, concern, tolerance, respect, and compassion!"*

Another option you have with wounded people is to become aware of how your inner family reacts to them. If you're trying to harmonize your inner crew and enable your Self, and a split (wounded) person interferes with that, a tough choice is whether to keep the other person in your life or not. That can't apply to dependent kids, but it *can* apply to mates, relatives, and co-workers. A challenging **part of true recovery from false-self dominance is recognizing and choosing to limit or end toxic relationships**. A related choice is recognizing and leaving low-nurturance groups, including families, employers, communities, churches, and organizations.

For wounded people you have to relate to, like a child, dependent relative, or co-parenting ex-mate, a class of options you have is learning how to balance relating to them in restricted roles, and detaching from them in others. This usually involves some form of "**tough love**": respectfully setting and enforcing firm boundaries that they don't like, and steadily giving them the responsibility of their own actions and decisions *without undue anxiety, guilt, or shame.* Your using all seven relationship skills with an =/= attitude, and working to resolve your inner conflicts, can be great helps in doing this effectively.

If you're recovering from false-self dominance, other choices you have are if, when, and how to talk about that with other people. Often describing your own inner family conflicts, inner wounds, and "parts work" is a safer way of raising wounded partners' interest than preaching, lecturing, threatening, or demanding. If they show significant interest, suggest they read this book, and/or the companion volume "Who's *Really* Running Your Life?" Another helpful book is "Embracing Each Other," by Hal Stone and Sidra Winkelman.

Sometimes your Self may decide that you need some form of assertive confrontation with a psychologically-wounded person: "*Nikki, I need you to know that I've studied the condition of psychological wounding, and I feel you have most of the symptoms. I am not saying you're bad or crazy. I am saying, I'm stressed by the symptoms of your condition, and I need to tell you that. Are you willing to hear more?*" See Chapter 7 for more ideas and guidelines on respectful assertion.

Once you _ become comfortable with the reality of your subselves, and you _ empower your Self, you can intentionally surround yourself with people who are either Self-led, or are committed to true (vs. pseudo) recovery from false-self dominance. This inevitably means reducing or ending existing personal or work relations with some wounded persons. If you're bonded (emotionally attached) to them, such endings create an important new need: to grieve the loss of your broken bonds, and whatever needs those people filled in your life.

Recap

This chapter offers 24 basic premises about _ you, _ relationships, _ relationship *problems*, and _ communication skills. **The premises provide a framework for evaluating what** *your* **premises are** in these four vital areas, and how well your inner rules are working for you (filling your relationship needs). Your awareness of *your* version of these premises will help determine how effectively the seven communication skills will help you get your true personal and social needs met every waking hour.

These are the key proposals in this chapter:

"Problems" and **"conflicts"** are unmet human *needs*: emotional-physical-spiritual *tensions*, or discomforts.

Need-conflicts occur inside you (between your subselves) and between you and others (your respective active subselves) all the time. Like the emotions they trigger, conflicts are intrinsically neither good nor bad.

High-nurturance relationships consistently fill many of both partners' true current needs. High nurturance *family* relationships are the primary bulwarks against bequeathing psychological wounds to young kids. Low nurturance ("dysfunctional") relationships tend to reproduce and foster others.

For need-conflicts you feel are significant, it's vital to dig down below surface (conscious) needs to illuminate the *true* needs underneath, and focus on filling them (Chapter 4).

Ultimately, *you* are responsible for filling your underlying true needs, and other adults are responsible for theirs. Kids depend on their caregivers to teach them how to fill their own needs—i.e. how to be *independent* and *self-sufficient*.)

A *relationship* **exists when** the behavior or well-being of a person has occasional or chronic effects on the wholistic health of another. Thus it's possible to have a live relationship with a dead or far distant child or adult, as well as people in your home and workspace.

Relationships range from low to high nurturance, and dependent to interdependent to independent. *Interdependent* relationships seem to form the most mutually satisfying and nurturing friendships and marriages. Low-nurturance ("toxic") relationships *always* indicate that a false self dominates one or both partners. They usually don't know that, or the seven communication skills.

If _ your Self is usually leading your inner family, _ you have a genuine =/= attitude of mutual respect and empathy for other people, and _ you know the seven mental/verbal skills well enough, then _ these premises and the problem-solving steps on p. 396 will empower you to solve *any* internal or social relationship problem well enough, over time.

Once you _ empower your true Self to lead your inner family and _ identify significantly-wounded people in your life, you have a range of relationship options. Two key ones are: _ let go of expecting a high-nurturance relationship with each of them, and being able to "fix" them; and _ choose to see them with compassion, vs. scorn.

Options

You can keep reading now, and/or do one or more of these:

Ignore these premises and options, and behave the way you always have. You (your true Self or other subselves) can elect to be aware of the outcome or not.

Re-scan this chapter to see if having all 24 of the premises in mind clarifies or emphasizes individual premises. Highlight or jot margin notes to help key awarenesses stand out.

Copy the problem-solving summary (p. 396) and discuss it with one or more key people in your life, in order to (do what?). If you're parenting minor kids, mull what you've been teaching them about these four topics (you, relationships, problems, and using the seven skills to resolve them). If you want to shift your teachings, do so. Option: spend time with each child discussing selected premises to raise their awareness, and learn what they think (if anything) about each belief.

If you're working with a professional on some personal or relationship problem, give them a copy of the problem-solving summary and these premises. Explore together to see if discussing and applying them frees anything up, or suggests new directions.

Journal about selected (or all these) premises to clarify what *your* (inner family's) premises are about the four topics in this chapter. Doing this grows your *awareness*, including seeing inner conflicts that may covertly inhibit your problem-solving effectiveness.

If you'd like to change one or more of your premises to improve your relationships and serenity, meditate on whether something or someone (e.g. a scared, distrustful subself) is in the way.

Use these 24 premises as a checklist to analyze one or more troublesome relationships you have with an adult or a child now. If it's useful, guesstimate the other person's beliefs on selected premises here to see if you two may have a significant (abstract) *values* or *belief* conflict. If so, consider your options, and let your Self determine what, if anything, you should do about this. Option: do this with each of your subselves, and journal about the process and the results.

Focus on each of your main childhood caregivers one at a time. Guesstimate what their beliefs were on each of the premises above when you were young, based on their actions. Then reflect on how that shaped your decoding of their actions, how your personality developed.

Put a summary of these 24 premises where you can easily access it, and *use* it to guide and refresh you in vexing and important relationship situations.

Pull back from the detail of these premises, and note the *process* they represent: intentionally identifying key beliefs about an important aspect of your life. Is there another area of your life that might improve if you did a similar belief-inventory, like assets, sex, spirituality, parenting, health, your life purpose, career, geographic location, and your current balance of work, rest, and play? **Option**: pick out the three or four aspects of your life that consistently generate the most "stress" (anxiety, frustration, and confusion), and patiently identify the key beliefs your subselves hold about each of them.

Add your own options . . .

What do you notice about this set of options? They demonstrate that in any life situation, you have *many* choices, if you choose to use your awareness and creativity to identify them! This reality is the heart of creative brainstorming, and effective inner and social conflict resolution.

The next chapter invites you to imagine the probable impact on your life if your dominant subselves choose to develop and apply these seven relationship skills.

11) What Would Your Life be Like . . .

...if you could double the *effectiveness* of your communication skills? You'd get twice as many of your daily needs met! This book and the companion volume "Who's *Really* Running Your Life?" show you a practical framework that can significantly increase your daily problem-solving effectiveness and satisfaction. If you're inner family of subselves is motivated, harmonious, and patient, you can use the framework to consistently identify and fill your most important *true* needs, in a way that pleases you and (often) those around you. This will promote your building high-nurturance relationships.

Reality check: Review your definition of "stress." Then identify the five most stressful relationships or aspects of your recent life:

1)
2)
3)
4)
5)

Consider that the "stress" (worry, anxiety, frustration, disappointment, hurt, anger, confusion, . . .) comes from unresolved need-conflicts _ inside you, _ inside each other person involved, and _ between your respective inner families.

Next, **list your recent life priorities,** judged by where you put most of your waking energy. See any relationship between your governing subselves' priorities and your "big five"? Is one of your stressors "*Often, I can't think, communicate, and problem-solve effectively*"? If you're not yet aware of your communication processes, that may not seem so.

This book offers you a framework of premises, attitudes, and learnable skills that can reduce or eliminate your half of each of these conflicts, over time. **Vividly imagine what your life would feel like** if you committed to doing that. Can you imagine waking up each day to . . .

. . . **feeling** clear on, and committed to, your life purpose?

. . . **feeling** confident you can _ identify and state your needs clearly, and _ resolve most inner and social disputes and conflicts effectively with most other people?

. . . **feeling** calm, balanced, alert, and *purposeful* most of the time?

. . . **genuinely** enjoying the majority of your relationships in peaceful and conflictual situations?

. . . **feeling** confident you can manage anger, anxiety, "mistakes," and guilt well in yourself and others?

. . . **living** increasingly by choice, rather than reacting to events around you?

. . . **the satisfaction** of modeling and teaching attitudes and skills to the young people in your life so they can have these blessings in *their* lives?

Notice your self-talk objectively, like a reporter. Do you have scared and skeptical subselves that earnestly propose that you can't attain these things?

Yes you *can*!

I've studied and taught communication skills for over 30 years, including clinical hypnosis. Twenty of those years have been working full time as a psychotherapist: a relationship facilitator, teacher, and problem-solver. Since 1981, I've listened to over 1,000 divorced and stepfamily co-parents and some kids struggle with a myriad of personal, marital, and co-parenting problems. Since 1988, I've studied and experienced my clients' and my own inner families of subselves. I've learned that **average people like you have never been taught how to solve their innerpersonal and interpersonal need conflicts.** Until you read this book, you were probably *unaware* of (1) your *inner* family of subselves, and who is usually leads it; and (2) effective communication basics (Chapter 1) and seven learnable relationship skills:

Inner and interpersonal *awareness* (Chapter 2).

Clear thinking (Chapter 3).

Digging down to the true needs underlying surface problems, and clarifying who's responsible for filling them (Chapter 4).

Metatalk: building a communication vocabulary, and using it and *awareness* to talk cooperatively about your behavioral sequences (Chapter 5), so you can identify and solve communication blocks.

Empathic listening: hearing with your *heart* (Chapter 6).

Respectful assertion: saying what you need in a way others can hear you (Chapter 7).

Problem solving: filling enough of your and your partner's true current needs (Chapter 8).

You also were probably unaware of (3) high-nurturance relationship basics (Chapter 9), and (4) how to apply these concepts to effectively resolve significant conflicts among your *inner* family members (Chapter 10).

You can study and master each of these four groups of concepts over time, if your ruling subselves _ care enough about the quality and productivity of your life, _ really *believe* that you can improve it, and _ commit to doing so. If you do, I believe you'll experience increasing serenity, self-respect, self-confidence, and a growing compassion for all past and present kids and adults in your life. Your spiritual awareness will probably grow and deepen, as well. These seven are really *life* skills.

Who's leading your inner family now? If a protective false self is in charge, you'll probably miss these priceless benefits because of a mix of excessive shame, guilt, and fears, and protective reality distortions. These will also probably limit your chance to teach these four groups of concepts to the young people you care about. I assume your childhood caregivers never knew these concepts, and gave you their best anyway.

Status check: See what you think about these self-assessments:

My Self is clearly in charge of my inner family now. (T F ?) When you feel some mix of *calm, centered, energized, light, focused, resilient, up, grounded, relaxed, alert, aware, serene, purposeful*, and *clear*, your true Self is probably leading.

On a scale of 1 (I really don't care about the quality of my life) to 10 (I'm deeply concerned with my own wholistic health and growth), I usually feel about a ___. "I" is your dominant subselves.

1 to 10, I'd rate my recent ability to resolve my major life problems effectively as a ___.

From 1 (I'm totally disinterested) to 10 (I'm intensely interested), my subselves' degree of motivation to learn and apply the four sets of concepts above is about a ___ right now.

I have a clear, steady vision of what I want to accomplish with my life: _ true _ false _ It's evolving _ I'm not sure.

Pause and notice your self-talk and emotions now. Which subselves are "speaking"?

Here's another way of assessing what you've gotten from reading this book so far. You encountered a set of questions on p. 19. See if you can answer them now, or identify where to find the answers.

How did you do? How do you feel about that? To help clarify or check your answers, use the summaries in the next section, the Glossary, and the index. Take heart: you don't have to know all of these answers now to improve your communications. What you do need is _ the motivation to keep studying the questions and answers, _ seeing how they apply in your relationships and daily problems, and _ learning where to find the answers when you need them.

With practice, you'll build your own set of experience-validated answers, and you'll only need this book in special situations.

We're done exploring seven skills you can grow to increase the satisfactions in your daily life. Here's a buffet of possible . . .

Next Steps

Recall why you first picked this book up: did you get what you needed? If your motives were surface ones, try digging down to see what your *true* needs were/are (Chapter 4). If you read the book without doing the # **Reality checks** or chapter-closing exercises, then you've gained some concepts, but probably little *experience*. Your valuing and believing these inner-family concepts and seven skills will only increase if you *try* them, with the focused curiosity of a Self-motivated student.

If you're at a busy or conflicted time in your life, experiment with these skills to *help you* regain life balance and control. Alternative: put this book somewhere in your sight, and create a reminder to return to it when your life has calmed down. Your Self will know what's best.

If you try these skills, your results will largely hinge on whether your true Self is guiding your subselves or not. I suggest you review the emotional symptoms of your Self being in charge (Chapter 1), and then honestly fill out the checklists in "Who's *Really* Running Your Life?" or [http://sfhelp.org/pop/assess.htm]. If you feel your false self is often in charge these days, switch from improving your communication effectiveness to recovering from significant false-self dominance. I recommend using Self-directed "parts work" and qualified clinical help.

Affectionately **expect your well-meaning false-self gang to be clever and persistent** in trying to discourage you from doing this. Note that true (vs. pseudo) recovery from inner wounds takes several years to start stabilizing. Benefits usually appear early, and escalate as you work on empowering your Self. Progress is more likely if you use a qualified recovery clinician, and perhaps a professionally-led recovery group, for at least part of your healing.

Using these skills is paradoxic: you won't really experience their power and value until you try them, and your motivation to try them may depend on your "seeing." The title of Wayne Dyer's interesting book comes to mind: "You'll See It When You Believe It."

If you can access the Web, follow the ["http://. . ."] links in this text, and use the Web articles and worksheets that supplement each chapter. If you can't **go online** yet, use the potential value of these relationship concepts and skills as motivation to do so.

These seven mental/verbal skills are sequential. Success with later ones depends on _ your Self being in charge, and _ "enough" fluency with earlier skills. **Option:** starting with *awareness*, **pick a skill a month** and experiment with it. Start your month by rereading the chapter on that skill, and using the resources noted in the skill's summary. Each skill is summarized in the last half of this book, so if you copy or tear them out, you don't have to lug the book around. Practice the skill, and journal about your experience several days a week.

Again: to fill your daily needs, you depend more on your ability to *communicate* effectively than on any other learned skill. Do you agree?

Option: If you can find one, **practice with an interested partner** who seems to be often led by her or his Self. If you can't find one, see if you can find a partner in recovery from psychological wounds to practice with. If you follow this scheme, you'll spend eight months practicing these combined skills, including resolving inner conflicts. That will give you a fair basis to judge whether the skills really do improve your serenity and satisfactions.

If you have a committed relationship, another powerful option you have is to **invite your mate to join you** in _ harmonizing your inner families, and _ growing fluent in these seven skills together. If your mate isn't genuinely enthused at this time, avoid trying to "sell" or persuade him or her on either project. Be patient: if you start using these skills, other people *will* notice a difference in you. They may get curious about "what you're up to," and grow their own motivation.

Are there any minor kids in your life now? An impactful choice you have at any time is to begin to teach them about their inner family, their Self, and these seven relationship skills. The long-term benefits of passing these concepts to the invisible fan of your descendents are beyond meaningful estimate. Reflect: if you had been patiently encouraged to learn and use these skills when you were young, how might that have affected *your* life? Would any of your kids' teachers or coaches be interested in these ideas? If you know of, or participate in, a parent-support group or PTA, consider alerting them to these ideas and skills.

Another option is to **use the ideas and resources in this book with a professional** therapist or counselor by yourself, and/or with your partner or a child. If you do, you'll want the professional to evaluate the four groups of concepts above, and tailor them to fit her or his own values and style, and your shared objectives.

Is there a person you want to, or *must*, relate to (e.g. parent, sibling, neighbor, stepchild, or co-worker), and are troubled with? Mull whether there might be mutual ($=/=$) advantage in alerting them to the ideas between these covers. "*No,*" and "*Not now*" are legitimate answers! Notice which of your subselves is deciding . . .

If you marked this book up as you read, another option is to go back over the pages and note the places where your energy was the highest, including anxiety, anger, doubt, skepticism, and pain. Meditate on which subselves got activated and why. See if that suggests a local action plan.

Put the book down, breathe well, and reflect quietly now. Use *awareness* to sense where your mind (inner family) wants to focus, and where your energy is. Quiet any inner chatter, and *listen* for your still small voice. What does it say is the next right thing for you to do in your life?

I'm glad to get your feedback on _ this book, the series, or the Web site; and _ these ideas and/or their impact on your life. Contact me online via [http://sfhelp.org] or pilgrim27@aol.com.

If you're in a divorced family or stepfamily, all the books in this [xlibris.com] series refer to this one. Growing these seven skills and teaching them to your kids is co-parent Project 2: [..02/project02.htm].

Namasté, fellow pilgrim: I salute the Spirit within you!

RESOURCES

Reading about the seven skills will probably make little lasting difference in your communication effectiveness (getting daily needs met). *Trying* them WILL improve your effectiveness over time. The degree of improvement will be proportional to your motivation, patience, focus, and efforts. To help you remember and apply each skill, this part of the book provides 13 resources:

A) Summary: communication basics

B) Sample: A Bill of Personal Rights

C) Summary: *awareness* skill

D) Summary: clear-thinking skill

E) Summary: dig-down skill

F) Summary: metatalk skill

G) Summary: empathic-listening skill

H) Summary: assertion skill

I) Summary: win-win problem solving skill

J) Common communication blocks

K) Selected readings

L) A Glossary of communication terms, and . . .

An index

Each skill summary includes pointers to additional resources: articles, worksheets, and practice exercises. These are available for free download from the Internet, and may be published as a separate workbook.

Options: copy the summaries and edit them to better fit you. Give copies to others you care about. Refer to the summaries as you practice, until the skills become automatic. Consider using a communication journal or log to realize and enjoy your progress, over time.

A) Summary: Communication Basics

These are key ideas from Chapter 1. Copy or tear this out and use it as a reference guide before or after important communication experiences. Add notes or hilights that make this digest more useful to you. Numbers in brackets [ ] below refer to chapters in this book. *Partner* below means "current adult or child communication partner." Add Web pointers [..**/ ***.htm] to [http://sfhelp.org/] to access referenced materials.

Normal human personalities are composed of a group of semi-independent *subselves* or *parts*. At any moment, the dominant subselves cause your and your partner's needs, thoughts, perceptions, and behaviors; i.e. they cause your communication. Your subselves communicate with each other and "you" (your body and conscious mind) all the time.

Any perceived behavior *or lack of behavior* of person (or subself) "A" that causes a mental, emotional, and/or spiritual change in person (or subself) "B" is *communication*. Therefore, it's impossible to *not* communicate, because we routinely decode implied meanings from silences, body language, and absences.

Internal and social communication is the learned skill that we adults and kids depend on the most to get our daily *needs* met. When people can describe and apply the seven mental/ verbal skills that promote effective internal and interpersonal communication, they're better able to _ fill their daily needs _ in a way that feels good enough often enough. Their (*your*) life productivity and satisfactions increase significantly.

Needs are emotional/spiritual/physical discomforts. **"Problems" are *need conflicts.*** *Problem solving,* and *conflict resolution* both mean, "filling (satisfying) your and my current true needs well enough."

The **six needs** that kids, adults, and subselves instinctively try to fill by communicating with others are to . . .

1) Feel *respected* (valued) enough by one's self and others involved. This need is a constant in any solitary or social situation. And we all periodically need to . . .

2) Give or get **information**; and/or to . . .

3) **Vent**: i.e. to feel deeply understood and accepted vs. getting fixed or lectured; and/or to . . .

4) **Cause or prevent change** (feel impactful). *Change* includes increasing or decreasing emotional distance (trust, respect, and intimacy) with your current partner.

5) Create **excitement** (reduce numbness and boredom), and/ or to . . .

6) **Divert** from some discomfort, like conflict, strong emotions, awareness, and silences.

You and each partner always have two or more of these communication needs at once. The needs flux *fast* during every behavioral interaction ("conversation"), as inner and outer environments change. Without motivation and *awareness,* people are often unconscious of *what* they need in important communications, specially if governed by a protective false self [1, 9].

The *effectiveness* of your communication (how often you get your current true needs met) can be intentionally improved with practice and adjustment, over time. **Effective** (vs. *good,* and *open and honest*) **communication happens** when each person _ gets enough of their *true,* vs. surface, current needs met, in their opinion; _ in a way that leaves them feeling good enough about _ themselves, _ all others involved, and _ the processes inside and between them.

This two-level definition implies that any two-person communication can have 16 possible outcomes. Only one of them is fully effective (win-win) for both people! Definitions of *"effective* verbal communication" vary widely, depending on many factors. In important situations, use metatalk [5] to discern if you partners share a compatible definition.

Effective **communication happens when** all partners' current communication needs match well enough, such as I need to vent, and you need to maintain our relationship and get information (about me). When our mix of current needs doesn't match, we have a *communication* (needs) conflict.

In conversation, we try to fill our needs (reduce our discomforts) by decoding up to **four messages at once, on each of three "channels":**

Message:	Communication "Channel"
"Now I feel . . ."	**Verbal:** (words and sounds)
"Now I need . . ."	**Paraverbal:** (voice tone + tempo + inflection + volume + accent)
"Now I think . . ."	**Non-verbal:** (face + body + hands + movement + touch)
"Now I see you as . . ."	

In most situations, "I see you as . . ." affects communication success the most. It is often decoded unconsciously, until you become *aware.* These **R(espect) messages have three possible decodings**: "Right now, you seem to value your needs, worth, and dignity . . .

. . . more than mine (**you're 1-up / superior**, and I'm 1-down)," or . . .

. . . less than mine (**you're 1-down / inferior**, and I'm 1-up)," or . . .

. . . equally with mine: **we're "=/="**.

Premise: **Communications may be fully effective** *only* when all partners consistently decode clear "=/=" respect messages from each other. Shame-based ("1-down") people often have trouble communicating well, until they evolve _ real Self-respect, and _ empathy for others.

Shame-based people, specially those who deny it, will often mistake your "=/=" (mutual respect) R-messages for attacks and put-downs, because they *feel* 1-down (inferior). You can metatalk [5] about this together if they're willing, but they have to *want to* change their own self-respect. *Accusing* them of such a decoding mistake will often make communication worse.

Face to face, **most of the meaning we decode from our partners comes through our** *eyes*; specially R(espect)-messages! Often the least of the meaning we decode comes from our words, but we've been taught to focus on them the most. *Awareness* rebalances that!

Many of our messages are decoded unconsciously. We "leak." People who are dominated by a false self often send conflicting messages via different channels: e.g. words say: "*Good to see you!*" and body, face, and voice tome imply "*I'm indifferent to you right now.*" Such double or mixed messages typically cause confusion, anxiety, and distrust.

Effective communication may (vs. will) happen when all people are undistracted enough internally and externally. That requires partners being guided by their Selves, *aware,* and intentionally focused on a common topic and the mutual communication process.

Seven interrelated communication skills any adult or child can learn and practice to fill their true needs more effectively are . . .

Awareness: what's happening now inside me, inside you, between us, and around us?

Clear (vs. fuzzy) thinking: _ building your vocabulary and _ using clear, appropriate words; and avoiding _ defocusing, _ fuzzy pronouns, and _ hand-grenade terms.

Digging down to current *true* needs, and owning your responsibility to fill yours.

Metatalk: talking objectively about *how* we communicate now, and/or over time.

Empathic listening: listening with your *heart.*

Assertion: stating respectfully and clearly what you need from others now; and . . .

Win-win problem solving (need fulfillment), vs. avoiding, and arguing, or fighting.

Each skill is best used in different situations:

Use *awareness* [2] all the time.

Use **clear thinking** [3], and digging down [4] when you're "significantly" uncomfortable.

Use **metatalk** [5] and the other skills any time you sense that your and your partner's communication needs are conflicting, or something else is blocking effective communication (p. 405).

Use **empathic listening** [6] _ when your partner can't hear you because they're currently distracted by intense emotions, sensations, and/or needs: their E(motion)-level is "above their ears; and _ to respond respectfully when your partner "resists" your assertion/s.

Use respectful **assertion** [7] to avoid or react to conflicts, and to give "dodge-proof" praise.

Use **problem solving** [8] any time you and a partner have significantly conflicting inner-family, communication, or other needs; specially those that recur.

Use **all seven skills** any time you have an internal conflict among two or more subselves [9].

Tips for "High-E" Situations

A "high-E(motion level)" situation occurs when one or more people experience emotional intensity that stays "above their ears": i.e. that distracts them from hearing their partner well, or at all. The emotions can be anything: joy, terror, guilt, confusion, shame, rage, pain, resentment, regret, anguish, overwhelm . . . Emotions may be caused or amplified by intense body sensations: pain, arousal, hunger, thirst, cold, cramps, and fatigue.

Stay clear on a definition of "effective communication" that works for you, and *use* it to guide your decisions.

Coach yourself to **become** *aware* **of your and your partners' E-levels** in important communication situations. That requires you to want to be aware of your awareness. If your partner's E-level is above their ears, choose empathic listening [6] until their hearing returns. This is *not* necessarily agreeing with them, or giving up your values, perceptions, and needs!

Ask: "**Is my Self and yours present now?** How do I know? [1] If not, what are my options?"

Option: do an awareness-bubble check. Are you aware of your partner's current needs, feelings, and inner-process as well as your own? Are they equally aware of yours? If not, use metatalk and problem solving to expand your bubbles.

Note without judgment whether the leader of your inner team of subselves sees **this high-E situation as an** *opportunity*, **or a chore, burden, or menace.** The latter suggests that a false self is probably in charge. Encourage yourself and partner/s to invest time in learning from your communication *process*, as well as trying to fill your other needs.

Do an inner and environmental **"distraction" check.** If anyone is physically, emotionally, mentally, or spiritually distracted, use metatalk [5] and assertion [7] to reduce those before continuing.

Patiently use digging down [4] to unearth your and your partner's current true (vs. surface) needs, and who's responsible for filling them. Break complex problems into small ones. Then prioritize those, and resolve them patiently one or two at a time, as =/= (mutually respectful) partners vs. opponents.

Assess together which of the four types of conflict you each are having: _ internal [9]; _ abstract (e.g. values, preferences, perceptions, expectations, and roles); _ concrete resource; or _ communication-needs. Review the options for solving each type [8], and help each other do that *as teammates.*

Intentionally choose an =/= attitude about your partner, despite any dissenting subselves (e.g. your diligent *Inner Critic.*) Intentionally promote or demote yourself to equal, in terms of human dignity and worth, with all subselves and communication partners. If helpful, build a Personal Bill of Rights (p. 362). Carry it with you and *use* it, until all your subselves accept its points as credible articles of faith and stop fighting it.

Objectively **assess what R(espect)-messages you're exchanging** with current partner/s. With *inner* conflicts, do the same with your subselves. If unsure, *ask* your partners or subselves if they're receiving credible "=/=" R-messages, or something else. Option: discern which subselves are sending your R-messages, and watch for opposing ones: a symptom of false-self dominance.

Get quiet, and **decide whether focusing on your "still, small voice" now** (your wise or spiritual subself), *and trusting what it says*, would help now. If you can't hear it or trust it, commit to learning which subselves are blocking that.

Use *awareness* [2] to re-check whether you're using the appropriate skills to match your and your partner's E-level mix:

Use empathic listening [6] if your E-level is low and theirs is high ("above their ears").

Use empathic listening and assertion [7] if both your levels are high. Then use assertion, and perhaps metatalk [5], when their level is low.

When both your E-levels are below your ears, use "normal conversation," or all seven skills if you have a conflict. Use =/

= *awareness* and clear thinking in all situations, regardless of E-level.

Help each other stay aware of the vital difference between your communication topics (*what* you talk about), and your inner and mutual processes (*how* you communicate.) Check to see if your and your partner's current communication needs (above) match or clash. If the latter, refocus and use metatalk [5] and the other six skills to resolve that.   ·

Consider breaking complex conflicts into three parts: your inner-family conflicts [9], your partner's inner conflicts; and "interpersonal" conflicts between your respective inner families [8]. Use all seven skills on each of these, internal conflicts first, to help reduce or resolve your major *surface* conflicts, over time.

If your inner and/or interpersonal communication needs clash now or repeatedly, **use the checklist of communication blocks** on p. 405 to brainstorm what may be going wrong.

More options:

Use communication-sequence mapping (p. 400) to grow your awareness of what's going on, and how to improve it. Be alert for repeating communication sequences (patterns), over time.

Keep your **inventory of communication** *strengths* handy and growing! [..02/evc-strengths.htm]

Any time you're aware of reducing a high-E situation to only two either-or options ("My way or the highway"), see who has blended with your and/or your partner's Self.

Identify communication hero/ines: people whom you see as *effective* communicators. Emulate their values and traits to the extent that's useful, without shaming your own efforts, or trying to become a clone. While building your own communication style and effectiveness, identify what they do or don't do that differs from less effective communicators.

Patiently practice the seven communication skills, ideally with a willing partner. For situations you deem "important," invest time in assessing the communication process/es that occurred, and decide *without blame* which of the 16 possible outcomes (p. 105) you achieved. Consider journaling about this as a way of increasing your awareness.

Discern what works (fills your and any partner's true needs), and what doesn't. Value and learn from your "mistakes," minimize self-blame, and keep practicing. *"Progress, not Perfection!"*

If your high-E-level partner is a child, note your option to model and teach them these basics, guidelines, and skills, starting with the inner family concept [1]. These are priceless life-skill gifts! You have the same option with adult partners who are unsplit and motivated to grow and learn with you.

When you've done all you can with a High-E situation, mentally review, or journal, what you learned, and what you want to remember. Appreciate yourself and your partner (=/=), even if you disagree with them. If helpful, remind yourself . . .

> "If I always do what I've always done,
> I'll always get what I've always got."
> —*Steve and Carol Lankton*
> and . . .
> "Nothing changes, if nothing *(in me)* changes."
> —Anonymous

Add your own tips . . .

To check your knowledge of these communcation basics, see p. 44 or [http://sfhelp/org/02/evc-quiz.htm].

B) A Personal Bill of Rights

Premise: every human being has basic rights, regardless of age, gender, race, religion, culture, or social rank. Kids need help to _ learn how to believe and assert these rights, and _ to *want to* accord them to other people. Clarity on and *belief in* rights like these are the foundation of self-respect and effective communication. To experience the power of rights like these, your true Self must consistently govern your inner family of subselves. See Chapter 1 and "Who's *Really* Running Your Life?" or [http://sfhelp.org/01/project01.htm].

These statements will clarify and remind me of my rights as a dignified, worthy, unique human being. I was not taught some of these as a child, and can strengthen my belief in them today. Doing this intentionally will free me of old inhibitions, and help me be assertive with others in a positive, realistic, respectful way. It is healthy for me to honor and respect my own rights and needs as much as I do those of every other adult and child. I *can legitimately proclaim and pursue these rights without shame, guilt, or fear, in any way that doesn't interfere with their equal rights.*

I Have the Right To . . .

1) all my emotions, including fear, sadness, anger, shame, uncertainty, confusion, anxiety, guilt, joy, lust, hope, pride, happiness, etc.—even "numbness." They are a natural part of being human. *All* my emotions are useful signals that I have needs to attend to. None are "negative."

2) tell others of my feelings if I choose to, *without* feeling guilty. I am responsible for this choice, but not for their reactions.

3) say "no" or "yes" without guilt or shame, and to be responsible for the consequences.

4) choose if, when, and how to meet others' expectations of me. If I choose not to meet them, *I need not feel guilty.* I am responsible for such choices.

5) _ choose my own friends and acquaintances, and how and _ when to spend time with them. I may, but don't *have* to, justify these choices to others.

6) make my own mistakes and profit by them, if I can.

7) choose if, when, and how to tell others how their actions are affecting me, and to take responsibility for doing so.

8) earn and maintain my own self-respect and pride, rather than depending on other people's opinions of me.

9) seek, accept, or decline help, without shame or guilt.

10) give others the responsibility for their own beliefs, actions, feelings, and thoughts, without feeling "selfish." Others have the same right to give me responsibility for mine.

And I have the right to . . .

11) seek situations, environments, and relationships that are healthy, growthful, and nurturing for me.

12) be spontaneous, play, and have fun!

13) develop and grow *at my own pace.*

14) appreciate my efforts and enjoy my achievements without guilt, anxiety, or shame.

15) act to fill my own wants and needs, rather than expect others to do so for me.

16) periods of rest, refreshment, reflection, and relaxation. These are as productive for me as times of work and action.

17) choose whom I will trust, when, and with what.

18) take on only as much as I can handle at any given

time, and to tell others if I feel overloaded, without **shame or guilt.**

19) nurture, love, and value my self as much as I do others who are special to me. In moderation, pride is not a sin, and never was.

20) choose the paths and goals I wish for my life, and to pursue them without guilt, shame, or having to justify them to others.

And I also have the right to . . .

21) take all the time I need to evaluate and make important life-decisions, even if this stresses others.

22) care for my body and soul lovingly and respectfully, in my own ways.

23) decide on my own priorities and limits at any given time, and act on them as I see fit.

24) distinguish between who my family, workmates, and friends say I am (or was) vs. who I really am.

25) be heard and understood. My thoughts, feelings, wants, and needs are just as legitimate, worthy, and important as anyone else's.

26) decide what *perfect* or *excellent* is in any situation, and to choose whether to strive for these or not.

27) choose how to spend my time, and own the current and long-term consequences of that.

28) tell others what I expect of them, realizing they may or may not choose to fulfill these expectations.

29) choose how and when to peacefully fill my spiritual needs, even if my choices conflict with others' values or wishes. I do not have the right to force my spiritual or religious views or values on other people.

30) heal past personal shamings and wounds, and replace unhealthy inner messages I've lived by with more appropriate ones.

31) listen to and heed my inner voice(s) with interest and respect, and to sort out my true voice(s) from others' I hear.

32) ask (not demand) of others how they feel about me, what they think about me, and what they want of me. They need not comply.

33) decide if, when, and how to forgive both my mistakes, and any hurts received from others. I affirm that such forgiveness promotes healing.

34) work respectfully and peacefully to change laws or rules I feel are unjust or harmful to me and/or others.

Add your own . . .

+ + +

Options

Note the spirit of this Bill, and thoughtfully edit it or compose your own. That's apt to feel more authentic than adopting this declaration word for word.

Grow the habit of reading your Bill out loud before making important assertions and confrontations.

Focus on a person or a subself who stresses you, and read each item in this Bill out loud as "*You* have the right to . . ." If you can *mean* this without ambivalence or qualification, you have the =/= attitude which is essential for effective communication. If you can't, a false self is probably controlling you.

Imagine your Higher Power speaking each of these rights to you, one at a time.

Review each right, and see if you need to amend it for minor children.

To add context and motivation to *use* such a Bill, review the wisdom at [..01/inspirations1.htm].

Other Web Resources:

A Web copy of this Bill of Personal Rights [http://sfhelp.org/02/rights.htm]

Assertion practice for partners:
[..02/assert-practice.htm]

Article on positive self esteem:
[..02/branden.htm]

C) Summary: Communication *Awareness*

Go within, or go without—Neale Walsh

These are key ideas from Chapter 2. **Premise**: A fundamental, learnable communication skill is becoming nonjudgmentally *aware* (conscious) of what's going on in four dynamic zones, moment by moment: _ the thoughts, feelings, and needs inside you and _ inside your partners, and _ what's happening *between* you and your partner/s and _ *around* you and them. Such awareness is vital in current solo and social situations you and/or any communication partner deem "important."

Building your awareness of what's happening in these zones enables you to discuss objectively *"What's going on in and between us now?"* (metatalk). This and the other five mental/verbal skills allow you to resolve most conflictual situations effectively, if your partner is led by their true Self. Common alternatives to clear *awareness* are denial, repression, numbness, minimization, exaggeration, projection, and defocusing. Bracketed [numbers, letters] below point to relevant chapters and other summaries, respectively.

Awareness Exercise

Get quiet and undistracted. Notice your breathing: shallow/

chest, or deeper/belly. Write down or meditate on these awarenesses *without judgment:*
   "Now I feel . . .
   "Now I think . . .
   "Now I (visually) see . . .
   "Now I need . . .
   "Now my body is saying . . .
   "Now I hear . . ."

Key Awarenesses

   In relationships and situations you deem important, key awarenesses to build are:
   Is either of us controlled by a false self? [1, 9]
   What R(espect)-messages are we decoding now, and over time; "1-up," "1-down," or "=/=" (mutual respect)? Non-=/= messages imply false-self dominance, and degraded communication effectiveness. [1, A]
   What communication needs do we each have now, besides self and mutual respect: _ give or get information, _ vent, _ cause change, or create _ excitement or _ distraction? Do our communication needs *match* now? [1, A]
   Are we focused together now, and over time? If so, what are we focused *on?*
   Are our E(motion)-levels above or below our ears? Based on that, which mix of communication skills should I use now? [1, A]
   If (I believe) we have a conflict, _ which of four types is it: _ internal [9], _ abstract, _ concrete (physical resource), or _ communication needs [8, I]); and _ what do we each *really* need, right now? [4, E]
   What are our communication outcomes _ now, and _ over time? Did we _ each get what we needed, _ in a way each of us feels good enough about? [1, A]
   For important relationships: **what are our key**

communication sequences and patterns over time specially when we're conflicted? [1, 5, I]

There are *many* more communication and relationship factors you can learn to be selectively aware of and use (via metatalk) to identify and resolve communication *process* problems. [F and L] In any situation, some of these awarenesses will be more relevant than others.

Other Awarenesses

Your and your partners' *attitudes* **about your rights** as dignified human beings. They are the basis for calm, firm assertions. If you're each not clear on your personal rights, the odds on getting your current true needs met well enough drop. Disagreements on personal rights are abstract *values* conflicts.

Environmental distractions around you and your partners. These include too much, and/or unexplained, noise, motion, unpleasant temperatures or smells, and too much or too little light. If you become aware of significant inner or outer distractions, use metatalk, respectful assertion and problem solving to reduce your distractions and sharpen your focus.

Your and each partner's *knowledge* of . . .

What _ significant false-self dominance is, _ the five other wounds it causes [1], and _ the typical symptoms of false-self dominance. [..pop/assess.htm]

Communication basics [1, A], including _ ways that communication effectiveness may be blocked, _ the specific blocks you and your partner are prone to, and _ specific options on resolving each of these blocks [J].

What "effective interpersonal communication" is. If you partners don't share a clear, compatible definition, your odds for achieving it drop. This book proposes two criteria for communication effectiveness: each partner feeling at the end _ "I got my current true needs filled well enough," and _ "On reflection, I feel good enough about me, my partner, and the process between us."

Options for resolving *inner* **conflicts** among your personality subselves. [1, 9]

High-nurturance relationship basics [10], including _ the primal human **needs** each of us can only fill for ourselves [4]; and _ what PVC (persecutor-victim-rescuer) *relationship triangles* **are** [10], _ why they're often toxic to personalities and relationships, and _ what to do about them. Such triangles usually indicate one or more of the three people is significantly split and controlled by a false self.

Differences between common male and female priorities, sensitivities, ways of thinking, and communication needs and styles. For details, see Deborah Tannen's book "You Just Don't Understand," and "Brain Sex," by Anne Moir and David Jessel. [http://sfhelp.org/02/gender.htm].

Other Web Resources

Checklist: your communication *strengths*:
[..02/evc-strengths.htm]

Awareness practice for partners:
[..02/aware-practice.htm]

Co-parent knowledge quiz: [..07/quiz.htm]

D) Summary: *Clear-thinking* Skill

This nets out key ideas from Chapter 3. If you don't agree with any of these premises, what *do* you believe?

One or more subselves causes your thinking by voicing their opinions, observations, and needs to your conscious mind; i.e. your thought streams, hunches, and images are the "voices" of your active subselves. When several "speak" at once, you feel *muddled* or *confused*. Subselves conversing cause "inner dialogs," including debates and fights. These can cause physical symptoms. [9]

Your subselves *think* in order to "make sense" of (decode meaning from) your current _ internal and _ external environments, so they can _ understand what you need now and in the future, in order to _ decide if and how to fill them (behave) now.

You think far faster than you speak, so your mind can "outrun your mouth," specially in crises. *Awareness* of your thinking and speaking can help keep them synchronized. Clear thinking may or may not promote clear speaking.

You *can* intentionally learn to improve your thinking effectiveness, within limits. Doing so will help you fill more needs more often, and promote your serenity, productivity, relationships, and wholistic health.

Effective **thinking** means the subselves using your

unconscious, semi-conscious, and conscious minds coordinate to _ identify and decode accurate *meaning* from your _ inner and _ outer environments; and then _ process the meanings in a way that leads to _ identifying and filling your current true needs well enough. Restated: Your thinking locally or chronically is *effective* if you feel you're getting enough of your true current needs met (p. 149).

Fuzzy thinking either _ makes distorted or no "sense" (meaning) of your inner and/or outer environments, and/or it _ processes your meanings in a way that doesn't meet your current true needs well enough. Your thinking is probably ineffective or fuzzy if you often feel worried, dissatisfied, anxious, sick, tired, lonely, or upset; and/or you often conclude "*I don't know what I need right now.*" These are common symptoms of normal *false self-dominance*: alarmed, distrustful subselves blending with and disabling your true Self. [1]

Logic is the art and science of assessing and describing how concepts, processes, or objects relate to each other (cause and effect). With study, awareness, and mental discipline, you can improve your logic. The subselves that operate your unconscious mind, and/or blend with your Self when excited, use a different kind of narrow-focus logic than your Self does. Therefore at times you behave *illogically* ("*I don't know what made me get a tattoo.*").

Assuming is a way of thinking. It is assigning a probable "truth" or meaning to something without adequate information about it ("*I assumed you were lying.*") *Awareness* and metatalk reveal if you or another is assuming, so you can act on that, if you wish.

Remembering, **imaging, associating, and physical and emotional** *feelings* provide raw material for thinking. The accuracy of your memory, and your awareness of your feelings and body sensations, affect how your subselves *process* that information (think).

Ways to Increase Your *Thinking* Effectiveness

Work to keep your Self in charge of your inner team of subselves [1]. S/He usually "sees" more "wide-angle" and long-range, and can make better conclusions and decisions than your other subselves. False selves tend to create muddled or fuzzy thinking.

In high-E(motion) times, choose to be more aware of _ *how* you think (focus, clarity, scope, pace) and _ which subselves are generating your thoughts. Note typical outcomes. Do you get your needs met?

Evolve your own definition of *effective* thinking, and grow the habit of using it to gauge your local status and long-term progress.

Awareness provides raw material for your thinking. **Intentionally replace mental and physical numbness with *awareness*,** by . . .

. . . avoiding tobacco. The chemicals from ingesting it reduce the transmission of oxygen by your blood, which numbs *awareness* of your senses and emotions.

. . . practicing breathing from your belly. False selves often cause unconscious shallow breathing, which mutes your awareness, emotions, and mental clarity.

. . . avoiding various chemicals, like marijuana and ethyl alcohol beverages. The latter is a poison that runs your car engine, and kills your liver and irreplaceable brain (thinking) cells; and . . .

. . . meditating and journaling regularly. Use the awareness exercise on p. 368 or equivalent.

Develop your awareness of bodily feelings that relate to _ false-self dominance and related fuzzy thinking (e.g. shallow breathing, numbness, tenseness), and _ your Self orchestrating your subselves' inner processing. [1]

Practice viewing *internal* and interpersonal "problems" as *need conflicts*. That promotes using awareness to dig down

[4] to discern "What do I *really* need right now?", which empowers effective thinking.

Regard *all* your emotions as useful signals from your subselves that they need something now. Discard old beliefs that some emotions are "negative." Distinguish between *feeling* your emotions and *acting* on them. Ignoring or muting emotional signals may lower your thinking effectiveness.

Coach yourself and those you love to **become "fuzzy word" and "hand-grenade word" hunters.** Fuzzy (ambiguous, vague) words include pronouns and phrases like *it, that, them, everybody, people, the issue, soon, sometime, sort of, maybe, the problem, thing, work on, deal with, and work through.* Example: *"We really have to sort of work through this issue,"* vs. *"You and I need to agree on evolving and following a budget this week, to stop our checks from bouncing and lowering our credit rating."*

Hand-grenade words carry high emotional charges. They can cause subselves to react, take over your or your partner's Self, and cause assumptions, misunderstandings, and impulsive behavior. Typical hand-grenade words are *rape, abuse, abortion, irresponsible, insensitive, selfish, liar, weak, pathetic, ridiculous, crazy, shameful, fanatic, addicted, childish, dysfunctional, stupid, pornography, molest,* and so on. See other examples in [3].

Intentionally build your vocabulary, perhaps in special categories like emotions, communications, families, and relationships. If someone uses a word you don't know, ask for a definition or use a dictionary. Learn one or several new words every couple of days. Option: start with the communication and relationship words (p. 418). Learn by *using* them in your speech and writing.

Thinking keeps you safe, comfortable, and healthy by filling your needs. With your Self in charge, **practice asking _ your** *inner* family members and _ any partner **questions like these**:

"Specifically, what do you (or I) need right now in general, and from me (or you)?"

"What have you (or I) tried, already, and what did you (or I) get?" and . . .

"Specifically, what do you (or I) feel is in the way (of getting enough of what you (I) need?"

In key situations, **practice identifying specifically what you *expect*** from you and others. **Then** coach yourself to notice how well your subselves **stay focused** on these, and what distracts (defocuses) them.

Patiently **grow your proficiency with the seven mental/ verbal skills** in this book. Then use the communication terms you're learning (9 above) to _ experiment with "mapping" communication sequences (p. 400) between _ conflicted inner-family subselves, and _ you and key other people. Use mapping specifically to spot situational or chronic fuzzy thinking.

Identify a trusted, supportive partner to give you periodic feedback on how clear or *effective* (3 above), vs. *logical*, they feel your thinking is.

Choose clear-thinking mentors and/or hero/ines. Study how they look and sound, and *why* you feel they're effective thinkers. Experiment, and incorporate the best of what you learn in your thinking style. Stay aware of the differences between *thinking* and *acting*, and *knowledge* (information) and *wisdom* (how you use your knowledge, which involves *thinking*).

If there are young people in your life, see if you can interest them in *how* they and other people think. Connect thinking, communicating, and *getting your needs filled* for them. Outline the inner-family concept to them [1], help them inventory their inner crew, and playfully ask, "Who's thinking that?" Fun and enlightening for everyone!

Use "parts work" to learn if you have a protective *Blocker* subself who "blanks out" your mind and/or emotions at certain times to protect a Vulnerable subself or someone else. If so, use parts work to grow *Blocker's* trust in your Regular subselves and true Self, and negotiate *Blocker* taking a new inner-family role.

Develop your *Observer's* **talent** for giving you factual feedback on what and *how* you think, with certain people, situations (like conflict), or moods. Become familiar with the experiences of _ mind *racing*, or *churning*, _ *assuming*, and _ *defocusing*, and assess yourself for those nonjudgmentally. They usually indicate several activated subselves, and false-self dominance (blending).

Work with a respectful, co-motivated partner towards clearer thinking. We can't avoid judging our thinking and behaving in distorted, subjective ways. This is specially true if we're controlled by a well-meaning false self. Exchanging clear supportive feedback with a respectful, unsplit, focused partner can safely expose and lower your (and their) distortions, and speed your work. It's also more fun!

Coach yourself to S-L-O-W *D-O-W-N*, and praise yourself when you do. Get interested in the subselves that feel uncomfortable when you do this (e.g. your *Driver-Achiever* and *Impatient One*), and help them toward an "attitude adjustment"! Premise: living *fast* and over-stimulated usually promotes hasty, impulsive, incomplete, semi-conscious, fuzzy thinking. Those promote unfilled true needs, "stress" (anxiety), and degraded wholistic health and relationships.

Pick a physical object you see every day (a "trigger") to remind you of these options to clarify your thinking.

List several things you can choose to do that will help upgrade the effectiveness of your thinking:

Options

Reread this summary or Chapter 3 monthly, for several months, to ground your awareness. Then journal about what happens in your life. See if you become more aware of _ the process and _ *effectiveness* of your thinking _ in general and _ in conflict, and _ its impact on getting your daily needs met.

Using your definition of *effective thinking*, _ rank yours in important situations or relationships, or over time. Do this to learn, not to shame. Option: use a scale like this: _ *very* ineffective _ fairly ineffective _ so-so _ fairly effective _ *very* effective

Awarenesses / To Do's ...

E) Summary: Dig-down Skill

This summarizes keys ideas from Chapter 4: dig down to your true needs. Bracketed [numbers and letters] refer to other chapters in this book, and their summaries. [..**/ ****.htm] points to a Web resource at [http://sfhelp.org/..].

Premise 1): Most inner-family and interpersonal "problems" (need conflicts) are surface *symptoms* of deeper semi-conscious true needs. By definition, a *true* personal need is one that only you can fill. See the examples on p. 149.

Premise 2) There are four levels of problem "ownership." Permanently solving recurring major conflicts requires all partners to _ dig down to levels three or four, _ identify their respective true needs, and _ accept responsibility for satisfying them. People whose inner family is consistently guided by their Self and Higher Power are more apt to succeed at this.

Level 1: *"I have no unfilled needs. I don't have a 'problem' right now. Maybe you do."* This may be true, or it may be subselves guarding you by denying, repressing, or distracting your bodily senses and consciousness from uncomfortable true needs. People at this level usually don't know about subselves and psychological wounding; and are low in *awareness* skill.

Level 2: *"I'm not controlled by a false self (blended, or split), and I do have a problem now. It's not my fault, and someone else is responsible for filling my needs."*

Level 3: *"I'm not split, and I am at least half responsible for filling the true needs under my surface problems. Someone else is responsible for the other half."*

Level 4: *"I am split, and I own full responsibility for _ enabling my Self, and then _ identifying and filling all of my true needs. I respectfully give other adults the same responsibility for their needs, without guilt, shame, or anxiety. I can choose to help others do this or not, and to ask for help with mine, or not."*

Premise 3) Problem-solving effectiveness is directly proportional to how clear participants are on their respective current *true* needs. Example: *"I need the car this afternoon"* is a surface need. The underlying needs are probably *"I need to lower my anxiety* now *by affirming I having a reliable way to get to my appointment at 3 PM on time, and then get home safely and easily."* Awareness like this opens up problem-solving options, like *"You take the car, and I'll take a taxi."*

How to Dig Down

In High-E(motion) situations, tailor these steps to fit. First, **reduce emotional and physical distractions, and use *awareness* to confirm** . . .

. . . **your** Self is leading your team of subselves. If s/he is, you'll feel some combination of *centered, grounded, light, clear, strong, sure, calm, focused, energized, purposeful, resilient, aware,* and *alert*. [1, ..01/innerfam1.htm]

. . . **your** E(motion)-level is. "below your ears." If not, use empathic listening [6, G], and/or ask for hearing checks from your partner/s.

. . . **you** have a steady two-person awareness bubble [2, C], and . . .

. . . **a solid** =/= (mutual respect) attitude [1] about your partner/s; and . . .

. . . **you** believe respectful digging down will probably benefit everyone.

When those are all true, ask your subselves and/or your partner *"What do you need right now?"* or *"What do you need from me, right now?"* Use empathic listening to make sure you hear their answer clearly.

Then ask *"OK, why do you need that?"* or *"And you need that now in order to . . .?"*

Then ask *"If you don't get that, what (bad thing) might happen?"* and then *"If that (bad thing) happened, what would that mean to you?"*

Keep digging down nonjudgmentally with each answer you get, using empathic listening to stay in synch. Practicing meditation; journaling; breathing-awareness; respectful silence; and *listening to* or *sensing* your mind + body + spirit. Those will often improve your *knowing*.

Helpful Dig-down Questions and Statements

"What do you need from me now?" (Then listen!)

"What I need from you here is . . ."

"I'm not clear what you need from me now."

"So you need me to . . ." (Goal: verify that you understand correctly, not to agree.)

"What do you think I need from you right now?"

"Who do you expect to fill that need (of yours)?"

"That's your need, not mine."

"I'm responsible for (filling this need.)"

"What's in the way of your (or my) filling this need now?"

"So you're asking me to help fill your need." (This verifies that you heard your partner clearly, It doesn't mean that you're responsible for filling their need!)

"Whose needs feel more important to you right now, yours or mine?" This is an *"=/="* attitude check. Sometimes an adult or child's local needs really are more important (intense, urgent) than their partner's!

"That feels like a surface need to me. Let's do some digging."

"I think I'm (you're) split now. I need to get my (your) Self back in charge."

"Which of your inner crew needs to feel heard, right now?" or *"Which of your subselves needs (whatever)?"* Here both partners need to know the inner-family concept [1, 9], and have an idea of their respective subself "rosters."

"Why are we communicating right now?" (What are your and my communication needs?) This works best if both/all people know the six communication needs (p. 354), and are developing their awareness [2, C] and metatalk [5, F] skills. If someone responds, "I don't know," summarize the seven communication skills [1, A] and/or check for false-self dominance. [1, ..pop/assess.htm]

Respectful, patient digging down works just as well with your Vulnerable and Guardian subselves as it does with young and adult people. **Option**: review chapter 10 to grow your awareness of how digging down promotes high-nurturance relationships between subselves and people.

F) Summary: Metatalk Skill

This summarizes key ideas in Chapter 5. Bracketed [numbers and letters] refer to skill and resource chapters. Add the pointer [..**/***.htm] to [http://www.sfhelp.org/] to access referenced Web resources.

Metatalk is talking objectively about *how* you communicate. It involves _ learning a group of communication concepts and terms below and [L], and _ using them with an =/= (mutual respect) attitude to discuss your recent or chronic _ internal and _ interpersonal communication sequences and patterns. A "meta-comment" is one or more nonjudgmental sentences describing an observation about your communication *process*.

This skill uses *awareness*, clear thinking, and dig-down skills to illuminate significant communication blocks (p. 405). Then empathic listening, assertion, and problem-solving skills empower you to resolve them.

Guidelines for Effective Metatalk

Use metatalk any time you're aware of a significant inner-family and/or social communication problem (communication needs aren't being met), current or chronic.

Before meta-commenting, check your R(espect) attitude. Metatalk works best when you genuinely (vs. dutifully or fearfully) respect the worth, dignity, needs, and opinions of any partner as much as your own (=/=). Any other attitude will send *"I'm 1-up"* or *"I'm 1-down"* R-messages to your partner, and probably diminish their hearing, patience, trust, and cooperation.

Assess your partner's E(motion)-level before metatalking. If it's "above their ears," use empathic listening to help lower it, until they can include you in their awareness bubble and can hear you.

Know *why* you're using metatalk. If it's to help you both get more of your needs met now, go ahead. If it's something else, your Self is probably disabled.

Use your partner's name occasionally in your meta-commenting (or in general) to affirm them. It may make it easier for them to hear you clearly.

Effective meta-comments are brief, factual, and specific. To promote this, describe specific environmental conditions and behaviors that could be recorded on film or tape (*"I notice you're not looking at me now."*), rather than abstract personality traits (*"You're pretty self-centered and rude."*)

In high-E(motion) situations like major conflicts and crises, **be aware of how you expect your partner to react to your metatalk.** If you expect them to reject or ignore your meta-comments, or attack you for them, or if you're split and feel unjustified or ambivalent in making them, your odds for being *heard* accurately drop. Be alert for "resistances" to your meta-comments, and use =/= empathic listening [6, G] to acknowledge them.

For major or volatile communication problems, **consider planning your meta-comments in advance.** Practice them alone or with an objective partner until they become more natural and spontaneous. Practice responding to possible "resistances" from your intended receiver, like defensiveness, blaming (attacking), withdrawing, or denials.

Through experimenting, **evolve your own metatalk style and skill over time**, rather than being "perfect" at it. *"Progress, not perfection!"*

Practice noting the difference between communication *content* (what we're communicating about) and *process* (how we're communicating _ now and _ over time.) Metatalk focuses awareness and discussion on your inner and interpersonal *processes*.

Add your own guidelines . . .

Metatalk Topics

- E(motion)-levels
- R(espect)-messages
- Nonverbal messages
- Embedded and double messages
- Eye contact
- Face and body language
- Voice dynamics
- Communication sequences and patterns
- Mind reading (assuming)
- Levels of meaning
- Levels of intimacy
- Levels of empathy
- Communication *styles*
- Distractions
- Inner-voice dialogs
- Communication blocks

- Communication pacing
- Six communication needs
- Surface and true needs
- Communication outcomes
- Seven skills
- Decoding meanings
- Concurrent feelings
- Minimizing
- Reflections
- Word associations
- Implications
- Concreteness
- Flooding (overtalking)
- Interruptions
- Insertions
- Discounting
- Focusing

The Glossary [L] describes each of these, and many relationship terms. For sample Meta-comments, see p. 195 and the Web pages below. Use them to practice forming appropriate meta-comments and *trying* them.

Other Web Resources

A recap of these guidelines, and sample meta-comments for many typical communication conflicts:
[..02/meta-wks.htm]

Guidelines for giving effective feedback:
[..02/evc-feedback.htm]

Practice worksheet for forming effective "I" messages (assertions): [..02/I-msg-wks.htm].

G) Summary: Empathic Listening Skill

Hearing With Your *Heart*

This summarizes key ideas from Chapter 6. Empathic listening is focusing on your partner, and briefly telling them your sense of what they're thinking, feeling, and needing at the moment *without judgment.* "Empathic" signals that your communication aims now are _ to sense as well as you can what it's like to be the speaker now, and then to _ summarize your impressions of this from time to time as they talk, without extra comment. Stay clear that you're not "giving in" or *agreeing* by doing this!

Empathic Listening Benefits Everyone

It signals your respect for, and interest in, the speaker. They feel valued by you (=/=), so they're more apt to keep talking, which builds trust, intimacy, and relationships. They're also more likely to listen well to you . . . later! Unlike saying "I hear you," empathic listening *demonstrates* whether you truly comprehend what the speaker means and feels. This minimizes misunderstandings. At the same time, empathic listening may help the speaker clarify their ideas, emotions, and needs, as they hear your nonjudgmental summaries.

Choose Empathic Listening When . . .

Your Self is clearly in charge of your inner family.

Your partner's E(motion)-level is "above their ears": i.e. their subselves are excited or upset about something, and their awareness bubble excludes you now.

You genuinely feel of equal worth with your partner (=/=), and . . .

You're genuinely interested in them, and . . .

You're not too distracted by the environment or your own current needs.

When you don't meet these five conditions, use all seven communication skills to get your mutual needs met.

How to Listen With Your Heart

The more you practice this skill, the more automatic these steps will become:

Reaffirm "Genuine listening is a gift, and it's not necessarily agreeing!"

If _ you meet the conditions above, temporarily _ set your own opinions and priorities aside, and focus *nonjudgmentally* on your partner. _ Watch their face, eyes, body, and hands: note postures, motions, expressions, and gestures, or lack of them; _ listen to their words and speech dynamics to estimate their main thoughts, feelings, and needs. Then . . .

When they pause, describe the essence of what you believe they're thinking, *feeling* (emotionally and/or physically), and needing . . .

. . . briefly . . . (use a few words or a phrase, at most);

. . . in your own words . . . (vs. repeating theirs);

. . . without questions, comments, or solutions.

Try to sense and include what's "in between their lines" and what they're feeling and needing, even if they don't describe those. What would it be like to *be* the speaker in the situation they're describing or right now?

Use _ attentive posture; _ comfortable eye contact; and _ gestures, _ expressions, and _ intensity that match the speaker's. When you're truly focused and empathic, these will happen automatically. If your partner doesn't pause, interject your brief summaries as they talk. Saying an empathic phrase while the other is talking (interjecting) is like sticking a knife into a stream of water parallel to the flow. Done skillfully, it won't deflect or splatter the speaker's thoughts or focus as interruptions and questions usually do.

Sincere empathic listening is win-win: the speaker will nod, and/or say "*Yes, and . . .*" or something like "*Uh, no, what I really meant was. . . .*" Either way, you both get clearer on their real meaning.

Some call this communication skill "active listening," because it involves intentional focus, awareness, and periodic comments by the listener; not just "sitting there nodding and grunting." This skill is also called "reflective listening" and "mirroring," because the listener returns only the gist of what they're getting, adding or subtracting nothing. In his useful book "The 7 Habits of Highly Effective People," Stephen Covey calls this skill *empathic* listening. This emphasizes the value of sensing your partner's current emotional experience as well as their thoughts.

Alternatives to Empathic Listening

Use *awareness* to see which of these alternatives you may do unconsciously: _ preaching; _ instructing or _ advising; _ lecturing; _ moralizing; _ criticizing or blaming; _ arguing, disagreeing, or denying; _ explaining, or justifying; _ monologing; _ changing the subject: _ intellectualizing (omitting feelings) or _ analyzing; _ generalizing; _ questioning; _ prolonged silence; _ threatening; _ reassuring or comforting; _ "overreacting" (responding with excessive or inappropriate emotions); _ withdrawing emotionally or physically; _ changing the mood (e.g. by joking), _ minimizing or trivializing; and/or _ pretending (faking) interest, understanding, or empathy. Each of these usually sends an embedded "I'm 1-up" R(espect)-message, which inexorably drops your communication effectiveness.

What Does Empathic Listening Sound Like?

"So you think that . . ."
"It seemed to you that . . ."
"You're really feeling . . ."
"What you need now is . . ."
"Wow! Really confusing!"
"So you were up against . . ."
"You're anxious about . . ."
"Really mystifying" (to you) "
"Now you look really . . ."
"Seems like you're unsure of . . ."
"You were furious with me!"
". . . Totally missed your point!"
". . . Pretty tough going!"
"Miraculous!" (you thought)"
"You hoped that . . ."
Note the absence of the pronoun "I."

Options

Ask your partner/s for "hearing checks": e.g. *"Norm, would you let me know the essence of what you just received from me?"* You can spontaneously **offer hearing checks** to partners, ask them for permission first, or explain what you're doing.

If a partner says something like "Why do you keep repeating what I say?" your options are to stop, apologize, or explain *"What you say is important to me. I repeat periodically to make sure I'm hearing you clearly."* Shame-based people can interpret empathic listening as implying they're not speaking clearly.

You can use empathic listening as an insincere ploy (covert attitude: "I'm 1-up"), or with genuine interest and respect. (=/=). The former usually degrades communication and relationships.

Other Web Resources

Add the pointers to [http://sfhelp.org/ . . .]:

Article: "The Art of Giving Empowering Personal Feedback" [..02/evc-feedback.htm]

Article: "Why Listening Is Good For You," by James J. Lynch. Our bodies react to effective listening! [..02/listen-lynch.htm]

Worksheet: a personal empathic listening inventory: [..02/listen-inventory.htm]

Exercise: practice empathic listening with a partner or a group: [..02/listen-practice.htm]

Awarenesses / To Do's . . .

H) Summary: Effective Assertion

This summarizes key ideas from Chapter 7. Bracketed [numbers and letters] refer to other chapters in this book and their respective summaries. Add the page names [..**/ ***.htm] to [http://sfhelp.org/ . . .] to access supplementary Internet articles and worksheets.

Assertion is the art and skill of saying what you need, think, or feel so someone can really *hear* you. Develop your assertion skill to . . .

. . . **prevent** inner-family or interpersonal conflicts;

. . . **protect** your integrity and self esteem by *respectfully* confronting others' broken commitments, and requesting or demanding acknowledgment and accountability; and assert to . . .

. . . give "dodge-proof" **praise**.

Two alternatives to mutually respectful (=/=) assertion **are** lose/win **submission** ("*Your needs come first, with me*") **or** win/lose **aggression** ("*My needs or opinions outrank yours.*") Assertion effectiveness is proportional to your fluency in four other skills: *awareness*, clear thinking, digging down to true needs, and empathic listening. To resolve communication problems, you'll also need fluency in metatalk skill.

Assertion Goals

Get _ your and _ your partner's current true (vs. surface)

needs met well enough, while maintaining or improving your _ self-respect and _ your relationship.

Effective-Assertion Steps

All nine steps are needed only for situations you rate as highly important.

1) Check: Is my Self leading my inner family? Symptoms: feeling a solid mix of *grounded, clear, calm, centered, aware, alert, energized, "up," strong, "light," purposeful, focused, and resilient.* If you don't feel those, correct that via "parts work" [1, A]; or expect impaired assertion and go ahead anyway.

2) Consciously *choose* to use these steps, vs. submit, hint, whine, complain, aggress, postpone, or endure, until the steps become a reflex.

3) Get clear on _ what you feel, _ why, and specifically _ what you *really* need from your partner right now. If you're not sure of these three things, pause to clarify them before you assert, if time allows.

4) Make four quick attitude checks on how your subselves all honestly feel about . . .
   Your partner's needs. If the consensus is *"They're as important as mine to me,"* go ahead. If not, lower your expectations about the outcome, or explore which of your subselves are blocking an =/= (mutually respectful) attitude. [1, 9, and ..02/a-bubble.htm]
   Asking for what you need. If you solidly feel "I have the right to say, ask, or demand this," go ahead. If your *Inner Critic* is running the show, s/he'll proclaim *"I'm being selfish / pushy / greedy / demanding / controlling . . ."*) Unconfronted, beliefs

like these cause your voice, face, and body to broadcast "*I'm 1-down*", which will degrade your assertion. See [B].

Your confidence in responding to your partner's reactions (e.g. anger, rejection, disagreement, attack) calmly. If you feel significantly anxious, work with your inner family to explore and heal subselves' ignorances and fears (mistrusts). See [..01/ innerfam1.htm]. Finally, get clear on . . .

Your expectations about the outcome. If you feel "*My partner and I can each get our needs met, and will probably feel OK about our exchange*," go for it. If you (some subselves) believe "*This assertion won't work*," it probably won't.

5) If your partner's E(motion)-level is "below their ears," **state your need simply and directly**, with steady eye contact. Avoid fuzzy pronouns and hand-grenade words. If their E-level is above their ears, use respectful empathic listening to lower it before you assert.

6) Nonjudgmentally, *expect resistances*, like your partner explaining, disagreeing, attacking, changing the subject, "forgetting," whining, "stonewalling," "blowing up," "collapsing," assuming, mind reading, clamming up, and/or physically leaving. These are normal protective human responses, specially if a false self is in control. They are *not* weakness, excuses, or character defects! When you get a resistance . . .

7) Use =/= empathic listening until your partner's E-level comes down, and s/he's able to hear you. Then . . .

8) Recycle steps 5-7 as needed: keep re-stating your need/ s clearly and directly, and using empathic listening with new resistances, until you . . .

. . . get _ a clear agreement, _ an acceptable compromise

or refusal, or _ new information that changes your needs or priorities; or . . .

. . . you're _ interrupted, _ distracted, or _ run out of time. In major assertions, arrange lots of time.

9) Note the outcome of your assertion. If _ you and _ your partner/s each got your main needs met _ in a way you feel good about, thank them and appreciate yourself! If someone didn't get all they needed, use *awareness* and metatalk to discover what would work better the next time.

Other Web Resources

Article: the Power of Positive Self Esteem, by Dr. Nathaniel Branden [..02/branden.htm]

An "I"-message (assertion) **worksheet**: [..02/I-msg-wks.htm]

Worksheet: rate yourself as an asserter: [..02/assert-profile.htm]

Exercise outline: practice assertion with a partner or a group [..02/assert-practice.htm]

Awarenesses / To Do's . . .

I) Summary: Win-Win Problem Solving

This is a digest of the ideas in Chapter 8. Add page-names [..**/***.htm] below to [http://sfhelp.org/] to access supplemental Internet articles and worksheets. Bracketed [numbers and letters] refer to skill and resource chapters, respectively.

Problem solving is a cooperative, intentional communication process between people or subselves whose current *needs* conflict internally and/or mutually. *Effective* problem solving is based on shared beliefs that _ meeting all partners' true (vs. surface) needs is the common win-win goal, and that _ the process will succeed well enough for everyone involved. Based on mutual respect (an =/= attitude), this skill focuses on meeting current *needs*, not power, control, punishment, fixing blame, or remaking personalities. Problem solving can be called "conflict resolution" or "joint needs fulfillment."

Common alternatives to problem solving are arguing, fighting, avoiding, hinting, denying, collapsing, demanding, threatening, procrastinating, pretending, changing the subject, blaming, giving in, whining, intellectualizing, analyzing, catastrophizing, mind reading (assuming), preaching (lecturing), pleading, decreeing, repeating, and monologing.

Consistent **success at problem solving requires** _ your Selves in charge, _ fluency in the other six communication skills, and _ knowing when to use each of them [1, A]. When each partner knows and uses all seven skills, most inner [9] and [..01/innerfam1.htm] and interpersonal conflicts can be resolved with everyone feeling respected and satisfied enough.

Problem-solving Options

The basic problem solving process offers you many choice points. Only the most complex, urgent, or persistent problems require all these steps:

1) Acknowledge that you have conflicting or unfilled needs, without guilt, anxiety, or shame. Common alternatives favored by untrusting false selves are denial (*"What problem?"*), minimizing (*"It's not that big a deal,"*), whining and complaining, (*"It burns me up that . . ."*), and avoiding (*"I'll tackle it later"*).

2) Check: Is my Self leading my inner family? Symptoms: feeling a solid mix of *grounded, clear, calm, centered, aware, alert, energized, "up," "light," strong, purposeful, focused, and resilient.* If you don't feel those, correct that via "parts work" [1, ..01/ifs1-intro.htm]; or expect impaired problem solving, and go ahead anyway. If your partner's Self is disabled, compassionately lower your expectations. Avoid rescuing or blaming, and consider =/= feedback [..02/evc-feedback.htm], "I"-message assertions [7], and/ or objective meta-comments [5, F].

3) If you have more than one problem, separate and rank them from simple to complex, and minor to urgent. For minor problems, _ get clear on your current needs, _ identify your options, _ pick the best, and _ do it. For complex, urgent need-conflicts with another person, review the steps below, and decide if you need to prepare in some way before asserting your needs to them.

4) Assert your need/s to your conflict partner. [7, H]. This may fill your needs, or it may lead you to . . .

5) Problem-solve with them. Pick appropriate steps from these:

Reaffirm that you're clear on _ your *true* **need/s**, and on _ specifically what you want from your conflict partner (vs. *opponent*). Common initial *communication* needs are genuine _ respect, and sincere _ agreement to problem solve with you.

If useful, _ **agree with your partner what "problem solving is**." (*"We're brainstorming to get your and my true needs met well enough."*) If they don't trust that you care about their needs as much as yours, _ consider adding, "rebuild trust" to your goals (needs). **Option**: if your partner doesn't know these steps, give them a copy of this summary and walk through it with them.

Do respectful _ E-level and _ attitude checks. If _ no one's E-level is "above their ears," and _ each partner seems to feel =/= (mutually respectful) now, and _ all expect problem solving to probably work, then go ahead. Otherwise, _ use empathic listening to bring E-levels down, and/or make achieving _ mutual respect (=/= attitudes) and _ realistically-optimistic attitudes your first problem solving goals. Both require awareness, clear thinking, and metatalk skills.

Agree to problem-solve as partners. Then _ use *awareness* to spot and reduce any major inner or environmental distractions.

Assess whether you have several concurrent problems. If so, _ separate and rank them, and _ help each other to stay focused on resolving one problem at a time.

On each focal problem, **use empathic listening and digging down** to confirm that _ you and _ your partner each _ clearly understand the others' real needs, and _ value them equally (=/=), unless there's an emergency.

Recall the difference between *what* you're talking about **(the content), and** *how* you're communicating (**your** *process*.) Use this to stay aware of where blocks to problem solving originate.

Agree on what *kind* **of problem** you're working to solve together:

If it's a *communication* **needs-clash**, use awareness and metatalk to identify which communication blocks you have [8] and [J]. If you have more than one, _ identify and _ separate multiple problems, _ prioritize them, and _ brainstorm resolution options one at a time. Use *mapping* (below) and other skills and Web resources here as appropriate. Option: read [1 or B] to each other for shared awareness and inspiration.

If your needs clash over a *concrete* **(tangible) resource**, like both needing the car at the same time, seek your true needs underneath, and creatively brainstorm all possible solutions, no matter how weird. Nutty ideas can lead unexpectedly to win-win outcomes. This step is not a contest. It can be fun or even hilarious, if Selves are guiding, E-levels are down, and nobody feels overly 1-down or anxious. Often, digging down [4, E] reveals hidden abstract conflicts underlying the concrete ones.

If your clash is abstract, see if it helps to decide which of these you're working to resolve:

A values conflict. These include things like differing _ priorities (*"Sergio, homework comes before TV"*), _ preferences (*"I like brussel sprouts, you hate 'em."*), and _ beliefs—(*"I worship Jehovah, and you're agnostic."*)

A perception conflict. *"Jeremy meant to insult me!"; "I don't think so, Rita."* "Misunderstandings" fit here.

A *loyalty* conflict: whose needs or worth ranks highest with one of you, between two or more people (*"Do I please my new mate first, or my child?"*)

A responsibility or role conflict over who's responsible for something (filling some needs)? *"You're responsible for telling your boss you missed work because of your hangover, not me."*

An inclusion or membership conflict whose needs and dignity should be considered "legitimate" by both of you? (*"I don't think we should invite Martha to the baptism, and you do."*)

An expectation or assumption conflict: *"I just took it for granted you'd pick up the tickets by Thursday."*

A ***power* struggle**: whose needs, opinions, or values will prevail? A form of this is which of you is acknowledged to be *right* or *better.* These are *always* surface clashes that mask someone's shame, guilt, ignorance, and/or fear, and usually signal false-self dominance.

Some other clash, or a combination.

Each of these types of abstract conflicts may have a unique type of solution. For instance, *preference* conflicts are best resolved via genuine (vs. dutiful or strategic) compromises, and agreeing to disagree. Trying to convert your partner implies *"My way is better, and you're 1-down."* If your or their response to this is *"Yes but . . ."* dig down further for a hidden true need.

As appropriate, use *awareness*, digging down, clear thinking, empathic listening, and assertion to explore below your or their surface needs to find the *true* discomforts motivating each of you [4, D]. Once you're clear enough, brainstorm your options; e.g. _ do internal problem solving first [9], _ accept what *is* (the problem is beyond your control), _ get more information, information, _ clarify or verify something, _ assert to someone, or _ re-do some problem solving steps. Help each other avoid defocusing, and/or slipping into 1-up or 1-down attitudes. Doing so means someone has blended: lost their Self's wise leadership.

For each focal problem, work to agree on the best-fit option, and see if each of you is satisfied enough. If not, avoid blaming either of you, and recheck your attitudes and expectations. Recycle these steps, if time, energy, and patience allow.

6) Assess your outcome. If your problem solving steps _ met each of your true needs well enough, _ in a way that left you feeling good *enough* about yourself, your partner, and your shared process; then appreciate each other! Option: explore together why your communication process worked well for you. If it "sort of" succeeded, or didn't satisfy these two criteria, avoid criticizing. Brainstorm how to problem solve differently the next time. Recall: *"Progress, not perfection."*

Mapping Communication Sequences

To co-operatively spot and resolve communication *process* blocks, diagram or map your behavioral sequence with a key partner:

Confirm that your Self is in charge of your inner family. If s/he's not, work to correct that first via "parts work" [..01/ recovery1.htm], or expect skewed mapping results.

Choose attitudes of curiosity, neutrality, and expectation of improved communication, rather than defensiveness, anxiety, or blame.

Recall that *communication* is an interactive sequence of inner and interpersonal behaviors that can have arbitrary beginnings and endings. You're about to map a portion of an ongoing behavioral sequence that might last two to 20 minutes. Pick a beginning event to start defining your map, like e.g. *"Nora felt hurt and angry at Ursula,"* or *"Ursula ended the phone call abruptly."*

At the top left corner of a large sheet of paper (e.g. two 8.5" by 11" sheets taped together), identify the person who "starts" the sequence. Draw a unique symbol (circle, square, diamond) to represent them, and/or write their initials or first name. Write brief summaries of your estimate of this person's . . .

Inner-family leadership: true Self or other subselves (false self)? If s/he was split, estimate _ which Guardian or Vulnerable subselves were controlling his or her inner family at that time, and _ whether s/he was aware of that.

R(espect) attitude toward their partner at that time: 1-up, 1-down, or =/=;

Emotions. Several at once is normal;

_ Communication **needs** (p. 354) and _ underlying *true* needs (p. 149).

Key thoughts: a representative phrase or summary sentence; and . . .

Estimate if her or his E(motion)-level was *above* or *below* their ears at that time.

Options:

Estimate (1) whether their **awareness bubble** included one or both people; and (2) their **focuses** at the moment: _ (me / you / us / other), and _ (past / present / future). Finally . . .

Like an objective reporter or scientist, **describe objectively and concisely what this person** *did* at that time, including "nothing." Describe facial expressions, gestures, body movements, and types of verbal behavior that affected the other person; e.g. *"Alex grimaced, broke eye contact, sighed, and shook his head."* With actions, be as specific, descriptive, and factual as you can. Note only those that could be audio or video taped. Include silences, and note eye contact, voice dynamics, and interruptions. *Avoid making assumptions or judgments.*

Example: in response to Teri's behavior now, Ruben . . .

Felt 1-down, and excluded himself from his awareness bubble; i.e. he was unaware of these factors. He also felt guilty, anxious, confused, and irritated.

Needed _ to feel respected, _ to vent, and _ to avoid unpleasant conflict with Teri.

Thought, *"This (communication snarl) is hopeless!"*

Was ruled by his *Catastrophizer*, *Scared Kid*, and *Shamed Kid* subselves, not his Self.

His E-level was above his ears, and he didn't know it.

Ruben was focused on _ Teri and _ the past, vs. _ himself and Teri _ right now; and he . . .

Laughed nervously, looked at the floor, and began to *explain* (justify) his past actions, vs. problem solve.

+ + +

Shift to the other person, and note on your map how they responded to (their perception of) the first person's behavior.

Summarize the same six to eight factors *objectively.* Use "?" if you're not sure of a factor, or list several possibilities.

Alternate summarizing these factors between the partners' actions and reactions until you choose an event that ends the sequence. (*"Ruben walked out of the room."*)

Estimate the outcome of the sequence: _ whose initial current needs got met or didn't? _ How did each of person feel about this communication sequence: frustrated, guilty, satisfied, elated, bored, regretful, anxious . . .?

Scan the whole sequence for significant patterns or changes in R-messages, E-levels, splitting (inner-family leadership), awareness bubbles, and focus.

If useful, widen your scope and **evaluate whether this sequence repeats** between these two people over time; i.e. whether it's a communication *pattern* with predictable steps and outcomes. Other choices . . .

Mapping Options

If you have clear sense of who comprises your inner family [1], [..01/innerfam1.htm], **map important sequences among your subselves.** Use surface symptoms as a guide, like "*I get really scared and angry around tax time.*"

if you mapped alone, **seek your communication partner's input to your map,** or ask them to make one of the same sequence. Compare and edit your maps until you both feel they're accurate enough. It's OK to have differing perceptions of your communication sequence. That's a helpful learning by itself. Avoid power struggles (*"I'm right!"* *"No, I am!"*) Try "*I see it differently,*" or similar.

For specially important events or persistent relationship problems, **assess whether there may be a third person involved directly or indirectly** in a Persecutor-Victim-Rescuer (PVR) "triangle" (p. 330). If so, consider expanding your map to include this third person's behaviors during this sequence. The goals are to understand the triangle roles *without blame*, and then work together to dissolve it, via metatalking, problem solving, and empowering =/= attitudes in all three people.

As you map, use this checklist of the common communication blocks [J] to help you see what's going on. Match any blocks you find to the sample meta-comments in [5] to help you see response alternatives that would improve the outcome of your sequence.

Review [10] to help discern missing relationship factors (unmet true needs) in the people you're mapping. Do this as partners working toward more effective communication, not opponents!

Map long sequences (e.g. a two-hour fight) by evaluating key events or factor-changes across the overall sequence. Use the awareness questions on pp. 368-9 as a guide as to what to assess. Doing this may lead you to map part of the long sequence in more detail (*"Let's discover where you first felt hurt, and why."*)

Watch for the "end' event in your sequence to (eventually) lead to a similar beginning event (*"Myra again felt ignored and disrespected by her stepdaughter, and felt hurt, resentful, and guilty."*) Details (topics) may change, but often the basic communication sequences (needs, strategies, reactions, and outcomes) repeat, forming *patterns* between people in relationship who aren't aware of their inner and mutual processes. This is specially true when false selves run the show.

Each action > reaction event in a mapped sequence is an opportunity for one partner to change any of their eight factors to improve your joint outcome. Because these factors occur simultaneously, there are usually *many* possible change points in even a five-minute sequence. Each partner has half the responsibility and the chances to improve the outcome of the next version of this sequence!

Use your metatalk vocabulary [5 and L] and skills as you map key communication sequences. That increases your mapping options and comprehensions, which can promote improved sequences and outcomes, unless a protective false self controls one or more of you.

Other Web Resources

Worksheet: Constructive and destructive problem-solving traits: [..02/evc-inventory.htm]

Summary: *Inner*-conflict resolution steps: [..01/ifs8-innr_cnflct.htm]

Summary: Tips for effective co-parent communication: [..02/evc-tips.htm]

Checklist: three sets of options for better problem-solving: [..02/evc-checklist.htm]

Outline: problem-solving practice exercise: [..02/prblmslv-practice.htm]

Article: "Respect—the Heart of Every Successful Marriage," by Annie Gottlieb: [..08/respect.htm]

Article: "Avoiding Couple Karate," by Anthony Brandt: [..02/karate.htm]

Awarenesses / To Do's . . .

J) Common Communication Blocks

People communicate to fill local needs (reduce discomforts). A communication *block* is anything that inhibits or prevents one or both partners from filling their true (vs. surface) current needs. Most are unconscious and related to false-self dominance, until partners _ put their Selves in charge, and _ learn and apply the seven skills.

Bracketed [numbers and letters] refer to skill and resource chapters, respectively.

Premises

Any perceived behavior that causes a "significant" emotional, physical, or spiritual effect on another person is "communication."

Communication aims to fill two to six personal needs (p. 354). Many combinations of these conflict. First steps: _ get clear on your and your partner's current communication needs, and _ value them equally! The need for "enough" self and mutual respect is subjective and constant. Shame-based people rarely get enough until in true recovery.

Effective **communication occurs when** each person _ gets their current true needs (p. 149) met well enough, _ in a way that promotes self and mutual respect and trust. Anything that hinders this is a communication "block."

Communication blocks can occur _ between your inner family of subselves and _ between people. Ineffective communication can be caused by blocks inside me, inside you, and/or between us.

The learnable skills of awareness and metatalk can help identify such blocks, and the other five relationship skills can resolve them *if* partner's true Selves are leading their inner families.

Typical blocks:

me/you

_ _ **1)** Someone gets a verbal or nonverbal **"R(espect)-message" they decode as "we're not equals** here and now." Such R-messages are usually implied by voice and body dynamics, despite contrary words. They're constantly being decoded by each communications partner, usually unconsciously. Communication works only when each person feels _ enough Self respect, and _ gets believable "=/=" (vs. "I'm 1-up" or "I'm 1-down") R-messages from their partner/s.

_ _ **2) Sender and receiver's communication needs don't match** (p. 81). For example, I want to vent, and you're distracted (can't really listen), or you want to persuade me to do something.

_ _ **3) The sender gives a double message**: their words say one thing, and their face, body, and/or voice imply something else: e.g. "I'm not angry!" (said loudly, fists clenched). Common (automatic) responses to double messages are confusion, frustration, and—if habitual—growing distrust of the speaker. Double messages are usually caused by the speaker being ruled by two or more subselves who disagree. Awareness and metatalk skills can help resolve this. See block 10 below.

_ _ **4) One or both people are distracted** (i.e. can't focus or hear well) by physical discomfort (pain, thirst, sleepiness, etc.), preoccupation (worry, anxiety, or other strong emotion), or environmental disturbances (noise, flashing lights, motions, temperature, etc.)—yet try important communication anyway.

_ _ 5) A "1-up" R(espect)-message is implied by a speaker who constantly interrupts their partner. This habit signals that the speaker is probably composing their response without really hearing the speaker. Interruptions can seem to mean "what I have to say now is more important than anything you need." That feels like a discount, or a putdown. If habitual, discounts hurt, and breed anger and resentment in the receiver. Frequent interrupting is often unconscious, and will continue unless the receiver is assertive about stopping it.

me/you

_ _ 6) **Either sender or receiver make wrong assumptions** about the other's intent, meaning, R-message, emotions, and/or key word/s. This is either unconscious, or an intentional way of discounting the other: "I know what you really feel or mean, no matter what you say (or don't say). Often this evokes a response of resentment, defensiveness, counterattack, and/or withdrawal and denial.

_ _ 7) **A common special case of mind-reading happens** when the receiver starts talking before the speaker finishes, because they "know what the speaker is going to say." Even if true, this can feel like a putdown. Conversely, the speaker may habitually repeat or be long-winded, and the receiver legitimately gets bored. The receiver may use a meta-comment like "When you string so many ideas and comments together without pausing, I get overwhelmed, and tune out."

_ _ 8) **The sender isn't clear on what s/he needs,** either personally, relationally, or from the communication process (see block # 2). The receiver will then probably feel uneasy and confused. A related problem is . . .

_ _ 9) **Either or both partners unconsciously using fuzzy thinking or fuzzy terms**, and/or vague or "hand-grenade" terms and phrases. The companion block is each person being unaware of these concepts, and their options to use respectful hearing checks to confirm that they're decoding the other person's meaning accurately.

me/you

_ _ 10) Either person may deny or minimize their true feelings to themselves and/or their partner. The receiver may feel they should be interested ("please go on, this is fascinating!"), when they're really bored or distracted.

Even when sent "skillfully," such denials usually result in a double message ("words can lie—bodies don't"). If habitual, such denials and deceptions breed confusion, and erode trust. Kids are specially quick to sense these "self-lies." See (3) above.

_ _ 11) Frequently withholding emotions from personal (non-business) communications, either on purpose or unconsciously, can leave the receiver unsure of the sender's full meaning. The listener may interpret this as "you don't trust me," or "you're hiding something bad." Over time, anxiety and distrust usually result.

The receiver may be doing something that makes the sender feel unsafe in honestly sharing their feelings (and the receiver isn't saying so), or the sender may be psychologically wounded, and emotionally numb. This communication block strangles intimacy.

_ _ 12) Focusing "too often" on the past or the future can prevent confronting and resolving problems in the present. A special case is when someone imagines a future event so vividly that they react to their partner in the present as though the imagined event had already occurred ("I know you'll be late again!")

_ _ 13) Habitually _ focusing on one's Self, or _ steadily deflecting the focus from one's Self will result at best in unbalanced and "shallow" communication. At worst, the other person may increasingly feel used and discounted, or "disconnected" and resentful, and develop impaired hearing. Awareness and respectful assertion may change this. You can use a flexible "awareness bubble" with metatalk to counter this block.

_ _ 14) Any participant being unaware of the true needs

under the conflicting surface goals or needs. For example "I want to talk to you" (surface need) may really mean "I need to reassure myself you still care about me, because you've seemed distant lately." Awareness, clear thinking, patient digging down, assertion, and empathic listening help unearth semi-conscious current true needs.

Old "issues" (conflicts) keep resurfacing and/or causing strong feelings because the true needs underneath them haven't been clearly acknowledged and filled.

_ _ **15) Either person can send a paradox.** These are messages that negate themselves and leave receivers confused and uneasy. "I insist that you want to talk to me!" and "Never say 'never'!" are examples. Demanding something which can only be given spontaneously (like love, trust, or respect) is usually a self-defeating communication. Other examples: "It's just no use talking about our communication problems!", and "I love you so much! Go away."

_ _ **16) Generalizing** can muffle or distort the current message, and prevent effective problem solving. "You're always inconsiderate!" will probably be received differently than "I'm mad, because you're 40 minutes late and I missed my ride!"

"You always . . ." or "You never . . ." are deadly because they imply the receiver is 1-down (unrespectable), and invite their feeling guilty and defensive about many past events as well as the present one. Normal responses to this block are to flee, tune out, and/or counterattack (vs. listen empathically and problem-solve).

_ _ **17) Preaching, moralizing, or advising** someone with a problem ("I'm just trying to help!") can erode relationships, if the "sufferer" just wants to vent (be respectfully heard and accepted). These reactions in the receiver promote dependence, helplessness, and imply "I-m 1-up: I know how to fix your problem, and you don't."

How common it is for busy parents to "fix" their child's problem before listening carefully, and considering if the best (long-range) help would be to encourage the child (or anyone) to find their own solution!

me/you

_ _ **18) Sarcastic, critical (vs. affectionate) name-calling** erodes both the receiver's self-esteem and the odds for cooperative problem solving. "You're stupid / lazy / spacey / nuts / weird / hopeless / a jerk / spastic" etc. hurts! The non-verbal version of this block is the withering "look" that a partner gives, which conveys a massive rejection and put-down. Do you ever name-call or use such a look? If so, what happens to your Self esteem, the receiver's, and your relationship? Who's present needs get met?

_ _ **19) Physical or emotional withdrawal** is a powerful communication that may imply "You scare or overwhelm me" [R(espect)-message: "I'm 1-down"], or "I don't care about you and your needs now," ("I'm 1-up"). Either way, the abandoned partner will probably feel hurt and frustrated—particularly if the withdrawer won't talk about withdrawing (i.e. won't metatalk). In resolving this communication block, respectfully explore if the sender is (or isn't) unconsciously doing something that triggers the withdrawal . . .

_ _ **20) Threats or demands (vs. requests)** often imply "my current needs are more important than yours!" They usually provoke hurt, resentment, and defiance, and everyone feeling badly about themselves and/or the exchange. The receiver needs to use assertive metatalk when this happens—e.g. (with steady eye contact) "I feel you're making demands (threats) now. When you do that, I feel resentful and combative. I need you to make your point another way."

_ _ **21) One person changing the subject** ("defocusing") repeatedly or suddenly without checking to see if their partner is done can imply that their current needs (and dignity) are superior to their partner's. The partner's responsibility is to _ notice the defocusing and how it feels, and _ be assertive about finishing their first topic, if they need to. However, the implied "you're 1-down to me" R-message still hit home . . .

me/you

__ **22) Hinting, or asking leading (indirect) questions** can be OK, or can imply "I don't trust one of us to deal squarely with my subject." Having a hidden agenda often results in sending double messages, which usually leave the receiver feeling confused, suspicious, discounted, and resentful.

__ **23) Habitual lack of appropriate eye contact,** speaking hesitantly, or constantly apologizing, all say "I feel 1-down now." This may seem OK, if the receiver is comfortable feeling 1-up. Over time, though, this style promotes loss of respect in both people—which breeds discounting, poor listening, and ineffective communications.

__ **24) Habitual nonstop talking** will probably condition regular listeners that nothing is expected of them—which is what the speaker will probably get. The jabberer's real communication need here may be to avoid stressful confrontation, surprises, or intimacy (keep their partner emotionally distant), or to avoid scary thoughts and feelings.

__ **25) The receiver may become overwhelmed** ("flooded") with information, ideas, or feelings. If the speaker doesn't pause, or if the receiver doesn't assert and ask them to, real hearing (and hence effective communications) will stop. This block often happens when the speaker needs to vent, lecture, or moralize without empathically caring what the listener's current need/s are (R-message: "you're 1-down to me now").

__ **26) Not making enough time to talk** clearly and thoroughly about important or conflictual issues. With lives filled with job, parenting, home upkeep, social, and other personal responsibilities, many couples put personal communications low or last in their day's priorities.

Because clear discussion is vital to nourishing and growing any relationship, lack of it takes an eventual toll. "We just don't have time" is code for "Communicating isn't important enough to me / you / us." Who's responsible in your relationship for making enough time to communicate?

me/you

_ _ **27) Not checking to see if you and your partner each got your real needs met** in key communication exchanges—specially in major disagreements. Omitting this lets one or both of you assume—perhaps wrongly—that the other is satisfied. "Unfinished business" will increase. Your trust that key communications between you two will work over time will probably shrink, too . . .

_ _ **28) Falling into an escalating conflict** or impasse with an opposite-gender partner **over unconscious gender-priority differences.** Research shows typical males and females differ—often sharply—over which priority to focus on in an interpersonal situation. For example, average females focus on relationships, cooperation, social harmony, feelings, and understanding, while typical males instinctively focus on logic, information, "fixing" things, power, and winning.

These priorities are biologically-based and socially imprinted, rather than right or wrong! In the best case, males and females recognize these complementary differences nonjudgmentally, and meld them rather than trying to convert each other ("Why can't a woman be more like a man?").

_ _ **29) Defensively denying that you're doing any of these blocks** without trying to investigate and verify is perhaps the most potent communication block of all. Note the difference between informing your partner of a communication problem (implication: "we're equals here,") vs. accusing them ("I'm 1-up.")

First, ask if your partner is open to feedback on their communication habits. Agree that such feedback doesn't mean "you're bad," or "I'm right." Most of us were never trained to know or use these ideas, so we're learners rather than "wrong"!

Add your own blocks:

Here's a general way partners can resolve each of these communication blocks:

Assess whether your Self or someone else is leading your inner family. If the latter, focus on correcting that, vs. these suggestion. See "Who's *Really* Running Your Life?" [xlibris.com] or [..pop/assess.htm].

Do your homework: study part 1 of this book.

Choose a mutual-respect (=/=) attitude, and start looking for such blocks (with awareness) in your communications with key people, including kids! And . . .

When found, **use respectful metatalk** to describe the blocks and their effects to your partner. If they're willing, use the other six communication skills together to resolve the blocks.

Review the communication basics in Chapter 1 to grow your perspective on learning and using these seven powerful relationship skills.

K) Selected Readings

The titles below focus on effective interpersonal communication. If you're reading this book and belong to a divorced family or stepfamily, see the selected readings on the Web at [http://sfhelp.org/11/booklist.htm]. This book is one in a series for co-parents in those families. For an overview, see http://sfhelp.org/books.htm.

No other authors explore _ inner-family dynamics or _ the true needs under those on the surface. Nonetheless, each book here adds wisdom, options, and vision to the topics of effective communication and high-nurturance relationships.

Between Parent and Teenager, by Dr. Haim G. Ginott; 1971. Avon Books, New York, NY. A classic, including a useful bibliography.

Brain Sex—the Real Difference between Men and Women, by Anne Moir and David Jessel; 1993. Doubleday Books, New York, NY. A well-researched, controversial explanation for lay people of why "male brains" and "female brains" work very differently. Very helpful in understanding and accepting (vs. resolving) gender-based communication conflicts. This complements Tannen's book below.

Couple communication I—Talking Together, by Sherod Miller, Elam Nunnally, and Daniel B. Wackman; 1991. Interpersonal Communication Programs, Inc., Minneapolis, MN. Also available: a four-session workshop guide with two audiotapes, based on the book.

The Dance of Anger, by Harriet G. Lerner, Ph.D.; 1985. Harper and Rowe, Publishers, Inc., New York, NY. Though slanted toward women, this is an excellent book for anyone wishing to express and use anger constructively.

Embracing Our Selves—The Voice Dialog Manual, by Hal Stone, Ph.D., and Sidra Winkelman, Ph.D.; 1989. New World Library, San Rafael, CA. A readable, practical paperback that introduces the many selves that clamor and compete within us.

Embracing Each Other—Relationship as Teacher, Healer, & Guide; by Hal Stone, Ph.D., and Sidra Winkelman, Ph.D.; 1989. New World Library, San Rafael, CA. An extension of their first book, examining how the selves within several people interact together.

Embracing Your Inner Critic—Turning Self-criticism Into A Creative Asset, by Hal Stone, Ph.D., and Sidra Stone, Ph.D.; 1993, Harper, San Francisco, CA. Using the ideas in their other books, (above), this suggests how to befriend and convert your *Inner Critic* into a steadfast ally.

Games People Play—the Psychology of Human Relationships, by Eric Berne, M.D.; 1996. Ballentine Books, New York, NY. A reissue of the 1964 classic on how false selves plot to get their true needs met with other people covertly.

Healing the Shame That Binds You, by John E. Bradshaw; 1988. Health Communications, Deerfield Beach, FL. The most practical, useful book I've found on identifying and converting shame into self-respect and self-love. Doing so is essential for effective assertion and problem solving. See also *The Six Pillars* below.

How To Talk So Kids Will Listen & Listen So That Kids Will Talk, by Adele Faber and Elaine Mazlish; 1980. Avon Books, New York, NY. A clear, helpful paperback.

If You Could Hear What I Cannot Say—Learning to Communicate With The Ones You Love; by Dr. Nathaniel Brandon; 1983. Bantam Books, New York, NY. A paperback text and workbook.

Inner Time––the Science of Body Clocks, and What Makes Us Tick, by Carol Orlock; 1993. Carol Publishing Group, New York, NY. This is a brief, readable introduction to the fascinating new field of *chronobiology*: the study of our body's many overlapping cycles. Besides general interest, this book may motivate you to learn when in a typical day, week, and month you're at your mental (and communication) best.

The Language of the Heart—the Body's Response to Human Dialog, by James. J. Lynch, 1986. Basic Books, New York, NY. Out of print, and worth searching for.

The NEW Peoplemaking, by Virginia Satir; 1988. Science and Behavior Books, Inc., Palo Alto, CA. An update of the classic on healthy personal and family relations.

P.E.T. (Parent Effectiveness Training) in Action, by Gordon, Dr. Thomas; 1976. Plume Books, New American

Library, Inc., New York, NY. A timeless paperback that applies to all relationships.

People Skills; by Robert Bolton, Ph.D.; 1979. Prentiss Hall, Inc. Spectrum Books; Englewood Cliffs, NJ. Another timeless book, selected by the American Management Association.

The Six Pillars of Self Esteem, by Dr. Nathaniel Branden; Bantam Books, New York, NY; 1995. A classic on healing old shame, which is vital for building effective assertion skill. See also *Healing the Shame*, above; and *Who's* Really *Running Your Life?* below.

The 7 Habits of Highly Effective People—Powerful Lessons in Personal Change, by Stephen R. Covey; 1989. Fireside Books, Simon & Schuster; New York, NY. An acclaimed framework for living life effectively.

Who's *Really* Running Your Life? Free your *Self* from Custody, and Guard Your Kids, by Peter K. Gerlach, MSW; 2000. Xlibris Corp., Philadelphia, PA. This describes how to identify and heal the six psychological wounds from significucant childhood neglect. Doing this is *essential* for effective thinking and communicating.

You Just Don't Understand—Women and Men in Conversation, by Deborah Tannen, Ph.D., 1990. Ballentine Books, New York, NY. A highly readable, practical paperback on the differing communication styles of men and women, by a linguistics professor. See also *Brain Sex* above.

L) Communication and Relationship Terms

*W*ords are symbols that societies, couples, and specialist groups like plumbers, pilots, parents, and hoboes, have agreed will represent specific ideas or concepts: units of *meaning.* Between societies, persons, and subselves, words' meanings may vary a little or a lot. For instance, in part of our culture, *"You are so* BAD!" is high praise.

The words and phrases below are keys to understanding and using the concepts and premises in this book effectively. The concepts of psychological wounds and *subselves* are used to redefine many of these words. These brief definitions aim to help you clarify your own meanings, strengthen your vocabulary, and to raise the odds you'll understand what I want to convey. Words are like a painter's palette: the more words you can use in context, the more vivid and impactful your communication "pictures" will be.

Clarifying what you and a communication partner *mean* by key words or phrases is one goal of the mental/verbal skills of awareness, clear thinking, empathic listening, and metatalk. The meanings your inner-family subselves decode from words or phrases are often affected by the way you perceive the sender expressing them. I offer these definitions not as "right," but as bases from which you can clarify your and your communication partners' meanings. Doing so will raise the effectiveness of your thinking and communicating, which will probably strengthen your relationships if your Selves are guiding you.

Option: scan or read these definitions, star or hilight terms that have special meaning for you, and use reflection and *awareness* to discern why. They're in alphabetical order.

Numbers in [brackets] below refer to chapters in this book. Add pointers in brackets [..**/****.htm] to [http://sfhelp.org/ . . .] to access referenced Web pages. The Latin phrase *quod videt* ("which see") is abbreviated "q.v." below.

+ + +

"1-up" (R-message): Decoding another person's behavior to mean that they believe their needs, opinions, dignity, and human worth are more important than, or superior to, yours right now. These R-messages usually mean one or both partners are controlled by a false self.

"1-down" (R-message): Un/consciously decoding another's verbal and non-verbal behaviors to mean *"Here and now and/ or over time, you feel inferior to me. You value my needs, opinions, abilities, and dignity more highly than your own."* This is a symptom of a dominant shame-based or fear-based false self.

"=/=" (R-message): Perceiving another person's verbal and non-verbal behaviors to mean *"Now and/or over time, I believe you genuinely value my needs, opinions, and dignity just as much as you value your own."* A core premise of this book is that to be truly effective, any innerpersonal or interpersonal communication exchange must yield credible =/= R-messages for all partners and subselves.

A

Abandonment is a primal trauma first experienced in early childhood. In extreme, it can cause wordless infantile terror of helplessness and *dying.* Kids in low-nurturance families automatically develop young Vulnerable personality parts who are terrified of emotional abandonment by people they depend on. In adulthood, these parts' terror can promote Guardian subselves who (protectively) cause excessive people-pleasing, approach-avoid relationships, submission (*"I'm 1-down"*), pseudo intimacy, and co-dependence, until true recovery helps them trust the person's true Self, *Inner Nurturer* (good parent), and a loving spiritual Higher Power. Before recovery, some wounded kids and adults abandon *themselves*. See *Fear* and *Loss.*

Abstract conflict: A "conflict" occurs inside you or between you and another person when you have opposing needs, values, beliefs, roles, or perceptions. You can't hold any of these factors in your hand or take a video of them. They're intangible and abstract, yet they have great emotional power. See *Communication conflict, and Concrete conflict.*

Abuse: In my experience, this *hand-grenade* word is often misunderstood and misused. That can harm self and mutual respect, trust, communication effectiveness, and relationships. True abuse must meet three conditions:

One person has *power* over another, like a boss, judge, landlord, or parent, and . . .

. . . **uses** it intentionally to fill their own needs with the dependent person in a way that causes the other significant emotional, physical or spiritual pain or harm (in someone's judgment); and . . .

. . . **the** victim can't safely escape or defend themselves.

Much adult "verbal abuse" is really *aggression*, because the receiving person can choose to defend or leave. People controlled by a false self often have trouble owning their responsibility to protect themselves, and *acting* on it. It's less provocative to say *"You were aggressive with me,"* than *"You abused me!"* The distinction is legally, emotionally, and conversationally important. In high-E situations, use *awareness* and metatalk to choose the right words!

Active listening: See *Empathic listening*

Addiction: a Guardian-subself's strategy for reducing

intolerable distress in one or more young Vulnerable subselves, like *Worthless/Unlovable (Shamed) Kid*. The four kinds of addiction all serve the same short-term self-comforting goal: *substances* (including fat and sugar), *activities* (like gambling or orgasm), *relationships* (co-dependence), and *emotional states* (e.g. love, excitement). Some chemical addictions are compounded by bodily cravings. An *Addict* subself usually partners with an *Illusionist* subself, who rationalizes or denies the addictive behavior (*"One more drink won't hurt. Go ahead!"*). See *Needy, Compulsion, False self, Guardian (subself), Obsess,* and *Vulnerable (subself)*.

Affect (noun): refers to the emotional tone or mood associated with a person's behavior now, or over time. This is a useful metatalk term in conveying whether a person has an *animated, labile* (changeable, fluctuating), or a *flat* (expressionless) way of behaving. Affect includes all three behavioral channels: verbal, paraverbal, and non-verbal. See *Animated, Expressionless, Feeling, Frozen, Labile,* and *Numbing*.

Aggression is any intentional or reflex behavior focused on filling your needs via another person, without truly caring about their needs, feelings, or dignity: i.e. "using" them as an object. Aggressive behavior *always* carries an embedded *"I'm 1-up"* R-message. That may intimidate or inflame receivers, if they're not numb (split). See *Abuse, Assertion, Boundary, Controlling, Fear based, Insensitive, Self-ish, selfish,* and *Submission*.

Agree to disagree: if both conflicted partners have mutual respect (=/=) and their Selves are leading their inner crews, this is the best solution to *abstract* disputes over preferences, beliefs, values, and unprovable perceptions or conclusions. Doing this implies the partners' value other things more than *winning* or *being right*, like their tranquility and relationship. See *Argue, Compromise, Debate,* and *Negotiate*.

Alienation is a relationship dynamic resulting in increased emotional "distance" (less respect, concern, caring, contact) between two emotionally bonded people. Adults from very low nurturance childhoods can feel alien (strange, and *different*) from less wounded people because of their personality limitations (e.g. difficulty trusting, self-loving, and bonding). Severely wounded kids and adults can feel alienated from society. See *Cutoff*, *Detach*, and *Intimacy*.

Alliance (relationship) is a group dynamic in which two or more people or subselves band together to resist or dominate other people. C/overt alliances are common in typical divorced families and stepfamilies, and promote stressful loyalty conflicts and relationship triangles. Guardian subselves can ally against a distrusted Self or other Regular subselves, to protect a troubled young Vulnerable. See *"1-up"*, *Conflict*, *Inner family*, *Multiplicity*, *R-message*, *Splitting*, and *Trust*.

Alone in a crowd is a metaphor for feeling alienated, unbonded, unaccepted or unnoticed, and "disconnected" from other people. If chronic, this feeling is a symptom of significant false-self domination and childhood deprivation. See *Bond*, *Emptiness*, and *Love*.

Ambiguity occurs when a person's subselves _ decode two or more different meanings from a partner's behaviors, and/or _ experience two opposed internal thought streams and/or feelings (self talk.) Skilled communicators may choose ambiguity to soften or add color and humor to their messages. See *Confusion*, *Double message*, *Embedded message*, *Implication*, *Levels of Meaning*, and *Pun*.

Analysis paralysis is a pop-psychology term describing a compulsive over-focus on intellectual explanations of some behavior, person, or event. This usually signals _ a dominant false self, who _ fears current *feelings* and/or *conflict*, and _ needs to appear concerned and proactive while fearing the latter. *Paralysis* implies "no action." See *Intellectual*, *Frozen*, *Numb*, *Superficial* and *Surface needs*.

Animated means using words, movements, gestures, and

voice dynamics that convey much emotion, variation, and "color." Too much local or chronic animation may come across as "hysterical" and "manic" to a receiver. People's tolerances for animation vary. See *Affect, Animated, Flat, Frozen, Expressionless, Intense,* and *Labile.*

Anxiety is emotional discomfort ranging from *unconscious* to *hysteria.* Emotional "comfort" is relief from anxiety, which probably drives most of your behavior. Synonyms; *Discomfort, Need, Stress, Upset, Uneasiness,* and *Worry.* Extreme anxiety is *panic.*

Approach-avoid relationship is one characterized by an ongoing cycle of trust and intimacy, and distrust and emotional and/or physical distance. Such relationships are *always* symptoms of one or both partners being significantly dominated by conflicted subselves. See *Double message* and *Symmetrical relationship.*

Arbitration: a communication process involving a neutral (=/=) third person working to clarify and facilitate compromise and lasting agreement between two or more conflicted subselves or people. See *Compromise, Mediate* and *Negotiate.*

Arguing: an ineffective alternative to win-win problem-solving. Competitive (vs. playful) arguing is characterized by blocked hearing, low communication awareness, and power struggles: *"I'm right." "No,* I'm *right!" Winning* becomes paramount, rather than filling both partner's needs respectfully. Local or chronic arguing probably indicates one or both partners' being controlled by a false self, and not knowing the seven communication skills. The other need arguing may fill is for excitement. In that case, the outcome is irrelevant. See *Conflict, Inner conflict, Power struggle, and "Yes, but. . .".*

Assertion: choosing to say clearly and directly to another person what you think, feel and need; in general, or from them. Alternatives are *submission ("I give in: your needs are more important");* and *aggression ("You will put my needs and opinions before yours, like it or not.")*

Association (mental/emotional): unconsciously attaching specific meanings and/or feelings to certain people, events, places, symbols, or experiences. For instance, notice what flashes into your awareness when you read *Walt Disney*, or *vomit*.

Assumption is an unconscious, semi-conscious, or conscious guesstimate at some truth about _ another person, the environment, or ourselves; or about _ an event (like a communication sequence outcome); or _ some relationship between things, events, or people (*"I assume you're interested in communication skills, because you're reading this book."*)

Attach (emotionally): See Bond, Grieve, Loss, Love, and Need.

Attitude: an evaluative mental judgment of a person, event, idea, relationship, or possibility that ranges from good to bad, right to wrong, useful to useless, clear to incomprehensible, safe to dangerous, truth to falsehood, moral to immoral, good to evil, and approval to rejection. Intense attitudes usually have associated emotional responses: revulsion, disgust, joy, excitement, fear, cynicism, guilt, shame, etc. *"He has an attitude"* is a vague term for holding a judgmental (critical) bias.

Avoiding is a popular Guardian-subself strategy to minimize expected discomfort by denying personal responsibility for confronting something. The protective false-self strategies of denial, defocusing, procrastinating, "forgetting," addiction, shallow breathing, withdrawing, and numbing are common ways of avoiding. When present, they imply subselves' fear of significant danger and pain, and distrust of the true Self's competence. Alternatives are admitting, confronting, and "owning" (taking responsibility).

Awareness: Here, this is the learnable mental/verbal skill on which the other six are based. Awareness skill focuses objectively on assessing what _ you think, feel, and need now; _ what any partner thinks, feels, and needs now; what's going on _ *between* your and your partner: now and over time; and _ around you both now. There are under 10 key awarenesses to cultivate for most situations, and scores of other communication variables. This glossary describes many of them. False-self dominance usually inhibits or distorts clear awareness.

Awareness "bubble": the field of awareness that figuratively surrounds the head and heart of each communicator at the moment. Awareness *bubbles* or *zones* can be restricted to "me only," "you only," "you and me right now, "you and me over time," or "neither of us." If two partners' awareness bubbles steadily include each other and they share =/= attitudes, they *may* be able to metatalk accurately on what each thinks, feels, needs, and perceives right now, if they know these seven skills. See [http://sfhelp.org/02/a-bubble.htm].

B

"Be-spontaneous!" paradox: is a self-defeating communication which requests or demands behavior from a partner which can only be spontaneous. Examples: *"Trust me!" "Love me!" "Respect me!" "Care about me!" "Agree with me!" "Accept me!"* and *"Desire me!"* If the partner complies, the sender may say, *"You only did that because I asked you to."* See *Double message, Game, Setup*, and *"Yes, but."*

Bill of Personal Rights: a clear statement of the social and relationship rights you or any person claims, as a dignified, unique human of undeniable worth. Your set of these beliefs, a genuine, mutual respect (=/=) attitude, and your fluency with assertion skills [7], shape your effectiveness in letting others know what you need from them (asserting). This is a core ingredient of effective problem solving. See *Aggression, Dignity, Empathy, Identity, Integrity, Reality distortion, and Wholistic health, and p. 362.*

Black/White ("bipolar") thinking: many of us from low-nurturance childhoods have Guardian subselves who master overwhelmingly complex social and emotional situations by reducing them to only two options, like *"My way, or the highway!;" "You're either part of the problem, or part of the solution;" "You're on time, or late, period."* Doing this avoids the uncertainty and anxiety of choosing among shades of gray; that is, it avoids wrestling with ambivalence or emotional overload, and/or making a shameful or painful "mistake." See *Fear-based,* and *Rigid.*

Blaming is arguably the single most destructive communication dynamic internally (*"It's all my fault."*) and socially (*"You caused this problem!"*) People who are centered and aware will choose =/= problem solving. That includes honest self-assessment for causing part of a conflict, and accepting responsibility for that without undue whining, guilt, explaining (justifying), or shame. Two shame-based adults or kids can get into an endless (exciting and/or wearying) shame-and-blame spiral in order to avoid feeling *bad* or *wrong* in someone's eyes, starting with their own. *Awareness* and clear, assertive "I" messages are a major antidote, after empowering your Self to lead your inner family. See *Arguing, Dig Down, Embarrassment, Fighting, Fear-based, Fighting, Guilt, Power, struggle,* and *Shame based.*

Blanking (out) is a protective mental/emotional reaction to something that one or more subselves perceive as scary. A Guardian *Blocker* subself can cause *blanking* or *blocking,* to soothe one or more frightened Vulnerable personality parts. A symptom of this your mind "going blank," if you're asked, "How do you feel (or think) about (something)?" See *Avoiding, Blocking, Denial,* and *Numbing.*

Blending (inner family) refers to the unconscious infusing of your true Self by one or more activated subselves, temporarily disabling your Self's wide-angle, long-viewed wisdom and judgment. Blending happens when a young Vulnerable and/or devoted Guardian subself distrusts or doesn't know your Self, and feels desperately that you (the host person) need to act in some way to prevent or reduce major physical, emotional, or spiritual discomfort. When you're blended, you experience the thinking, perceptions, feelings, and goals of the subselves who have taken your Self over. This is usually outside conscious awareness, until you develop inner-family knowledge and perception. See Chapter 1, *False self,* and the book "Who's *Really* Running Your Life?" (xlibris.com, 2000).

Blocking is a protective strategy by a distrustful Guardian *(Blocker)* subself which distracts a communicator's attention, defocuses their conscious mind, and may numb out normal emotional reactions to a sender's behavior. Common symptoms are the listener thinking or saying, "*I don't know how I feel (or what I think)*" about their partner's actions. Blocking can also refer to one or more attitudes and/or behaviors that hinder or prevent effective communication or mourning. See *Avoiding, Blanking, Denial, Guardian (subself), Numbing,* and *Repression.*

Bond (verb): emotionally and spiritually *attaching* to (caring about) another person or living thing. Bonds (noun) develop naturally between members of high-nurturance families, and with selected other kids, adults, living things, ideas, rituals, and objects. People from low-nurturance families and ancestries may not be able to truly bond with other some or all other people, including their own children, because of the mix of psychological wounds from false-self dominance: shame, guilt, distrust, fear, and reality distortion. The ability to bond creates _ possible abandonment and loss, and _ the need to grieve well. "I *care about* you" is different than "I *need* you." See *Attach, Cutoff, Distance, Love, Needy, and Relationship.*

Borderline personality disorder: a clinical diagnosis for people whose inner families are particularly chaotic and leaderless. The "border" referred to is the one between mental health and "illness." The label can be a hand-grenade word, because it evokes fear, pity, and shame. See *Dissociate* and *Splitting.*

Boundaries (relationship) are felt and expressed personal limits that define where you stop, and another person "starts."

A set of clear mental and verbal boundaries helps to determine your personal *identity*, which builds your personal security, self-concept, and self-confidence. Respectful (=/=) *assertion* is the healthy language of describing your current true needs and boundaries to other people. Restated: boundaries define what you will and won't tolerate or do; "*I'll eat salmon, but not grasshoppers*;" or "*You can say I'm lazy, but not* stupid." See *Assertion, Comfort zone, Consequence, Enabling, Payoff, Sequence, Submission,* and *Victim.*

Brainstorming is a cooperative, creative process between mutually-respectful subselves or people seeking to identify all possible options toward resolving a current conflict. Common alternatives are threatening, manipulating, black/white thinking, hinting, assuming, dictating, complaining, procrastinating, persuading, arguing, explaining, and playing *"Yes, but . . ."*

Breakdown: *Personal* breakdown is the experience of extreme mental and emotional disorientation and overwhelm that occurs (I believe) from situational or sustained inner-family chaos. That happens when one or more personality parts are terrified, needy, and hysterical, and the Self is distrusted and unable to calm them. A *communication* breakdown occurs when partners are _ too controlled by agitated false selves, and _ don't know or trust the seven communication skills. See *Centered, Cutoff, Go to pieces, "Lose it,"* and *Meltdown.*

C

Catastrophizing is the mental/emotional process of vividly imagining and obsessing on the very worst possible outcome to a situation, regardless of liklihood. This is a well-meant protective strategy by a Guardian subself who _ doesn't trust the Self to lead well enough, and _ wants to make the host person aware of, and prepared for, the worst; to avoid expected overwhelm and disaster. See *Reality distortion.*

Centered: describes the mind-body-spirit "state" that occurs when your Self is _ trusted and solidly in charge of your inner troop of personality subselves, _ focused steadily on the present moment, and _ is actively getting your true needs met. Sustained *awareness* is most likely when you're inner family is centered and harmonized. See *Blending, Grounded, Defocused,* and *Fragmented.*

Change: See First-order change and Second-order change.

Channel (communication): any of three concurrent ways humans exchange information: (1) words and sounds (verbal channel), (2) voice dynamics (paraverbal channel), and (3) facial and body expressions, posture, touch, and movement (non-verbal channel). Many people believe there is a fourth *telepathy* or *extra-sensory* channel ("ESP"), available to us all. See *Awareness* and *Double message.*

Character: See *Personality*

Character defect: an implicitly shaming concept and phrase fostered by generations of recovering addicts following the well-known "12 steps" espoused by Alcoholics Anonymous and related recovery programs. This term implies *"I am defective (and bad),"* which promotes semi-conscious shame: one of the six major psychological wounds coming from low childhood nurturance. A recovery-promoting alternative (in my opinion) is *"I am or was blended, and controlled by a false self."* See *Embedded message, Hand-grenade terms,* and *Shame-based.*

Childish (adult behavior) usually comes from temporary dominance of one or more Vulnerable subselves ("Inner Children.") When chronic, childish behavior in a man or woman indicates major false self-dominance. Trying to scold or blame such adults (*"Just grow up, will you?"*) frustrates both people, because without inner-family awareness and reorganizing, the split person *cannot* "grow up" (free their Self to lead). See *Assuming, Discount, Labeling, and Name calling.*

Churning (mental): See *Mind racing.*

Co-dependence is obsessive, unconscious over-focusing on another person's welfare, appearance, and behaviors, and losing your own identity and life goals in the process. Some say this condition is "relationship addiction," because it has the same compulsive, progressive, harmful attributes as craving a toxic substance. The term grew out of *co-alcoholic* and *co-addiction* in the 1980's. Co-dependence is clear evidence of major false-self dominance. See [.. 01/co-dep.htm and ..11/booklist.htm].

Comfort (noun): the absence of emotional and physical pain. Seeking to create and maintain enough comfort drives all behavior (communication) and relationships. (Verb): to comfort is behaving in a way that reduces your or another person's emotional, physical, or spiritual tensions, longings, cravings, or pain. In major traumas, the need for comfort (including security) supercedes all other emotional needs. See *Needs*

Comfort zone: means _ the physical and/or emotional closeness your subselves can tolerate with other persons before feeling "invaded" (unsafe and distracted); or _ the types of social or solo behaviors that your subselves can tolerate before blending (taking over) your Self. See *Distraction, Heart talk, Intimacy, Non-verbal channel,* and *Trust.*

Communication is any *perceived, assumed,* or *sensed* behavior in or by someone that causes an un/conscious emotional, mental, spiritual, and/or physical reaction in another person. This also applies to behaviors between any two subselves in your inner family, like your Self and your *Inner Critic,* or *Shamed Child.* There is no such thing as "no communication" between people or subselves in a relationship, for the perceived absence of behavior usually suggests assumed meanings to the receiver. See *Communication needs, Double message, Embedded message, Levels of meaning, Outcome,* and *Payoff.*

Communication block: any thought, attitude, reflex, or response that hinders effective *inner* personal or interpersonal communication [J]. With true =/= (mutually respectful) attitudes and true Selves leading, partners can use the seven skills to identify and resolve *any* communication block. See *Arguing, Defocusing, Distraction, Fighting, Fuzzy thinking, Lose-lose, Outcome, R-message, Triangling,* and *Win-win.*

Communication conflict: occurs when two or more people have incompatible local communication needs: e.g. you need to vent, and I need to cause action or excitement. Any time a communicator interprets an "I-m 1-up," or "I'm I-down" R(espect)-message from their partner, there is an implied communication conflict, since the need for at least self respect exists in all communication exchanges. The skill of Metatalk helps identify such conflicts, and the other six skills can resolve them if partners' Selves are in charge.

Communication needs: the six tensions causing subselves and people to communicate: _ build and keep respect; _ give or get information; _ vent; _ cause change or feel impactful; _ create stimulation, or _ avoid discomfort. Two or more of these motivate every communication exchange between people and subselves, as the need for respect is constant. Partners' communication needs are concurrent with other surface and underlying true needs.

Complaining is a popular false-self strategy to avoid taking risky responsibility for acting to fill your current true needs. See *Avoiding, Blaming, Catastrophizing, Defocusing, Postponing, Whining,* and *"Yes, but . . ."*

Compromise: a communication-sequence process and outcome in which each partner or subself in a conflict chooses to give up filling one or more needs completely, to fill other needs they value more. This strategy works best for abstract inner and social conflicts over values, preferences, limits, and beliefs. When each person or subself is centered (Self-led), genuine (vs. pseudo) compromise may permanently resolve the need, value, resource, or perception, dispute. See *Arbitrate* and *Negotiate.*

Compulsion: an uncontrollable, repeated *physical* behavioral ritual or sequence that may be unhealthy or harmful. I believe compulsions usually indicate significant false-self dominance. Brain chemistry and wiring is another factor. See *Addiction* and *Obsession.*

Concrete (resource) conflict: a dispute over a physical resource like a tool, currency, vehicle, appliance, money, food, or clothing, etc. If E-levels stay unusually high in these conflicts, the odds are high that _ one or more people are dominated by a false self, and _ there are major true needs underneath the disputed resource, like respect, pride, security, and/or physical comfort. See *Abstract conflict, Communication conflict,* and *Inner conflict.*

Conflict: two or more opposed internal or interpersonal values, perceptions, or opinions; or emotional, spiritual, and/ or physical *needs* (discomforts). Conflicts can be conscious or unconscious; over differing communication, concrete, or abstract needs; individual or group, and situational or chronic. Common synonyms are *impasse, dispute, dilemma, standoff, battle, war, disagreement, problem,* and *"issue."* The seven mental/verbal skills in this book exist to satisfy needs and reduce or end conflicts. See *Argue, Fight, Impasse,* and *Problem solving.*

Confrontation is a type of communication sequence in which one partner, or a Self, chooses to assert observations, requests, or demands for acknowledgement or change from a partner or other subselves. Assertions can range between respectful and calm, to disrespectful and emotionally intense and overwhelming. See *Avoiding* and *Denial.*

Confusion is a mental/emotional *feeling* which indicates _ your personality subselves are reorganizing and/or _ conflicted, and/or _ you're *growing*: shifting from one life-state to another. Transiting from childhood to adulthood or independence to parenthood is pretty *confusing* for most people. So are approach-avoid relationships and inner-family anarchy. See *Ambiguity, Double Message, Mind racing,* and *Defocusing.*

Consequence: a planned or impulsive behavioral reaction to a communication or action. Describing *and enforcing* clear consequences (*"If you choose to spend money at the racetrack and lie to me about that again, I'll file for divorce."*) is a key ingredient to effective child discipline, and to setting effective personal boundaries with another person. Realistic consequences are a vital ingredient of effective assertions. Well designed and respectfully enforced, they promote self-respect, inner-family harmony and security, increased intimacy, and effective problem-solving. Consequences designed to c/overtly embarrass, hurt, punish, or scare a partner are *always* caused by false selves, and *always* degrade self-respect, trust, and relationships, long term. See *Boundaries, Fear-based, "I" message, Payoff, Power struggle,* and *Revenge.*

Content (communication) is the conscious topic/s under discussion between two or more subselves or people. See *Awareness, Focus,* and *Process.*

Context: the frame of meaning with which a behavior (communication) or relationship is evaluated. For example: depending on the context, avoiding an explosive confrontation can be viewed as "*prudently keeping the peace,*" or "*enabling a low-nurturance relationship, and sacrificing self respect for short-term security.*" In conflict-resolution, discerning different contexts invites partners to assess that context is more important to them individually, and whether their respective contexts are part of the conflict, e.g. "*I'm working on our marriage,*" vs. "*I'm more concerned with our child's development.*" See *Levels of meaning* and *Reframing.*

Controlling (behavior) can range from minor to obsessive, and unconscious to intentional. It can apply to your own behavior ("*I controlled my urge to yell.*"), and/or attempts to evoke desired behavior in others to fill your own un/conscious needs. Excessive control implies distrust of either one's own thoughts and feelings, or of your partner's judgment or reactions. Habitual over-controlling implies significant false-self dominance, and ineffective inner and interpersonal communication. See *Aggression, Black/white thinking, Manipulation,* and *Rigidity.*

Co-parent: an adult who willingly or dutifully takes on the role of occasionally or regularly providing some level of emotional, spiritual, and/or physical nurturance to a minor or dependent child. S/He may or may not have genetic or legal connection to the child, and/or to the child's biological parent/s. *To co-parent* means to nurture, guide, and protect a dependent child with one or more other caregivers. See *Needs, Nurture,* and *Wholistic health.*

Crisis is a subjective label for a personal or social situation that threatens or causes great harm or change to the subselves or person/s affected. What one person feels is a crisis may be a *challenge* or *problem* to another, depending on many factors. Impulsively or strategically used, "crisis" can be a hand-grenade word. See *Association, Catastrophizing, Framing, Loss, Meaning, Panic, Reality distortion, Second-order change, Trauma,* and *Overwhelm.*

Cutoff (relationship noun and verb) occurs when one person temporarily or permanently refuses to exchange verbal or written communication with another. When no clear, genuine explanation is offered (*"I've lost all trust and hope that you and I can communicate civilly, so I won't respond to you any more"*), cutoffs can be easily misunderstood and misinterpreted (*"Jan just feels too embarrassed and guilty to face me."*). Most long-standing cutoffs result from two opposed false selves, ineffective communication skills, high distrust and disrespect, and indifference to, or denial or ignorance of these. Many divorced parents who are scorned as "uninvolved" (cut off) and "not caring about their children," often cannot bear the pain (guilt, remorse, longing) of contact with a beloved child. Some cutoffs are symptoms of a false-self inability to bond. See *Avoidance, Bonding, Pseudo intimacy,* and *Divorce.*

D

Deal with is a vague (fuzzy-thinking) phrase people use when they're not clear on what they really need, as in *"You'll just have to deal with my bluntness."* Using cooperative dig-down, metatalk, and empathic listening skills can get closer to what the speaker really means or needs. Avoiding this in important situations risks ineffective communication. See *Discuss* and *Work through.*

Debate (noun or verb) can be an internal and/or social communication sequence to entertain, stimulate, clarify, teach, compete, persuade, or help make a complex decision (like debating pros and cons). When excessive, compulsive, or chronic, inner or mutual debates can serve to _ avoid silence and awareness, _ avoid the risk of (wrong) decision, and/or to _ shame or dominate another subself or person. *Effective* debates imply all participants have genuine mutual respect (=/ = attitudes), stable, common focus/es, and are led by their respective true Selves. See *Agree to disagree, Argue, Compromise, Fight, Justify, Negotiate, Persuade, Problem solve,* and *"Yes, but . . ."*

Decoding is deducing meaning from your or another person's perceived verbal and non-verbal behaviors. "Misunderstandings" occur when you decode a different message than the sender (consciously) intended. *Hearing checks* can reduce misunderstandings in important communications. See *Assumption, Double message, Levels of Meaning,* and *R-message.*

Defensiveness is a shame-based false-self trait: often interpreting another's implied or actual behaviors as *attacks* (criticisms), and reflexively explaining, defending, and/or counterattacking. Two unaware shame-based partners can fall into a destructive sequence of (blame > defend > counterattack) that erodes their self esteems, mutual trusts and securities, and faith in their communication abilities. Like *over-sensitivity, over-defensiveness* is a subjective judgment. When used often in a relationship, it suggests significant psychological wounding in the speaker and/or receiver. See *Assertion, Boundary, Dignity, Discount, Name calling, Scorn,* and *Shame.*

Defocusing happens when any communication partner or

subself is distracted toward, or chooses, a new topic or focus before the present topic is "done enough." This may be a semiconscious or intentional strategy to avoid risk or discomfort. The person may also be controlled by volatile subselves who have different agendas (focuses). See *Avoiding* and *Confusion*.

Delusion or Illusion: a convincing survival-oriented reality distortion caused by one or more Guardian subselves (q.v.) that don't trust their host person's Self or inner delegates to act safely on a current stressor. Some delusions are organically caused. See *Assuming, Catastrophizing, Decoding,* and *Denial*.

Demand: a communication message which implies or states, "I will not tolerate (accept) you're responding 'No,' 'Not now,' and/or 'Not your way' to my needs without taking assertive or aggressive action." Voice tone and body language can determine whether the demand is respectful (=/=), "1-down" (timid), or "1-up" (disrespectful). See *Boundary, Consequence, Hinting, Pleading, Submission,* and *Request.*

Denial: a common Guardian-subself strategy to protect Vulnerable subselves from expected or current discomfort (*"Nah, this chest pain will go away. Just something I ate."*) Denials can mute or numb emotions (repressions), distort perceptions, promote self-neglect and/or aggression, and cause constant inner and interpersonal conflicts. The master denial is of denial itself. See *Resistance.*

Dependent relationship is one in which one or both partners feel they can't live a secure-enough life without the presence of, and emotional connection to, the other. Our earliest relationship experience is total dependence on our caregivers. Self-led (mature) adults learn to balance self-sufficiency and voluntary interdependence with one or more others, and often with a benign Higher Power. See *Approach-avoid, Bond, Co-dependence, Isolation, Needy,* and *Symmetrical relationship.*

Despair: feeling no credible hope that _ painful or overwhelming inner and/or social conditions will get better (i.e. that key unmet needs may be filled); and/or that _ the sufferer can do anything to bring relief. A period of despair may be normal in the process of healthy grief. Prolonged despair usually signals a disabled true Self. See *Catastrophizing* and *Victim.*

Detach is the opposite of *attach:* intentionally or unconsciously reducing emotional/spiritual bonding ("caring") for a vision, ideal, hope, or living thing. If perceived as meaning *"I care less: You're a bad or inadequate person"* relationship detachment feels like personal discounting and rejection. That can trigger shame, guilt, and fear of abandonment via major false-self activation. See *Cutoff* and *Loss.*

De-triangling: intentionally dissolving a Persecutor–Victim–Rescuer relationship triangle (q.v.) by declining the role you've chosen or accepted.

Dig down is one of seven learnable relationship skills. It requires *awareness,* clear thinking, and your Self in charge of your inner family; and aims to objectively look "underneath" internal and social *surface* problems, to discern communication partners' (semi-conscious) *true* needs, and who's responsible for filling them [4].

Dignity is the respect, importance, and worth you accord yourself (and your Self) and other persons, including those you're conflicted with. A true =/= (mutually respectful) relationship attitude implies "I see you and me as people of equal dignity and worth, despite our differences." See *Identity, Integrity* and *R-message.*

Discount (communication noun and verb): an incoming message which is decoded as *"I think your feelings, thoughts, needs, or values are invalid, wrong, and/or of little value."* Without clear awareness of this, the receiver may automatically add *". . . and (you think) I'm a bad person."* Intended or (mis)perceived discounts usually promote hurt, guilt, shame, irritation, and either defensiveness, withdrawal, or counterattack. Synonyms: *slam, criticism, put down, insult, invalidation, label,* and *demean. Awareness* and clear, assertive "I" messages are far more effective. Chronic discounting usually signals a shame-based false self in charge in sender and/or receiver. See *Abuse, Aggression,* and *Awareness bubble.*

Discuss is a fuzzy catchall term like "talk about," "step up to," or "talk over" ("Let's talk *this thing* over") which may include one or more of these: venting, clarifying, asserting, negotiating, hinting, asserting, blaming, defending, explaining, requesting, demanding, informing, arguing, negotiating, compromising, and/or problem-solving. A *discussion* is a communication sequence (q.v.) including some mix of these, and may or may not be *effective* communication. Discussions occur between subselves and humans to fill local surface and true needs. See *Deal with* and *Fuzzy thinking.*

Dissociate: to lose focus and coherent mental awareness of yourself and your surroundings. Dissociation is a primal neural *survival* strategy to protect against intolerable immediate terror, injury, or pain. Kids and adults living or working in very low-nurturance settings may dissociate often or all the time. I believe all levels of dissociation (mild and temporary to chronic Dissociative Identity Disorder) are caused by rioting subselves who don't trust the true Self, other people, or a Higher Power to create enough local safety and comfort. See *Blending, Breakdown, Centered, False self, Go to pieces, Multiplicity, Reality distortion, Recovery, Serenity,* and *Splitting.*

Distance (relationship): the variable intensity of emotional concern, attraction, intimacy, trust, (q.v.) and bonding a person feels for a partner. See *Bond, Co-dependence, Cutoff, Independent relationship,* and *Love.*

Distraction: something internal (emotional, physical, and/or spiritual), or environmental that significantly hinders clear conscious *awareness,* and stable focusing on one or a few communication topics or goals. Distractions usually indicate a false self (q.v.) is in charge. See *Content, Defocus,* and *Process.*

Divorce is a (potential) hand-grenade term meaning _ the emotional/spiritual *process* of ending an important relationship bond, and altering the bonds, roles, and self esteems of related people; a legal _ *process* and _ *event* which formally demarks the end of a socially and religiously sanctioned sexual relationship and a related family; and _ a potentially shaming personal, parental, and multi-generational "failure" and/or _ a religious "sin."

In my experience, emotional or legal (re)divorce strongly suggests _ unrecognized false self-dominance in one or both partners, _ their low-nurturance ancestries; _ unawareness of these seven skills, and _ likely early splitting in any dependent kids involved. Many lay people and professionals mistakenly focus on the impact of the legal divorce process and event on adults and kids, rather than on the emotional/developmental impacts of low family nurturance and ineffective communication skills that led to a divorce. See *Avoidance, Co-parent, Cutoff, Grieve, Loss, Marriage, and Second-order change.*

Double (mixed) message: any verbal, paraverbal, or non-verbal behavior from which the receiver decodes two or more contradictory meanings; e.g. *"I love you; You're disgusting."* Typically, local or chronic double messages imply that the sender is dominated by a false self, and isn't aware of that. Synonym: *double entendre.* See *Assumption, Embedded message, Implication, Innuendo, Levels of meaning, and Pun.*

Doubt is mental + emotional + spiritual confusion and uncertainty that signifies _ false-self dominance, distrust of self or a partner, and inner conflict in one or both partners; or _ a true Self and advisors in the process of assessing known information and options toward making a firm decision. See *Ambivalence, Minds, and Trust.*

Dysfunctional (relationship, group, family): See *Low nurturance,* and *Wholistic health.*

E

Effective communication occurs (I believe) when each person or inner-family subself _ gets enough of their current true (vs. surface) needs met, _ in a way that leaves them feeling good *enough* about themselves, their partner/s, and the processes in and between them. The adjective *effective* is less apt to provoke shame and guilt than *good* or *bad* communication. Effective communication may or may not be "open and honest," depending on local needs and perceptions. See *Communication needs, Lose-lose, Outcome, Payoff, Problem solving, Resolution, Sequence,* and *Win-win.*

Ego (Latin: "I"): normal to exaggerated self-importance. I believe *egotistic* people are governed by a Guardian subself devoted to protecting a deeply shamed young Vulnerable. A companion *Magician* subself may cause the person to deny this to avoid more shame. See *Entitlement, Narcissism,* and *Self-centered.*

Egotism: See *Entitlement, Grandiosity,* and *Narcissism.*

Embarrassment is "shame made public." Behaving "shamefully" in front of others, or describing shameful private behaviors to others, causes one or more subselves to feel shame, and infuse your Self and body with it. Embarrassment usually has a garnish of guilt and various anxieties. Moderate embarrassment helps regulate social behavior. Excessive or chronic embarrassment, or excessive fear of that, is a sure sign of psychological wounds. See *"1-down," Co-dependence, Discount, Moralizing, Oversensitive, People pleasing,* and *Rules.*

Embedded (implied) message: an implied message within a message. Communication is the exchange of *meaning* over verbal, paraverbal, and non-verbal channels. "Messages" on each of these channels can contain surface meanings, and concurrent implied or embedded meanings. Satirist Mark Twain noted this when he wrote *"There are 17 different ways of saying 'No'."* See *Context, Double message, Levels of Meaning,* and *Pun.*

E(motion)-level refers to the current intensity of your or your partner's *feelings* (emotions + physical sensations). These can range from *calm* or *numb* (no perceived feelings), to serene (feeling *peaceful* and *calm*), to *uneasy*, to *upset* or *agitated*, to *overwhelmed*, to *hysterical*, or *berserk*. Choosing which of the six communication skills besides awareness to use varies with whether your and your partner's E-levels are "above or below your ears." That is, whether emotional intensity is high enough to distract either of you from mental focusing and effective *listening*. See *Awareness bubble* and *Venting*.

Empathic listening is "hearing with your *heart*." I feel this term, coined by Stephen Covey, improves the traditional labels *active* listening, *reflective* listening, and *mirroring,* by emphasizing the vital emotional half of our communication process. Empathic listening is the learned skill of *nonjudgmentally* sensing what the speaker feels, needs, and thinks, and periodically summarizing those *without inner or spoken evaluation or comment.* See *Hearing check.*

Empathy is the ability to accurately *sense* what another person is currently feeling and experiencing, and what those mean to the other person now. Relationship quality depends partly on each partner's ability to empathize with the other. The ability to empathize depends partly on whether your true Self is leading your inner family. See *Awareness bubble, Bonding,* and *Numbing.*

Emptiness is a metaphor for feeling one's life has little or no purpose, and/or for having minimal or no emotional-spiritual bonds to other living things and/or a Higher Power. Difficulty bonding is one of six personality-splitting wounds from a low-nurturance childhood [1]. *Losses* (broken emotional/spiritual bonds) cause temporary emptiness, which promotes normal grieving (acceptance) and forming new bonds. Infants and young children whose caregivers are unable to bond (nurture) may feel that emptiness, dubbed "A hole in the soul," is *normal* and unremarkable. See *Abandonment, Alienation, Alone in a crowd, Apathy, Attach, Bond, Cutoff, Depression, Distance, Intimacy,* and *Love.*

Enabling is compulsively taking responsibility for filling another person's needs, and unintentionally blocking them from healing, and/or growing self-competence and confidence. The classic example is an addict's mate calling in "sick" for their hung-over partner, instead of helping by letting him or her experience the consequences of their own behaviors. Guardian subselves can justify enabling as *kindness*. See *Co-dependence, Denial, Dependent relationship, People pleasing, and Rescuer.*

Entitlement is an emotional belief that says *"I deserve (something.)"* Often, *excessive* entitlement and related aggression signal that Guardian subselves are protecting Vulnerables from shame and guilt, about wanting something unattainable, or feeling resentful others have "it." Healthy (moderate) entitlement underlies integrity and =/= self-respect. Excessive or me-only entitlement damages communication effectiveness and relationship health. See *"1-up," Assertion, "Be spontaneous!" paradox, Boundaries, Controlling, Dignity, Grandiosity, Integrity, Jealousy, Manipulation, Narcissism, Selfish, and selfish.*

Exaggerating: is a way of humorously or defensively distorting something in thought and/or speech to make it bigger than it is; e.g. *"The length of this glossary shows clearly that effective communication is impossible for the average person."* Chronic exaggeration and/or minimizing are reality distortions that signal protective false-self dominance. See *Lying* and *Reality distortion.*

Expectations (communication): Based on past history and/or social conditioning, people in active relationships build semi-conscious expectations (forecasts) of how their typical communication sequences (mutual behaviors) will go. If they're unaware of their expectations, they can assume the outcome, and react to it before it happens. (*"I know Pat won't really care about what I think or need, though she'll never admit it."*) Personality subselves act on expectations all the time, which can cause stress if they're living in the past, or influenced by a Guardian *Illusionist*. See *Assumption* and *Fuzzy thinking*.

Explaining: is either providing useful information, or a false-self reaction to feeling blamed or criticized by a partner. Unaware, shame-based communicators can get stuck in an (attack > explain > counterattack) cycle that leaves both people feeling frustrated, unheard, and disrespected. Wounded people tend to over-explain, or say little. Both cause relationship tensions. See *Defensiveness, Justifying, Rationalizing, Whining,* and *"Yes, but . . ."*

Expression (facial) usually describes the arrangement of a communicator's head posture, facial muscles, skin tone, and eye behaviors. Infants seem pre-programmed to decode meaning from facial expressions in their caregivers like smiles, frowns, and looking disinterested. From this beginning, all of us have learned to *unconsciously* associate fine nuances of facial expressions with meanings or feelings (*"Jenny looks troubled."*) In major interpersonal conflicts, it can help to objectively assess and use metatalk to learn whether assumed meanings of, or unconscious reactions to, facial expressions and voice dynamics are fueling the problem. (*"My Dad used to roll his eyes like that when I disappointed him, and I felt so ashamed."*)

Expressionless: having a face, body and voice that shows or implies little or no emotion during communication. This may indicate the person is chronically fear-based, or is situationally choosing to not reveal some or all of their emotions. Common reactions to an overly-expressionless person range from "vague unease" to anxiety, suspicion, and distrust. See *Affect, Blocking, Frozen, Intense, Labile,* and *Numbing*.

Extra-sensory Perception (ESP) is the widely documented ability that some of us have to *sense* or *know* things about events and other people in the past, present, or future that we have "no way of knowing." Relationship decisions, and behaviors based on *sixth senses* have high potential for mistrust, scorn, and conflict, because "logic" and "rationality" don't apply and our faith in the power of reason and natural (observable) laws are shaken. See *Guesstimate, Hunch,* and *Intuition.*

Eye contact: If "eyes are the windows of the soul," then withholding or avoiding eye contact can be decoded as, "*You don't trust me to view your soul.*" That in turn can imply "*You have something to hide,*" and/or "*You don't trust me.*" Habitually avoiding eye contact sends an "*I'm 1-down*" R-message, which invites unconscious distrust and discounting. It often implies a fear-based or shame-based inner family, controlled by a protective false self. *Awareness,* respectful metatalk and/or true recovery can shift eye-contact behaviors.

F

Fall apart: a metaphor for inner-family uproar and chaos. See *Break down, Confusion, Defocusing, Go to pieces,* and *Meltdown.*

False self is one or more personality parts (subselves) who activate and "blend with" (infuse and take over), your true Self. They do this because the subselves don't yet trust your Self to get their needs met well enough. Being controlled by a false self _ usually inhibits or blocks effective thinking and interpersonal communication, _ causes and amplifies relationship and health "problems," _ is self-camouflaging ("I'm *not controlled by a false self!*"), and _ can be identified and healed, over time, via Self-motivated "parts (inner family) work" with a competent helper. See [1 and 9].

Family: two or more people connected by some mix of genes, names, legal documents, traditions, roles, responsibilities, and mutual bonding. Families persist in every era and culture because they fill certain human needs for acceptance, protection, procreation, nurturing, and intimacy better than non-families. See *Inner* family system.

Family secret: one or a series of events, or an ancestor's traits, that are so shameful that each new generation is told

openly or covertly *"We don't acknowledge or talk about that."*
This mimics the Christian tradition that all humans are tainted
and require Divine redemption because Adam and Eve
disobeyed God. Family adults create the secrets by following
their parents' and society's moral rules. Who defined the secret
and why can become lost, but the intense shame and "No talk"
rule continue until someone challenges it. Family secrets
promote semi-conscious shame, guilt, and anxiety; and
psychological wounding in the next generation. See *Avoidance,
Black/white thinking, Cutoff, Denial, Embarrassment,
Moralizing, Reality distortion, Rigidity, Rule conflicts, and
Threats.*

Family system: the present and absent people comprising
a nuclear or extended (multi-generational) family, and the
values, bonds, rules, roles, rituals, scripts, assets, memories,
and boundaries that separate them from their social and physical
environment. See *Inner* family system.

Fear is a primal protective neorochemical reaction to
perceived potential or present danger. We each have our own
opinions about what is "healthy" or "too much" fear. This
emotion is *natural,* vs. negative nor positive. Our own and
others' *reactions* to our fears can be toxic or nurturing. See
Anxiety, Panic, Terror, and *Overwhelm.*

Fear-based (personality) is an inner family often dominated
by one or more significantly scared Vulnerable subselves and
their protective Guardians. Common primal fears are of _
abandonment (being alone and uncared for); _ emotional
overwhelm (and therefore fear of intimacy, strong emotions,
and conflict); _ the unknown; fear of _ "failure" (feeling inept,
unworthy, shameful, and guilty); and of _ "success" (feeling
guilty, undeserving, and unworthy); and _ fear of the emotional
state of excessive fear. Ultimately, fear is (some subself's) distrust
of Self and the environment, including distrust of a caring
Higher Power. See *Shame-based.*

Feedback is giving conscious *and/or unconscious* reactions to another person's behavior. Feedback may be invited or not; supportive or shaming; real or assumed; verbal, visual, audible, and/or tactile; and may be decoded with any of three embedded R-messages. Use awareness and metatalk to distinguish among all these in any situation.

Feeling can mean either _ a bodily (sensory) experience: *"I feel hot (physically)"*; _ an emotion or mood *"I feel hot (angry);"* or _ a hunch, intuition, or "sense." In conflicts or confusions, distinguishing what "feel" means may help clarify true needs, and avoid misunderstandings. See *Affect, Emotion, Expressionless, Numbing,* and *Oversensitive.*

Female brain: See *Gender* and the book "Brain Sex" (p. 414).

Fighting (communication) is a popular lose-lose alternative to cooperative problem solving. Fighting usually indicates false selves control one or more people, and no one knows the seven skills in this book. See *Arguing* and *Conflict.*

First-order change is a superficial or cosmetic shift in attitude and/or behavior. Diets that "don't work" are first-order changes. So is "controlling" one addiction (e.g. alcohol) and starting another (smoking, gambling, overeating, or sex.) This concept and term is useful in building *awareness* of personal and relationship behavioral choices and patterns. (*"I think you're proposing a first-order change."*) Major and repeated first order changes (*"This is the fifth therapist I've tried."*) usually signal denied psychological wounding and false-self conflict (*"Change!" / "No!"*) and dominance. See *Second-order change.*

Flat affect: showing no emotions on any communication channel (verbal, paraverbal, and non-verbal). When chronic, this is usually a symptom of major false-self dominance. The implication is that the governing subselves don't believe that expressing emotions is safe. Synonyms are *implacable, inscrutable,* "cold," and *stony-faced.* See *Blocking, Controlling, Expressionless, Labile, Numbing,* and *Passionate.*

Flooding occurs when a communicator gives too much

information to the receiver without pausing to let them respond. If chronic, this degrades communication effectiveness and relationships. The embedded R-message is *"My need to express myself is more important to me than my need to know how you're feeling, and what you need now. I'm 1-up."*

Usually, false-self dominance causes the speaker's awareness bubble to exclude their partner, so eventually the receiver feels ignored (discounted) and used. Shame-based people will endure flooding, blow up, or withdraw. True Selves will confront respectfully with meta-comments and "I"-message assertions (*"When you talk on and on, I feel discounted and resentful, and lose interest in what you're saying."*) See *Assertion, Awareness "bubble," Monologing, Preaching, Rambling, Submission, Venting,* and *Victim.*

Focus is the current or repeated target of individual or group behaviors. Clear, shared focus usually promotes effective communication, and vice versa. Significant false-self control hinders productive mental and conversational focusing. "Attention Deficit Disorder (A.D.D.)" in adults and kids may indicate major psychological wounding. Key communication *awarenesses* are *"Are we focused (over time)? On what?"* See *Confusion, Defocus, Distraction, Mind racing,* and *Overtalking.*

"Forgetting," specially if chronic, can be a protective false-self strategy to spare a young Vulnerable subself from discomfort. It can also be a neorochemical deficit in one or more of the mind's several memory areas.

Fragmented (personality) can refer to the normal psychological multiplicity of all people, or to the erratic, inappropriate thinking and behavior of a child or adult dominated by a chaotic group of subselves. See *Blending, Breakdown, Go to Pieces, Fall apart, Fuzzy thinking, Meltdown,* and *Splitting.*

Framing is a particular way of interpreting the nature, meaning, or value of a situation, person, event, relationship, loss, or idea. E.g. *confusion* may be framed as "a negative mind-body condition that hinders progress and productivity," or "an exciting symptom of important personal growth and second-order (core attitude) change." See *Context, Idealism, Levels of meaning, and Reframe.*

Freudian slip: Psychoanalyst Sigmund Freud noted the human foible of saying something "accidentally" that reveals unconscious motives or associations. A male radio announcer's bread-commercial blooper is a classic example; *"For the breast in bed, get . . ."* The commonality of such slips affirms our neural multiplicity, and widespread *normal* personality splitting. See *Leaking, Slip of the tongue,* and *Subliminal cues.*

Frozen is a metaphoric adjective describing the emotional/physical state of "feeling nothing" (*"Hank was frozen with fear and shame."*) Some adults from low-nurturance childhoods learned to adaptively freeze their breathing, bodies, and/or facial muscles, to guard against painful retaliation for expressing their feelings to their caregivers. In adult recovery, they can learn to "thaw," over time. See *Affect, Blocking, Animated, Fear based, Expressionless, Impassive, Numb,* and *Labile.*

Frustration is a helpful automatic mind-body reaction that signals one or more subselves are unable to fill one or more current *needs.* They feel blocked from reducing current mental, emotional, spiritual, and/or physical discomforts. The learnable skill of *awareness* [2] helps to note this feeling, and selective *digging down* [4] can unearth the real needs underneath the surface ones. Then the other five communication skills can help fill the needs. When they don't, we can feel frustrated with our (subselves') frustration. Chronic or explosive frustration and/or repressing it suggests significant psychological wounding and inner conflict. See *Anger, Communication needs, Denial, Dig Down, Expectation, True Needs, Perfectionism, Reflex, Triangling,* and *Upset.*

Functional (relationship, family, group): See *High nurturance and Wholistic health.*

Future self is a concept suggested by therapist Nancy

Napier: imaging and dialoging with your older self, e.g. shortly before your future death. Depending on many factors, people can experience this self as very real, and have meaningful discussions with her or him. Others will ridicule this, because accepting it means too great a change in (some subselves') definition of "reality." During parts work, I have witnessed many people dialoging with their Future self. See *Subself.*

Fuzzy thinking is defocusing, using vague or inappropriate words or phrases, and erratic or no logic, to form thoughts and related speech. This is characteristic of people with major inner-family turmoil, and can be intentionally reduced, once identified. Clear thinking is one of the seven mental/verbal communication skills you can develop. [3] See *Avoiding, Awareness, Deal with, Defocus, Denial, Discuss,* and *Work through.*

G

Game (communication): attitudes and related communication strategies that aim to covertly get a certain payoff from a communication partner. Doing this satisfies one or more true needs of the game player (e.g. to feel *powerful, impactful,* and *safe*); which are usually markedly different than their surface goals (*"Have some fun."*). By definition, behavioral games are "1-up" and insincere, vs. clear, honest, and direct communication transactions. Unless meant in fun ("kidding"), they typically leave the receiver feeling *uneasy, used, resentful, wary, disrespected,* and *distrustful.* See *Double message, Embedded message, Framing, Levels of Meaning,* and the book "Games People Play," by Eric Berne.

Gender factors in communication: significant preference, sensitivity, and information-processing differences innate to "male brains and "female brains." See the books "Brain Sex" by Anne Moir and David Jessel; and "You Just Don't Understand," by Deborah Tannen. For a summary, see [..02/gender.htm].

Generalizing is the communication dynamic of taking a specific trait, feeling, or circumstance and applying it to "everyone" or "all situations": "*All snakes are slimy*," "*Conflict is never productive*," "*Dictionaries are always intellectual and boring*," etc. The spoken or thought words *never* and *always* are indicators. Generalizing can seriously hinder effective problem solving by leaving the true current need undefined. This reflex usually indicates unawareness, fuzzy thinking (q.v.), and perhaps protective Guardian subselves in charge. See *Vague terms*.

Genuineness or authenticity is "*Saying what you mean, and meaning what you say.*" It usually signals that a speaker's true Self is currently in charge of their inner team of subselves. People "walking their talk" (acting on their *integrity*) are experienced as genuine. Some false selves are very adept at faking this. The opposite is being *phony, plastic, glib, political, sly,* or *insincere*. See *Integrity, Intimacy,* and *Trust*.

Glibness is insincere or phony behavior on one or more communication channels that leaves the receiver feeling uneasy, distrustful, guarded, and/or irritated. Glibness implies the sender's dominant personality parts don't trust that being honest (sincere) is locally safe. That can come from Vulnerable subselves' unconscious or conscious fear of internal and/or social criticism and rejection or loss. Chronic glibness usually indicates a fear-based and/or shame-based false self reigns.

Go ballistic: See *Blending, Centered, "Lose it," Meltdown,* and *Rageaholic*.

Go to pieces is an unconsciously accurate metaphor for being dominated by distrustful, chaotic subselves. It's the opposite of *grounded, integrated,* and *centered*. See *Breakdown, Irrational behavior, Lose it, Meltdown,* and *Panic*.

Golden rule (of communications): "Feel the same steady respect for your partner's needs, feelings, opinions, values, and dignity as you wish them to feel for you." See R(espect) message and "=/=".

"Gotcha" is a (false self) communication strategy designed to embarrass your partner, and prove you're *right* or *better* ("1-

up") in a current dispute. The theme is covertly setting the other person up, and then forcing her or him to admit that they're wrong about, or at fault for, something. See *Game, Hidden agenda,* and *Setup.*

Grandiosity (egotism) is having an exaggerated opinion about your personal worth, talents, and/or social value or status. I believe people burdened with this trait are *always* ruled by a shame-based false self trying to compensate for an agonizing semi-conscious feeling of worthlessness, emptiness, and unlovablity. See *Arrogance, Awareness "bubble," Bonding, Ego, Empathy, Entitlement, Exaggeration, False self, Idealism, Love, Narcissism, Reality distortion, Respect,* and *Shame.*

Grieving is the instinctive mental + emotional + spiritual process of adjusting to major life losses (broken attachments), to make room for new bonds. Healthy grief (mourning) hinges partly on communicating emotions (shock, rage, sadness) and thoughts (confusions, questions, impacts) to caring, empathic others. Significantly-wounded kids and adults may have trouble bonding, and little to mourn. Blocked grief can significantly hinder inner-family harmony, social relationships, and effective communication. Healthy grief has its own vocabulary. See *Bond, Blocking, Denial, Flat affect, Loss, Numbing,* and *Venting.*

Grounded: A mind + body feeling that occurs when your Self is unblended and solidly in charge of your personality (inner family of subselves), regardless of outer circumstances. See *Centered, Go to pieces, Lose it, Meltdown,* and *Serenity.*

Guardian (subself): a type of personality part whose ceaseless aim is to control the host person and other people to comfort or protect one or more young Vulnerable subselves. Common Guardians are your *Inner Critic, Perfectionist, Magician (Illusionist), Rebel, Victim, Loner, Procrastinator, Addict, Warrior, Worrier,* and *Catastrophizer.* See *Blending, False self, Multiplicity, Personality, Regulars, Splitting,* and *Vulnerables.*

Guesstimate: an intentional or impulsive conclusion based partly on fact and rational estimation, and partly on intuition, hunch, and "guesswork." See *Assumption, Reality distortion,* and *Logic.*

Guilt: is the normal human emotion rising from the un/conscious belief that we have broken or violated someone's important rule: a *should* (not), *must* (not), *ought* (not), *cannot, dare not* or *have to.* Chronic guilt promotes excessive shame, which cripples communications, health, and relationships. Excessive (toxic) guilt can be reduced to normal. A common Vulnerable subself is our *Guilty Child.* See *Emotion* and *Shame.*

Guilt trip is a covert relationship strategy to control another's behaviors, and raise local comfort (*security*). The "tripper" uses sensed or known behaviors to activate the receiver's *Guilty Child.* That activates Guardian subselves like the *Pleaser, Inner Critic, Rebel, Warrior,* and/or *Amazon.* Guilt trippers are usually badly wounded and shame-based. They're unaware of _ that, _ their true needs, and _ the seven communication skills, and _ don't know how to assert their needs effectively without using guilt. See *"1-up," Controlling, Manipulation, Persecutor, Rigidity, Triangle, Used,* and *Victim.*

H

Half truth is a common false-self strategy to compromise between filling two or more opposed needs "*I should or must be honest,*" and "*I don't feel safe being honest.*" The withheld half may be factual information, an opinion, an intention, and/or an emotion. See *Assuming, Conflict, Double message, Fear, Integrity, Leaking, Lying, Persuasion* and *Truth.*

Hand-grenade term, expression, gesture, or phrase: one that delivers an explosive emotional charge of implied meaning, usually intense scorn or threat. These promote the receiver's false-self activating, defocusing, and losing the wise leadership of her or his Self. Option: evolve a list of words and behaviors that trigger *very* strong feelings in you and/or any partner. See

Association, Defensiveness, Discount, Embedded message, Innuendo, and *Oversensitivity.*

Happiness is the temporary mental + emotional + spiritual state of having _ enough current true needs met, _ enough inner-family peace and contentment, and _ a glass-half-full outlook. See *Serenity* and *Joy.*

Harmonize: to cause all parts of a group or system to work smoothly together toward some goal or purpose. The goal of "parts work" (inner family therapy) is to harmonize all subselves into a cooperative team, led by the resident true Self and a (or *the*) Higher Power. See *Integrity, Joy* and *Serenity.*

Hear, Hearing: can have a range of meanings:

"I receive audible sounds from you,"

"I decode some mental meaning from the sounds I perceive you're making, and I don't register or decode your emotions;"

"I consciously decode the mental-emotional content you meant from these sounds,"

"I consciously decode coherent meaning from the combined sounds, voice dynamics, and non-verbal signals I perceive you making, and I'm aware of my mental-emotional-spiritual-physical response to that meaning."

The last is *full* hearing, which is required for effective win-win assertion and problem solving. These same four hearing levels apply to each of your subselves communicating with the others, including with your Self. When both communication partners are *aware* of whether they're listening *empathically* (with "their hearts"), truly effective communication is possible (vs. guaranteed.) See *Awareness, Decoding, Levels of Meaning,* and *Empathic listening.*

"Heart talk": Thanks to therapists Buddy Portugal and Bob Mark for this term. It implies clear, honest, deeply personal exchanges, including caring confrontations, between two trusting people. The opposite of heart talk is casual, shallow, superficial, or intellectual conversation, whose focus is not on either partner or their relationship. See *Genuineness, Intimacy* and *Trust.*

Hidden agenda: a covert reason for communicating. The agenda may be hidden from the receiver, or both people if the sender isn't aware of who's leading her or his inner family. Hidden agendas imply that the sender fears being open and direct, with themselves, and/or with their partner/s. See *Denial, Double message, Guilt trip, Hinting, Leaking, Lying, Manipulation, Pretending, Pseudo Intimacy, and Suggestion.*

High-E(motion) situations happen when _ one or more of your subselves and/or _ a communication–partner's inner family is very emotional. High-E situations usually mean the subself or person is so flooded with emotions ("above their ears") that _ they can't really hear you now, and _ their awareness bubble (q.v.) excludes you. If your Self is leading, use sincere, respectful (=/=) empathic listening to bring E-levels down, and re-empower hearing. See *Awareness bubble, Dissociate, Go ballistic, Intense, Meltdown, Panic, and Passionate.*

Higher Power: a personally-meaningful non-denominational supreme Being or Force that offers attentive, loving, reliable support; specially in times of great danger, pain, loss, or chaos. Arguably, more human misery and death has been caused by groups insisting *"My Supreme Being is better than yours"* than any other human cause or belief. My experience is that true recovery from psychological wounds both requires and promotes accepting a personally-credible Higher Power. I write this as a converted atheist, raised in a home without spirituality.

High nurturance: a relationship, environment, or group that steadily fills most members' true wholistic (mental + emotional + spiritual + physical) needs. Synonyms: "functional" and "healthy" (relationship/family). See *Dysfunctional, Low nurturance* and *Wholistic health.*

Hinting is a Guardian-subself communication strategy used to imply a need to another person without openly declaring it.

This minimizes the risk of possible criticism, scorn, anger, and rejection (i.e. *pain*). If those occur, the hinter can deny responsibility or intention, covertly blaming their partner for any upset. Hints are double messages, which may promote anxiety and distrust in the receiver. Chronic hinting implies false-self dominance. See *Double message, Embedded message, Half truth, Innuendo, Intuition, Leaking, Levels of Meaning, Lying, Subliminal Cues, Suggest,* and *Trust.*

Hot potato: an exciting or frustrating lose-lose communication sequence in which unaware partners try to avoid owning responsibility for their share of someone's discomfort: *"It's your fault!" "No, it's* yours!" This game usually indicates one or both people are unaware of _ being controlled by a false self; _ their inner and mutual processes; and _ their false selves focusing on avoiding the pain of shame and/or guilt, rather than =/= (win-win) problem solving. Self-motivated recovery from inner wounds, *awareness*, and metatalk can significantly reduce this lose-lose game, over time. Relationships based on this style of problem-solving, including parent-child, usually self-destruct legally and/or emotionally. See *Arguing, Blaming, Dig Down, Fighting, Guilt trip, Mapping, Power struggle, Problem solving,* and *Surface need.*

Hunch: a semi-conscious sensing or "knowing" something that can't be clearly explained. Subselves who can't form thought streams or images may use hunches, dreams, "senses," and intuitions to communicate with other inner-family members, including your Self. See *Assumption, ESP, Guesstimate, Intuition, Sixth sense,* and *Unconscious mind.*

I

"I" message: a respectful (=/=) two or three-part assertion statement with this general format:

"When you . . ." (describe a partner's specific behaviors nonjudgmentally); **"I . . ."** (describe the specific effects of their behavior on you); and optionally state specifically what you need now from your partner, if anything: **". . . and I need you to . . ."**

In doing this, it can help to imagine that you're an impartial news reporter describing something you can tape or video record. Calmly describe the behaviors you hear and see, rather than your partner's (unrecordable) personality traits. For example:

"Gina, when you repeatedly talk to me and choose to do something else with your hands . . ." (Recordable behavior), *". . . I feel discounted, unimportant, and irritated."* (Concrete effect on you.) *"Except for emergencies, I need you to really attend me when we talk."*

Instead of clear, respectful "I" messages, unaware or shame-based communicators often use "You" messages (*"You're never on time."*) These are usually decoded as putdowns, implying blame and a disrespectful *"I'm 1-up"* attitude. "You" messages usually hinder or wreck communications, specially if partners don't shift to cooperative metatalking about them.

Idealism: being locally or chronically controlled by a Guardian subself who feels it's useful to vividly imagine and dwell on perfect or unrealizable outcomes or conditions. Moderate idealism can be an motivational asset. Compulsive idealism is usually a harmful, fear-based reality distortion that breeds frustration, conflict, and self doubt. See *Perfectionism.*

Identity (personal): is the set of personal traits, values, beliefs, body and genetic attributes, dreams, talents, limits, and reflexes that defines you as a unique human being. A false self usually controls people who aren't clear on, or have a distorted sense of, their identity. You're clear on your identity when you can meaningfully answer *"Who am I?"*, and people who know you well would agree. See *Boundary, Dignity, Genuineness, Grandiosity, Integrity,* and *Personality.*

Immaturity can be a factual description of a person early in their emotional growth, or an insulting ("1-up") label implying the receiving adult should act according to the speaker's standards of behavior. Since we mature across our entire lives, most arguments over "maturity" are silly, tragic, or toxic. Do you think that's a mature point of view? See *Discount* and *Name calling.*

Impasse is a communication block occurring when two or more people or subselves have conflicting needs, values, or perceptions, and _ can't find a compromise, or don't want to, _ can't agree to disagree, and _ see no resolution options.

Typically such stymied partners _ are ruled by false selves, and aren't aware of _ their inner families, _ their *true* current needs, and/or _ the seven communication skills. Common reactions to important inner and social impasses are to blame, fight, argue, withdraw, numb out, postpone, explain endlessly, threaten, con, and/or give up. All are lose-lose, compared to patient =/= inner and mutual problem solving.

Impassive describes someone whose face, voice tone, and body offer few clues to what s/he is thinking, feeling, or needing. Local or chronic impassivity signals fear of expressing these, which implies a low-nurturance social environment, and/or a fear-based false self in charge. See *Affect, Animated, Expressionless, Flat affect, Frozen, Labile, Numbing,* and *Subliminal cue.*

Implication, Implied message: is a playful, strategic, or unintended multi-level communication that carries an unspoken meaning. *Generalizing* is a common way of implying: "saying something without saying it;" e.g. *"People who smoke in public are pretty thoughtless"* implies *"You smoke, and I think you are thoughtless, but I'll avoid responsibility for owning that opinion and risking guilt and/or conflict."* See *Association, Decoding, Double message, Embedded message, Hinting, Innuendo, Levels of meaning,* and *Suggesting.*

Indecision: specially if chronic or extreme, is a symptom of false-self dominance and inner conflict between antagonistic or distrustful subselves. Developing fluency with the seven skills to reduce or avoid inner conflicts [Chapter 9] significantly reduces indecision and personal "stress." See *Abstract conflict, Ambivalence, Confusion, Doubt, Impasse, Procrastination, Worry,* and *"Yes, but . . ."*

Independent relationship: one where one or both partners feel *"I don't need you much or at all to get my key personal needs met."* This applies to most acquaintanceships, some sibling relationships, and loveless marriages. See *Bonding, Dependent relationship, Distance, Interdependent relationship, Intimacy, Isolation, Pseudo intimacy,* and *Symmetrical relationship.*

Inference is implying something without saying it. See *Association, Assuming, Double message, Embedded message, Hinting, Implication, Innuendo, Levels of meaning,* and *Suggestion.*

Inner conflict happens when two or more of a person's inner family of subselves have opposing needs, opinions, perceptions, or values. Common manifestations of this are *"I'm torn about," "I blow hot and cold over . . ." "One part of me thinks . . ." "One the one hand, I . . .", "I'm having trouble making up my mind about . . .",* and *"I changed my mind."* The seven communication skills apply to subself conflicts as effectively as with other people. Chapter 9 focuses on resolving these conflicts. See *Ambivalence, Approach-avoid, Blending, Doubt, Inner family, Multiplicity, Indecision, Splitting, Subselves,* and *Uncertainty.*

Inner dialog: an interactive sequence of thoughts and reactions between two or more subselves. The dialog may or may not be "conscious," and involve feelings, memories, fantasies, perceptions, and needs. See Chapter 9 for examples, *Thoughts,* and *Sequence.*

Inner family: the group of semi-autonomous Vulnerable, Guardian, and Regular "parts" or subselves which comprise your personality, and govern your perceptions, thoughts, feelings, needs, and behavior. See *Family system, Multiplicity, Personality, Splitting,* and *Subself.*

Inner voice: a discrete thought-stream, with or without related inner images, memories, associations, emotions, and bodily symptoms. I agree with those who propose that each inner voice comes from an individual personality part or subself, and that parts constantly "talk together" in our conscious mind. Another premise is that adults and kids routinely "hear" (experience) inner voices all the time, often simultaneous and conflicted. Mental/emotional "confusion" and "overwhelm" occur when a person's inner voices and related feelings become chaotic. The several books by psychologists Hal Stone and Sidra Winkleman Stone (e.g. "Embracing Each Other") have much of interest to say about our inner voices. See *Inner conflict.*

Innuendo: a multi-level message (behavior) with a surface meaning, and a covert meaning which is often derogatory or sexual. With sarcastic inflection, *"You're so thoughtful,"* can mean just the opposite. Innuendoes usually imply the sender distrusts that it's safe to be explicit and direct. See *Association, Double message, Embedded message, Hinting, Implication,* and *Levels of meaning.*

Insensitive: means distracted, psychologically wounded, and/or unaware. See *Awareness bubble, Bonding, Empathy, Focus, Narcissism, Oversensitive, and selfish (little "s").*

Instinct: a primal brain-stem ("wired-in") survival impulse to act without thinking, usually triggered by an environmental change that implies danger to you or someone you value. I'm unsure whether *instincts* are caused by activated subselves, as many other reactions are. What do you think?

Insult: See *"1-down," Discount, and R-message.*

Integrity: To "integrate" is to "make all the pieces fit together stably," or "add a new piece to an existing set." *Disintegrate"* means to "come apart." Your *integrity* is _ having all your subselves accept each other as dignified and valuable, vs. rejecting, exiling, repressing, disowning, or paralyzing some; and _ having all subselves united in manifesting a common life purpose, under the trusted leadership of your Self and Higher

Power. See *Boundaries, Dignity, Identity, Personality, Pride, Recovery,* and *Wholistic health.*

Intellectual, intellectualize: may mean a person or communication exchange is focused largely on information ("data"), opinions, and ideas, not current feelings, conflicts, or personal needs. Partners' needs may clash on how much intellectual discussion is OK, vs. venting, or emotionally-rich heart talk. Sometimes, excessive intellectualism (in someone's opinion) signals moderate blending with an *Anesthetist (Guardian)—Analyzer—Observer* trio running the inner family much of the time. See *Affect, Analysis paralysis, Expressionless, Frozen, Heart talk, Intimacy, Labile, Numb, Superficial, Trust,* and *Vulnerability.*

Intense: behavior or situations where one or more people feel and express extreme emotion, verbally and/or non-verbally. Fear-based (fragmented) people are often paralyzed or easily agitated (blended) by a partner showing *intense* anger (rage), fear (terror), scorn, shame, or lust. See *Affect, Animated, Blocking, Expressionless, E(motion-level), Fear, High-E, Idealism, Numbing,* and *Passionate.*

Interdependent relationship: a shared, conscious core attitude between voluntary partners: "*I can live well enough without you, and I choose to live with you.*" Alternative attitudes are *dependent* ("*I can't live without you*") and *independent* (low emotional bond) relationships. To choose and sustain a stable, interdependent relationship, both partners' usually need their true Selves to lead their inner family of subselves. The ~50% U.S. first-divorce rate testifies how unusual this is. See *Bonding, Boundaries, Dependent relationship, Divorce, Heart talk, Identity, Independent relationship, Integrity, Intimacy, Love, Neediness, Symmetrical relationship, Trust,* and *Vulnerability.*

Interject: a listener periodically saying respectful verbal summaries of a speaker's verbal and non-verbal behaviors. Empathic-listening *interjections* aim to affirm the listener's understanding of the speaker, and not distract them from their focus. The alternatives are silence, or interruptions that defocus the speaker. See *Empathy, Hearing, Metatalk, Process,* and *Sequence.*

Interrogating: differs from respectful questioning via an implied or overt "I-up" attitude: *"I'm going to aggressively find out something about you may not want to reveal, (and I may use it to shame or hurt you)."* Interrogating is more about power and judgment than about seeking information and clarity. It usually implies Guardian subselves are in control, specially if the interrogator denies their intentions or behavior, and/or blames the receiver (*"I have to, because you're too weak to tell me the truth."*) See *Aggression, Lying, Persecutor, Power struggle, R-message, Relationship triangle, Trust,* and *Victim.*

Interrupt: acting in a way that breaks a communicator's thought focus. Impacts of interruptions range from trivial to highly insulting, specially if they're a chronic response. Depending on the context, interruptions can imply *"I value my opinion and/or need to speak more highly than yours. I'm 1-up."* Some low-awareness speakers invite interruptions because they monolog endlessly without caring what their partner feels or needs. See *Awareness bubble, Boredom, Boundaries, Communication conflict, Context, Discount, Empathy, Flooding, Interjection, Respect, R-message,* and *Venting.*

Intimacy: voluntary personal emotional, physical, and spiritual disclosure to another person in the face of possible misunderstanding, criticism, and rejection. Or, *"Intimacy is the relationship state that occurs when one or both partners let the other inside their most private boundaries."* Significant inner wounds in one or both partners makes sustained intimacy difficult or impossible, until true recovery. See *Approach-avoid, Bond, Empathy, Heart talk, Intellectualizing, Love, Pseudo intimacy, Superficial, Trust,* and *Vulnerability.*

Intuition: a kind of inner communication that has no

conscious factual basis. See *ESP, Feeling, Hunch, "Knowing,"* and *Sixth sense.*

Irrational (behavior) is someone's judgment about their or another's decisions or actions. It says, *"That behavior isn't appropriate or logical in this context,"* according to the judge's set of values and definitions. Depending on voice tone and expression, *"You're irrational"* can imply major criticism (*"I know better than you: you're 1-down!"*). A major source of conflict and stress in and between psychologically-wounded people occurs because their governing subselves have their own short-term, survival-oriented logic (rationale), which doesn't match accepted norms of "rational" behavior.

Issue (problem): See *Conflict.*

J, K, L

Jealousy is a universal human mental/emotional state of envying the possessions, status, freedoms, achievements, abilities, and/or features of another person, with minor to major resentments. I believe significant jealousy is *always* a symptom of personal insecurity, shame, reality distortion, and unrecognized false-self dominance. Jealousy is often caused or amplified by a Guardian personality subself who has intense needs for *fairness* and *entitlement* (*"I* deserve _____*!"*). Where present, such a subself is usually fiercely protecting an agonized *Shamed Child.* See *Co-dependence, Compulsion, Entitlement, Grandiosity, Narcissism, Neediness,* and *selfish.*

Joking and kidding is a communication behavior that can be decoded as _ playful, light, friendly, and respectful (=/=); _ sarcastic, demeaning, and hurtful (R-message: *"I'm 1-up!"*); or _ both at once: a false-self double message. When confronted, some shame-based people say reflexively, *"Can't you take a joke? (What's wrong with you!)"* to avoid their shame and guilt.

Joy is a subjectively defined experience of peak mental + emotional + spiritual + physical pleasure, elation, contentment, hope, satisfaction, and fulfillment: "extreme temporary happiness." Some psychologically wounded people rarely or never experience this blissful state until well along in personal recovery. They may confuse other (artificially-induced) states with joy, in their longing for it. See *Centered, Happiness, Harmonize, Love,* and *Serenity.*

Judgmental: having a right/wrong, good/bad opinion about someone or something. Paradoxically, many kids are taught that being *judgmental* of other people is *wrong* or *bad.* Forming such opinions about others and ourselves is as reflexive as breathing. Any good/bad impact comes from the basis for the judgment (e.g. facts vs. assumptions or hearsay), how such opinions are expressed, to whom, and for what purposes. Respectful (=/=), honest confrontations based on right/wrong judgments can lead to constructive change and enhanced relationships, *if* the receiver is open to well-meant feedback, and is led by their Self. See *Abstract conflict, Assertion, Discount, Empathy, Guilt, "I" message, Labeling, Name calling,* and *Praise.*

Justifying can be useful clarification of behavior, or part of an ineffective communication sequence that leaves both partners feeling unheard: *"You (did something wrong or bad.)" "Well here's why I did it (justification)." "That (doesn't excuse your behavior)." "Yes, but . . ."* Without awareness, this can escalate into a power struggle: *"I'm right." "No you're not!"* Empathic listening [6] and problem solving [8] are more effective responses. See *Defensiveness, Explaining, Power struggle, Whining,* and *"Yes, but . . ."*

Kidding: See *Joking.*

Knowing is an instinctual feeling or sense that something is true, without factual evidence. Young and spiritual personality parts (subselves) probably cause this universal "sixth sense" experience. It may increase as *awareness* skill does. See *Awareness, Decoding, ESP, Hunch, Intuition, Meaning, Sixth sense, Subliminal cues,* and *Unconscious mind.*

Labeling is the reflex to assign evaluative (good / bad, right / wrong, sane / crazy) adjectives and names (labels) to someone's choices, thinking, and/or behaviors. If used constructively in mutually-respectful metatalk, labels may help. I can't think of another instance where they do, including most "mental health" diagnostic labels like "Schizo-affective disorder." Some labels, like *schizophrenic* and *abuser,* can be "hand grenade" terms. See *Association, Black/white thinking, Embedded message, Innuendo, Levels of Meaning,* and *Name-calling.*

Labile means emotionally reactive and changeable; passionate, expressive, or "unstable." The opposite of labile is phlegmatic, frozen, impassive, and inscrutable. *"Marge and Harry are perfect opposites: she's labile, and he's a stump."*

"Leaking" is giving small verbal and non-verbal cues that indicate our true (hidden) feelings, thoughts, and needs. This universal human reflex causes the saying *"Words may lie, but bodies don't."* It demonstrates that subselves control glands, neurons, and muscle cells despite our conscious efforts to prevent that. As a trained hypnotist, I've seen a wide range of people respond to subliminal cues without their conscious awareness. Leaking often causes relationship "unease" or something "not feeling right." See *Hunch, Embedded message, Intuition, Knowing, Sixth sense,* and *Unconscious mind.*

Lecturing can be a communication block, when an unaware partner chooses to instruct or explain something at length without evaluating what their partner needs. Without invitation, empathy, and awareness, lecturers risk _ being perceived as "1-up," (so their partner feels judged as stupid and inept); _ exceeding their partner's attention span, and _ unconsciously promoting resentment, frustration, and defiance or opposition. See *Awareness "bubble," Explaining, Monologing, Rambling, Preaching,* and *Venting.*

Levels of Meaning: In complex situations, it may help to distinguish that a word, phrase, or behavior can have several meanings at once. For example, a confrontational "intervention" with a chemical addict in lethal denial can be seen by the receiver as *brutal, insulting, aggression, betrayal,* and *shameful;*

and by others as *caring, courageous, kind, assertion, and morally right.* Different subselves can interpret different meanings from a partner's behavior at the same time; as in *"Her avoiding eye contact means she's hiding something,"* vs. *"She's concentrating on trying to express what she feels."* Some meanings are conscious, and others unconscious. This is why *awareness* is so critical in key relationships and conflicts. See *Association, Assumption, Context, Double message, Embedded message, Framing, Hint, Innuendo, Meaning, Metaphor, Pun,* and *Reframing.*

"Light" can mean a pleasant mood or "mind set," and/or mental clarity and understanding, as in "I see the light." The alternative is feeling "heavy": oppressed, gloomy, and depressed. Feeling *light* is one symptom of a true Self leading other subselves. See *Happiness, Peace, and Serenity.*

Listen, listening: See *Empathic listening* and *Hearing.*

"Lose it" is slang for chaotic, distrustful subselves blending with (controlling) the Self. The lost "it" is the Self's calm, wise wide-angle, long-range rational judgment, and inner-family harmony. See *Blending, Centered, Confusion, Defocus, Doubt, Go to pieces, Irrational behavior, Melt down, Mind racing, Panic,* and *Splitting.*

Lose-lose is a communication sequence or pattern in which no subselves or partners get their true needs met well enough. See *Outcome* and *Win-win.*

Loss is a broken emotional/spiritual bond with a cherished living thing, vision (dream), idea, ability, freedom, or belief. Venting about our losses is vital for effective three-level grieving, which is a key component of intimate relationships. People dominated by false selves often have trouble bonding, grieving well, and supporting other grievers. Many unaware people associate loss and grieving only with the death of a loved one.

Love is the intense mix of emotions and responses that well-bonded people and other living things spontaneously feel for each other. Effective communication of these attitudes and feelings is an innate ability that springs freely from the heart and soul, vs. any manual or textbook. *Self*-love is one requirement for effective assertion [7] and interdependent relationships [10]. Reducing shame-based false-self dominance is essential for self-love and unfettered love for others. When significantly wounded people say *"I love you,"* they may unconsciously mean *"I desire / fear / need / feel obligated to / feel responsible for / pity / you."* See *Bond, Empathy, Interdependent relationship, Intimacy, Loss, Pretend, Pseudo intimacy, Respect, Splitting,* and *Trust.*

Low nurturance: Here, nurturance means *effectively* filling the true spiritual, bodily, emotional, and mental needs of yourself or another person. Childhoods, families, relationships, communication sequences, organizations, nations, and cultures can be judged as being low to high nurturance, over time. My experience is that children in significantly low-nurturance families adapt by developing a protective false self and up to five toxic psychological wounds. As adults, such people _ unconsciously pick each other as friends, co-workers, and lovers; _ pick, create, or endure low-nurturance work and social settings; _ have chronic difficulty thinking and communicating effectively, and _ *unintentionally* pass on inner wounds to dependent kids.

I prefer *low nurturance* to *dysfunctional* because it's less apt to evoke blame, shame, and guilt. Effective communications promote high-nurturance ("healthy") relationships and inner families. See *Alienation, Dignity, Emptiness, Happiness, Integrity, Joy, Love, Neediness, Serenity, and Wholistic Health.*

Lying is un/consciously withholding or distorting information. It means the "liar" _ doesn't trust their partner to receive the truth without responding painfully (e.g. criticizing, shaming, or distancing); and/or the "liar" _ can't tolerate their inner reaction to facing and disclosing the local truth to themselves or others: usually great fear, shame, and guilt. Communication outcomes and relationships improve by focusing on making it safe to tell the truth, rather than making moral judgments about the *badness* and *wrongness* of (protective) lying. See *Avoidance, Defensiveness, Denial, Half truth, Reality distortion, Trust, Truth,* and *Vulnerability.*

M

Male brain: See *Gender factors*

Manic means extreme uncontrolled excitement or behavior. Chronic manic behavior implies either a neuro-chemical imbalance, and/or serious psychological wounding. The latter may promote or cause the former. If true, medicating to reduce manic behavior may *block* a true remedy like parts work (inner-family harmonizing). The opposite of manic is *depressive* or *apathetic* moods and behavior. People cycling between with both behaviors are clinically labeled "bi-polar." I believe "dominated by a false self" is more accurate and less stigmatizing (shaming). See *Affect, Expressionless, Flat, High-E, Serenity,* and *Type "A" behavior.*

Manipulate: the pejorative meaning is getting someone to fill your need, without *really* caring equally about *their* needs, values, and feelings. Wounded people can have some personality parts that don't want to "use" or manipulate others "selfishly," and other parts that do. The usual result is double messages (behavior), guilt, and denial. Subtle to blatant manipulative behavior always implies "*I'm 1 up,*" and "*I've lost my true Self.*" See *Controlling, Games, Guilt trip, Hidden agenda, Lying, Pretending,* and *Persuasion.*

Mapping (here) is a communication analysis scheme (p. 402) based on the ideas that all communication exchanges are a multi-level sequence of identifiable actions > reactions > reactions > . . . Each step in a mapping sequence estimates for a given partner: You *thought,* you *felt,* you *needed,* you *did,* and you were *led by your Self or not.* Mapping effectiveness depends on *awareness* and true Selves being in charge. See *Sequence* and *Pattern.*

Marriage has many concurrent meanings: _ a legal ceremony socially sanctioning the emotional, financial, parental, and sexual union of two partners; _ a religious celebration and sanction of a holy union deemed insoluble by many believers; _ a set of new roles (responsibilities) and related rules for each partner and any relatives (*"Now I'm a husband and spouse."*); _ a mutual personal commitment to relationship priority and exclusivity; _ a model of a committed primary adult relationship for dependent kids; _ a legal contract of rights and responsibilities, specially relating to child conception and rearing, between two consenting adult partners; _ a component of each mate's personal identity; _ a normal stage of the human individual and family developmental cycle; _ a basic unit ("institution") of societal stability; and _ a focus of economic trade in most cultures. See *Co-parenting, Divorce, Needs,* and *Relationship.*

Meaning is the mentally computed or "sensed" relationship of ideas, events, things, or perceived human behaviors to each other, and/or to a person's current needs. *Thinking* is the constant decoding of the *meaning* of environmental events by conscious "inner voices" and the unconscious mind. An infant *senses* meaning from a parent's facial expression and voice tone, though the baby has no words (vocabulary) to *think.* The instinctive human drive to "understand" ultimately relates to filling one or more true current needs. Different subselves can compute different meanings from a given event or perceived behavior, causing inner and social conflicts. See *Assumption, Confusion, Context, Double message, Embedded message, Explaining, Hint, Innuendo, Levels of Meaning, Message, Reframing, Sequence, Subliminal cues,* and *Pun.*

Mediate: See Arbitrate, Compromise, Demand, Negotiate, Problem solve, and Request.

Meltdown (behavioral) is Nuclear-age slang for major inner-family chaos. Synonyms: *lose it, come unglued, have a spaz-attack, break down, go to pieces, throw a fit, go ballistic, freak out, bonkers, go nuts,* etc. See Centered and Dissociate.

Mental illness is an outmoded catchall term for some behaviors and traits causing personal and social anxiety, pain, and conflict. Like *alcoholism*, the term is based on the "disease model" of human behavior. I believe this model mistakenly equates many mental, emotional, spiritual, and physical conditions to non-organic "sickness" rather than to psychological fragmenting from ancestral childhood nurturance-deprivation trauma. See *Trauma, Nurture,* and *Wholistic health.*

Message is the conscious and unconscious *meanings* kids and adults decode from another person's perceived behaviors. Personality subselves decode incoming messages concurrently on verbal, paraverbal, and non-verbal channels. Different subselves may decode the same perceived behavior differently (*"She's lying!" "No she's not!"*). This causes confusion, unease, and doubt: inner-family and social conflict.

Meta-comment is a descriptive, non-judgmental (respectful) observation about *how* someone is thinking and communicating (your *process*), vs. what you're communicating about (your *content*). See *Metatalk.*

Metaphor is a word picture that stands for something else, like *"He was as jumpy as a long-tailed cat in a room full of rocking chairs"* (Tennessee Ernie Ford). Using metaphors well is a learnable communication skill that can help make communication more interesting; convey abstract, emotional, or complex concepts more clearly; or present a sensitive idea in a different mood. See *Association, Framing, and Levels of meaning.*

Metatalk is one of seven learnable mental/verbal communication skills. It uses *awareness* to (1) focus nonjudgmentally on the communication processes, sequences, and patterns _ *within* you or a partner, and _ *between* you two; and (2) cooperatively discuss aspects of those. Metatalk requires a special vocabulary about communication and relationship variables (p. 384 and this glossary). This skill aims to identify communication conflicts, to help resolve them via the other six skills. See *Mapping, Need, Outcome, Pattern, Payoff, Process, and Sequence.*

Mind is the mysterious human component that can *remember, imagine, sense,* and *reason* (think); i.e. that can *process* sensory signals to produce coherent "meaning." Philosophic, medical, psychological, and metaphysical debates continue about what, exactly, constitutes our mind, where it's located in our body, and how it relates to our three brains and our *spirit* and/or *soul.* Many people now believe we have unconscious, semi-conscious, and conscious minds, which each process information differently and have limited interconnection. Each mind can cause physiological reactions. See *Splitting, Meaning, Multiplicity, Psychosomatic,* and *Thinking.*

Mind racing or churning is the local or chronic experience of having ceaseless jumbled semi-conscious and conscious thought streams, mental mages, memories, and feelings without a clear theme or focus. This is usually caused by several or many agitated subselves expressing themselves at once, with the true Self unable to bring them all to order and focus on one thing at a time. Excessive churning leads to chaotic or goalless behavior, causing anxiety and social judgments. Doing effective parts work can significantly reduce churning, over time. See *Confusion, Defocus, Doubt, Harmonize, Indecision, Inner conflict,* and *Meltdown.*

Mind reading: See *Assumption.*

Minimizing: See *Discounting, Exaggerating,* and *Reality distortion.*

Mirroring: See *Empathic listening.*

Mixed message: See *Double message.*

Monologing is talking on and on, usually with little or no awareness of the listener's reactions or needs. False selves choose this strategy to avoid unpleasant silences, feelings or thoughts; and/or unsafe interaction with the listener.

Monologing is a reliable sign of local or chronic false-self dominance. See *Awareness bubble, Defocusing, Explaining, Flooding, Justifying, Preaching, Rambling, Self-centered,* and *Venting.*

Moralizing is a communication in which one partner implies or expresses moral (right/wrong, good/bad) judgments about themselves, and/or some aspect of another person. However well meant, moralizing usually carries an implied "I'm 1-up" R-message. This may activate the receiver's *Guilty* or *Shamed* young (Vulnerable) subselves, and their vigilant Guardians. Inappropriate or excessive moralizing (preaching) signals a false self is in control. It often causes blanking out, withdrawal, boredom, defensiveness, anxiety, irritation, and/or disinterest in the receiver. See *Discount, Explaining, Lecturing, Monologing, Preaching,* and *Venting.*

Multiple Personality Disorder (MPD) was designated as a legitimate "mental illness" in the 1980s by the American Psychiatric Association It is characterized by behaving as though there were several different unrelated people ("alters") inhabiting the same body. MPD, now called "Dissociative Identity Disorder," is the extreme version of normal personality splitting [1]. Its existence seems to validate the innate human neural capacity to "split," or "fragment" in varying degrees. People diagnosed with DID usually report major childhood trauma. See *Dissociate, Multiplicity, Splitting,* and *Subself.*

Multiplicity is the undeniable ability of normal human brains and neural networks to develop semi-independent, interactive regions that process sensory information concurrently. This has been visually observed in the last generation via new Positron Emission Tomography (PET) scanning technology of living brains. These observations suggest the reality of (universal?) "personality splitting" into *parts,* or *subselves,* which may explain many "illogical" and "irrational" behaviors and non-organic "mental illnesses." The multiplicity concept invites applying (family) systems theory to the dynamics of our *inner* families of subselves, toward reducing personal and interpersonal conflicts and distress. See *Blending, False self, Identity, "I", Inner family, Mind, Parts work, Personality, Self, self, Split personality,* and *Splitting.*

N

Name-calling is thinking or speaking judgmental labels to or about you or another person. The names can be endearing or demeaning; e.g. "You are (your behavior is) *stupid, asinine, ridiculous, wimpy, lazy, dumb.* . . . Or "You are a *jerk, moron, imbecile, pervert . . ."* Whether situational or chronic, the name-caller _ is unaware or uncaring about the effects of these loaded terms on the receiver; _ has a "1-up" (superior) attitude; _ is uninterested in, or ignorant of, effective communication skills; and _ is probably controlled by a spiteful or resentful inner child (Vulnerable) and/or their Guardian subself, like their *Judge* or *Bigot.* See "=/=", *Awareness bubble, Dignity, Discount, Hand grenade terms, Empathy, Labeling,* and *Respect.*

Narcissism is a misleading, shaming mental-health and pop psychology label for a person controlled by a shame-based, fear-based false self. The term comes from the myth of Narcissus, who was cursed by falling in love with his own reflection in a pool. I believe the symptoms of "narcissism"— excessive self-absorption, grandiosity, and little (real) selfless concern for others—are caused by childhood shaming and fragmenting. This condition can be reduced through skilled parts work and personal recovery. See *Awareness bubble, Bonding, Ego, Empathy, Entitlement, False self, Insensitivity, Love, Monologing, Name calling, Pretending, selfish, Self-centered, Self-ish,* and *Splitting.*

Need is a spiritual, physical (cellular/chemical), mental, or emotional discomfort, or tension. Human needs are _ concurrent, _ conscious and unconscious, _ normal and universal, _ neither god or bad, _ dynamic and ceaseless, and _ interactive: some needs cause, amplify, or reduce others. Daily satisfaction and human relationships are shaped by each person trying to fill their perceived current mix of surface needs, and the shadowy underlying *true* needs, *well enough*. We *communicate* ceaselessly to fill current true needs even when attending ("helping") other people.

"Needy" can be a guilt-inducing or shaming judgment of yourself or another, as in *"You are too (weak and) needy."* That judgment often follows growing up in a family where kids' needs and emotions were minimized, trivialized, or ignored; and self-sufficiency, repression, and stoicism were prized. True recovery from psychological wounds fosters clear awareness of, and co-equally honoring the value of, felt emotional, spiritual, and physical needs in yourself and others.

Neglect is paying little attention to key needs in yourself or another person. *Parental* neglect is not providing adequately for the spiritual, emotional, physical, and/or mental needs (wholistic health) of a dependent child. Such neglect is the main source of low-family nurturance, which promotes significant childhood personality splitting. Child neglect passes down the generations, and promotes *self* neglect, based on core shame. It is fueled by caregiver wounding (false self dominance), unawareness, denials, self-rejection. This unconscious toxic bequest can be stopped by *awareness*, and true (vs. pseudo) personal recovery from psychological wounds. See *Abuse, Bonding, Love, Needs, Nurturing, and Toxic.*

Negotiation is a type of conflict-resolution process that two or more subselves or people may choose. Popular alternatives are collapsing, manipulating, threatening, explaining, whining, avoiding, deferring, demanding, pleading, arguing, and submitting. In the best case, negotiating is a good-will attempt between people of equal dignity and respect (=/=) to find a solution that fills their respective true need well enough for now. *Mediation* and *arbitration* use an objective third person to focus, guide, and moderate the negotiation process. See *Arguing, Conflict, impasse,* and *Problem solving.*

Neurolinguistic programming (NLP) is a sophisticated communication concept proposing that each person has an unconsciously preferred sensory way of communicating: visual (imagery), audible, tactile (physical sensations), or kinesthetic (movement). The skill of *awareness* promotes assessing a partner's preference from their speech patterns, and intentionally choosing words to match the preference can improve communication effectiveness. NLP is specially useful for professional communicators like therapists, clergy, teachers, psychologists, and salespeople.

Non-verbal communication is any observed or sensed physical behavior (facial expression, eye contact, body language, hand gestures . . .) that changes something in a relationship partner. No physical response ("her face was frozen"), and/or local or continued silence, are powerful non-verbal behaviors that can *imply* meanings to shamed, guilty, needy, and/or anxious subselves. Some researchers suggest perceived non-verbal behavior accounts for most of the meaning we decode from other people's perceived actions. See *Association, Blocking, Channels, Expression, Eye contact, Flat affect, Intuition, Meaning, Mind reading, Paraverbal, Sensing, Subliminal cues,* and *Verbal.*

Numbing (behavioral) is the unconscious reflex of muting or blocking awareness of bodily and emotional feelings to protect from overwhelm or agony. Some seriously-wounded adults and kids develop a Guardian subself (*"Anesthetist"*) whose special protective talent is situationally or chronically blocking awareness of *feelings.* This results in expressionless behavior and flat (emotionless) speech and appearance. These often evoke anxiety in partners, and may inhibit effective communication.

Nurturance refers to the degree that any child or adult got, or is getting, all their true wholistic needs met. High-nurturance ("functional") homes and childhoods consistently fill most or all of a young person's emotional, spiritual, and physical (developmental) needs *and* their caregivers' true needs. *Toxic* (low-nurturance) childhoods, homes, relationships, and communication inhibit one or more people from filling their true needs. See *Abuse, Bond, Love, Needy, Neglect, Surface needs,* and *Wholistic health* and [..01/health.htm].

O-P

Obsess: having uncontrollable, repetitive thought-and-emotion sequences that may range from personally and socially harmless to harmful, like co-dependence and excessive control. I believe obsessions usually indicate denied false-self dominance (a disabled Self). See *Addiction, Blending, Compulsion, Pattern,* and *Mind racing.*

Outcome (communication): each participant in an inner-family and/or interpersonal communication exchange can have two key conclusions at the end of any communication exchange:

I got my main true (vs. surface) needs met well enough, or I didn't; and . . .

In this exchange, I feel good enough about _ myself, _ my partner/s, and _ our shared communication process, or I don't. Most people are hazy on the outcome of their non-crisis exchanges, unless they're "very bad" or "really good."

Intentionally growing your communication *awareness,* and selectively using the diagnostic technique of *mapping* (p. 400), can illuminate internal, local, and habitual communication outcomes. See p. 105, *Awareness "bubble," Dig down, Lose-lose, Needs, Pattern, Payoff, Sequence, Surface needs,* and *Win-win.*

"Oversensitive" is an opinion that a person reacts too quickly or too intensely to some event or behavior. Depending on voice tone and context, *"You're just oversensitive"* can feel like a "1-down" criticism. *Inner Critics* can label us *oversensitive* as well as other people. The opposite condition is *numbness.*

The judgment is really about the receiver's discomfort and unawareness. See *Animated, Awareness bubble, Blocking, Empathy, Expressionless, Fear-based, Flat affect, Labile, Numb,* and *Style.*

Overtalking can mean _ several people or subselves talking at once and no one really listening; or _ *flooding* and *monologing:* speaking at length without awareness of the listener's needs. Both indicate major false-self dominance. See *"1-up," Arguing, Awareness bubble, Communication conflict, Empathy, Hearing, Interrupt, Metatalk, Mind racing, Preaching,* and *Self-centered.*

Overwhelm is major mental/emotional discomfort from local inner-family chaos, where no personality parts are in consistent control, and emotions and feelings "run riot." Subconscious fear of overwhelm _ comes from childhood experience of it, and _ can promote avoidance of conflict, healthy risks, and real intimacy. People who are dubbed "controlling" are probably dominated by subselves who are terrified of feeling overwhelmed (again). "Reasoning" (using *logic*) with such people will rarely cause second-order change. See *Blending, Blocking, Centered, Confusion, Dissociate, False self, Focus, Go to pieces, Inner family, Meltdown, Multiplicity, Recovery, Self, Serenity,* and *Splitting.*

Oxymoron describes a term or phrase with two or more opposed meanings, like "a mournful reveler," or "healthy abuse." See *Association, Confusion, Double message, Levels of meaning,* and *Pun.*

Pace (communication): Do you know someone who usually thinks and speaks much faster or slower than you do? What emotions do you feel in a lengthy conversation with them? Impatience, frustration, and guilt (at feeling judgmental and frustrated) are common, which may distract from effective hearing. Awareness and respectful metatalk can help identify and mediate *pace*-conflicts. See *"I" message* and *Style.*

Panic is extreme fear, symptomized by rapid heartbeat,

shallow breathing, mental confusion or narrow focus, time distortion (perhaps), and impulsive (instinctive) actions. True panic usually signals a false self is in local control. "Controlled panic" is an oxymoron. See *Break down, Catastrophize, Crisis, Fear, Go to pieces, Overwhelm, Terror,* and *Trauma.*

Paraverbal communication is one of three communication "channels:" *how* words and sounds are said, and what that means to both sender and receiver. One subself may locally determine what words you think and speak, and other subselves may control the nerves and muscles that determine *how* you speak. See *Association, Channels, Decoding, Double message, Levels of Meaning, Meaning, Message, Non-verbal (channel), R-message, Verbal (channel),* and *Voice dynamics.*

Partner (communication) is any child or adult you have a temporary or ongoing relationship with. By definition, true partners share equal dignity, common goals, and mutual respect, though their values, priorities, opinions, knowledge, and perceptions may differ. A symptom of true partnership is each person feeling genuinely respected by the other, in calm and conflictual times. Ideally, mates feel like true partners. Option: see people you're conflicted with as communication partners with equal dignity and value, vs. opponents or "the enemy." See *"=/=", Arguing, Boundaries, Fighting, Dignity, Identity, Integrity,* and *Relationship.*

Parts work (*inner* family therapy) is the intentional process of meeting the subselves (*parts*) that comprise your personality, and harmonizing them over time under the wise leadership of your true Self and Higher Power. See *Change, False self, Integrity, Multiplicity, Personality, Pseudo recovery, Recovery, Self, self, Serenity, Subself, Splitting, Wholistic health,* and "Who's *Really* Running Your Life?" [www.xlibris.com]

Passionate can describe sexual desire; zeal about a cherished belief, goal, or activity; or a style of expressing intense feelings on all three communication channels. Clarifying the intended meaning of this word may reduce situational confusion and misunderstandings. Excessive passion can scare or worry some Vulnerable subselves, and cause their protective Guardian parts to "shut down" (emotionally numb out) their host person. Some shame-based passionate people try to minimize emotional expression. They usually "leak," causing unease and distrust. See *Animated, Affect, E-level, Emotion, Expression, Intensity,* and *Labile.*

Pattern (communication) is a repeated sequence of inner and/or interpersonal communication sequences, over time (*"Every time I mention sex, you break off eye contact and start to fidget."*) *Awareness* and *metatalk* skills and the technique of *mapping* (p. 400) can reveal such patterns. Doing this may help illuminate and resolve chronic *internal* and/or interpersonal communication conflicts. See *Compulsion, Lose-lose, Needs, Outcome, Payoff,* and *Process.*

Payoff means (here) the degree to which current or chronic behaviors fill true needs or not. Short-term "positive" payoffs (e.g. gaining local comfort from an addiction) may yield long-term toxic payoffs (guilt, shame, regret, divorce, and premature death.) Communication payoffs are judged by which of each partner's set of two to six needs (p. 46) got met well enough, at the end of an exchange. See *Communication, Enabling, Focus, Meaning, Needs, Outcome, Pattern, Response, Sequence,* and *Transaction.*

Peace implicitly means "current freedom from unmet inner and social needs (discomforts)." I propose that two core requisites for sustained personal peace are _ having your Self consistently leading your inner family, and _ an aware relationship with a or *the* benign (vs. toxic) Higher Power. Added requisites for *group* peace are all members _ knowing and using these seven skills, and _ helping each other getting enough of the factors at [..01/health.htm].

People-pleasing is a compulsion to "be nice," "help other people," "be tolerant and understanding," and avoid disagreement or conflict. When chronic and done at the expense of balanced self-nurturance, this trait strongly indicates false-self dominance, low self esteem, and unreasonable fear of inner or outer criticism, rejection, and social isolation. The primal core fear is of being alone and dying. See *Abandonment, Avoidance, Co-dependence, Denial, Enabling, Fear-based, Nurturance, Shame, Submission, Victim, and Wholistic health.*

Perfectionism is a common trait of fear and shame-based kids and adults in denial. Adults who were chronically criticized and scorned as young kids often have evolved Guardian subselves who criticize them mercilessly just like their original caregivers. Three such common well-meaning subselves that work at this zealously together are the *Perfectionist, Driver/ Achiever, and Inner Critic.* Often a *Catastrophizer* adds to their impact. Until true recovery, people controlled by such subselves take superior achievement as "normal," so they take little pride in outstanding performance. See *Compromise, False self, Idealism, Reality distortion, Splitting,* and *Subself.*

Persecutor is one of three roles in a PVR relationship triangle. The adult or child in this role causes significant discomfort in the person playing the *Victim* role. The *Persecutor* usually does that by aggressive ("1-up") verbal and nonverbal behaviors that are labeled as blaming, criticizing, ridiculing, ignoring, abusing, insensitive, neglecting, discounting, humiliating, frustrating, demeaning, and so on. The Victim's discomfort activates the person playing the *Rescuer* role. By definition, people in such triangles are wounded, and aren't using effective problem-solving skills. Their true needs usually go unmet. See *Abuse, Aggression, Conflict, Enabling, R-message, Submission, Role conflict, and Triangling.*

Perseverate: to compulsively repeat words, phrases, gestures, expressions, or ideas, despite the listener understanding them the first time. I believe perseveration is a clear symptom of false-self dominance, perhaps with neuro-chemical factors. Effective Self-motivated parts-work may reduce or stop this, and perhaps reduce stuttering, over time. See *Obsess* and *Compulsion.*

Personality is the unique mosaic of values, priorities, talents, traits, thought patterns, reflexes, limits, and quirks that distinguish each adult and child from all others. In this book, *personality* is defined as the inner family of semi-independent subselves (brain regions) that cause these unique characteristics. See *Blending, Boundaries, False self, Identity, Inner family, Integrity, Multiplicity, Parts work, Self, self, Splitting, and Subself.*

Personality "part": See *Blending, False self, Inner family, Inner voices, Multiplicity, Parts work, Splitting,* and *Subself.*

Persuasion is overt or covert behavior to get another person to think, believe, or act the way we want them to. Persuasion can range from genuinely altruistic (*"It's for your own good!"*) to covertly and "selfishly" filling our own needs with little or no genuine concern for our partner. See *Assertion, Controlling, Demand, Hidden agenda, Hinting, Lying, Manipulate, Needs, Request, R(espect) message, Suggest, and Used.*

Pleading is a dignified or desperate "1-down" problem-resolution strategy used by people or subselves who see no options like =/= assertion and problem solving to fill their current needs. Pleading promotes the ruling subselves in a partner assuming a "1-up" relationship position. That fosters conflictual (Persecutor-Victim-Rescuer) relationship triangles and ineffective communication. See *Assertion, Dependent relationship, Dignity, Enabling, Guilt, trip, Integrity, Manipulation, Negotiation, R-message, Request, Submission* and *Whining.*

Power struggle is a communication sequence between two or more opposed subselves, or psychologically wounded people. The aim is not mutual problem solving, but seeking control or dominance of a dispute, conversation, situation, or relationship. Often, ongoing power struggles are fueled by false-self control, denied shame and fear, compulsions to be *right* or *best*, and ineffective communication skills. They inevitably erode relationships and promote conflicts. See *Argue, Conflict, Controlling, Fight, Guilt trip, Hot Potato, Lose-lose,* and *Manipulation.*

Praise is a judgmental attitude and declaration of approval and respect for someone. Adults and kids ruled by shame-based false selves often have trouble giving or receiving genuine praise. That lowers the quality of their self-respect and their relationships. One of three ways to use *assertion* skill [7] is to give another person or subself "dodge-proof" praise. See *Assertion, Happiness, "I" message, Love, Judgmental, and R-message.*

Preaching (communication) is moralizing, interpreting, and dictating opinions to a partner without _ being asked for them, or _ caring about the listener's current needs. Zealous *unaware* parents preach to their kids, and unwittingly cause them to tune out. Uninvited and excessive preaching contains embedded *"I'm 1-up!"* R-messages. These usually raise the listener's E-level, and hinder or block their hearing. See *Awareness bubble, Feedback, Lecturing, Monologing, Moralizing, Rambling,* and *Venting.*

Pretending is a protective false-self ploy to avoid discomfort and possible losses from honest behavior. When Self-led communicators learn how to give respectful "I"-messages [7] and meta-comments [5], their need to avoid and pretend often drops. See *Co-dependence, Denial, Double message, Enabling, Genuineness, Lying, Pseudo agreement, Pseudo intimacy,* and *Trust.*

Pride is a feeling of genuine satisfaction, admiration, and pleasure about your or another's behaviors or achievement. Pride is the opposite of *shame.* People and families have unspoken rules about feeling and expressing pride. Some interpret the Christian Bible as saying that pride is a (shameful) sin, and that God sternly decrees *humility.* If carried to extreme, this bias promotes low-nurturance relationships, false-self control, guilt, and anxiety. One goal of inner-wound recovery is to generate anxiety-free, non-egotistical pride: i.e. self-esteem and non-egotistical self-love. See *Happiness, Joy, Perfectionism,* and *Serenity.*

Problem: In the context of wholistic personal and relationship health, a *problem* occurs when one or more people have significant unfilled mental, spiritual, emotional, and/or physical *needs.* The needs may be conscious or not, and surface (symptomatic) or *true* (underlying, core - p. 149.) Problems may be internal or interpersonal, abstract, concrete, or communication-process. Each of these is best resolved differently. See *Argue, Brainstorm, Conflict, Dig down, Fight, Impasse, Needy,* and *Resolution.*

Problem solving or resolution is the process of filling significant current needs in one or more subselves and/or people. Win-win (=/=) problem solving aims to fill the current needs of all participants equally. See *Conflict, Deal with, Dig down, Needs, Negotiate,* and *Work through.*

Process: *Noun:* a sequence of events with a beginning, an ending, and an impact or outcome. *Verb:* to analyze a solo or social behavioral sequence, and draw contextual meanings from its elements and character, as in *"Let's process how we got into that fight last night, and why it turned out the way it did."* Meta-processing is processing how you process, which can be a useful communication exercise if it's cooperative (=/=). See *Awareness, Content, Dig down, Focus, Mapping, Needs, Metatalk, Outcome, Payoff, Sequence,* and *Transaction.*

Procrastination is a protective false-self ploy to avoid immediate discomfort. It always implies _ some subselves don't trust the resident Self (or a Higher Power) to handle the feared thing, and _ inner conflict [9]. Intentional, reasoned *deferring,* vs. procrastinating, can be a best-option decision by your Self. Our English term comes across centuries from the Latin word for *tomorrow.* See *Guardian (subself).*

Projection (psychological) is an *unconscious* (involuntary) false-self strategy to avoid emotional discomfort by imagining an unpleasant or detested personal trait to belong to another person, rather than admitting (owning) it oneself. *"You're the liar here, not me!"* If confronted, projection is usually denied, and always indicates a false self is in control. Arguing about denied projections brings predictable conflict and frustration, vs. resolution. See *Guardian (subself), Inner family,* and *Subself.*

Pseudo agreement occurs when one or both conflict partners' false selves pretend to go along with the other's needs or opinions, but are really ambivalent or opposed. Pretending or implying agreement suggests one or both persons are controlled by a false self, and don't feel safe internally or socially stating their truth (*"I disagree."*) Pretended agreement is a double message (q.v.). It can usually be sensed semi-consciously by the receiver, breeding unease (anxiety), distrust, and doubt. Saying respectfully *"I see it differently"* feels very different than pretending to agree, or saying *"You're wrong (1-down)"*. See *Abandonment, Assertion, Co-dependence, Double messages, Enabling, "I" message, Lying, People pleasing, Pretending,* and *Trust.*

Pseudo intimacy occurs when a person *pretends* to think, feel, and desire emotional and physical closeness and relationship equality. From childhood abandonment and wounding, they may be unable to bond, and must pretend otherwise to themselves and/or their partner to avoid the horrifying truth. Over time, the partner usually "senses" the pretense, and feels confused, distrustful, uneasy, and anxious. I believe pseudo intimacy or pseudo "mutuality" *always* indicates major unseen psychological injuries and a low-nurturance childhood. So does denying, enabling, and tolerating pseudo intimacy. See *Approach-avoid, Avoidance, Bond, Co-dependence, Double message, Enabling, False self, Independent Relationship, Love, Lying, Pretending, Reality distortion, Symmetrical relationship,* and *Trust.*

Pseudo recovery occurs when people controlled by a false self think, talk, and act as if they're harmonizing their inner family, but their core beliefs, values, and reflexes don't change. Some subselves want to change, and others are too scared to. People in 12-step and some Christian programs refer to this as "not walking the talk." See *Avoiding, Denial, False self, First-order change, Procrastination,* and *Wounds.*

Psychosomatic (illness or condition): a body condition (e.g. migraine, allergy, back pain, stomach or digestive disorder, facial tic, muscle spasm) that is caused by "emotions" (neuro-chemical reactions) rather than organic (cellular/chemical) malfunction or germs. I believe such conditions are real, widespread, and are caused by subselves trying to express something they can't communicate otherwise. Evidence is overwhelming that there is a little-understood human "mind-body-soul" connection that influences our inner-family and social communication effectiveness. See *Nurturance* and *Wholistic health.*

Pun is a phrase with two or more, often humorously opposed, meanings. See *Association, Decoding, Double message, Embedded message, Joking, Levels of meaning,* and *Oxymoron.*

Punish: intentionally inflicting physical and/or emotional discomfort (like guilt, shame, and anxiety) on someone in retribution for an action or behavior. Punishment *always* implies aggression and self-absorption: "*I'm 1-up. I care more for my needs than yours, now.*" It usually signals false-self control, and it promotes power struggles, fear-based relationships, and relationship triangles. Unaware caregivers who discipline kids via *punishment* (vs. natural consequences) unintentionally promote the six pyschological wounds (p. 37). Shame-based people may habitually punish *themselves,* replicating early childhood caregivers' behaviors. See *Abuse, Aggression, Assertion, Controlling, Embedded message, Fear-based, "I" message, R-message, Revenge,* and *Shame.*

Q-R

Questioning is a communication dynamic whose impact can range from a helpful request for information (*"Can you summarize what you just heard me say?"*) to avoiding a direct response (*"Before I answer, tell me . . ."*) to criticism and attack. (*"So how long have you been addicted to pornography?"*) Questions may have multiple intents, and may be implied or direct. Empathic listening experts suggest not reflecting a speaker's communication with a question, because that risks refocusing the speaker on the listener's needs and world view. See *Communication needs, Interrogating, Intellectualizing,* and *Levels of Meaning.*

Rageaholic is (often) a disparaging label for someone who seems addicted to (unable to control) feeling and expressing intense anger. Rageful Vulnerable or Guardian subselves usually control "perpetually angry" people. They need to protest or protect against some past or feared calamity. Dominance of such subselves may also indicate the person is unable to grieve some major losses. Digging down respectfully [4] can reveal some indescribable past *hurt* underlying the rage, like childhood neglect or abuse. See *Aggression, Addiction, Controlling, Emotion, Family secret, Narcissism,* and *Type-A behavior.*

Rambling is talking on and on with little focus or concern about the listener's present communication needs. Ramblers' awareness bubbles exclude their partners. That often signifies a disabled Self. So does the listener tolerating too much rambling, vs. using respectful "I"-message assertions to confront and stop it. See *Aggression, Defocusing, Explaining, Flooding, Lecturing, Monologing, Preaching, selfish, Submission, Venting,* and *Victim.*

Rationalizing is a false-self strategy to make a harmful or unethical action appear legitimate, useful, or acceptable (*"I had to steal the money because they were going to repossess my car, and I'd lose my job."*) Avoidances, psychological wounds, and addictions are often elaborately rationalized (*"I use pot to relax and lighten up. I can quit any time I want to."*) The payoff is usually providing short-term comfort for an upset Vulnerable subself, despite painful long-term consequences. See *Denial, Inner family, Neglect, Resistance,* and *Reality distortion.*

Reality distortion is an unconscious misinterpretation of a subself's or person's behavior, or environmental events. Distorting is one of six common inner wounds (p. 37). Most Guardian subselves are talented at protecting Vulnerable subselves from pain by distorting sensory perceptions in creative ways like denying, repressing or numbing feelings, "neuroses" and "paranoias," minimizing or exaggerating, intellectualizing, catastrophizing, mis-remembering or forgetting, projecting, rationalizing, and mind reading (assuming.) See *Blending, Decoding, Denial, Guardian (subself), Inner family, Meaning, Message, Splitting,* and *Understanding.*

Reasoning is a type of inner or social communication which attempts to _ "make sense" of inner or environmental events or conditions, or _ persuade someone via "logic" to *want to* change their attitudes or behavior. The former is a survival-based reaction. The latter is an overt or covert attempt to satisfy the persuader's surface or true needs, and often sounds like *"Don't you see? You'll feel better, if . . ."* See *Controlling, First-order change, Manipulate,* and *Persuasion.*

Recovery (from false-self dominance) means the *intentional* process over time of meeting and reorganizing inner-family subselves (personality "parts") to know and trust _ each other, and the leadership of _ the true Self and _ a personal Higher Power. This usually involves increasing *awareness*, reducing excessive shame, guilts, and fears; rebalancing trusts, strengthening the ability to bond with other living things, reducing reality distortions, and living increasingly free of the impulsivity and narrow focus of a protective false self team. See *Blending, Family system, Multiplicity, "Parts work," Pseudo recovery, Second-order change, Splitting,* and *Wholistic health.*

Reflex: an automatic thinking, bodily, and/or behavioral response that bypasses conscious awareness and choice. A common one is shame-based people reflexively apologizing (*"Oop, Sorry!"*) if they bump into furniture or a doorway. Before developing *awareness*, most of us have a large inventory of reflexes like interrupting, avoiding eye contact in conflict, and using *"we"* instead of *"I,"* that shape the outcomes of our communication. Often whole communication sequences over minutes or weeks follow a reflexive pattern, without partners' awareness. One or more protective Guardian subselves may cause any given reflex. See *Association, Black/white thinking, Pattern, Process, Sequence, Thinking, Subliminal cues,* and *Unconscious mind.*

Reframing is intentionally changing a topic's frame of reference to shift its meaning and/or emotional tone (e.g. pessimistic/discouraging to realistic/hopeful). For example, being fired from a job can be reframed from being shameful personal and role *failures* to *"A chance to learn more clearly what your real talents and life mission are."* See *Association, Context, Decoding, Framing, Meaning, Levels of meaning,* and *Second-order change.*

Regular (subself type) is any personality part that usually shapes or controls a person's experience and behavior when their Vulnerables and Guardian subselves are "quiet." Typical Regulars include a *Do-er, Pusher, or Achiever; an Observer or Reporter; a Historian; a Planner-Organizer; an Adult ("Common Sense"); a Spiritual One; a Wise One; a Nurturer; a Creative One; and a Self (capital "S").* See *Guardian (subself), Inner family, Multiplicity, Personality, Self, Serenity, Subself, Recovery, Splitting,* and *Vulnerable (subself).*

Relationship (interpersonal): a temporary or sustained *caring* (emotional/spiritual reactivity) between two or more people, caused by various *needs* and perceptions in each partner. When a partner no longer gets their needs filled, they emotionally, physically, or legally "pull back," (distance) or leave the relationship. Relationships can range between . . .

+ high-nurturance to toxic (low-nurturance),
+ faked to superficial to intimate and committed,
+ forced to chosen,
+ dependent to interdependent to independent,
+ mutual to one-way,
+ human to spiritual, and . . .
+ business to platonic to romantic/sexual.

The depth, type, and emotional closeness of a given relationship shift over time, like the need-mix of each partner, and their abilities to satisfy their needs themselves and/or with other people. Awareness, clear thinking, and effective communication are key relationship nutrients or stressors. This is true also for the relationships between your inner-family members. See *Approach-avoid, Bond, Cutoff, Family, Family system, Interdependent relationship, Needs, Roles, Subself, Symmetrical relationship,* and *Wholistic health.*

Repression (emotional) is a common Guardian-subself strategy to protect young Vulnerable parts from being overwhelmed by intense confusion, guilt, shame, and terror. Repression manifests as not feeling these emotions fully or at all, and may involve protective "forgetting." Usually repression is coupled with *denial* (*"I'm not repressing anything!"*) It's one of an array of reality distortions that Guardian subselves use, like minimizing, exaggerating, "forgetting," projecting, catastrophizing, numbing, and denials. See *Blocking, Numbing, Reality distortion,* and *Vulnerable (subself).*

Request: a communication in which the sender asserts a need to someone, and can genuinely tolerate the other saying *"No," "Not now," "Not that way,"* and *"Maybe."* Unlike demands ("I'm 1-up") or pleas ("I'm 1-down"), effective requests carry embedded =/= R-messages. See *Assertion, Demand, Guilt trip, Hint, Innuendo, Manipulate, Pleading, Questioning, Suggestion,* and *Threat.*

Rescuer is one of three "PVR relationship-triangle" roles. The adult or child choosing this role focuses on the welfare of the perceived Victim, and unconsciously sends "*I'm 1-up*" R-messages to people in the Victim and Persecutor roles. Rescuers are usually unaware of false-self dominance and the seven skills, so their communications with the people in the other two triangle roles are guaranteed to be ineffective. This will continue or escalate until one or more people quit their triangle roles and behaviors, and assume a genuine =/= attitude. See *Alliance, Awareness, Co-dependent, Conflict, Enabling, Game, Outcome, Reality Distortion, Second-order change, Triangling,* and *True needs.*

Resistance (behavioral) is any conscious or reflexive inner or outer behavior that blocks _ truly acknowledging personal responsibility for something, and/or _ acting to resolve a mutual conflict (need clash). Common resistances are denying, repressing, "forgetting," arguing, blaming, intellectualizing, analyzing, questioning, shifting the focus or topic, monologing, justifying, "collapsing," withdrawing emotionally or physically, aggressing, pseudo-agreeing, procrastinating, silence, rambling, preaching, over-apologizing, pretending, and numbing or blanking out. Every one of these is a Guardian-subself strategy to avoid expected discomfort, because the Self and other Regulars aren't trusted to manage the situation. See *Alliance, Avoidance, Guardian subself, Inner family, Multiplicity, Parts work, Process, Self, Splitting, Trust,* and *Vulnerable subself.*

Resolution (conflict) is the outcome of effective two-level communication. Each partner or subself feels they got their current true needs met well enough, so their "problems" (need conflicts) were "solved." See *Awareness, Conflict, Compromise, Lose-lose, Negotiation, Outcome, Sequence, Pattern, Payoff,* and *Win-win.*

Respect is a feeling and attitude of acceptance, approval, and admiration of a person, idea, group, or goal. It implies seeing significant *worth* and *value* in any of these, regardless of differences, defects, or conflicts. The need to feel enough respect from other people and yourself, now and over time, is one of six reasons adults, kids, and subselves communicate. False-self dominance implies active Guardian subselves don't trust or respect the Self as a competent personality leader. See *Awareness bubble, Dignity, Discount, False self, Integrity, R-message,* and *Subself.*

R(espect)-message is a signal embedded in every perceived behavior of a communication partner, including no behavior, which can be decoded in one of three ways: *"Here and now, I (your communication partner) see you as having . . .*

Less worth and dignity than me: *"I'm superior to (1-up on) you;"*

More worth and dignity than me: *"I'm inferior (1-down) to you;"* or . . .

Equal worth and dignity as me: *"We're =/= (co-equals) here."*

Communications are likely to be effective *only* if all participants (people and subselves) steadily receive credible =/= R-messages. See *Assertion, Channels, Dignity, Double message, Embedded message, Empathy, Implication, Innuendo, Integrity, Meaning, Reality Distortion, Recovery, Respect,* and *Wholistic Health.*

Response: the (emotional + mental + physical + spiritual) reaction in one person or subself to the behavior of another person or subself. Silence, or no apparent reaction, *is* a response, for it causes implied meanings in the sender and receiver. Responses are neutral. How responses are decoded on three different communication "channels" determines if they're "good," or "bad" (whether they fill current true needs or not). See *Association, Communication Meaning, Needs, Outcome, Pattern, Payoff, Process, Sequence,* and *Transaction.*

Revenge is a uniquely human behavior that usually means *"You hurt me, so I'll hurt you"* to "get even." It manifests in early childhood, and seems to be an instinctive, primal attempt to assert boundaries with aggressors to raise security and avoid future pain and injury. Revenge in adults is a clear symptom their inner family is dominated either by a young Vulnerable (inner child), and/or a narrow-visioned Guardian protecting some Vulnerable.

Two such people (or nations) form self-stoking "feuds," and "animosities" until one or both true Selves regain inner control, or society intervenes. Revenge between ex mates can signal blocked grief, which is another symptom of significant psychological wounding. See *Abuse, Aggression, Boundaries, Controlling, Entitlement, Lose-lose, Narcissism, Power struggle, Rageaholic, Threat,* and *Punish.*

Rigidity is resistance to change, uncertainty, or compromise. Excessive rigidity (in someone's opinion) can indicate a fear-based inner family whose dominant members equate change with *danger, pain, failure* (shame), *overwhelm,* and *Self distrust.* See *Black/white thinking, Controlling, Idealism, Manipulation,* and *Perfectionism.*

Role conflict: A *role* is a set of responsibilities and behavioral rules that govern how pairs or groups of people relate to each other. Usually roles come in pairs, like parent-child, boss-employee, friend-friend, teacher-student, vendor-customer, husband-wife, and author-reader. Each person's subselves judge how their and their partner's roles "should be" performed. They form good/bad, right/wrong opinions of their own and their partner's behavior, based on those *rules* (shoulds, oughts, have-to's, and musts).

Each inner-family member has self-selected functional roles, like *Inner Critic, Nurturer, and Rebel*, which combine to form your personality. When subselves and/or people disagree on the responsibilities or rules of a role-pair, they have an abstract *role* conflict. See *Abstract conflict, Arbitrate, Argue, Compromise, Dig down, Family system, Fight, Negotiate,* and *Rule conflict.*

Royal "We" comes from medieval Europe, where kings and queens sought to avoid appearing grandiose by avoiding the pronoun "I." In our culture, many people who were taught to devalue themselves feel unconsciously uneasy owning their thoughts and feelings. They reflexively say *you* ("*You get frustrated when people don't look at you.*") or *we* instead of "*I.*" Discomfort using *I* and *me* is often a sign of shame-based, false-self dominance. See *Assertion, Co-dependence, Dignity, Fuzzy thinking, Generalizing, Genuineness, "I" message, Integrity, Pride, R-message, Shame-based, Submission,* and *Victim.*

Rudeness is a subjective judgment of someone's behavior as being disrespectful or uncaring about another person's needs, comfort, or dignity. Labeling behavior as *rude* always implies "I'm 1-up." People who tolerate rudeness to avoid conflict are *enabling* the rude person, and modeling the *Victim* relationship role. That risks lowering self and others' respect. See *Aggression, Awareness bubble, Boundaries, Dignity, Discount, Empathy, Interrupt, Respect, Self-centered,* and *selfish.*

Rule conflict: Here, a *rule* is any mental or spoken definition of how people expect or demand each other to behave in various situations; e.g. "*It's OK to cheer at (most) sports events, not at funerals or abortions.*" Adults and kids have thousands of un/conscious rules that govern how they behave: i.e. how, when, and what they communicate and respond to others. All living systems, including your inner team of subselves, evolve rules to avoid chaos.

"Breaking (someone's) rules", e.g. *shoulds, oughts, musts, and have to's,* causes *guilt,* shame, and anxiety. Subselves and people can disagree on what rules apply to a current life situation, and/or on who makes the rules, or the consequences for breaking the rules. These are abstract *values conflicts.* See *Abstract conflict, Blaming, Family system, Inner Family, Guilt, Moralizing, Preaching, Resolution,* and *Role conflicts.*

S

Sarcasm is sent or received when a person's non-verbal behavior and/or voice dynamics (tone, inflection, tempo, accent) are perceived to mean "*I'm 1-up (superior)*." Depending on the context, sarcasm can be socially funny, or personally wounding and painful; like a (shame-based) father saying with burlesqued pride to his son "*I'm* thrilled *that you're in a ballet class, Billy.*"

Chronic sarcasm usually causes hurt, distrust, and emotional and behavioral caution, specially if the sender denies or defends it. Local or chronic "biting (two-level) humor" usually indicates an insecure false self in control. See *Aggression, Discount, Double message, Judgmental, Labeling, Levels of meaning, Name-calling, R-message, Toxic,* and *Verbal abuse.*

Satisfy means to reduce a physical, emotional, or spiritual tension (fill a need) to *tolerable* or below. Daily life is a stunningly complex struggle to satisfy a ceaseless, dynamic mosaic of unconscious and conscious *needs.* Inner-family and interpersonal *communication* is a universal strategy to try to accomplish this. Aware communicators dig down below surface needs to satisfy the true needs "underneath." See *Comfort, Dig down, Happiness, Joy, Needy, Serenity,* and *True needs.*

Script (relationship): a set of unconscious beliefs and commands inherited from ancestors or key others that unconsciously shape core life decisions and trajectories. Psychologist Claude Steiner wrote "Scripts People Live" (1974), identifying basic common script types like *Loveless, Mindlessness,* and *Joylessness.* I believe scripts are real, come from early childhood experiences, and are manifestations of major psychological wounds. True recovery can unearth and revise toxic life scripts. See *Identity, Family secret, Future Self, Parts work, Personality, Rules, Suggestion, Threat,* and *Unconscious mind.*

Scorn is the shame-promoting attitude that decodes as "I'm *way* 1-up" to you—you're a flawed, bad, worthless person, and/ or your decisions and behavior are contemptible." Kids and adults can experience scorn from their *Inner Critic* and/or the false self of another person. It usually activates a *Shamed Child,* (subself) which activates one or more Guardian subselves. Without awareness, this usually disables the receiver's Self. See *Shame*.

Second-order change is a shift in personal core attitudes, beliefs, values, or priorities that causes permanent behavior change. Often, such changes are caused by traumas, accumulated pain and weariness, and epiphanies (profound new awarenesses). Harmonizing a chaotic inner family under the guidance of your true Self is a second-order change. See *Avoidance, First-order change, Procrastination,* and *Resistance*.

self (small "s") means your body, mind, soul, and all subselves together. So does *myself*. If your Self isn't leading, *self* can also mean the personality part that is locally controlling your perceptions, sensations, motivations, and behaviors. See *Blending, False self, Identity, Inner family, Multiplicity, Parts work, Personality,* and *Splitting*.

Self is a resident Regular personality part that kids in high-nurturance settings develop from birth. Its key talent is consistently *effective* inner-family leadership, in normal and crisis situations. Your true Self (capital "S") is like a skilled athletic coach, aircraft captain, musical conductor, military commander, CEO, or committee chairperson. If your Self is distrusted by or unknown to your other subselves, they will "blend" with him or her at crucial times. That causes narrow-viewed, impulsive (ineffective) use of your senses, muscles, and bodily organs to do what they feel is right. Communication effectiveness is directly related to whether each partner's Self is currently leading their inner families. See *Awareness, Blending, Centered, False self, Guardian (subselves), Inner family, Joy, Multiplicity, Parts work, Personality, Recovery, Regular (subselves) Serenity, Subself, Splitting,* and [..01/ f+t_selves.htm].

Self-centered means locally or chronically focusing on one's own needs, feelings, and opinions. This is reliable symptom of a disabled true Self, and a dominant *Narcissist* or *Egotist* subself.

Because this attitude is socially scorned, self-centered people can develop camouflages, denials, and justifications for their false-self's strategy. See *"1-up," Aggression, Awareness bubble, Bond, Demand, Discount, Ego, Empathy, Entitlement, Grandiosity, Narcissistic, selfish,* and *Rude.*

Self-ish (capital "S") means valuing your own needs, integrity, and dignity *as much as* other people's, without undue guilt, shame, or anxiety. Alternatives are being *selfish ("My needs and integrity are more important to me than yours now"),* or *submissive ("My needs, opinions, feelings, and worth are less important than yours now.")"* See *Abuse, Assertion, Aggression, Awareness bubble, Bill of Personal Rights, Dig down, Dignity, Golden rule (of communication), Integrity, Narcissistic, R-message, Respect, Self,* and *True needs.*

Sequence (communication): a series of two or more multi-level actions and reactions (transactions) between two subselves or people in a local or sustained relationship. Five levels in any re/action are thinking, feeling, needing, perceiving, and acting. Cooperative communication "mapping" of inner-family and interpersonal sequences and patterns (sequences of sequences) can help partners clarify and resolve complex and high-priority communication conflicts. See *Awareness, Mapping, Metatalk, Outcome, Pattern, Payoff, Process,* and *Transaction.*

Serenity is a prized, transitory mind-body-spirit state of relaxed contentment that indicates all your major current *true* (vs. surface) needs are satisfied enough, according to all your active subselves. Using "parts work" to harmonize your *inner* family of subselves under the guidance of your Self and Higher Power greatly increases the frequency and duration of serenity and joy. The alternative state is some level of significant un/conscious *anxiety* and *neediness.* See *Centered, Grounded, Happiness, Joy, Needy, Recovery,* and *Wholistic Health.*

Serenity Prayer: An inspiring, timeless gift from theologian Reinhold Neibuhr to the AA recovery community in 1935: *"God grant me the serenity to accept the things I cannot* *change, Courage to change the things I can, and Wisdom to know the difference."*

People burdened by false-self dominance are often unable to follow the wisdom and truth in this, despite agreeing with it intellectually. See *Centered* and *Higher Power.*

Setup is a semi-conscious c/overt behavior sequence with predictable results: often the discomfort of you and/or a partner. Plotting setups is a sure symptom of false-self dominance, and unawareness of problem-solving skills. See *"1-up," Aggression, Controlling, Games, Gotcha, Hidden agenda, Lose-lose, Manipulate, Outcome, Payoff, Persecutor, Process, Power Struggle, Punish,* and *Revenge.*

Shame-based (personality): Shame is the painful belief and feeling *"I'm flawed, bad, worthless, damaged, and unlovable."* It first appears in infancy (wordless feeling: *"Bad me!"*) when we perceive rejection or displeasure in our caregiver/s. In low-nurturance childhoods, excessively shamed and frightened kids protectively split their personalities. One or more of the resulting subselves carries this agonizing *shame* feeling into adulthood. When this subself (usually a Vulnerable) activates, often because of scathing criticism from our *Inner Critic* and *Perfectionist,* we (the person) are flooded with *shame.*

If some subselves believe other people perceive our worthlessness, we feel *embarrassed.* We protectively develop Guardian subselves to soothe or numb our shamed part/s like an *Addict, Liar, Bully, Fugitive, Con, Denier, and Blamer.* An adult or child whose behaviors are largely controlled by shamed Vulnerables and their Guardians has a "same-based" personality.

Such people often have major trouble sending or receiving =/= R-messages, so their communication is often ineffective. That increases their shame (low self esteem). Self-motivated recovery converts this into feeling appropriate self-respect, self-love, and love for others. See *Avoiding, Defensive, Denial, Explaining, False self, Family secret, Embarrassment, Fear-*

based, Guilt, Justifying, Inner family, Low nurturance, Multiplicity, Respect, Self, Toxic, and *Splitting.*

Sincerity (genuineness): behaving honestly and congruently with your basic beliefs and priorities, without hidden agendas or relationship ploys. Sincere behavior can send either =/= or "I'm 1-up" R-messages to a partner ("I'm sincerely more important than you are.") See *Integrity*

Sixth sense: See *Hunch* and *Intuition.*

Slip of the tongue is a verbal behavior that reveals what a distrustful, hidden subself is feeling or thinking. See *Freudian slip, Leaking, Mind, Subliminal cues, Subself,* and *Unconscious mind.*

Split personality means having distinctly different, often opposed, attitudes, values, and behaviors; like being "a nice guy" and "a raging maniac" at different times. This term validates the human ability to *dissociate,* based on normal neural *multiplicity.* The nature and degree of "splitness" varies by situation and person. Because moderate personality splitting seems to be our cultural norm, it is unacknowledged and denied. I believe "split" people are *always* _ from low-nurturance ancestries, and are _ often governed by protective false selves, until they decide to recover from that. See *Blending, Dissociate, Double message, Guardian (subself), Inner conflict, Inner dialog, Inner family, Mental illness, Multiple Personality Disorder, Nurture, Parts work, Personality, Regular (subself), Recovery, Parts work, Self,* and *Vulnerable (subself).*

Splitting (personality) can mean _ the original fragmenting of a young personality into subselves, or _ the local (situational) blending (infusing) of the true Self by alarmed, distrustful subselves. See *Dissociation, False self, Guardian subself, Inner Family, Multiplicity, Personality, Regular subself, Subself,* and *Vulnerable subself.*

Standoff: See *Compromise, Conflict, Cutoff, Impasse, Problem,* and *Rigidity.*

Stress is a vague term usually based on _ personal

unawareness, _ false self dominance, _ inner-family confusion and chaos, and "too many" situational or chronic inner and social conflicts. The ultimate cause of personal "stress" is inner family disharmony, a disabled true Self, and "too many" unmet true needs. These can be amplified by a low-nurturance environment. See *Problem, Conflict, Happiness, Needs, and Peace*

Stubbornness is a common personality trait that suggests _ significant inner wounding, _ dominant subselves' high need to be *right* and/or *independent*, and often _ their distrust (fear) of *change* and *compromise* based on subliminal insecurity and distrust of Self and High Power to manage new conditions safely. See *Arguing, Black/white thinking, Compromise, Conflict, Fighting, Negotiate, Perfectionism, Power struggle, Rigidity, Resistance,* and *Problem solve.*

Style (communication): Master therapist Virginia Satir suggested that each child and adult develops a characteristic way of communicating. She proposed that over time, our typical behavioral sequences with certain or all others will have one of these themes:

Domineering, aggressive, and controlling ("1-up");

Submissive, timid, or apologetic (1-down");

"Clear" (direct, focused, and respectful, or =/=); and . . .

Defocused, scattered, or distracted (split and variable).

Objective *awareness* of your and a partner's styles can start to resolve problems caused by style mismatches (e.g. two Aggressives battling to be "1-up.") Only the *clear* style indicates a true Self is guiding your or a partner's inner family. Style *awareness* can help you decide the state and leadership of your or their inner family. See *"=/=," Arguing, Awareness bubble, Distraction, Feedback, Mapping, Metatalk, Neurolinguistic programming, Pattern, Power struggle, R-message,* and *Sequence.*

Subliminal cues are tiny vocal (e.g. pace, accent, and inflection changes) and non-verbal behaviors (e.g. eye flickers, muscle twitches, skin color changes, faint smells) that signal what our governing subselves *really* think, feel, and need now, despite our words or silences. Ancient mammalian survival depended partly on developing exquisite sensitivity to such tiny signals in other living things. Most of us have subselves who retain muted awareness of such cues in our and our partners' bodies and behaviors. On some level of consciousness, decoded communication *meanings* are shaped by these tiny cues. See *Awareness, Intuition, Knowing, Reflex, Sixth sense,* and *Unconscious mind.*

Submissive behavior manifests an *"I'm 1-down"* (inferior) relationship attitude. That usually implies that a shame-based and/or fear-based false self is in control. Chronic submissive behavior invites disrespect, aggression, and/or pity, which all detract from high-nurturance relationships and effective communication. Chronic submissive attitudes and behaviors invite personal recovery work focused on raising one's true Self to inner leadership, and (re)building genuine self respect, dignity, and integrity. See *Aggression, Assertion, Bill of Personal Rights, Dignity, Fear-based, Guilt, Inner family, Integrity, Pride, R-message, Shame, Shame-based,* and *Style.*

Subself: any one of three or four functional types of personality "parts" (semi-independent brain regions) that constantly influence your mind, body, and spirit. I and others believe normal kids and adults have an "inner family" of subselves, whose collective needs, values, perceptions, and roles cause "behavior." See *Blending, False self, Future Self, Guardians, Multiplicity, Parts work, Personality, Recovery, Regulars, Self, self, Splitting,* and *Vulnerables.*

Suggestion: a clear respectful recommendation of action or interpretation to a partner (*"I think what your boss meant was . . ."*), or a covert *implied* message aimed at the receiver's unconscious mind, and avoiding the appearance of directing or judging. (*"I heard somewhere that some people in situations like yours often choose to . . ."*) In a trance state, our unconscious mind is often more receptive to accepting covert suggestions literally, without evaluation. See *Association, Demand, Double message, Embedded Message, Hint, Implication, Innuendo, Judgmental, Levels of meaning, Request,* and *Subliminal cues.*

Superficial: focusing on safe impersonal topics, and avoiding the anxiety of honest disclosure and/or discussion of current core personal feelings, needs, and conflicts. Partners agreeing to have an independent relationship often have superficial conversations, which fill the need to be "social," and don't risk real intimacy. Wounded kids and adults unable to truly bond with others may only be capable of superficial communication, and until in true recovery, see nothing "wrong" with that. See *Awareness, Distance, Focus, Genuineness, Heart talk, Intimacy,* and *Vulnerability.*

Surface need: a spontaneous, unexamined thought or spoken expression of a desired event or thing, like "*I want to see this movie tonight.*" Digging down below this casual description unearths true needs "underneath" (lower in awareness): "*I* really *need stimulation, companionship, and temporary distraction from my shame, guilt, and anxieties from having just lost my job.*" In high E-level situations, communications are far more effective when partners and/or subselves help each other dig down [4] to the true needs below the surface. See *Awareness, Communication needs, Needy, People pleasing,* and *Superficial.*

Symmetrical relationship: one where partners' needs for power and control (dominance), dependence, and autonomy are stably balanced, over time. Unsymmetrical relationships are usually characterized by ongoing stress and conflict, which are usually signs of significant false-self control and ineffective communications in both partners. See *Interdependent relationship.*

System (family): See Family system and *Inner* family

T

Terror is extreme fear. The experience of terror usually implies some hyper-scared subselves have blended with (taken over) the Self, because they don't really trust her/him to cope well enough with some current or possible threat or trauma. The reverse is "staying cool under fire." In some contexts, *terror* can be a hand-grenade word, because of implied meanings, like *"You terrified me (and are a bad person)."* See *Anxiety, Association, Blending, Fear, Go to Pieces, Panic, Uneasy,* and *Worry.*

"The *Look*" is a special facial expression that is associated with great discomfort from shame, guilt, frustration, and anxiety. If part of a communication pattern, the *Look* (or the *Face,* or *Glance,* or *tone of voice*), becomes shorthand behavior that condenses long critical lectures or outbursts, and delivers the same searing *"You're 1-down"* message. Few kids have the awareness, permission, vocabulary, and communication skills to confront the "looker," and get different behavior. See *Association, Controlling, Embedded message, Expression, Guilt trip, Manipulation, R-message, Shame-based,* and *Nonverbal channel.*

Thinking, Thoughts: Here, *thinking* means the automatic neuro-chemical process of collecting information from various brain and body centers, and decoding it for *meaning* in one or more of our unconscious, semi-conscious, and conscious minds. Thinking is a primal strategy to *survive.* See *Association, Assumption, Double message, Hunch, Inner voices, Instinct, Knowing, Logic, Meaning, Mind racing, Process, R-message, Self-talk, Sequence,* and *Transaction.*

Threatening: implying or forecasting some painful consequence if the listener doesn't do (or stop doing) something. Chronic threats suggest the partners _ can't problem solve effectively, _ have low communication and personal awareness, _ are probably psychologically wounded, and _ the sender's false self feels unable to fill her or his needs without using threats. Non-humorous threats always include an embedded "*I'm 1-up!*" R-message. Fear-based people may perceive threats where none are intended (reality distortion). See *Abuse, Aggression, Alliance, Assume, Catastrophizing, Controlling, Fight, Manipulation, Persecutor, Power struggle, Triangling,* and *Victim.*

Toxic: relative to attitudes, behavior, relationships, and human groups, *toxic* means "hindering true Self leadership and recovery from excessive, shame, guilt, anxiety, numbness, conflict, distortion, and confusion." The opposite is *nurturing*: promoting pride, compassion, empathy, balance, serenity, forgiveness, teamwork, awareness, growth, and satisfaction. A sign of true recovery from false-self dominance is intentionally shifting relationships and social settings from toxic to nurturing, starting with your relationship with your Self. See *Abuse, Addiction, Controlling, Low nurturance, Neglect,* and *Wholistic health.*

Trance: a common mind/body state characterized by focusing conscious awareness inward on thoughts, feelings, and images, and reducing awareness of the local environment. Entranced (undistracted) people are more receptive to in/direct suggestions. Hypnosis is the art of inviting people into the trance state, and possibly offering useful *suggestions* to their unconscious mind. See *Embedded message, Focus, Hinting, Innuendo, Paraverbal channel, Suggestion,* and *Unconscious mind.*

Transaction (communication): a multi-level exchange of perceived behavior and related meanings between two need-driven people, resulting in *payoffs* (need fulfillments or frustrations). A *sequence* is a series of transactions, over time. A communication *message* is one unit of behavior/meaning in a transaction. See *Channel, Communication needs, Mapping, Outcome, Process, Response,* and *Surface needs.*

Transactional Analysis (TA): a useful scheme of analyzing and explaining internal and social communication transactions between inner Parent, Adult, and Child subselves. TA was originated by psychiatrist Eric Berne and colleagues ("Games People Play"). See *Awareness, Channels, Embedded message, Game, Mapping, Pattern, Process, Sequence,* and *Scripts.*

Trauma means any sensory experience that overwhelms, shocks (disorients), and/or harms an adult or child; usually leaving a major long-lasting psychological injury. This usually is some form of psychological wounding. Traumas occur suddenly and violently (e.g. rape, car wreck, explosion, stroke, earthquake), or silently over time (like young children being deprived of emotional-spiritual nurturances every day).

The definition, impacts, and morality of social traumas are subjective. Kids and adults displaying significant false-self traits strongly suggest major childhood trauma, even if none is remembered. Trauma reactions (e.g. nightmares and flashbacks) can be traumatic themselves. See *Abandonment, Abuse, Aggression, Breakdown, Dissociation, Crisis, Framing, Go to pieces, Grieving, Loss, Neglect, Recovery,* and *Overwhelm.*

Triangling (relationship): three adults and/or kids *unconsciously* taking on the relationship roles of Victim (1-down), Persecutor (1-up), and Rescuer (1-up or down). Triangles can occur once or repeatedly over time. They can interlock ("*I'm a Victim here, and the Persecutor there.*") Triangles can be dissolved if one of the three decides consciously (via *awareness*) to disengage, or shift to an =/= (mutual respect) stance. Triangles usually indicate two or all three people are dominated by a false self, and aren't aware of that.

Communication among triangled people is rarely effective, and tends to promote or amplify the three unconscious roles, despite "common sense." *Triangling* and *de-triangling* are useful metatalk concepts and terms. See *Aggression, Alliance, Arguing, Enabling, Persecutor, Power struggle, Process, Rescuer, Role conflicts, R-message, Splitting, Submission,* and *Victim.*

True needs: Any one of a mosaic of fluctuating primal

mental, emotional, spiritual, and emotional *tensions, or* discomforts, which underlie all behavior, including internal and social communication. Ultimately, we each are responsible for filling our own true needs, including asking for help with that. Typical true needs are listed on p. 149. See *Approach-avoid, Assertion, Avoidance, Communication needs, Conflict, Denial, Dig down, Happiness, Needy, Outcome, Problem solving, Procrastination, Projection, Resistance, Resolution, Serenity,* and *Surface needs.*

Trust is a mental/emotional belief and *feeling* that a situation, person, or relationship will reliably cause comfort, not pain. Until in true recovery, people from low-nurturance childhoods often trust too easily and are repeatedly betrayed; or they trust too little, and suffer chronic isolation and anxiety. Talking about dis/trust, including self distrust (uncertainty), is grist for metatalk. Subselves distrusting the competence of the resident true Self and a Higher Power cause psychological blending. See *Boundary, False self, Fear-based, Feedback, Intimacy, Needy,* and *Pretending.*

Truth A relative term which depends on each partner's perceptions, awareness, vocabulary, intentions, needs, and event associations. Millions of humans have died trying to force others to acknowledge that their truth is morally or factually "right." When partners' Selves lead their inner families, they can agree *"Your truth (perception or belief) and mine don't match. Let's explore that as partners, and/or agree to disagree."* Disclosing personal truth (*honesty*) is the basis of interpersonal trust, and therefore intimacy. See *Arguing, Fighting, Half truth,* and *Lying.*

Type "A" behavior is associated with people whose actions are *manic, driven, perfectionistic, ambitious, demanding, fast-paced, impatient, and aggressive.* I believe such people are *always* dominated by subselves like the *Driver* or *Achiever, the Perfectionist, the Star (Egotist), the Idealist, the Inner Critic, the Creative One/s, the Illusionist or Pretender; a Denier, a Shamed Child,* and sometimes a *Messiah and a Bully.*

Effective communication with such people is often unlikely or impossible because their Self is disabled, their E-level is often "above their ears," and their awareness bubble often includes only themselves. See *Addiction, Aggression, Alliance, Black/white, Controlling, Demand, Manic, Manipulation, Narcissistic, Obsess, Passionate, Perfectionism, Persecutor,* and *selfish.*

U–Z

Unconscious mind: Sigmund Freud and many other researchers propose that normal people have three levels of awareness: unconscious (never knowable), semi-conscious (eventually knowable), and conscious. Clinical hypnosis unquestionably confirms the existence and operation of our unconscious-mind brain region. It seems to have its own rules for decoding meaning from inner and environmental stimuli (events) which affect our body organs and other two minds. It may be the seat of intuition, impulses, and *hunches,* and operate in the stem, the most primitive of the three main parts of our brains. See *Association, Assuming, Channels, Double messages, Embedded messages, Freudian slip, Implied messages, Leaking, Mind, Reflex, Slip of the tongue, Subliminal cues, Trance,* and *Thinking.*

Understanding: the survival-motivated, automatic reflex of trying to make clear current *meaning* from inner and outer current events, and event-patterns over time. Understanding seems to involve a complex concurrent mix of thinking, feeling, intuiting, remembering, and associating in our unconscious, semi-conscious, and conscious minds. Your minds may decode perceptions and conclude, "*I understand (assume) your meaning,*" when they really don't—i.e. they *misunderstand.* False-self dominance (splitting) and ineffective communications promote misunderstandings between inner-family subselves and people. See *Assuming, Context, Decoding, Double message, Embedded message, Framing, Hint, Innuendo, Levels of Meaning, R-message, Reframing, Suggestion,* and *Thinking.*

Upset: a vague catch-all term unaware people use to describe being "off-center," "disturbed," or "ungrounded." Digging down usually reveals that *upset* stands for some mix of *anxious, guilty, ashamed, excited, hurting, frustrated, confused, and angry.* It may also include physical and spiritual discomforts. The alternative is *comfortable, content, peaceful,* and *serene.* Feeling "upset" means one or more subselves *need* something now. See *Argue, Breakdown, Conflict, Centered, Defocused, Feeling, Fuzzy thinking, Go to pieces, Happiness, Inner conflict, Melt down, Needy, Power struggle, Serenity,* and *Surface need.*

Used: the emotional/mental reaction that some subselves have when they decode another person's behavior as being disrespectful, discounting, selfish, and treating you like an (unimportant, unfeeling) object, with no concern for your dignity, needs, or well being. Adults bearing the false-self symptom of *Narcissism* (inability to empathize and bond + excessive shame + grandiose perceptions) often evolve elaborate strategies deny or to minimize their partners' feeling used. See *Aggression, Assertion, Boundaries, Controlling, Delusion, Denial, Guilt trip, "I" message, Manipulation, Persecutor, Persuasion, Submission, Triangling,* and *Victim.*

Vague terms: a common detriment to sensitive communications and negotiation is someone thinking and speaking vague words and pronouns like *it, them, that, those, him, her, the problem, the issue, those people,* and *these things.* Sometimes the context makes those terms clear to all partners. Other times, specially high-E situations and any time one or more partners is psychologically wounded, those words can cause misunderstanding, confusion, frustration, and distrust.

For example, *"The last three times we've barbequed, you've overcooked the spareribs."* promotes more effective problem solving than *"You never do it right!"* Clear thinking and speaking is one of seven learnable communication skills (Chapter 3). See *Association, Assumption, Decoding, Double* message, *Focus, Fuzzy thinking, Hearing check, Hinting, Levels of Meaning, Meaning,* and *Understanding.*

Values conflict: a personal *value* is a unique preference, priority, belief, or evaluation (good/bad, right/wrong) of something or someone. Any two adults or kids will have a range of values agreements and disputes. Since tastes and preferences are subjective vs. absolute, trying to persuade another person to *want to* adopt your value is like trying to levitate.

Effective communication aims to _ identify this kind of conflict via *awareness* and metatalk, and then to _ agree to disagree, with mutual (=/=) respect. See *Abstract conflict, Arguing, Communication conflict, Concrete conflict, Fighting, Impasse, Moralizing, Negotiate, Payoff, Power struggle, Preaching, Problem solving, Process, R-message, Role conflict,* and *Rule conflict.*

Venting is one of six primal reasons humans communicate. It fills the need to feel and verbally express (release) current high-emotion topics to one or more receptive people. A venter's current communication needs are _ to feel respected, _ to give information, and _ to perceive empathic acceptance (listening) back. Typical males and some females respond to venting by *mis-assuming* that the speaker wants help, and trying to "fix" their "problem." Subselves have the same need to vent and be respectfully accepted by your Self and other people. See *Animated, Affect, Communication needs, E-level, Expression, Hearing, Hearing check, High-E, Passionate, True need,* and *Upset.*

Verbal abuse is a widely misused label describing spoken behavior that significantly demeans, scares, shames, or harms the receiving infant, child, or adult. Most "verbal abuse" of non-handicapped adults is really *aggression* because, unlike minor kids, the adults have the option of defending themselves and/or leaving. See *Assertion, Boundaries, Conflict, Confrontation, Dignity, Fighting, Hot potato, "I" message,*

Integrity, Interrupting, Labeling, Name calling, R(espect)-message, Sarcasm, Splitting, Trauma, and *Yelling.*

Verbal channel is one of three ways that non-deaf people use to exchange communication messages: audible sounds, including words. Some researchers suggest this is the least important of the three, in terms of meaning transmitted. See *Paraverbal* and *Non-verbal.*

Victim (here) means a local or chronic relationship role in which the adult or child (i.e. their ruling subselves) un/consciously sacrifices their dignity, needs, and physical and emotional comfort in deference to those of other people. Their behavior broadcasts an *"I'm 1-down"* R-message, which often provokes others to take complementary "1-up" *Rescuer* or *Persecutor* role. This guarantees ineffective communications. People chronically choosing the Victim role are usually dominated by a fear-based, and/or shame-based, false self. See *"=/=," Bill of Personal Rights, Boundaries, Dignity, Fear-based, Integrity, Shame-based,* and *Submission.*

Voice dynamics are *how* words and sounds are expressed, like voice quality (soft–harsh), volume (low–high), tone (e.g. sensual or menacing), accent (e.g. "southern"), pitch or intonation (nasal), pace (slow–fast), intensity (mild-fierce) and inflection (emphasizing certain syllables, words and phrases). These traits are often semi-consciously decoded by the receiver as conveying their own meaning. The decoded meaning/s may or may not match the verbal content of the words being expressed, or the face and body (non-verbal) language. Awareness and metatalk skills help to define and interpret these. See *Association, Assumption, Awareness, Channel, Decoding, Hunch, Inner voice, Intuition, Metatalk, Non-verbal, Meaning, Process, Sequence,* and *Patterns.*

Vulnerability: choosing to reveal thoughts, feelings, beliefs, and past or present behaviors that have a significant risk of evoking criticism, scorn, and rejection (pain) from a valued subself or person. This trait is required for *heart talk* and true intimacy, and is usually a sign of true-Self inner leadership. See *Abandonment, Fear-based, Genuineness, Interdependent relationship, Lying, Neediness, Pretending, Pseudo-intimacy, Shame-based, Superficial,* and *Trust.*

Vulnerable (subself type): any of a group of "Inner child" personality subselves who are developmentally young, emotionally reactive and impulsive, self-centered and shortsighted, sensitive to inner and outer events, and naïve. When a Vulnerable subself activates, one or more vigilant Guardian subselves will usually activate to comfort or protect them because the former are *vulnerable* to harm. If the Guardians don't know or trust the Self to keep the Vulnerables safe, they blend with and disable the Self. "Childish" adults are often dominated by charming, beguiling, needy, or rebellious Vulnerable subselves. See *Blending, Guardians, Inner family, Multiplicity, Parts work, Personality, Regulars, Splitting,* and *Subself.*

Whining is an irritating or satisfying "1-down" communication style which usually implies "*I'm a pitiful, helpless (1-down) victim.*" Chronic adult whining suggests being controlled by one or more subselves who feel incompetent, needy, and overwhelmed, and fear taking responsibility for reducing current discomfort. It also suggests an imagined or real Persecutor-Victim-Rescuer relationship triangle. See *Aggression, Approach-avoid, Assertion, Co-dependence, Complaining, Denial, Guilt trip, Hidden agenda, Explaining, Justifying, Persecutor, Triangling, Victim,* and *"Yes, but . . ."*

Wholistic (holistic) health: the degree to which an adult or child has their true (mental + spiritual + emotional + physical) needs met, and their mind, body, emotions, and spirit are in natural balance, over time. See *Nurture, Needs, Neglect, Serenity, Spirituality,* and *Toxic.*

Win-win is a communication attitude, sequence, or pattern where all _ partners value their true needs equally and _ get them filled well enough, in their respective judgments. The alternatives are lose-win, win-lose, and lose-lose communication outcomes. See =/=, *Communication needs, Happiness, Needs, Outcome, Payoff, Process,* and *Respect.*

Work through (a conflict) is a vague phrase used by people unaware of what they really need, as in "*We need to work through this thing about money.*" Patience, awareness, metatalk, and digging-down skills can disclose partners' true needs beneath this phrase ("*We need to admit and resolve our values conflict about saving vs. spending.*") Doing so can help achieve win-win outcomes in high-stakes inner and interpersonal conflicts. See *Deal with, Fuzzy thinking, Issue, True needs,* and *Vague terms.*

Worry is another word for *anxiety.* Many of us have competent Worrier (Guardian) subselves who try to forecast pain, so we can avoid it. See *Catastrophize, Doubt, Fear, Go to pieces, Mind racing, Panic,* and *Upset.*

Wounds (personality-splitting, or psychological): toxic traits of a dominant false self, like excessive shame, guilt, and fears. See [1], *Parts work,* and *Recovery.*

Yelling can imply messages on verbal, paraverbal, and non-verbal levels. It may signal "*I'm really frustrated with feeling unheard!*" to "*I REALLY need to vent now, or (something very bad will happen!);*" or "*I'm really scared if I don't interrupt or defocus you, some catastrophe may occur!*" or "*I'm being controlled by a tantruming young Vulnerable part who doesn't know any other way to express itself,*" Often the receiver's dominant subselves decode an "*I'm 1-up!*" R-message embedded in one or more of these levels, and get anxious, combative, or paralyzed. Subselves of unaware, fear-based (wounded) kids and adults can misinterpret a raised (*intense,* vs. loud) voice as "yelling." If accused of "yelling," their partner can feel disoriented, because they don't experience themselves as doing that (being very loud.) See *Association, Double message, Embedded message, Fear-based, Implication, Paraverbal channel* and *Reflex.*

"Yes, but . . ." is a frustrating or stimulating communication sequence or game where an adult or child _ c/overtly moans or complains, _ their partner offers solutions, and _ the moaner discounts them, and may hint *"Try again."* This sequence or pattern *always* indicates false-self dominance in the complainer. If their partner keeps playing the game, they're probably split also, and neither player is aware of that.

True selves will spot the sequence after a few rounds, and shift to *"I'm sorry you're uncomfortable. What do you see as your options here?"* or *"What do you need from me, now?"* *"I don't know"* is an invitation to keep playing. See *Boundaries, Controlling, Game, Guilt trip, Payoff, Power struggle, Process, Rescuer, Sequence, Triangling,* and *Victim.*

Index

V

W

Y

Z

Printed in the United Kingdom
by Lightning Source UK Ltd.
100890UKS00001B/221